A Concise History of the Middle East

Other Titles of Interest

The Government and Politics of Israel, Don Peretz

Muslim-Christian Conflicts: Economic, Political, and Social Origins, edited by Suad Joseph and Barbara L. K. Pillsbury

Armed Struggle in Palestine: A Political-Military Analysis, Bard O'Neill

Archaeological History of the Ancient Middle East, Jack Finegan

A Concise History of the Middle East
Arthur Goldschmidt, Jr.

This introduction to the history of Southwest Asia and Egypt from the beginnings of Islam to the present is distinguished by its broad scope, balanced coverage of various groups and countries, and use of recent scholarship to correct many glaring misconceptions. The author focuses on the evolution of Islamic institutions and culture, the influence of the West, the struggle of various peoples for political independence, and the development of the Arab-Israeli conflict. The organization of the book makes it ideal as a text for the college student.

Arthur Goldschmidt, Jr., is associate professor of history at Pennsylvania State University and chairman of the university's undergraduate program in Middle East studies. Educated at Colby College, the American University of Beirut, and Harvard University, Dr. Goldschmidt has lectured and conducted research in several Middle Eastern countries.

A Concise History of the Middle East

Arthur Goldschmidt, Jr.

Westview Press • Boulder, Colorado

Dawson • Folkestone, England

Copyright © 1979 by Westview Press, Inc.

Published in 1979 in the United States of America by
  Westview Press, Inc.
  5500 Central Avenue
  Boulder, Colorado 80301
  Frederick A. Praeger, Publisher

Published in 1979 in Great Britain by
  Wm. Dawson and Sons, Ltd.
  Cannon House
  Folkestone
  Kent CT19 5EE England

Library of Congress Catalog Card Number: 79-4189
ISBN (U.S.): 0-89158-251-7 (hardcover)
ISBN (U.S.): 0-89158-289-4 (paperback)
ISBN (U.K.): 0-7129-0889-7 (hardcover)

Printed and bound in the United States of America

To the memory of
AGNES INGLIS O'NEILL
teacher, counselor, and friend

She taught every subject with a spirit of fun
and each pupil in a spirit of love

Contents

Maps and Tables

Preface

When I started to teach Middle East history, I was sure that I would never write a textbook. Nothing in my graduate training or early research experience led me to esteem writing for beginners in my field. Textbooks were the means by which second-rate minds made their reputations and feathered their financial nests. Now I wonder whether what follows will reveal a deflated self-image or a touch of avarice. Will it meet a general need?

I know that I would not have spent so much time and energy on *A Concise History of the Middle East* if existing textbooks had met *my* needs in teaching undergraduates who have never before studied anything about the Middle East. I have grown tired of choosing among textbooks that reflect the best scholarship of the 1920s, ponderous tomes addressed to fellow scholars, and partisan diatribes that reinforce political and ethnic biases, whether Arab or Jewish, Turkish or Iranian, British or American. Our students deserve a better book. So do members of the public who want to know how the Arab-Israeli conflict began or why the Middle East became so important in meeting our energy needs.

More and more scholars, both Middle Eastern and Western, are enlarging what we know about the history of the area. We can and must teach the gist of their findings to college and university students, both to stimulate their interest in the Middle East and to make them more aware of themselves through confrontation with other life-styles, other areas, and other eras. If we cannot hide all of our biases, let us at least make sure that our students see more than one side to the burning issues of the past and present. Let us also make what we know accessible to the wider public, which also cares about the current Middle East situation and how it got to be what it is now.

Any work of art or scholarship follows certain conventions. In a book introducing a recondite subject to students and general readers, the author must spell out those he plans to follow. The English system of weights and measures is giving way to the metric system; this book uses both. Prices expressed in non-American currencies, ancient or modern, are given 1978 U.S. dollar equivalents. All dates are according to the Gregorian calendar. Western readers are warned, however, that Muslims follow a twelve-month lunar calendar dated from the year when Muhammad and his close associates moved from Mecca to Medina. They quite naturally use this calendar in teaching or studying Islamic history. Conversion between the two systems is cumbersome and prone to error. Personal names in languages using the Arabic script are transliterated according to the Library of Congress system, except for a few persons and places frequently mentioned in the press. The same applies to technical terms that cannot be simply and accurately translated into English.

This book has an immense number and variety of sources. Almost every book or article that I have read and most people with whom I have conversed have left some imprint on what I think and write. Footnotes, which are apt to distract the reader, are omitted, but there is a long bibliographical essay at the end. In some places I have specifically named scholars who have influenced my treatment of a topic, especially if I think that their names should be recognized by beginning students of Middle East history. No doubt I have omitted others, but I expect college and university instructors to fill in the gaps for their students.

In writing this book, I have tried to find a middle ground between telegraphic brevity and boring thoroughness. If it is to be used as a teaching tool for undergraduates, I would suggest a collection of original sources in translation, as supplementary reading. I make my beginning students follow the Middle Eastern news in the *New York Times*, but this is partly because my home institution offers no courses on the politics or economics of the area. Students should be exposed to pictures of Islamic art, monuments of architecture, factories, oil wells, landscapes, famous people, or anything else that will illustrate the textbook, the original sources, and lectures.

I tested a mimeographed draft version of this volume in my large survey classes for three ten-week terms. My students (totaling about 240 in 1977-1978) helped me improve the style and coverage of this book by their comments and criticisms and also by what they showed, in written and oral tests and in classroom discussions, was understandable or obscure. Several gathered for informal seminars at my house to review the book in minute detail while I was revising it for publication. In this regard, let me thank Michele Berg, Jay Berman, Gary Capkovic, Mohamed Chougui, Pamela Cottam, Robert Deer, Jon Hardy, Joseph Majestic, Joseph Ross, Robert Steinberg, Ann Whitfield, Don Wright, and most especially Patricia Kozlik-Wright for their time, effort, and advice. I am also grateful to

Lawrence Conrad for correcting some errors I made in writing about early Islamic history and to Charles Correal for sharing with me his senior honors thesis on the rise of Saudi Arabia.

Professors James Jankowski of the University of Colorado and Glenn Perry of Indiana State University critiqued many parts of the manuscript. My wife, Louise, answered many of my questions and patiently endured my efforts to formulate my ideas out loud. Their comments and criticisms have benefited the book greatly, but I take full responsibility for the errors that remain. In addition to the advances made in our scholarship, changes are now occurring so rapidly in the Middle East that I will periodically need to bring this book up to date. Please share with me any suggestions you have for its revision.

Westview editors Lynne Rienner, Patty Hodgins, and Lisa DeGrazio supplied lots of advice, prodding, copyediting, and moral encouragement. Ilene Glenn rescued my wife and me by typing much of the manuscript. Donald Kunze (aided by Barbara Droms) drew the maps to my sometimes protean specifications. I should also acknowledge financial assistance received from the Department of History and from the Central Fund for Research of the Pennsylvania State University for the cost of reproducing the manuscript, as well as from my parents, Arthur E. and Elizabeth Wickenden Goldschmidt, for various other expenses.

They will, I hope, be surprised but pleased by my dedication of the book to a remarkable schoolteacher and principal whose knowledge, ideas, and enthusiasm live on in thousands of her former pupils.

Arthur Goldschmidt, Jr.
State College, Pennsylvania

A Concise History of the Middle East

Introduction

This book is intended to introduce the Middle East to students and to other readers who have had no previous exposure to the area. The Middle East is a somewhat imprecise term describing a geographical region or culture area, and I plan to make the term clearer in the opening chapter. First I must justify my belief in history as the discipline best suited for an introduction to the Middle East. After all, it is also possible to look at the Middle East through its systems for allocating power and values, using the discipline of political science. An economist would focus on the ways by which its inhabitants satisfy their material needs. A student of comparative religions would learn about their different systems of belief and worship. Geography would treat the interaction between the people and their physical surroundings. The disciplines of sociology and cultural anthropology would analyze the institutions and group behavior of the various peoples who constitute the Middle East. It is also possible to treat the various cultures or life-styles of the region through literature, architecture, arts, crafts, and possibly even cuisine.

Why history? Some of you may have picked up a rather dismal picture of history from schools or books. History is supposed to be the study of events that took place in the past. These events have been carefully gathered together, checked for accuracy, and written down in chronological order by historians, who shamble between dusty libraries and musty archives. History teachers pass the events along to young people by means of textbooks and lectures. These are organized by the reigns of rulers or the life spans of nation states, divided into manageable chunks of time. Students memorize this "history"—as little as they can get away with—in the form of facts, names, and dates. Only an occasional concept, casually communicated and dimly grasped, adds some seasoning to the stew. A kind teacher may tell a class just to learn the "trends." These are interpreted by the students to mean vague statements unsupported by evidence from the teacher's unheeded lectures or from the unread textbook. History, in this

1

all too popular conception, is a dreary bore, a dead subject suited only to cranks, to antiquarians, or perhaps to a few students looking for bits of small talk with which to impress their peers. It is not useful. It will not get students jobs. It cannot predict what will happen in the future. Although historians repeat other historians, history does not repeat itself.

But let me respond. I do have some better ideas about what history is, how it should be studied and taught, and why we bother to learn it. Some of my ideas may seem obvious if you have already taken several college or university courses in history. Or you may already be an avid reader of history books. My ideas may be wrong or subject to change in the years to come. In time you may want to set me straight. But first let me tell you what I think about this subject and its relevance to your introduction to the Middle East.

History belongs to all of us. Whenever you talk about something that happened to yourself, your friends, your community, or your country, you are relating history through events that took place in the past. Everyone does this at least some of the time. History has no technical vocabulary, except what is needed to describe a particular time or place, society or culture. It can deal with politics, economics, life-styles, beliefs, works of art and literature, cities or rural areas, events you remember, stories older people can tell you, or subjects you can only read about. Everything that has ever happened up to the moment you read these lines is, broadly speaking, history, or the study of the past.

As an academic discipline, though, history is usually limited to those aspects of the past that have been written down or passed along by word of mouth. Historians cannot write or teach about an event that was never recorded. The unrecorded event may be trivial: What did Columbus have for breakfast on 12 October 1492? Or it may be a big question: When Muhammad was dying on 8 June 632, whom did he want as his successor?

Historians do not treat all recorded events as being equally important, any more than you would if you were writing a letter home just after you had arrived in a new place. They evaluate past events, stressing some, while downgrading or even omitting others. What historians think is worth mentioning can also change over time or vary from place to place. I plan to explore this historiographical dimension later on.

How do historians pick the events they want to stress? Usually their decision is based on how events affected what happened later on. Just as chemistry goes beyond looking at the elements on the periodic table, history deals with more than just isolated occurrences. Historians examine cause-and-effect relationships. Bostonians threw crates of tea into the harbor in 1774 *because* they resented Britain's imposing new taxes without their consent. Russian intellectuals, workers, and peasants could not stand the autocratic and inefficient rule of Tsar Nicholas II; *therefore*, they organized revolutionary movements until they overthrew it in 1917. We want to know not just *what* events occurred, but *why*.

Sometimes we argue about causal relationships. Did the institution of slavery cause the American Civil War? Was the creation of Israel in 1948 the result of Hitler's attempt to wipe out the Jews of Europe during World War II? Was it Israel's policies, Egypt's economic problems, or Nixon's appointment of Kissinger as secretary of state that provoked the Arab leaders to go to war on 6 October 1973? When we deal with cause-and-effect relationships, we are studying processes: What makes individuals or groups act, react, make decisions, or refrain from doing anything? The answer usually depends on the time and the place. As we study events close to the present, we may feel we know more about what made the people tick, but then our own feelings may also color our views. We may also have to do without some of the sources we need, such as memoirs and government documents, which are often held back for at least a generation to protect people's careers and reputations.

There is still another dimension to history, one we often overlook even though it influences our thinking. What makes our society or culture or civilization different from others existing at the same time? How does American society in the 1970s differ from what it was in the 1770s? On the other hand, does our modern age have certain common or universal qualities that make contemporary America and Egypt, for instance, more similar to each other today than both countries are to what they were a century or two ago? Do the English have certain characteristics that span differences of period or region, so that an English person of 1800 and one of today are more like each other than either is like, say, an Iranian of corresponding dates? In short, historians like to make comparisons.

The last paragraph brings up another issue. What are the most meaningful units of historical study? In the West there is a strong tradition of studying national history: the United States, Britain, France, Russia, or for that matter China or Japan. In some other parts of the world, including the Middle East, political boundaries have changed so often that we cannot use nation-states as meaningful units. In the Islamic and Middle Eastern tradition, historical studies are cut up into dynasties (ruling families), whose time spans and territories vary widely. For example, the Ottoman Empire, about which you will learn a lot in this book, was a large state made up of Turks, Arabs, Greeks, and many other ethnic groups. Its rulers, called sultans, all belonged to a family descended from a Turkish warrior named Osman. Middle East historians are starting to develop a system of periodization that is less political and more closely related to the changes in the people's economic and social life. This book, which tries to show the present state of the art in Middle East history, will straddle the issue. Sometimes I will use the old dynastic divisions of time and space, or in the modern period a country-by-country approach, using major wars and crises as points of division. At other times I will examine the history topically, in terms of "Islamic civilization" or "westernizing reform." As you (and professional historians generally) become more learned about the Middle East, I expect we will become more systematic and sophisticated.

On the basis of what we now know about Middle East history, I believe that our most meaningful unit of study is not the dynasty or the nation-state, but the civilization. Although the term is easier to describe than to define, this book will focus on a particular civilization as an interlocking complex of rules and subjects, governments and laws, arts and letters, cultures and customs, cities and villages, a civilization that covered most of western Asia and northern Africa from the seventh to the twentieth centuries, sustaining its solidarity through the religion of Islam. You will see how Islamic beliefs and practices produced specialized institutions for all aspects of Middle Eastern life. Then you will learn how Muslim patterns of belief and action have been jarred by the impact of the West. We will look at some of the ways in which the peoples of the Middle East have coped with Western domination, accepting the best and rejecting the rest. We will see how they have won back their political independence and have started to regain their autonomy as a civilization. I believe this to be the best way to approach the study of the Middle East for the first time.

You may wonder why anyone would want to study the Middle East, let alone the history of Islamic civilization. In a sense, I must argue that the study of any subject, from philosophy to physics, is potentially an adventure of the mind. Islamic history is a subject worth studying for its own sake. Confronted by distances of time and space, and by differences of thought patterns and life-styles, we learn more about ourselves: our era, area, beliefs, and customs. Islam is somewhat like Christianity and Judaism, but not entirely so. The peoples of the Middle East (like those of the West) are partial heirs of the Greeks and the Romans. However, unlike us they are direct successors of the still earlier civilizations of Egypt, Mesopotamia, and other lands of the ancient Middle East. As a result, they have evolved in a different direction than we have. They are rather like our cousins, neither brothers nor strangers to us.

In another sense, our culture has been their debtor. Our religious beliefs and observances are clearly derived from those of the ancient Hebrews, but also from Greeks, Arameans, Persians, and Egyptians living in the Middle East before Islam. Yet many Westerners do not know what they owe to Islamic culture. Some of the technical aspects of cultural transmission, especially in philosophy, mathematics, and science, I will save for later. For now, a short excursion into the derivation of some everyday English words should serve to illustrate my point.

We start with what is closest to ourselves, our clothes. Several things we are apt to wear have Middle Eastern backgrounds: cotton (from the Arabic *qutn*), pajamas and sandals (both words taken from Persian), and obviously caftans and turbans. Muslin cloth used to come from Mosul (a city in Iraq), and damask from Damascus. The striped cat we call "tabby" got his name from a type of cloth called "Attabi," once woven in a section of Baghdad having that name. Some Arabs claim that the game of tennis took its name from a medieval Egyptian city, Tinnis, where cotton cloth (that might once have been used to cover the balls) was woven. This may not be so. But the implement with which you play the game, a "racquet," has been traced back to an Arabic word meaning "palm of the hand." Polo, chess, backgammon, and probably playing cards came to the West from the Middle East. The "rook" in chess comes from the Persian word *rukh* ("castle") and "checkmate" from *shah mat* ("your king is dead"). In the area of household furnishings, we have taken the divan, sofa, mattress, and of course the afghan and ottoman.

You may know the Middle Eastern origin of foods like shish kebab and yogurt. Some of our other eatables have simply been naturalized longer: artichokes, apricots, ginger, lemon, lime, orange, saffron, sugar, and tangerine. Need I mention where the word "hashish" comes from? Both "sherbet" and "syrup" come from the Arabic word for drink. Muslims may not use intoxicating liquor, but the very word "alcohol" comes from Arabic. So do some other favorite beverages: coffee, soda (derived from the word for headache, which the Arabs cured with a plant containing soda), and julep (from a Persian word meaning "rosewater").

The guitar can be traced back to the Arabic *qitar.* Other Middle Eastern instruments include the lute, tambourine, and zither. "Mask" and "mascara" both derive from an Arabic word meaning "fool." Let some miscellaneous words round out the digression: "alcove" (from *al-qubbah,* meaning "a domed area"), "admiral," "tariff" (from *ta'rifah,* or "a list of prices"), "talc," "magazine" (in the sense of a storehouse), and "almanac" (from *al-manakh,* meaning "weather"). The history of the Middle East gives us some background to what we have, what we do, and what we are.

For more practical purposes, we look to the recent history of the Middle East to help us understand what is happening there now. This area gets more than its share of the news: the Arab-Israeli wars, airplane hijackings, assassinations, arms races, oil diplomacy and petrodollars, the Greek-Turkish conflict in Cyprus, the civil war in Lebanon, and Iran's revolution have made headlines. Current events in the Middle East affect us as individuals, as members of religious or ethnic groups, and as a nation. Can history give us clues as to how we should respond? I believe it can. This book will try to relate some past events to current ones. As an historian, I care about what happened, how it happened, and why it happened. But we also want to know what is important for us now about these happenings.

As this caravan (originally a Persian word) of Middle East history starts off, let me wish you *rihlah sa'idah, nasi'ah tovah,* and may you have a fruitful intellectual journey.

1

The Physical Setting

WHAT IS THE MIDDLE EAST?

Before I can write anything about its history, I have to settle on a definition of the Middle East. Historians and journalists throw the term around, but not everyone agrees on what it means. It makes little sense geographically. No point on the globe is more "middle" than any other. What is "east" for France and Italy is "west" for India and China. It would be more logical to speak of "Southwest Asia," but what about Egypt or European Turkey? Our conventional view of the "Old World" as having three major continents—Europe, Asia, and Africa—breaks down once we think about their physical and cultural geography. Do Asia and Africa divide at the Suez Canal, or the current line between Israel and Egypt, or somewhere east of Sinai? What differences are there between peoples living east and west of the Ural mountains (or the Bosporus, for that matter)? Continents are really not logical either.

So I will be lazy and write about a "Middle East" that the press, radio, and TV have made familiar to us. Its geographical limits may be disputed, but for the purposes of this book the Middle East runs from the Nile Valley to the Muslim lands of central Asia (roughly, the valley of the Amu Darya or Oxus River), from extreme southeast Europe to the Indian Ocean. Sometimes I may portray the area as more, sometimes less, when the political realities of a certain period of history alter the conventional outline. After all, the lands south and east of the Mediterranean were *the* East to our cultural forebears, until they started traveling to India and China, whereupon the Muslim lands became the Near East. World War II made it the Middle East, and so it has remained, despite UN attempts to rename it "West Asia." For navigation and aviation, for peacetime commerce and wartime strategy, and for journalism and politics, the area is very much in the middle, flanked by centers of population and power.

7

SOME DESCRIPTIVE GEOGRAPHY

History waits upon geography. Before you can have a play, there must be a stage. Perhaps we should spend a lot of time on topography, climate, flora and fauna, and other aspects of descriptive geography. Actually, it is necessary to master only a few geographical points before starting the study of Middle East history. Let us stick to the fundamentals, adding the details later as we need them.

Climate

The Middle East tends to be hot and dry. Most parts get some rainfall, but usually in amounts too small or too irregular to support settled agriculture. Yet the world's oldest agricultural villages have been unearthed in the highlands of Anatolia (Asiatic Turkey), Iran, and Palestine. Others have been found in the western Sahara. What happened? It seems that, as the polar ice caps (from the last "great ice age") retreated some ten thousand years ago, rainfall started diminishing in North Africa and southwest Asia. Hunting and food-gathering peoples, living in an area that had once been like the Garden of Eden, had to learn how to control their sources of sustenance. Rain-watered areas became farther and farther apart, and some peoples wandered into the marshy valleys of the great rivers: the Nile, the Tigris, and the Euphrates. By 3000 B.C. or so, they had learned how to tame the annual floods to water their fields. Other peoples became nomads; they learned how to move up and down mountains or among desert oases to find forage for their sheep, goats, asses, and eventually camels and horses.

The peasants who tamed the river valleys needed governments to organize the building of dams, dikes, and canals for large-scale irrigation that would regulate the distribution of the flood waters. In addition, they needed protection from wandering herdsmen. The latter group, the nomads, sometimes helped the settled peoples as soldiers, merchants, and purveyors of meat and other animal products. But they also became the bane of the peasants and their rulers when they pillaged the farms and sacked the cities. Herdsman and peasant often fought each other, like Cain and Abel, and yet they also needed each other. In arid lands having long hot summers and cold winter nights, both had to coexist in order to survive.

Map. 1. Physical Map of the Middle East. Source: Department of Defense, Defense Mapping Agency and the Topographic and Hydrographic centers, Washington, D.C.

Location

The Middle East is the natural crossroads of the "Old World" or the Afro-Eurasian land mass. It is also the "land of the seven seas." It lies athwart the water route from the southern Ukraine to the Mediterranean, via the Black Sea, the Bosporus, the Sea of Marmora, the Dardanelles, and the Aegean Sea. At various times in history an area between the Nile Delta and the Sinai Peninsula has been adapted to accommodate shipping between the Mediterranean and the Red Sea. Since the taming of the one-humped camel around 3000 B.C., people have crossed the deserts with their merchandise, flocks, and household goods. Even the high mountains of Anatolia and Iran did not bar passage to men with horses, donkeys, or two-humped camels. Invaders and traders have entered the Middle East from central Asia, Europe, and Africa ever since prehistoric times. Rarely in the past four thousand years have the peoples of the Middle East known any respite from outside pressures or influences.

Consider what this accessibility means for the Middle East, compared with some other parts of the world. The civilizations of China and Japan developed in relative isolation; invading "barbarians" were first tamed and then absorbed into the political and religious system. The people of England lived for centuries in what they smugly called "splendid isolation" and regarded foreign affairs as "something, usually unpleasant, that happens to someone else." The United States long felt free from any fear of outside invasion. Writing as an American to my fellow citizens, who may sometimes feel like criticizing the political attitudes and actions of Middle Eastern peoples, I suggest that we ask ourselves some questions: When did we last fight a war on American soil? When did we last experience a foreign military occupation? When did we even fear hostile raids from across our borders? By contrast, Middle Eastern peoples have known foreign conquest, outside domination, and a continuing exchange of people and animals (but also goods and ideas) with both the East and West.

Resources

Nature did not endow the Middle East as lavishly as North America or Europe. There are no more grassy plains. Over nine-tenths of the forests have been cut down. Drinkable water is scarce, hence precious, almost everywhere. Some coal and lignite are mined in Anatolia. A few mountainous areas harbor deposits of copper, iron, and other metals, often worked since ancient times. These resources do not amount to much. More plentiful are sand and limestone, other building materials, and sunlight (which is good news if solar energy becomes the major source of power).

But what about oil? It is true that some areas, especially around the Persian (or Arab) Gulf, have immense petroleum deposits, about two-thirds of the world's known reserves. The oil has magnified the importance of the Middle East lately. Its blessings, though, are showered on a few countries, mainly Saudi Arabia, Iran, Kuwait, Iraq, and the United Arab Emirates. Exploitation of Middle Eastern oil did not start until this century; it became large-scale only after 1945. For most of history, crude petroleum was a medicine, a pitch for caulking riverboats, or the cause of mysterious fires that were objects of religious veneration, but not the source of wealth and power that it has now become. And who knows how long it will last?

Human Diversity

The Middle East's geography has helped create the diversity of its inhabitants. Varied landscapes—mountains and plains, river valleys and deserts—make for differing life-styles. Relatively inaccessible mountains, further isolated in winter and spring by fast-flowing streams, have protected religious and ethnic minorities in countries like Lebanon and Yemen. On the other hand, frequent invasions have brought new races, religions, and languages into the Middle East. The result is a vast mosaic of peoples, a living museum of physical types, belief systems, languages, and cultures.

This diversity may not always show up on statistical tables like Table 1. Even when it does, remember that the religion of nine-tenths of the people in the Middle East is Islam. Half the population of the area speaks Arabic; the other half primarily speaks Turkish or Persian. The mosaic of separate ethnic and religious groups is starting to crumble. General primary schooling, the transistor radio, and now TV are spreading universal culture, especially among young people. Rising oil revenues, industrialization, and the growth of cities have also made the people seem more alike.

But cultural and religious differences remain politically relevant, as the following examples illustrate. Lebanon's civil wars of 1958 and 1975-1976 were partly caused by the feeling of many Muslims that they did not enjoy equal power and prestige with the Christians, who claimed to be the majority in the country. The present leadership of Syria comes disproportionately from a minority sect of Islam, the Alawis, who used the officer corps to rise to power within a society otherwise dominated by Sunni Muslims. Christian Arabs, especially the Greek Orthodox, who make up less than 5 percent of Syria's population and about 10 percent of Lebanon's, outstripped the Muslims in promoting the early growth of Arab nationalism in those countries. Iraq's politics are bedeviled by differences between Sunni and Shi'i Muslim Arabs, both of whom oppose the desire of the Kurds (almost a fifth of the country's population) for a separate state. Israel, though predominantly Jewish, has an Arab minority of over half a million living within its pre-1967 borders and currently administers lands

TABLE 1
Basic Statistics for Middle Eastern Countries

Country	Area (sq. mi./km^2)	Population (year)	Languages	Religions (C = Christian M = Muslim)
Afghanistan	252,100/653,000	20,330,000 (1977)	Pashto Persian	99% M
Bahrain	256/662	256,600 (1976)	Arabic Persian	96% M, 3% C
Cyprus	3,572/9,251	639,000 (1976)	Greek Turkish	82% C, 18% M
Egypt*	386,900/1,102,000	38,228,200 (1976)	Arabic	93% M, 7% C
Iran	636,293/1,648,000	33,591,900 (1976)	Persian Turkish Kurdish	98% M
Iraq	168,928/437,522	11,505,000 (1976)	Arabic Kurdish Turkish	95% M, 5% C
Israel*	7,992/20,700	3,590,700 (1977)	Hebrew Arabic	85% Jewish 10% M, 5% C
Jordan*	36,833/95,396	2,779,000 (1976)	Arabic	94% M, 6% C
Kuwait	6,532/16,918	994,800 (1975)	Arabic	95% M, 4% C
Lebanon	3,950/10,230	2,961,000 (1976)	Arabic French	50% M, 45% C
Oman	120,000/300,000	791,000 (1976)	Arabic	100% M
Qatar	4,400/11,400	180,000 (1975)	Arabic	99% M
Saudi Arabia	865,000/2,240,000	7,200,600 (1975)	Arabic	100% M
Sudan	967,500/2,505,813	16,126,000 (1976)	Arabic various languages	70% M, 5% C 25% animist
Syria*	71,498/185,180	7,595,000 (1976)	Arabic	87% M, 13% C
Turkey	300,948/779,452	40,197,700 (1975)	Turkish Kurdish Arabic	98% M
United Arab Emirates	32,300/83,600	656,000 (1975)	Arabic Persian Urdu	96% M
Yemen Arab Republic	77,200/200,000	5,237,900 (1975)	Arabic	100% M
Yemen, South	111,074/287,680	1,749,000 (1975)	Arabic	99% M

*Area figures and population estimates are based on boundaries existing on 4 June 1967.

Source: 1978 Britannica Book of the Year (Chicago: Encyclopaedia Britannica, 1978), passim.

containing over 1.1 million more Arab Muslims and Christians. Even the Jews of Israel are divided between those of European origin (called Ashkenazim) and those of Asian or African background (often called Sephardim or Orientals). I realize that these sectarian and ethnic differences are confusing at first, but I plan to deal with them in more detail later. If you want to have the terms defined now, you can find them in the glossary.

CONCLUSION

The interaction between human beings and their physical surroundings is a much more fascinating subject than most students realize. The bad old ways of teaching geography by making schoolchildren memorize the names of mountains, rivers, capitals, or principal products still scares away many readers. I intend to bring in the facts and names as I need them. Once we get into the history of the various peoples of the Middle East, you will have little trouble absorbing the geographical data, as nomadic tribes confront peasants, as urban centers absorb invading soldiers, or as oil discoveries bestow sudden benefits on backward areas. History is not limited to shaykhs and shahs, or to presidents and politicians; it is also the story of tradesmen and teachers, artisans and peasants, herders of goats and warriors on horseback. In the chapters that follow, you will see how they used the mountains, plains, and valleys that appear on the first map, and how they filled the Middle East with cities, dynastic kingdoms, and contending nation-states.

2

The Middle East
before Muhammad

Every profession has its own special hazards. For historians, it is the urge to trace causal relationships as far back as they can go. We are trained to see that no event or trend simply emerged, like Venus from her seashell, without some prior reason, which must in turn have been caused by something else. But where does the concise history of the Middle East begin? If history can be defined as mankind's recorded past, then the Middle East has had more history than any other part of the world. The human species probably originated in Africa, but our best available evidence shows that the main breakthroughs to civilization occurred in the Middle East. It was here that most staple food crops were initially cultivated, most farm animals first domesticated, and the earliest agricultural villages established. Here too arose the world's oldest cities, the first governments, and the earliest religious and legal systems. Writing and the preservation of records were Middle Eastern inventions. Without them history would be inconceivable.

Also inconceivable would be a complete coverage of all aspects of Middle East history in a concise narrative. It is easy to cut out trivia, but I hate to omit the entire span of history from the earliest civilizations in the valleys of the Nile and the Tigris-Euphrates region up to the decline and fall of the Roman Empire. This subject is by no means trivial, but its omission reduces our time span from sixty centuries to fifteen. My excuse is that courses in the history of Western civilization or the ancient world commonly drop the Middle East after the fall of Rome. The conventional date of this event is 476, but you probably know that the center of Roman power and culture had already shifted to the eastern Mediterranean, where it would last for almost another thousand years. It is precisely where traditional Western civilization courses leave the Middle East that this concise history should start.

A MINIMUM OF ANTIQUITY

There is something admirable about the way human beings adapt to seemingly adverse living conditions: the heat of Libya or the cold of Siberia, the crowds of Calcutta or the vast emptiness of the Great Plains, the bureaucratized anonymity of a big university or the insularity of a small college. People often turn adversity to advantage: the Yankee farmer scrabbles a living from his rocky hillside, the camel nomad finds seasonal water and vegetation in the desert, and the architect designs a handsome structure to fit an oddly shaped city block. I see much of this adaptability in the history of the ancient Middle East.

During the last ten thousand years before the birth of Christ, the peoples of the Middle East developed various skills to cope with their changing environment. They tamed asses and cattle to bear their burdens and share their labors. They built ovens hot enough to fire clay pottery. As the uplands became dry and parched, they learned to harness the great rivers to support the cultivation of their food supply. They made tools and weapons from bronze and later from forged iron. They devised alphabets suitable for sending messages and keeping records on tablets of clay or rolls of papyrus. They developed cults and rituals to give meaning to their lives. They absorbed Medes and Persians invading from the north and various Semitic peoples from Arabia. They submitted to Alexander's Macedonians between 334 and 323 B.C., but acculturated them within a short time. Finally, in the last century before Christ, the lands east and south of the Mediterranean were absorbed into the Roman Empire.

ROME AND PERSIA

You may be surprised to learn that Rome took many pages from the books of ancient Middle Eastern empires. During the period of the Achaemenid dynasty (550-330 B.C.), Persia, the land that we now call Iran, had ruled over various ethnic and religious groups in an area stretching from the Indus to the Nile. The kings and nobles followed the religion of Zoroaster, who had lived in the sixth century B.C. He believed in a supreme deity, Ahura Mazda ("Wise Lord"), creator of the material and spiritual worlds, source of both light and darkness, founder of the moral order, lawgiver, and judge of all being. There was an opposing force, Ahriman, represented by darkness and disorder. Although Zoroaster predicted that Ahura Mazda would ultimately win the cosmic struggle, all people were free to choose between Good and Evil, Light and Darkness, the Truth and the Lie. Zoroastrians venerated light, through a network of fire temples tended by a large priestly class. Zoroastrianism appealed mainly to

Persians. The Achaemenid kings tolerated the diverse beliefs and practices of their other subjects as long as they obeyed the laws, paid their taxes, and sent their sons to the Persian army. When Alexander humbled the Achaemenids and absorbed their empire into his own, he hoped to fuse Hellenic (Greek) ways into the culture of the Middle East. Egyptians, Mesopotamians, and Persians found many of their ideas, institutions, and administrators co-opted into his far-flung, short-lived realm.

Something similar happened to Rome later on. By bringing together under one rule all the peoples of the Mediterranean world, the Roman Empire stimulated trade and the interchange of peoples and folkways. Several Middle Eastern religions and mystery cults spread among the Romans. Two of these were Mithraism, which had grown up in Persia, and Christianity, originally a Jewish sect whose base of support was broadened by Paul and the early apostles. It is interesting that most of the early church fathers lived in Anatolia, Syria, Egypt, and North Africa. These areas— later Islam's heartland—were the scene of the first development of most Christian doctrines and institutions. By the late third century, Christianity (while officially banned) prevailed in many parts of the eastern Mediterranean. Its appeal, relative to other religions, was probably due to its successful incorporation of the attractive features of earlier belief systems. To give an example, the Egyptians could identify the risen Christ with Osiris, one of their ancient gods.

When the Emperor Constantine (r. 311-337) converted to Christianity (a slower process than we might think), he redirected the course of history, both Middle Eastern and Western. Rome became a Christian empire. The emperor ordered the construction of a new capital, strategically situated on the straits linking the Black Sea to the Aegean. He called it Constantinople, after himself. Its older name, Byzantium, survives in the parlance of historians who call his "new" state the "Byzantine Empire." Actually, it would be better to go on calling it Rome, just as people did in the fourth century (and long afterwards). Even now, when Arabs, Turks, and Persians speak of "Rum," they mean what we term the Byzantine Empire, its lands (especially Anatolia), or the believers in its religion, Greek Orthodox Christianity. Rum was far from the Italian city on the banks of the Tiber, but the old Roman idea of the universal and multicultural empire lived on in this Christian and Byzantine form. Later on, Arabs and other Muslims would pick it up.

Roman rule benefited the peoples of the Middle East. Their trading and manufacturing cities flourished, just as before. Greek, Syrian, and Egyptian merchants grew rich from the trade between Europe, Asia, and East Africa. Arab camel nomads, or bedouin, carried cloth and spices (plus the proverbial gold, frankincense, and myrrh) across the deserts. Other

Middle Easterners sailed through the Red Sea, the Persian Gulf, and the Indian Ocean, to the lands farther east. Surviving remains of Roman buildings at Leptis Magna (Libya), Jerash (Jordan), and Ba'albek (Lebanon) give us a hint of the grandeur of Rome in the Middle East.

But Roman dominion had its darker side. Syria and Egypt, the granaries of the ancient world, were taxed heavily to support large armies of occupation and a top-heavy bureaucracy in Rome and Constantinople. Peasants, fleeing to the great cities to escape taxes, could find no work there. Instead, they became part of a rootless mob, rioting frequently over social and religious issues. In principle, an urbane tolerance of other people's beliefs and customs was the hallmark of a Roman gentleman. But we also know that Roman soldiers tried to put down a Jewish rebellion by destroying the Temple in Jerusalem. Many of Jesus' early followers were tortured or killed for their refusal to worship the emperor.

Christian Rome proved even more intolerant. The spread and triumph of Christianity brought it into the mainstream of Hellenistic (or "Greek-influenced") philosophy. This led to some major doctrinal crises, as Christians debated the precise nature of Christ. The points at issue are hard to grasp nowadays and are apt to puzzle Christians (as well as everyone else). Let me simplify things a little. The essence of Christianity, what makes it distinct from Judaism and Islam (the other monotheistic or "one God" religions), is its teaching that God, acting out of love for an often sinful humanity, sent His son, Jesus, to live on earth among men and to redeem them through his suffering and death on the cross. Anyone who hopes to be reunited with God in the next world must accept Jesus as Christ (Greek for "messiah" or "anointed one") and as his personal lord and savior. The centrality of Jesus Christ as mediator between God and man led the early Christians into many disputes over his nature.

Dissident Christian Sects

One Christian group, the Arians, who arose in the early fourth century, taught that Christ, though divinely inspired and sired, was still a man not equivalent to God. Opponents of the Arians argued that, if Christ were merely human, his crucifixion, death, and resurrection could not redeem mankind. They won the church's acceptance of Christ's divinity at a council held in Nicaea in 325. Arianism became a heresy, and its followers were persecuted as if they were traitors to the Roman Empire. Most Christians accepted the Nicene Creed, which incorporated Christ into the divine trinity: Father, Son, and Holy Spirit. Did this make Christ the same as God? If so, then what about the Gospel stories of his mother's pregnancy, his birth, baptism, mission, and suffering—all essentially human attributes? The early church fathers, heirs to a rich tradition of Hellenistic thought, worried about these problems. Even for the poor, the humble, the unlettered masses, the nature of Christ was a burning issue, especially in the great Christian centers of the Middle East: Antioch, Alexandria, and Constantinople. While learned scholars disputed, Christian mobs brawled, rioted, and pillaged over the true nature of the Prince of Peace!

In Antioch grew up a school of theologians called the Nestorians, who saw Christ as two distinct persons, divine and human, closely and inseparably joined. A church council at Ephesus condemned this view in 430, after which the emperor and the Orthodox church tried to suppress Nestorianism throughout the Byzantine Empire. Many Nestorians took refuge in Persia, sending out missionaries to central Asia, India, China, and even southern France. Some of their opponents, called Monophysites, went to the opposite extreme, claiming that Christ had only a single and wholly divine nature within his person. Especially strong in Alexandria, this Monophysite position won many followers in Egypt, Syria, and Armenia (an independent kingdom in eastern Anatolia). But the majority of Orthodox bishops, meeting in Chalcedon in 451, declared it to be a heresy too. The Orthodox church sought a compromise formula between the two extremes: Christ the savior was at the same time the perfect God and perfect man. These two natures, though separate, were combined within the single person of Jesus Christ. Whenever the Byzantine emperor supported the Chalcedonian formula, the Orthodox bishops would use the government to persecute Egyptians and Syrians who would not recant their Monophysite heresy. This policy effectively alienated them from Constantinople and paved the way for the seventh-century Arab conquests and the subordination of Eastern Christianity to Islam.

This issue seems petty now. Some modern historians think that material motives account for the differences among Middle Eastern Christians. No doubt Egyptians and Syrians resented the high Byzantine taxes. Others disliked the subordination of their bishops to the Constantinople patriarch. Ancient Middle Eastern mysticism inevitably clashed with Hellenistic rationalism. In addition, there were personality conflicts and power struggles: Christian bishops were all too human. But when all is said and done, Christological issues were vital to these Middle Eastern peoples, whose lives in this world were guided by religion in preparation for the Judgment Day and the life to come. Someday, perhaps, our descendants will wonder why we fought so vehemently about abortion, busing, and gun control!

Rome's Persian Rivals

The Roman Empire never monopolized the Middle East. There was always a rival state in Persia, which covered an area larger than today's

Iran. It usually included what we now call Iraq (Mesopotamia) and lands east of Iran, such as present-day Pakistan, Afghanistan, and Soviet central Asia. Large mountain ranges, such as the Zagros in the area north of the Persian Gulf, the Elburz just south of the Caspian Sea, and the highlands of Khurasan, accumulated enough rain and snow to support hundreds of hillside agricultural villages. The Persian peasants were also clever in channeling groundwater through subterranean *qanats*, a sophisticated irrigation system that supported farms and homes in otherwise parched lowlands. The Persians were far superior to the Romans in bronze casting and iron working. Both Eastern and Western cultures drew heavily on Persian architectural motifs, such as the dome mounted on squinches, the shaded courtyard, and huge bas-relief murals.

During the four centuries surrounding the birth of Christ, Persia was ruled by the Parthians, a dynasty that historians have tended to underrate because so little is known about it. Part of the problem is that the written histories of the Parthian dynasty have come from the Romans, who tried unsuccessfully to conquer them, and the Sasanids, the Persian dynasty that succeeded them in A.D. 226. We cannot expect these sources to be sympathetic. But archaeological excavations have proved the Parthians to be enthusiastic hunters and horsemen, talented artisans and architects, and devoted to the preservation of Persian culture and Zoroastrianism, though tolerant of Buddhism and Judaism.

Their successors, the Sasanid dynasty, usually get credit for Persia's revival. Between the third and seventh centuries, they built up an extensive empire (shown on map 2), established Zoroastrianism as the state religion, and set up a strong and centralized administration. The early Sasanids sent scholars to many other countries to collect books, which were then translated into the Pahlavi (Middle Persian) language, and to gather scientific and technical lore. Many foreign scholars were attracted to Persia, a tolerant kingdom where Nestorian Christians, Jews, and Buddhists could worship and proselytize freely. When the Byzantine bigots drove out the Nestorians in the fifth century, some of their scholars found refuge at the great Persian university of Jundishapur, which thus became a center for the preservation of Hellenistic culture—indeed, the humanistic culture of the whole ancient world. Scholars and students from all parts of the world came to teach and to study, unhindered by racial prejudice, religious dogma, or political restrictions. Zoroastrianism remained almost exclusively Persian, but it gave birth to a more popular dualistic faith called Manichaeism, which spread throughout Europe and Asia during the Sasanid era. Meanwhile, Persian art influenced architecture, sculpture, painting, and even jewelry and textile design from Western Europe to

China. Ctesiphon, the Sasanid capital slightly south of what is now Baghdad, had vaulted buildings higher and wider than any to be found in the Roman Empire. Small wonder that this rich and cultivated kingdom defied the Romans and their Byzantine successors. With the help of their bedouin allies in Arabia, Persian soldiers managed to overrun Syria, Palestine, and Egypt early in the seventh century. However, this climax would prove short-lived.

THE ARABS

It was not the proud Persians who put an end to the Hellenistic age in the Middle East, but their camel-driving allies, the Arabs. The domestication of the camel, sometime before 1000 B.C., enabled bands of men to cross the vast deserts of Arabia, eastern Iran, and eventually North Africa. The Arabian dromedary, or one-humped camel, is famous for its ability to go for days across great distances without needing water. This is due to its prodigious capacity—twenty-five gallons in ten minutes' drinking time— its retention of the water it takes in, and its memory for water holes. Compared with other animals, the camel loses little water by perspiration, skin evaporation, and urination. Padded feet, short hair, and a high ratio of skin surface to body mass all help it stand the heat. Camels can subsist on thorny plants and dry grasses that other animals cannot digest. They store fat—not water—in their humps as a reserve against scarcity. It is hard for us Westerners to learn how to ride and guide camels, but their reputation for stubbornness and spitefulness is ill-deserved. Our jokes and songs about camels reveal our ignorance rather than their character.

The people who tamed the camel, probably first for food and later for transportation, were Arabs. No one is sure where they came from. Popular legends have identified the Arabs as descendants of Ishmael, Abraham's son by his Egyptian maid Hagar. It is generally thought that the Arabs are very much like the ancestors of other peoples who speak Semitic languages, such as the Hebrews, the Assyrians, and the Arameans. The difference is that the latter originally settled in the Fertile Crescent (Syria and Mesopotamia). In ancient times there were groups of people who would become sedentarized, while others would move out of settled areas. When population outstripped the means of subsistence in well-endowed areas like the Fertile Crescent, some groups took to herding sheep and goats in lands unsuited for cultivation of crops. A few ventured farther away and migrated from one desert oasis to another (just as others moved up and down mountains) to find seasonal water and vegetation for their flocks. Those who had mastered the camel were able to move even farther away

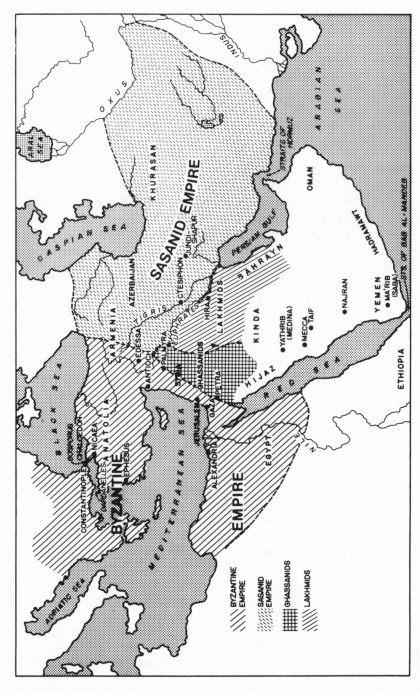

Map 2. Byzantine and Sasanid Empires circa 600

from the lands of the peasant, the shepherd, and the tax collector.

Conditions in Arabia

The Arabian peninsula was just such a place: desolate, bereft of rivers and lakes, cut off by sand and sea from all but the bravest invader. An exception to this was the Yemen mountains near the southern tip, which I will discuss later. The prevailing west winds from the Mediterranean, which brings winter rain to Syria and Anatolia, rarely carry moisture as far south as Arabia. What rain does come is usually stopped by the hills of the Hijaz, the western part, leaving central and eastern Arabia bone dry. An occasional freak storm can send floods coursing down the dry valleys, but most of the water runs off because the ground is too hard to absorb it. Fortunately, underground water does reach the surface in springs, water holes, and oases, where date palms flourish. The Arabs learned to migrate continually, following the seasonal availability of groundwater and forage for their animals. Milk and dates—occasionally meat and bread—were their staple diet.

It would have been hard for an individual or even a small band of people to survive in such a harsh environment. The Arabs were organized into clans and tribes, which were extended kinship groups that migrated together and held property in common. Significantly, the tribes protected their members against other nomads and the settled peoples. The Arabs were belligerent and zealous in defending their honor. Tests of strength, which took the form of raiding and skirmishing, were common. Each tribe was governed by a council of adult men, representing the various clans or smaller family groupings. The council chose a leader, called a shaykh, usually the member of the tribe most respected for his bravery and generosity. In a few tribes the leadership was hereditary, but election of the shaykh was more common. The council decided on questions of war and peace, since the tribe augmented its meager income by raiding other tribes and "protecting" the commercial caravans that plied between Syria and the Indian Ocean. Some bedouin tribesmen served as auxiliaries in the Persian or Roman armies; one of the third-century Roman emperors was named Philip the Arab. Others built trading cities on the fringes of the settled areas, like Palmyra in Syria, Petra in Jordan, and Najran in Yemen. And still others reverted to farming land, such as the region around Yathrib (now called Medina). But camel breeding and raiding were most Arabs' favorite (and most respected) activities.

Arabian Culture

If the bedouin Arabs, due to their adaptation to desert life, lacked the refinement of the Romans or the Persians, they were not wholly uncivilized. They were warlike; hunger or habit led them to prey on one another or on outsiders. Their constant movement gave them little chance to develop architecture, sculpture, or painting. However, they did possess a highly portable form of artistic expression—poetry. Pre-Islamic poetry embodied the Arab code of virtue, the *muruwwah*: bravery in battle, patience in misfortune, persistence in revenge (the only possible justice where no governments exist), protection of the weak, defiance toward the strong, hospitality to the visitor (even a total stranger), generosity to the poor, loyalty to the tribe, and fidelity in keeping promises. These were the moral principles people needed to survive in the desert, and the poems helped to fix them in their minds. Recited from memory by the Arab tribesmen and their descendants, these poems expressed the joys and tribulations of nomadic life, extolled the bravery of their own tribes, and lampooned the faults of their rivals. Some Arabs loved poetry so much that they used to stop wars and raids for an annual festival where poets might try out their new verses and match wits with one another. Pre-Islamic poetry helped to shape the Arabic language, the literature and culture of the Arabs, and hence the thoughts and behavior of Arabic-speaking peoples right up to the present.

Southern Arabia

During the time when Rome and Persia seemed to dominate the Middle East, there was actually a third power, far-off and little appreciated. Southern Arabia, with its monsoon rains and lush vegetation, seemed like a world apart, but it fostered the growth of several ancient city-states. Saba (whence came the mythic Queen of Sheba who visited King Solomon) is the best known. Long before the time of Christ, its people, the Sabaeans, had developed a thriving trade across the Indian Ocean. They were the first people to make India and its products known to the Roman world and to colonize the East African mainland. The Sabaeans dammed up mountain streams and terraced the Yemen hillsides to support an elaborate agriculture. Their main export crop was frankincense, used by the pagan Romans, who cremated their dead, to mask the offensive odor. The spread of Christianity, which replaced cremation with burial, hurt the frankincense trade. When Ethiopia turned Christian and teamed up with the Byzantines, the Arabs of Yemen, whose kings had converted to Judaism, found themselves caught in the middle. A dam break, an Ethiopian invasion, and a commercial depression combined to weaken southern Arabia in the sixth century.

Conditions in the Sixth Century

The political situation in sixth-century Arabia ranged from complex to chaotic. The last of the great South Arabian kingdoms had been reduced in 525 to a dependency on Ethiopia. Three outside powers contended for control: the Byzantine Empire, champion of Orthodox Christianity; Sasanid Persia, officially Zoroastrian but harboring Nestorian Christians, Jews, dissident Manichaeans, and other sects; and Ethiopia, which espoused the same Monophysite Christianity as the Byzantines' rebellious Egyptian subjects, the Copts. Each empire had a client Arab tribe that it paid well and furnished with the trappings of monarchy in return for military service. The peninsula was frequently ravaged by wars among these three tribes: the pro-Byzantine Ghassanids of the northwest; the pro-Sasanid Lakhmids with their capital at Hira near the Euphrates; and the Christian tribe of Kinda, situated in central Arabia and friendly to Ethiopia. Other Arab tribes, some still animist, others partially Zoroastrian, Jewish, or Christian (though usually not Orthodox), would mix in their quarrels. Southern Arabia experienced two consecutive foreign occupations: Ethiopian (ca. 525-575) and Persian (ca. 575-625).

Mecca

Most of central and northern Arabia remained precariously independent. In periods of peace the area was crossed by the camel caravans of the overland trade route between Syria and Yemen. Despite the declining market for frankincense, overland trade was gaining in importance as the shoals and pirates of the Red Sea made sailing hazardous. The Byzantine-Sasanian wars also tended to divert trade toward western Arabia. One of the Arabian towns, formerly tied to the Sabaean kingdom as a religious shrine, was emerging as a major station for caravan traders. This was Mecca, set inland from the Red Sea among the mountains of the Hijaz. It was a hot, dry place unsuited for farming. Mecca acquired some of its wealth and power from trade. But its primacy among Arab towns stemmed from three additional assets: an annual poets' fair at neighboring Ukaz; nearby Mount Arafat, a pilgrimage center even in pre-Islamic times; and its Ka'bah, a cube-shaped structure of unknown antiquity that housed idols (reportedly 360) of the various gods and goddesses venerated by the Arab tribesmen. Also close to Mecca were lesser shrines honoring individual goddesses, notably al-Lat, al-Uzza, and al-Manat, worshipped by the pagan Meccans themselves.

Later on, some Muslims would portray pre-Islamic Mecca as a sinkhole of wanton vice and corruption, although they also believed that Abraham and Ishmael had personally built the Ka'bah for the worship of the one true God (it had later been corrupted). Mecca was probably an amalgam of goodness and iniquity, a small businessman's paradise. Its rulers belonged to a sedentarized Arab tribe called the Quraysh, later to become both famous and infamous in the annals of Islamic history. Every Muslim caliph for more than six centuries would trace his ancestry back to this family of traders, shrinekeepers, and politicians. Under their leadership, the centers of Middle Eastern power would shift from the Mediterranean Sea and the Iranian plateau to the Arabian Desert and the Fertile Crescent. In the conventional usage of historians, this shift marked the transition from the ancient to the medieval era. The prime cause of the transition will soon become clear: Muhammad, the last and the greatest of the prophets of Islam, was a Meccan of the Quraysh.

3

The Prophet of Mecca

Around the year 570 (by our reckoning), an Ethiopian army marched northward from Yemen, with a baggage train of elephants, and tried to take Mecca. It failed. Smallpox broke out among the Ethiopians, and they withdrew to Yemen. Soon afterwards they were driven out of Arabia entirely. From then on, the "Year of the Elephant" was remembered by Arabs—especially Meccans—as a lucky one. It is generally thought that Muhammad was born in that year, a few months after his father's death. Before Muhammad was six, his mother also died. His grandfather, assuming responsibility for the boy, sent him out to live with some bedouin Arabs. Meccans often farmed out their small children so that they might learn to speak better Arabic and get a healthier start in life. When his grandfather died, Muhammad's upbringing was taken over by his uncle, a caravan merchant named Abu-Talib, and so he learned the business of buying, selling, and transporting goods. Muhammad's family was called the clan of Hashim, or Hashimites. They were a reputable, though impoverished, branch of the ruling Quraysh tribe.

MUHAMMAD'S EARLY LIFE

Nowadays, when many historians look to psychology as a key to understanding great men and women of the past, it is frustrating to know so little about Muhammad's childhood. To be sure, the Quran (the book containing God's revelations to Muhammad) tells us a little about his formative years. Pious early Muslims, gathering all they could about the man they call "the Seal of the Prophets," have furnished more information. The documentation on Muhammad far exceeds what we have on the life of Christ. But we wonder how heredity and environment combined to produce this deeply religious man who was also a brilliant political leader. What truths lurk behind the legends, recorded by early Muslim biographers, about the angels who opened five-year-old Muhammad's chest to cleanse his heart, or about a Christian hermit who later identified a mark of prophethood between the lad's shoulders?

We do know that Muhammad, despite the handicaps of being orphaned and without property in a highly materialistic society, developed into a capable and honest merchant. During this period of his life a widow named Khadijah entrusted him with the care of her caravan. When he acquitted himself well, she proposed marriage to him. Although she was supposedly forty, fifteen years older than Muhammad, the marriage proved to be a happy one. She bore him six children, and Muhammad took no other wives during her lifetime. The business (and hence his reputation) did well. In the normal course of events, Muhammad should have become one of Mecca's leading citizens, even though the Umayyads, the strongest clan within the Quraysh tribe, looked down on the Hashimite family to which he belonged.

Confrontation with Pagan Arab Values

Muhammad was not entirely happy. The *muruwwah* code of ideal Arab behavior, which parents still taught to their children, was no longer upheld by the Meccan leaders, whose money-making activities as merchants or shrine keepers had made them acquisitive and self-centered. Bravery in battle and generosity to the poor were noble ideals for nomads (what, the Meccans wondered, did they have to give away?), but the sedentarized Arabs of Mecca admired the ability to drive a hard bargain in the marketplace.

What did they believe in, then? The Arabs' polytheistic animism and ancestor worship, a major source of Mecca's income, no longer constituted a living faith, even though pilgrimages to the Ka'bah and other shrines went on. The tribesman believed in his gods only so long as they did what he wanted. He was more apt to fear the jinns, invisible creatures who could do both nice and nasty things to people. There were some Christians in Mecca, just as there were tribes and cities elsewhere in Arabia that had adopted Judaism or some sect of Christianity. There were other pious people, neither Christian nor Jewish but leaning toward monotheism, known as Hanifs. But the Meccan businessmen, profoundly practical, scoffed at ideas like the bodily resurrection or the day of judgment, and at holy laws that might interfere with their pursuit of money and more money. To Muhammad, however, the Jews, Christians, and Hanifs just might have answers to the problems that were gnawing at the core of Meccan society. Many nights he would go to a nearby cave to meditate.

First Revelations

One night in 610, during the Arabic month of Ramadan, Muhammad heard a clanging of bells, out of which came a voice exhorting him to read aloud. In awe and terror, he cried out, "I cannot recite" (for Muhammad, most Muslims believe, was illiterate). The voice replied:

> Read: in the name of thy lord who created
> created mankind from a blood-clot
> Read: for thy Lord the most generous
> he has taught by the pen
> taught man what he knew not. (Quran, 96:1-5)

Fearing that he had gone mad, Muhammad rushed home and asked Khadijah to cover him with a warm coat. His quaking subsided, but then he heard more bells and the voice sounded:

> O thou who are shrouded in thy mantle,
> rise and warn!
> Thy Lord magnify,
> Thy robes purify,
> And from iniquity flee! (Quran, 74:1-5)

Now Khadijah had a cousin who was a Hanif (or, some say, a Christian). He assured her that Muhammad, far from being mad, was God's long-awaited messenger to the Arabs. She went back to her husband and reassured him. He then realized that what he had heard was God's exhortation to proclaim His existence among the Arabs. He must also warn them (just as God had sent earlier prophets to warn Jews and Christians) of an imminent Judgment Day when everyone would be called to account:

> When the earth shall quake with a predestined quaking,
> When the earth shall bring forth her burdens,
> and men shall ask, "What ails her?"
> Upon that day shall she tell her news
> with which thy Lord has inspired her,
> Upon that day shall men come out in scattered groups
> to be shown what they have done.
> Then he who has done one atom's weight of good shall see it
> And he who has done one atom's weight of evil shall see it. (Quran, 109:1-8)

This was an awesome task for an unlettered, middle-aged merchant, an orphan who had gained a precarious hold on a little wealth and status. It would have been tempting to shirk the responsibility. Luckily, he received no more divine messages for quite a while. This gave him time to keep asking himself whether he really was a prophet, to win a few of his friends and relatives, and thus to convince himself that his mission was real.

The Early Muslims

The first believers, though they came from all classes and many of the clans of Meccan society, were mainly young men from the upper middle stratum—the "nearly haves" from which so many revolutions elsewhere have sprung. Some converts were sons or younger brothers of the leading merchants; others were important men who had somehow lost (or failed to attain) the status they wanted within pagan Mecca. A few were "weak," which meant they came from outside the system and had no clan to protect them against harm from other Arabs, or perhaps their families lacked the political clout of the Umayyads or the Hashimites. In this regard, it is interesting that Muhammad's uncle and protector, Abu-Talib, never embraced Islam. Yet Abu-Talib's son, Ali, raised in the Prophet's own home, was one of his first converts. Ali would later marry Muhammad's daughter and play a major role in early Islamic history. Other early converts were Abu-Bakr, Muhammad's best friend and a man of some wealth and social standing; Arkam, a very young member of a prestigious clan, who allowed the first Muslims to meet at his home; Umar, an imposing figure from a weak clan; Uthman, an elegant but quiet youth of the powerful Umayyad family; Bilal, an Ethiopian slave set free by Abu-Bakr; and Zayd ibn Harithah, a captured Christian Arab who lived in Muhammad's household.

Even if the early Muslims had kept a low profile, they would have attracted the notice—and the hostility—of the Meccan leaders. After all, some of them were relatives. Muhammad's message disrupted families and threatened the established order. W. Montgomery Watt, a British scholar whose books on the life of the Prophet have won wide acceptance, has summarized this message in five main points: (1) God is good and all-powerful, (2) God will call all men and women back to Himself on the Last Day and will judge and reward them on the basis of how they acted on earth, (3) people should thank God, through worship, for the blessings He has given the earth, (4) God expects people to share their worldly goods with others needier than themselves, and (5) Muhammad has been designated as God's messenger to his own people, the Arabs. Perhaps I might add that, later on in his mission, Muhammad saw himself as a prophet for all humanity.

Let me put in a semantic point here. During Muhammad's mission, those who believed in him as God's messenger came to be known as Muslims. The Arabic word *muslim* means "one who submits"—to the will of God. The act of submission is *islam*, which became the name of the religion. Its adjective can be either "Muslim" or "Islamic." It is wrong to speak of

"Mohammedanism," although you may see it used for "Islam" in older books. "Moslem" is the same as "Muslim." Please do not say "Ali became an Islam" when you mean "Ali became a Muslim." Do not say "Mecca is an Islam city" for "Mecca is a Muslim (or Islamic) city." Some usages are confusing. An "Islamic scholar" may be a learned Muslim, but the same term is used for a non-Muslim who has studied a lot about Islam. "Islamic history" may mean the story of Islam's development as a religion, or of the community of Muslims as distinct from non-Muslim states, or of any Muslim peoples wherever they have lived. Further clarification is often necessary.

Meccan Opposition

The Meccans who rejected Muhammad's message feared that he might try to take away their wealth and power. What right did he have to attack business practices that they deemed necessary for their success? If God had chosen to reveal Himself then and there, why had He not chosen one of Mecca's leaders? If the pagan tribes accepted Islam, would they stop making their annual pilgrimage (or hajj) to the Ka'bah and the other sacred shrines? We now realize that Muhammad respected the Ka'bah and never wanted to displace it as a center for pilgrims. Nor was he trying to undermine Mecca's economy. Some accounts depict Muhammad as having been so eager to gain the acceptance of the Meccan leaders that he even conceded that three pagan goddesses, al-Lat, al-Uzza, and Manat, were "sacred swans" worthy of veneration. This horrified some of the Muslims. When Muhammad realized the full meaning of what he had done, he emphatically disowned what he had supposed to be a revelation from God, blamed it on Satan, and added:

What, would you have males and He females?
that would indeed be an unjust division.
They are nothing but names you and your fathers have named,
God has sent down no authority touching them. (Quran, 53:21-23)

Muhammad's turnabout on the issue of the three goddesses angered the Meccan leaders, for the keepers of their nearby shrines were Mecca's allies. Unable to attack Muhammad while he had Abu-Talib's protection, the Meccans tried a boycott of the whole Hashimite clan. It failed. Still they could make life miserable for the most vulnerable Muslims, some of whom fled to Christian Ethiopia. Then Muhammad told an even more unlikely tale. He said he had made a miraculous journey one night on a winged horse, first to Jerusalem, then up to the seven levels of Heaven, where he saw the celestial Ka'bah and (by some accounts) talked with God. The pagan Arabs scoffed at these claims, especially after Muhammad's wife said that he had spent that whole night sleeping in his bed.

In 619 Muhammad lost two persons who had helped him significantly in his early mission: Khadijah and Abu-Talib died. Muhammad married many women after that, but none other could match the loyalty and support of his first wife. Without his uncle, Muhammad had no protector within the Hashimite clan, and so the persecution grew worse. The Muslims realized they had to leave Mecca. An attempt to take refuge in nearby Taif failed, and Muhammad had to abase himself to find a new Meccan protector so that he and his followers could safely return home. Their situation in Mecca had become untenable, but where else could the Muslims go?

THE EMIGRATION (*Hijrah*)

During the pilgrimage month in 620, Muhammad was visited by six Arab tribesmen from an agricultural oasis town called Yathrib (now Medina), located some 270 miles (430 kilometers) north of Mecca, just after they had completed the pagan hajj rites at the Ka'bah. They told him that fighting between the two pagan tribes of Yathrib had become so bad that they could no longer protect themselves against the three Jewish tribes with which they shared the oasis. They wanted Muhammad to come and, because of his reputation as an honest man, arbitrate their quarrels. The next year a larger number of pilgrims from Yathrib came to Muhammad. In return for his services as an arbiter, they agreed to give sanctuary to the Meccan Muslims.

This was a great opportunity for Muhammad. He was quick to realize that his mission as a divine spokesman would mean more once he became the chief judge of a city, even if only a motley collection of settled tribes, rather than the spiritual leader of a persecuted band of rebels split between pagan Mecca and Christian Ethiopia. Besides, the presence of Jews in Yathrib made him hope that he might be accepted as a prophet by people who were already worshippers of the one God revealed to them by earlier scriptures. In the following months, he arranged a gradual transfer of his Muslim followers from Mecca to Yathrib. Finally, he and his closest companions went.

This emigration, called the *hijrah* in Arabic, was a major event in Islamic history. It should not be called a "flight," for the *hijrah* was a carefully planned maneuver by Muhammad in response to an invitation by the citizens of Yathrib. It enabled him to organize his followers as a community, as a nation, or (to use the Arabic word that is so hard to translate) as an *ummah*. From then on, Muhammad was both a prophet and a lawgiver, both a religious and a political leader. Islam was both a faith in one God as revealed to Muhammad (and the earlier prophets) and a sociopolitical system. No wonder the Muslims, when they adopted their own calendar, made the first year the one in which the *hijrah* had occurred.

The Struggle for Survival

The establishment of the *ummah* in Yathrib, renamed Medina (or *madinat al-nabi,* the "city of the Prophet"), created new problems for Muhammad. The Arabs of Medina did not all convert at once to Islam, their quarrels proved hard to settle, it was harder still for Muhammad to win the allegiance of the city as a whole. If the Jews of Medina ever harbored any belief in Muhammad as the Messiah or the messenger of God, they were soon disillusioned. His revelations did not agree with what they knew from the Bible, and they rejected his religious authority. Muhammad, on the other hand, saw Islam as the first and most natural monotheism, not a pale imitation of Judaism or Christianity. His revelation from God, collectively known as the Quran, repeatedly called Abraham a Muslim, a man who submitted to God's will. He hoped the Jews would realize that Adam, Noah, Abraham, and the other prophets had lived before there was Judaism as they knew it. He even tried to incorporate into Islam some Jewish practices (as he understood them), such as observing the fast of Yom Kippur ("the Day of Atonement") and leading the Muslims in prayer facing Jerusalem. The Jews were not convinced. Even the Medinan Muslim converts, called *ansar* ("helpers"), got tired of supporting the Meccan emigrants, who showed no aptitude for farming, the economic basis for their oasis. Commerce, which the emigrants did know how to conduct, was impossible so long as pagan Mecca controlled the caravan routes and paid protection money to the nearby bedouin tribes.

If Muhammad was to become the leader of Medina's Jews and *ansar,* the emigrants would have to become self-supporting. The immediate answer was to raid the Meccan caravans. Perhaps, in time, they could gain enough control of the trade route between Syria and Mecca to compete. This was not as easy as you might think, for the Meccan caravans usually went armed and had many of the bedouin tribes on their side. Muhammad and his men were several generations removed from desert life and knew little about the techniques of raiding. But raid they did and, after a few fiascoes, they hit the Meccans hard enough to hurt. To do this, they attacked even during the sacred month, when raiding was forbidden because of the traditional pagan pilgrimage to Mecca. This shocked many of the Arabs, but a Quranic revelation stated:

> They will question you about the holy month and fighting in it,
> Say: "Fighting in it is wrong, but to bar from God's way,

and disbelief in Him,
and the sacred Ka'bah, and to expel its people from it—
that is more wicked in God's sight;
and persecution is more wicked than killing. (Quran, 2:213)

The pagan Meccans saw matters differently. In the second year after the
hijrah—March 624 to be exact—the Muslims were zeroing in on a rich
Umayyad caravan returning from Syria, just as Mecca sent out a
retaliatory army of almost a thousand men. They met Muhammad's forces
(86 emigrants, 238 *ansar*) at a village called Badr, southwest of Medina.
The Muslims won the conflict more because of good tactics than any real
superiority. But nothing succeeds like success. To Muhammad's people,
victory was a tangible sign of God's favor. It also meant prisoners and
booty. The latter was divided up among the warriors, except for a fifth that
(according to a recent revelation) was assigned to the Prophet to support
needy members of the *ummah*.

In addition, the victory at Badr enhanced the prestige of Islam—and of
Medina—in the eyes of the Arab tribesmen. Even though the Meccans got
their revenge by defeating the Muslims at Uhud in 625, they could not go on
to take Medina. The *ummah* survived. Islam was taking root and could not
be eradicated. In 627 Mecca sent out a larger force to capture Medina, but
the Muslims foiled the army by digging a trench around vulnerable parts of
the city. The ditch was too broad for the Meccan horses and camels to
cross, so they turned back in disgust. Meanwhile, Muslim raids from
Medina were making the Meccan caravan trade extremely risky.
Gradually, the tribes started breaking with Mecca and making treaties with
Muhammad that enabled them to take part in these lucrative attacks.

MUSLIM LIFE IN MEDINA

On the domestic front, Muhammad was becoming the head of both a
large household and a small state. Revelations from God now dealt with
laws about marriage and divorce, inheritance, theft and other crimes, and
interpersonal relations, more than with God's power and the Judgment
Day. Besides, on those practical matters where the Quran was silent and
where old Arab customs were no longer applicable, Muhammad's own
sayings and actions were becoming an authoritative guide for Muslim
behavior. For the most part, a non-Muslim can readily admire the humane
common sense that underlay Muhammad's conduct of his public and
private life, and thus appreciate his role as a model for Muslims. But
Westerners are sometimes troubled about two accusations that hostile
critics have leveled against him: his lust for women and his hostile

treatment of the Jews. Here, of course, we run the risk of judging a seventh-century Arab by the standards of our own time and place. All I can do is present a few facts and let you draw what conclusions you will.

Muhammad's Marriages

Before Islam, Arab men used to take as many wives as they could afford (unless they happened to belong to a tribe in which the women were dominant), and various forms of extramarital sexual relations were also accepted. The Quran specifically allowed Muslim men a maximum of four wives, and then only if they treated them all equally. After Khadijah died, Muhammad gradually took other wives, possibly as many as ten, plus a couple of concubines. Some were the widows of his slain followers he married out of charity. Other marriages were with the daughters of tribal chieftains whom Muhammad wanted as allies. Aishah, who became his favorite, was the daughter of Abu-Bakr, his best friend. More troubling to moralists was his marriage to Zaynab, with whom he became infatuated while she was married to his adopted son, Zayd. A Quranic revelation sanctioned her divorce and remarriage, but Muhammad's detractors have been quick to criticize the whole affair. Muhammad believed that his marriages were prescribed for him by God. Anyway, he enjoyed the company of women and never apologized for his sexuality. Likewise, he forbade wailing at funerals until one of his infant sons died, whereupon that rule was forgotten. He could forgive many of the foes he faced on the battlefield, but never a poet who made fun of his mission. Prophets were human beings, not plaster saints.

Muhammad and the Jews

Muhammad's relations with the Jews of Medina got progressively worse as his own power grew. This disturbs many Westerners, partly because it has taken us a long time to get over anti-Muslim prejudices that go back to the Crusades, but also because of inferences we are apt to draw concerning the modern Arab-Israeli conflict. Muhammad recognized many Biblical figures as prophets, or men to whom God had spoken. Jews and Christians were respected as "People of the Book," since they worshipped God as revealed by sacred scriptures. Why could he not have been magnanimous in Medina? Part of the problem was that he expected the Jews to recognize him as God's messenger, just as he had accepted their prophets. However, there was no way they could reconcile his Quran with their sacred scriptures. There were too many discrepancies. He also felt that they were turning some of the less sincere *ansar* against him, trying to trick him with sophisticated arguments and mocking him and his followers in public. The Jews may have seen the Muslims as potential competitors in the marketplace, but we do not have records of their point of view. The split widened. Responding to a Quranic revelation, Muhammad changed the direction of prayer—south toward Mecca instead of north toward Jerusalem. The twenty-four-hour fast of Yom Kippur was dropped, and Muslims started fasting instead during the daylight hours of Ramadan, the month in which Muhammad's first revelation had come. Sabbath observance was replaced by congregational prayers with a sermon on Friday noon. The dietary laws were loosened somewhat. Islam was becoming more distinct and also more Arabian.

Following his victory at Badr, Muhammad expelled one of the Jewish tribes for conspiring with his Meccan foes, but let its members keep their property. The Muslims expelled another Jewish tribe after the defeat at Uhud, seizing its groves of date palms. The last of the three tribes suffered the worst fate: the men were put to the sword; the women and children were sold into slavery. Muhammad believed that the tribe, despite the outward appearance of loyalty, had sided with the Meccans during their Siege of the Trench in 627. He put the case before an associate who seemed neutral, but who really wanted the Jews' property. The resulting slaughter enriched some of the Muslims and raised Muhammad's stature among the Arab tribesmen, for it showed he had no fear of blood reprisals. We should understand, though not necessarily condone, what he did. The Jews were not defenseless. On the other hand, the Muslims feared they might lose their grip on Medina and fall prey to the Meccans and their tribal allies. Neutralizing their enemies seemed essential for their security, if not indeed their survival. Partly because of these incidents, the Quran contains some harsh words about Jews. This did not mean that later Muslim-Jewish relations were usually bad or that Muhammad's policies were the main cause of what we now call the Arab-Israeli conflict.

The Winning of Mecca

It is one of the ironies of history that the pagan leaders of Mecca who had persecuted Muhammad finally gave in to him and prospered under the new order; while the Jews of Arabia, whose beliefs were closer to his, rejected him as a prophet and then suffered severely. The story of Mecca's final capitulation is almost anticlimactic. The emigrants in Medina missed their homes, their families (many were the sons and daughters of leading Meccan merchants), and the Ka'bah, so in 628 Muhammad led a band of would-be pilgrims toward Mecca. They encountered Meccan troops at Hudaybiyah, slightly north of the city, and the two sides hammered out a truce ending their state of war. The Muslims had to go back to Medina but would be let into Mecca the following year to perform the Arab pilgrimage rites. In effect, the Meccans were recognizing the Muslims as equals. Three months after the Hudaybiyah truce, two of the best Arab fighters, Khalid ibn al-Walid and Amr ibn al-As, embraced Islam. They would go on to greater glory as warriors for the *ummah*. Muhammad made more key converts during the 629 pilgrimage. The next year he collected a force of ten thousand men and marched on Mecca. The Meccan leaders, overawed, quickly submitted, and the Muslims occupied the city with very little bloodshed. After that almost everyone in Mecca became Muslim.

Bolstered by Meccan troops, the Muslims defeated a large coalition of Arab tribes from around Taif. The Hijaz was now united under Islam. From then on, other clans and tribes, recognizing Muhammad's power, began sending delegations to Medina, which remained the capital of the new state. As a condition for his support, Muhammad required the tribes to accept Islam and even to pay taxes, a condition that the Quraysh had never been able to impose. Traditional accounts say that by 632 nearly all the Arab tribes were Muslim. It is more likely that certain clans, factions, or individuals within each tribe had embraced Islam. Even today some bedouin tribesmen are Muslims only in name.

Muhammad's Death

The Prophet's last years were clouded by worries about would-be rivals in Arabia, heavy political responsibilities, marital problems, the death of his infant son and several daughters, and failing health. He did manage to lead a final pilgrimage to Mecca in March 632. Thus he finished incorporating into Islam the rituals of the hajj, cleansed of its polytheistic features. In his final sermon he exhorted his followers, "O ye men, listen to my words and take them to heart! Know that every Muslim is a brother to every other Muslim and that you are now one brotherhood."

Soon after his return to Medina, Muhammad retired to Aishah's apartment. He designated her father, Abu-Bakr, to lead public worship in his place, and on 8 June 632 he died.

ASSESSMENT

How do we evaluate Muhammad and what he did? For Muslims he has always been the exemplar of Muslim virtues, such as piety, patience, humor, kindness, generosity, and sobriety. Non-Muslim Westerners, remembering battles and disputations with Islam, have often judged him harshly. He has been called a renegade bishop frustrated in his ambition to become pope, a businessman turned brigand, an imposter who summoned mountains to come to him, an epileptic, and (by some students) a madman. Such statements are unfounded, of course. On the other hand, these different assessments point out the fact that observant Jews and sincere

Christians do not believe, as Muslims must, that God really spoke to Muhammad.

The life of any famous person serves as a lens or mirror by which other people, individually or in groups, view themselves and the world. The biographer or the historian stresses some facts and omits or downplays others. The reader seizes upon certain points and expands them to fit a preconceived image. How then to judge Muhammad? I see him as a kind and sincere man, urban but not urbane (he resented the poets' mockery, for instance), with an overwhelming faith in God and in himself as His final messenger, a warner to Arabs and other people about an impending Judgment Day, and the organizer of the *ummah*, a community in which Muslim believers could best prepare themselves for that dread occasion. He must have been a skilled political and military tactician; how many other leaders have succeeded in uniting the Arabs? I could say more, but let me not inhibit you from forming your own conclusions or studying more about this remarkable man.

What Is Islam?

When we think about Islam—or any religion that has lasted for a long time—we should remember that it has evolved through history and will continue to do so. It has varied from time to time, from place to place, and perhaps even from one person to another. Religions as personal belief systems are difficult to describe: How do you speak or write about someone else's thoughts? Let me try to answer the question anyway.

BASIC BELIEFS

Islam is the act of submission to the will of God ("Allah" in Arabic). In the broadest sense, every object in the universe has its own "islam," meaning that it conforms to God's rules, or to what atheists might call the laws of nature. Human beings, creatures capable of reason, have been made free to choose whether and how to submit to God's will. Many refuse out of ignorance, or because they have forgotten the divine commandments they once knew. Some Christians and Jews may have been misled by their scriptures, or rather by the way they have interpreted them. But anyone who submits to God's will, worships Him, and expects His reward or punishment is, broadly speaking, a "muslim."

God

In common usage, though, a Muslim is anyone who believes that God last revealed Himself through the Quran to Muhammad on behalf of all mankind. What is God? It is not easy to describe the Infinite. To the Muslim, God is all-powerful and all-knowing, the creator of all that was and is and will be, the righteous judge of good and evil, and the generous guide to mankind through His messengers and His scriptures. He has no peer, no partner, no offspring, and no human attributes that might limit Him.

"La ilaha ill' Allah, wa Muhammad rasul Allah"—there is no god

whatever but the one God, and Muhammad is the messenger of God. This is the first of the famous five pillars of Islam; it can be found in the muezzin's call to prayer; it is emblazoned in white letters on the green flag of Saudi Arabia. Presumably anyone professing Judaism or Christianity agrees that there is only one God, but monotheism is more than rejecting a pantheon of gods and goddesses. There can be no other Absolute Good; all else is relative. All material blessings—our houses, furniture, cars, clothing, and food—must be valued less highly than the one true God. The pleasures we pursue are (if lawful) fine, but finer yet is the satisfaction of God's commands. Spouses and consorts, parents and children, friends and colleagues may be dear to us, but must be second to God in our hearts. God is the giver of life and death. Some Muslims say that He has predestined all human actions. But most now argue that He has given us free will, making us strictly accountable for what we choose to do. God wants willing worshippers, not human robots.

Angels

Muslims believe that God works in a universe inhabited by various creatures, not all of whom can be seen, heard, or felt by human beings. Jinns (or genies) do much good and evil here on earth and are addressed in some Quranic revelations. More important in God's scheme of things, however, are His angels, who are Heavenly servants obedient to His will. God did not reveal the Quran directly to Muhammad; He sent the Angel Gabriel to do so. Angels taught him how to pray. An angel will blow a horn to announce the Judgment Day. When each of us dies, we will be questioned by a pair of angels. The Devil, called Iblis or al-Shaytan in Arabic, was an angel who flouted God's command to worship Adam. Having fallen from grace, he now tries to corrupt mankind. He seems to do well.

Books

How did God make His existence known to mankind? How does the Infinite reveal Himself to finite minds? Christians say that the Word became Flesh and dwelt among us: God became a man or sent down His son. But Muslims argue that God revealed Himself by the words He put into the mouths of certain righteous men called prophets. These words have taken the form of books: the Torah (first five books of the Bible) of the Jews, the Gospels of the Christians, and the Quran of the Muslims. They also believe that God's earlier revelations, in the form we know them, were corrupted and had to be corrected by the Quran. Modern scholarship has shown that the books of the Bible were not written down until some time had passed after they were revealed. Muslims wonder, therefore, whether the Jews changed some passages of the Torah to depict themselves as God's chosen people (a concept Islam rejects) or whether Christians rewrote the Gospels to prove the divinity of Jesus of Nazareth. The Quran, however, is God's perfect revelation. It has existed in Heaven since the beginning of time and will never be superseded. After Muhammad's death it was carefully compiled ("from scraps of parchment, from thin white stones, from palm leaves, and from the breasts of men," wrote an early Muslim) by his followers. Some parts had actually been written down while Muhammad was still alive. If any passage had been wrongly read, a Muslim who had heard Muhammad deliver the passage would surely have put it right.

The Quran is not easy reading. It is the record of God's revelations to Muhammad, containing laws, historical narratives, and devotional pieces meant for guidance and recitation, not literary entertainment. Most of its 114 chapters bring together passages revealed at different times. The chapters, except for the first, are arranged in order of length. Those revealed in Medina, filled with legal injunctions and prohibitions, generally precede the Meccan chapters, which stress God's power and warn of the coming Judgment Day. Because it was revealed in Arabic, many Muslims do not think it can or should be translated into any other language. Since its usage reflects that of seventh-century Meccans, even Arab Muslims may need help in understanding parts of what they read. The language of the Quran is rhymed prose (not metrical like poetry), but it can sound lyrical when chanted by a trained reciter. Try to hear one if you can. Muslims venerate the Quran for many reasons: its language and style are inimitable, the book differentiates Islam from all other religions, and many of its teachings have stood the test of time. The speech and writing of pious Muslims are studded with Quranic expressions. No other book has affected so many minds so powerfully and for so long.

Messengers

God's books were revealed to mortal men called prophets or messengers. Although Islam stresses that Muhammad was the last of the prophets, Muslims recognize and venerate many others, including Adam, Noah, Abraham, Moses, Jonah, and Job. Many Biblical personages (like King Solomon) reappear in the Quran as prophets. Of special interest to Christians is the inclusion of Jesus among the messengers of God. The Quran affirms that he was born of a virgin, but denies that he was crucified or that he should be called the son of God. All prophets must be respected; no one prophet (not even Muhammad) may be exalted above the others. No more will come before the Judgment Day. Many people misconstrue the role and attributes of a prophet. He does not predict what will happen or perform miracles (unless God enables him to do so); he is just a good man chosen by God to bring His message to other men and women.

Judgment Day

Among Islam's basic tenets, none was preached more urgently by Muhammad than belief in a final Judgment Day, from which no one can escape. On this day of doom all living people will die, joining those who have gone before them. All will be summoned before the Heavenly Throne to be judged for the good and the bad things they have done. Later Muslims built up the imagery: a tightrope will stretch across the fires of Hell, and only the righteous will cross over safely into Heaven. The Quran depicts Paradise as a shaded garden with cooling fountains, abundant food and drink, and beautiful maidens for the eternal bliss of righteous men. Righteous women, too, will enter Heaven, but the Quran is less specific on what they will find. Popular Islam says they will resume being the age at which they were most beautiful. Both men and women will know peace, live in harmony, and see God. Hell is everything that is horrible in the Arab mind: fearsome beasts, fiery tortures, noxious vapors, foul-tasting food to eat, and boiling water to drink. There will be no peace, no harmony, and the torments will never end.

Naturally Muslims would like to prepare for the great Final Examination, but God alone knows the hour and the day when the Judgment will come. Folk Islam has identified various warning signs: comets; natural disasters; the coming of the Antichrist followed by the return of Christ; and especially the appearance of a mahdi, a divinely guided Muslim who will lead others back into God's good graces. What about the leaders who fired up their troops with promises of booty if they won and instant Heaven if they fell in battle? Martyrdom and death for a righteous cause surely benefits a Muslim in the afterlife, but there will be no way around the Judgment Day. Only by obeying God in this life can the believer find Paradise in the next.

THE FIVE PILLARS OF ISLAM

How can the believer obey God? What are His commands? The Quran and Muhammad's teachings are full of dos and don'ts, more than this book can cover. However, they are symbolized by five obligatory actions: the five pillars of Islam.

Witness (Shahadah)

I have already mentioned the first duty, witness or testimony that there is no god but God and that Muhammad is the messenger of God. Anyone who says these words—and really means them—is a Muslim. Any Muslim who associates other beings with God, or denies that Muhammad is a prophet, is no longer a Muslim, but an apostate. Apostasy can be punishable by death.

Worship (Salat)

The second pillar of Islam is worship, a set sequence of motions and prostrations, performed facing in the direction of the Ka'bah and accompanied by brief Quranic recitations. Worship reminds men and women of their relationship to God and takes their minds off worldly matters. It occurs five times each day, at fixed times announced by the muezzin's call from the minaret (tower) of a mosque, a building constructed for congregational prayers. Muslims may pray almost anywhere, but men are encouraged to do so in congregation, while women usually pray at home. All men should go to a mosque on Friday noon, since congregational worship at that time is followed by a sermon and sometimes by major announcements. Muslims must wash their hands, arms, feet, and faces before they pray. The rules on how to perform worship are elaborate and vary among the different rites.

Fasting (Sawm)

Muslims are required to fast during the month of Ramadan. From daybreak until sunset they refrain from eating, drinking, smoking, and sexual intercourse. Good Muslims spend extra time during Ramadan praying, reciting from the Quran, and thinking about religion; lax ones are apt to sleep in the daytime, for the nights are filled with festivities, bright lights, and merrymaking. The discipline of fasting is supposed to teach the rich what it is like to be poor, and certainly the shared discomfort of fasting creates common bonds among Muslims. Here is the place to point out that the Muslim calendar has exactly twelve lunar months in each year. With no month occasionally put in, as in the Jewish calendar, the Muslim year consists of only 354 days. Thus Ramadan advances 11 or 12 days each year in relation to our calendar and to the seasons. As you might have guessed, the fast is easy to observe in the northern hemisphere when Ramadan occurs in December; it requires great self-discipline when it falls in July (as in the early 1980s). A Muslim who gets sick or makes a trip during Ramadan may put off all or part of the fast until a more suitable time. Growing children, pregnant and nursing mothers, soldiers on duty, and chronically ill Muslims are exempt. But nearly every Muslim who can fast does so, even if he has given up all other outward observances of his faith.

Tithing (Zakat)

All Muslims must pay a specified share of their income or property to help provide for the needy. This payment is called *zakat,* often translated as "alms," though it began as a tax levied on all adult members of the *ummah*. Nowadays, in countries where the *zakat* is no longer collected by the government, Muslims are supposed to make equivalent charitable donations. Many wealthy and pious Muslims make additional gifts or bequests to feed the hungry, cure the sick, educate the young, or shelter the traveler. Many fountains, mosques, and hospitals have been founded and maintained by a type of endowment called a *waqf*, about which I will write more later. In essence, the fourth pillar of Islam is sharing.

Pilgrimage (Hajj)

The fifth duty is the hajj, or pilgrimage to Mecca during the twelfth month of the Mulsim year. Every adult Muslim should perform the hajj at least once in his lifetime, if he is well enough and can afford to make the journey. Each year, from all parts of the world, observant Muslims, their heads shaven (or veiled) and their bodies clad in identical unsewn strips of cloth, converge on Mecca to perform rites hallowed by the Prophet, though in some cases taken from earlier Arab practices. These include circling the Ka'bah, kissing the Black Stone set in one of its walls, running between the nearly hills of Safa and Marwa, throwing rocks near Mina, sacrificing sheep there, and assembling on the plain of Arafat. Some may have begun as pagan rites, but Muhammad reinterpreted them in monotheistic terms. Thus Muslims believe that Abraham and Ishmael found the Black Stone and erected the Ka'bah around it. Running between Safa and Marwa seven times recalls Hagar's frantic search for water after Abraham had expelled her and Ishmael from his tent. The sacrifice of a sheep commemorates Abraham's binding of Ishmael (Muslims believe it was not Isaac) at God's command and the last-minute sacrifice of a lamb that an angel provided. The day of the sacrifice is a high point of the hajj and is also the occasion for a major Muslim feast throughout the world. The pilgrimage rites have served throughout history to bring Muslims together and to break down racial, linguistic, and political barriers among them.

Other Duties and Prohibitions

The five pillars do not cover all Muslim duties. There is another, sometimes called the "sixth pillar of Islam," which is the jihad, or the "struggle in the way of God." Westerners often think of the jihad as a Muslim holy war against all other religions. This is not entirely true. To be sure, the Quran (9:29) commands Muslims to "fight those who do not believe in God or the Judgment Day, who permit what God and His messenger have forbidden, and who refuse allegiance to the true faith from those who have received scriptures, until they humbly pay tribute." This would mean fighting Christians and Jews under some circumstances, and pagans in any case. But Islam also decreed tolerance toward the older monotheistic faiths.

Just how militant should Muslims be? I can give part of the answer now, elaborating on it in the next two chapters. Muslims strove to expand the territory controlled by their *ummah,* not to convert conquered Christians or Jews. Those who agreed to live at peace and to pay tribute were entitled to Islam's protection; those who resisted or rebelled against Muslim rule were crushed. Modern Muslims often interpret jihad to mean defending Islam against attacks, whether military or intellectual, from non-Muslims. Furthermore, each Muslim must also purify his own soul and straighten out his family and friends in order to defend the *ummah.*

Prohibited to Muslims are all intoxicating liquors, all mind-affecting drugs, eating the flesh of pigs or of any animal not slaughtered in the name of God, wearing silk clothes, gambling, and usury. The Quran lays down harsh penalties for murder, theft, and some other crimes. There are also punishments for Muslims who make or worship idols, but this does not mean a total prohibition against artistic depictions of living creatures, as some Westerners suppose. It is true, however, that Muslims have not traditionally sculpted statues, and pictures of living creatures are seldom found in mosques. I will write more about Islamic art in chapter 8.

Islam teaches that sexual relations are primarily for the purpose of having children and should therefore not occur outside marriage. Most marriages are arranged by the parents of the bride and groom; in olden times the young couple often met for the first time on the wedding day. There also used to be strict rules separating the sexes in order to ward off undesirable love relationships. These rules led in practice to the seclusion of women from the mainstream of political and social life and subjected them to their fathers, brothers, and husbands. Wearing the veil, required by the Quran only for Muhammad's wives, became the rule for all Muslim women, at least in the cities. Nowadays they are less apt to veil their faces, but many continue to cover their hair. Adults of both sexes dress modestly and shun situations requiring nudity. Islam forbids homosexual acts and masturbation. Even if some Muslims flout some of these rules, acceptance of the prohibitions remains the norm.

Cleanliness is close to godliness. In addition to ritual ablutions before worship, Muslims also must wash themselves after performing an act of nature, before eating, upon awaking, and after handling certain objects considered unclean. Total immersion in running water is required after sexual intercourse and, for women, after menstruation and childbirth as well. Traditionally Muslim men shaved or cropped their heads, but let their beards grow.

CONCLUSION

This chapter has barely scratched the surface of its topic. Hundreds of books have been written and thousands of speeches given on "What is Islam?" Every life lived by a Muslim is a statement about Islam, which now has well over half a billion adherents living in every part of the world (though most heavily concentrated in the southern third of Asia and the northern two-thirds of Africa). The religion prescribes a way of life. In later chapters you will learn about the Shari'ah, or sacred law of Islam, which was developed and codified during the first three centuries after Muhammad's death. Let me say for now that the Quran, combined with the teachings and practices of Muhammad, provided a comprehensive and coherent life-style for Muslims. They had no bishops or priests. Even the ulama, the men learned in Islamic doctrines and practices, were not set apart from other Muslims. In the eyes of God, all Muslims were equal except in their obedience to His will. Men and women, young and old, friends and neighbors—all had mutual rights and responsibilities within Islam. All could find freedom, together with a feeling of security, in this world and the next. It was more than a faith; it was a way of life.

5

The Early Arab Conquests

Muhammad's death left a great void within the community of his followers, the Islamic *ummah*. As long as he was alive, he had been prophet, arbiter, lawgiver, and military commander. In fact, just about any issue that arose among Muslims had been referred to him. How could they manage when he was no longer there? This posed a crisis for the *ummah,* but Muhammad's survivors found new leaders. These men proceeded to meet the challenge of an Arab tribal rebellion, increasing the lands under their control. The mightiest empires of the Middle East, Byzantium and Persia, were humbled by the Arab warriors for Islam. Later on, internal dissension led to sectarian splits that have never completely healed. However, the momentum of Islam's expansion would be broken only briefly. The ability of the early Muslims to overcome these crises helped assure that Islam would last.

THE SUCCESSION ISSUE

During his lifetime Muhammad never named a successor. Many people say this was his biggest mistake, but it was not customary for Arab leaders to designate their successors. Furthermore, how would he have sorted out the functions he could pass on to someone else? He probably did not expect to die so soon; his death came suddenly. He may not have thought of designating another prophet. He was incensed by other Arabs who claimed to be prophets. Although the Quran does not say so, Muhammad and nearly all Muslims since his time have maintained that he was the last of the prophets. No one after his death could receive divine revelations. Since the Judgment Day was supposed to come at any time, perhaps no more would be needed. But even if there were no successor-as-prophet, the *ummah* would need some sort of political leader comparable to a tribal shaykh who could direct its affairs until the hour of doom.

A leader was needed right away. Before Muhammad's body was cold, the *ansar* were trying to choose a leader of their own. Given the smoldering rivalry between their tribes, we can imagine how hard it would have been for them to agree on anyone from Medina. And how could a Medinan control the nomadic tribes only lately converted to Islam? The best hope would be to take a leader from the prestigious Quraysh tribe, not one of the ex-pagan tormentors of Muhammad, but one of the early converts who had emigrated with him to Medina. Umar, the strongest and most decisive of Muhammad's companions, carried the day by naming Abu-Bakr, who came (as did Umar) from a clan of the Quraysh that was neither Umayyad nor Hashimite. Abu-Bakr was a modest man with an encyclopedic knowledge of the Arab tribes. He had been Muhammad's closest friend, the first convert the Prophet had made outside his household, the father of his beloved wife Aishah, and the designated prayer leader during his final illness. Later on, some Muslims would say that a member of Muhammad's family should have been chosen. Since Muhammad had no surviving sons, they argued that his successor should have been his cousin and son-in-law, Ali, son of Abu-Talib. But his name did not come up in 632. Surely, if Muhammad had favored Ali, it would have.

Abu-Bakr as First Caliph

Abu-Bakr took the title of *khalifat rasul Allah* ("successor of the messenger of God"), usually shortened to *khalifah,* or "caliph" in English. In common usage, the caliph was called *emir al-muminin* ("commander of the believers"). Abu-Bakr surely earned the title. As soon as the Arab tribes heard of Muhammad's death, most of them broke with the *ummah.* Later Muslim historians would call it "apostasy" (*riddah*), seeing the break as a renunciation of Islam. To the tribesmen, however, the death of the leader had ended the treaty requiring them to pay the *zakat*—a form of tribute—to Medina. Abu-Bakr realized that if they got away without paying, the finances of the *ummah* would suffer and the unity of the Arabs would be broken. Islam might well disappear. So he sent two of his greatest generals, Khalid ibn al-Walid and Amr ibn al-As, to force the tribes back into the *ummah.* The *riddah* wars were costly, but the tribes capitulated, one by one, and were eventually forgiven. But what, beyond a superficial adherence to Islam and the power of the caliph's police, could hold the Arab tribes together?

THE INITIAL CONQUESTS

The brilliant answer of Muhammad's successors was to turn the bedouins' combative energies away from one another and toward the settled lands to the north, the territories of the Byzantine (Roman) and the

Sasanid (Persian) empires. Abu-Bakr's successor pardoned the tribes that had renounced Islam and enlisted them in the service of the caliphate, in a jihad to expand the lands of the *ummah.* This momentous decision would lead to the capture of Rome's Middle Eastern possessions (Palestine, Syria, Egypt, and Cyrenaica) in little more than a decade. Within a generation the whole Sasanid empire would be absorbed. Within a century Muslim soldiers would be stationed from Spain in the west, across North Africa and the Middle East, to the borders of China in the east. To some Western historians, the victories of the Arab tribesmen were the main events separating the ancient world from the Middle Ages. The peoples of Europe were just about isolated. Christianity was set back, especially in the lands of its birth. The Arab conquests brought together the diverse cultures of North Africa, Egypt, Syria, and Iran. Out of this combination would grow a new civilization that would match those of ancient Greece and Rome.

Reasons for Their Success

If you had asked someone in the streets of Damascus (or anyplace else) around 625 to predict who would be ruling the Middle East a generation later, he might have named the Byzantine emperors, the Sasanid shahs, or perhaps some new Roman or Persian dynasty. No one would have expected the rulers to be Arabs from Mecca. The speed of the Arab conquests amazed everyone, then and now, and people still ask why they succeeded. As you try to come up with an answer, let me suggest some points to keep in mind.

1. The Arab armies were small, usually less than ten thousand men, fewer in number and less well equipped than their Roman or Persian foes. They fought few engagements, but their victories were decisive ones that enabled them to gain vast expanses of territory. Their horses, usually a luxury for bedouin, were the essential ingredient in their speed, but their camels gave them endurance and mobility in the desert. Arab victories usually happened in the desert, or close enough so that they could get away from Roman or Persian legions if they had to. A common Arab tactic was to draw the enemy forces into a nearby wadi ("valley") and use the terrain to trap them. One of the Arabs' decisive victories over Rome, the Battle of the Yarmuk River Valley in 636, was due to a dust storm, which Khalid knew how to turn to his advantage. This victory gave the Arabs control over Syria. Another dust storm enabled the Arabs to defeat the Persians in 637 at al-Qadisiyah and hence to overrun Iraq.

2. Not all Arab warriors were, as popular histories suggest, fired up with Muslim zeal. A few were, but others belonged to Christian tribes estranged from the Byzantine Empire. Some of the leading Muslim individuals and tribes may have believed in predestination and martyrdom as a quick

passport to paradise. Most tribesmen believed in looting, for bad economic conditions in Arabia had brought many of them to the verge of starvation. In fact, the Arab conquests laid the groundwork for a great Semitic emigration from Arabia comparable to those of the Akkadians and the Arameans (among others) in ancient times.

3. Years of fighting between the Sasanid and Byzantine empires had depleted the resources and manpower of both. Up to about 620, the Sasanid Persians seemed to be taking over the entire Middle East. Then the Byzantine emperor, Heraclius, managed to reorganize his armies and push the Sasanids back to Iraq and Iran. Remember also that each side relied heavily on mercenaries, many of them Arabs. However, the Byzantines had become too poor to go on paying the Ghassanid tribe, so southern Palestine was open to Muslim penetration even in Muhammad's last years. The Persians, on the other hand, thought they were rich enough to get along without supporting their Lakhmid vassals. As a result, by 632 the pro-Byzantine and pro-Sasanid Arabs had both become unreliable, and some were defecting to Islam.

4. The subject peoples, especially those under Byzantine rule in Syria and Egypt, were discontented. Although cultural and economic grievances were the probable causes, the open point at issue was theological, or rather Christological. The Byzantine Empire held the Orthodox (or Chalcedonian) view, explained in chapter 2, that Jesus Christ combined in his person both a divine and a human nature. The Egyptian Copts and the Syrian Jacobites believed in his single and wholly divine nature, the Monophysite doctrine. Emperor Heraclius, anxious to keep their support, proposed a compromise: Christ combined two natures within one will. Almost nobody (except the Maronites of Mount Lebanon, whom I will write about later) bought that solution. The disgruntled Syrian and Egyptian Christians saw the Muslim Arabs as their liberators from the Byzantine yoke and often welcomed them. For example, the Christian bishops of Egypt, disloyal to Byzantium, delivered their country between 640 and 642 to an Arab force commanded by Amr and numbering, even with reinforcements, less than ten thousand. Likewise the Jews, numerous in Palestine and Syria, chose Muslim indifference over Byzantine persecution.

5. The sudden collapse of Sasanid Persia, after having been master of Egypt, Syria, and much of Arabia as recently as 625, created a vacuum that the Arabs were quick to fill. Persia was falling back because of political chaos in Ctesiphon, the capital. Power struggles weakened the central administration, whose control was needed for the irrigation system along the Tigris and Euphrates rivers. Farm production fell and discontent rose. Besides, the Christian, Jewish, and Manichaean peasants of Iraq had little

sympathy for the Zoroastrian priests or the Sasanid absentee landlords who lived in the Iranian highlands. But once Iraq fell, following the Battle of al-Qadisiyah (637), the Sasanid state broke up. The Arabs picked up one Persian province after another, until the last Sasanid shah died, a fugitive, in 651.

Extension of Arab Power

When Muhammad died in 632, the lands of the *ummah* had been limited to western Arabia as far north as the Gulf of Aqaba, plus parts of the rest of the peninsula where the Arab tribes had supposedly embraced Islam. Under Abu-Bakr, the government at Medina had faced the challenge of the tribal rebellion (*riddah*) and overcome it. The conquest of the adjacent lands in Syria and Iraq had started under Abu-Bakr during the repression of the *riddah*. Upon his death in 634, Umar became the new caliph. Granting a blanket pardon to the rebellious tribes, Umar turned what had been a few forays into a systematic policy of territorial acquisition. During his caliphate and that of his successor, Uthman, all of Syria, Iraq, Iran, Egypt, and Cyrenaica were brought into the lands of the *ummah*. You can readily imagine the stress this put on the primitive government in Medina, where Muhammad and Abu-Bakr used to buy their own food in the market, mend their own clothes, cobble their own shoes, and dispense justice and money in the courtyards of their homes.

THE BEGINNINGS OF ISLAMIC GOVERNMENT

Umar, strong-willed and hot-tempered, an early Meccan convert who came from a minor clan of the Quraysh tribe, was the man on the spot. He was shrewd enough to see that the Arab tribes, easily led into battle with the lure of booty far richer than they had ever known, might be unruly when they were not fighting. Military discipline sat lightly on the shoulders of these Arab warriors, especially if their commanders did not come from their own tribe. What would happen when centers of civilization fell under the sway of these bedouins? Would they wreck the palaces and libraries first, or would the bars and dancing girls undermine their martial skills and religious zeal?

Military Discipline

For centuries nomads and foreign armies have overrun the settled parts of the Middle East, only to find themselves conquered in short order by their own captives. Umar did not want his Muslims to be corrupted and subverted in this way. It was no mere quirk of character that made him stride through the streets and bazaars of Medina, whip in hand, ready to scourge any Muslim who missed the prayers or broke the Ramadan fast. Umar may have admired Khalid's skill at beating the Romans and the Persians in battle, but not his reported habit of taking their women and making love to them on the blood-soaked battlefield! Khalid's bathing in wine and hiring poets to sing his praises (poets were the publicity agents of the seventh century) infuriated Umar. He sent Khalid an angry letter of dismissal, making him an example to other Arabs.

The troops had to be kept under strict discipline between military engagements. Umar's policy was to settle them on the fringe between the desert and the cultivated lands in special garrison towns, notably Basrah and Kufah in Iraq and Fustat just south of what is now Cairo, Egypt. The purpose was to keep the Arabs and the settled peoples apart. The Arab soldiers were forbidden to acquire lands outside Arabia. Their right to take over buildings and other immovable war booty was restricted. Even one-fifth of the movable prizes of war had to be sent back to Medina, where Umar set up a diwan (register) that carefully divided the spoils into shares for the members of the *ummah,* ranging from widows and companions of Muhammad down to the humblest Arab soldier.

Civil Government

Although Arab generals and Meccan merchants tended to take over the top posts of the newly won provinces, the civil administration was left almost untouched. That previously mentioned man in the streets of Damascus would not have found life in 650 much different from what it had been in 625. Local administrators continued to run affairs as they had before. Land and house taxes were lighter than in the bad old days; they now went to Medina instead of Ctesiphon or Constantinople. The languages of government remained as before: Greek and Coptic in Egypt, Greek and Aramaic in Syria, Persian and Syriac in Iraq and Iran. The people, of course, went on speaking the languages they were used to. Few Christians or Jews rushed to convert to Islam, since they were protected as "People of the Book." Zoroastrians and Manichaeans in Iraq and Iran were less tolerated and more apt to become Muslim, but even they changed slowly. It seems to have been hard for the early Muslims to get used to the conversion of non-Arabs to Islam. Having assumed that Muhammad was God's messenger to the Arabs, they would confer honorary Arab status on any foreign convert. They did this by making him a client member (*mawla*; plural, *mawali*) in an Arab tribe. Persians and Arameans who flocked to garrison towns like Basrah and Kufah were especially apt to turn Muslim. Soon the garrison towns had more *mawali* than bona fide Arabs living in them. This is ironic when you consider that Basrah and Kufah had been set up to protect the Arabs from the corrupting influences of Persian culture! Now they were melting pots and centers of cultural interchange.

DISSENSION IN THE *UMMAH*

The garrison towns also became hotbeds of dissension and intrigue, especially after the guiding hand of Umar was removed by assassination. Before he died, Umar appointed a *shura,* or "committee of electors," to choose the third caliph. Some Arab writers have pointed to the *shura* as proof that early Islam was democratic. To be truthful, it consisted of six Meccan companions of Muhammad, all from the Quraysh tribe and all in the caravan trading business. Owing perhaps to their personal rivalries, they ended up choosing the only member of the *shura* who belonged to the prestigious Umayyads, the clan that had long opposed Muhammad.

Their choice to succeed Umar, Uthman, has come down in history as a weak caliph, eager to please the rich Meccan merchants and put his Umayyad kinsmen into positions of power. This is unfair to Uthman, who had defied his clan when he became one of Muhammad's earliest converts. He defied many of Muhammad's companions also when, as caliph, he established a single authoritative version of the Quran and ordered the burning of all copies that contained variant readings. Many of the reciters were appalled when their cherished versions of the Quran went up in smoke, but would Islam have fared better with seven competing readings of its sacred scriptures? Lately, this story has been challenged. M. A. Shaban, an Egyptian historian of early Islam, argues that the detractors of Uthman were Arab "villagers," members of tribes that had stayed loyal during the *riddah* wars and had been entrusted with managing the first conquered lands, and not Quran "reciters." The two words are almost the same in Arabic. The current debate among Middle East historians illustrates the problem we have in using early texts that lack not only vowels, but most other pronunciation guides. If Shaban is correct, Uthman's first opponents were tribesmen who had been loyal to his predecessors and resented his favoritism toward other Arab tribes.

As for the issue of Uthman's relatives, it is true that some of them lusted after power and that others were incompetent drunkards he should never have appointed. Uthman's intention, though, was to use his family ties to assert greater control over the government. His cousin Mu'awiyah governed Syria very well. He and his foster brother in Egypt built Islam's first navy, used to conquer Cyprus in 655. The trouble with Uthman is that he carried on Umar's policies without having Umar's force of character. The Muslims of the Iraqi garrison saw this and started plotting against him.

Uthman's Troubled Caliphate

Traditional accounts make much of the contrast between the second and third caliphs of Islam. "The luck of Islam was shrouded in Umar's winding-sheet," remarked some of his survivors. Uthman is said to have complained from the pulpit of Muhammad's mosque to the men of Medina: "You took it from Umar, even when he whipped you. Why then do you not take it from one who is gentle and does not punish you?" While Umar slept on a bed of palm leaves during his caliphate and wore the same woolen shirt until it was covered with patches, Uthman amassed estates worth about a million dollars during his.

Modern scholars play down the personality contrast, however, and stress changing conditions within the *ummah.* The influx of money and treasure enriched Medina and Mecca far beyond anything Muhammad could have anticipated and eventually beyond what his companions could assimilate. Greed and vice proliferated, especially among the young (according to their elders). Once the early conquests had reached their limits (Cyrenaica in the west, the Taurus Mountains of Anatolia in the north, the highlands of Khurasan in the east, and the Indian Ocean and the upper Nile in the south), the Arab tribesmen could not change from border warriors into military police. They sat idly in their garrison towns, bewailed the lost opportunities for booty, and plotted against the caliphate in far-off Medina.

From about 650, Uthman's rule was menaced by a strange assortment of people: pious old Muslims, mostly Medinans, who resented the way the Umayyads were taking control of the *ummah* they had once tried to destroy. Quran reciters who had suffered from the establishment of a single authorized version; and Arab tribesmen who chafed at being deprived of new lands to seize and plunder. Of the various garrison towns, Kufah was the most restive. An open revolt broke out there in 655, spread to Arabia, and reached Medina in 656. The insurgents besieged the house of Uthman, who got no protection from any of Muhammad's companions. A group of rebels from Egypt broke in, killing the aged caliph as he sat with his wife, reciting from the Quran. Five days later, with great reluctance, Ali agreed to become the fourth caliph.

Ali's Caliphate

Thus began the first *fitnah* (time of troubles) in the history of Islam. It should have ended with Ali's accession to the caliphate. After all, he was the son of Muhammad's uncle and protector, possibly his first male convert, the husband of Muhammad's daughter Fatimah, and hence the father of the Prophet's only grandsons, Hasan and Husayn. Ali had risked his life to get Muhammad safely out of Mecca during the *hijrah.* He had fought well in the early battles against the pagan Meccans, accompanied the Prophet on most of his expeditions, and advised the earlier caliphs on various questions of dogma and policy. He was pious and generous. Unfortunately, he was a weak caliph. Either Ali came too late to do the office any good, or the caliphate came too late to do him any good.

Battle of the Camel

Soon after his accession, Ali left Medina never to return; Kufah would serve as his capital. But when he reached Basrah, he was challenged by two of Muhammad's companions, Talhah and Zubayr, joined by Aishah, who branded him unfit to rule because he had not tried to protect Uthman. It was a strange accusation, since none of the challengers had liked or defended the third caliph. Their real motives were political and personal. Ali had supposedly denied government posts to Talhah and Zubayr, and Aishah had never forgiven him for once accusing her of infidelity to Muhammad. Ali and his troops defeated the challengers in a bloody affray, the Battle of the Camel, so called because it raged around Aishah's camel-borne litter. Talhah and Zubayr died in battle (as did, reportedly, 13,000 others), and Aishah was sent back to Medina. The Battle of the Camel was the first instance in which two Muslim armies fought against each other. It set an unhappy precedent.

Battle of Siffin

Ali's more serious challenge came from Mu'awiyah, Uthman's cousin and governor of Syria. The Umayyad clan was understandably outraged when Uthman was murdered and replaced by Ali, a Hashimite, who seemed reluctant to find and prosecute the assassins. Mu'awiyah displayed the bloodstained shirt of Uthman and the severed fingers of his widow, who had tried to protect her husband, thus playing on the revulsion felt by many good Muslims after what seemed like a political murder. Arab tradition called for seeking revenge, especially once it became clear that the assassins would not be brought to justice. Mu'awiyah had a loyal garrison of Arab troops in Syria, and they challenged Ali. The two sides met in a series of skirmishes at Siffin in June and July 657. Finally, when Ali's side seemed to be winning, wily old general Amr advised Mu'awiyah's men to stick pages of the Quran on the tips of their spears and to appeal for a peaceful arbitration of the quarrel. Ali suspected a trick, but his troops persuaded him to accept.

Ali and Mu'awiyah each chose a representative and agreed to let them decide whether or not the Umayyads were justified in seeking revenge for Uthman's murder. Soon afterwards, some of Ali's men turned against him for agreeing to the arbitration. Called Kharijites ("seceders"), these rebels gave Ali trouble for the rest of his caliphate, even after he had defeated them at the Nahrawan canal (in Iraq) in 659. By that time, the appointed arbiters of Ali and Mu'awiyah had met. Emboldened perhaps by the Kharijite rebellion against Ali, Mu'awiyah's representative, Amr ibn al-As, tricked Ali's arbiter into agreeing to his master's deposition from the caliphate. Ali did not resign, but the arbitration undermined his authority. His followers faded away. One province after another fell into the hands of Mu'awiyah, who had himself proclaimed caliph in Jerusalem in 660. Finally, in 661, Ali was assassinated by a Kharijite seeking revenge for Nahrawan.

CHANGES IN THE GOVERNMENT OF ISLAM

Ali's death ended the era known to Muslim historians as that of the Rashidun ("rightly guided") caliphs. All four were men related to Muhammad by marriage and chosen by his companions. Later Muslims would look back on the period as a golden age to which many longed to return. They contrasted the simple governments in Medina and Kufah with the swollen bureaucracies of Damascus and Baghdad, headed by kingly caliphs who succeeded by heredity. Indeed, some of the Rashidun caliphs were admirable and all four were interesting, but theirs was a period of frequent strife, many crises of adjustment to changing conditions, and much improvisation. The very institution of the caliphate had started as a stopgap measure, taking on most of what would be its permanent form under Umar. It had become the linchpin for a state that was doubling and redoubling in area, population, and wealth. Now, upon Ali's death, it seemed to be in peril.

Mu'awiyah

The man who saved the *ummah* and the caliphate from anarchy was the Umayyad governor of Syria, Mu'awiyah. He never wavered in his determination to discredit Ali for the murder of Uthman, and his Syrian-Arab troops (many of them Christian) rewarded him with their support. He possessed a virtue highly prized among Arabs, the ability to refrain from using force unless absolutely necessary. As he himself put it, "I never use my sword when my whip will do, nor my whip when my tongue will do. Let a single hair bind me to my people, and I will not let it snap; when they pull I loosen, and if they loosen I pull." When Ali died, some of his die-hard Kufan supporters pushed his son Hasan into contesting the caliphate. Mu'awiyah got him to withdraw his claim by sending what amounted to a blank check. Hasan retired, a rich man, to Medina, where he married (and divorced) some ninety women until one of them poisoned him.

It is interesting that Mu'awiyah first claimed the caliphate in Jerusalem.

What if he had made that city his capital, something no Arab or Muslim ruler has ever done? But Mu'awiyah started his adult life as a Meccan merchant and he valued Damascus, which had been his provincial capital, because it was closer than Jerusalem to the major trade route between Syria and the Yemen. Mu'awiyah seemed to have viewed Syria as a stepping-stone toward capturing the whole Byzantine Empire. We see this in various ways. When the Arab conquests resumed after the first *fitnah,* the big push was against Byzantium. Each summer Mu'awiyah's armies would push their way into the mountains of Anatolia. Meanwhile, his navy chased the Byzantine fleet from the Mediterranean and twice during his reign besieged the very capital of the empire. But Byzantium withstood the onslaught. The Arabs had to console themselves by advancing westward across Tunisia and eastward through Khurasan.

Administrative Changes

Mu'awiyah, once called the "Caesar of the Arabs" by none other than the Caliph Umar himself, aspired to be a new Roman emperor. Patriarchal government, namely what had grown up in Medina on the model of the Arab tribal system, modified somewhat by the Quran and the practices of the Prophet, could not meet the needs of a sprawling empire of many peoples and religions. Mu'awiyah adopted the customs of the Byzantine rulers and the bureaucratic practices familiar to Egypt and Syria. Many of his administrators and some of his warriors were Syrians or Christian Arabs, often survivors or sons of the old Byzantine bureaucracy and soldiery. Mu'awiyah recognized his dependence on the Arab tribes for most of his military manpower, and he was wise enough to flatter their sense of racial superiority. But each tribe had to send a representative (really a hostage) to his court in Damascus. Troublesome areas like Iraq, where Arab tribes had terrorized the countryside during Ali's caliphate, were brought to heel by ruthless provincial governors. The most notorious of these was Ziyad, "the son of his father" (whom Mu'awiyah won over from the pro-Ali faction and acknowledged as his own half-brother). Upon taking charge in Basrah, Ziyad warned the people from the pulpit of its main mosque:

> You are putting family ties before religion. You are excusing and sheltering your criminals and tearing down the protecting laws sanctified by Islam. Beware of prowling by night; I will kill everyone who is found at night in the streets. Beware of the arbitrary call to obey family ties; I will cut out the tongue of everyone who raises the cry. Whoever pushes anyone into the water, whoever sets fire to another's home, whoever breaks into a house, whoever opens a grave, him will I punish. Hatred against myself I do not

punish, but only crime. Many who are terrified of my coming will be glad of my presence, and many who are building their hopes upon it will be undeceived. I rule you with the authority of God and will maintain you from the wealth of God's *ummah.* From you I demand obedience, and you can demand from me justice. Though I may fall short, there are three things in which I shall not be lacking: I will be ready to listen to anyone at any time, I will pay you your pension when it is due, and I will not send you to war too far away or for too long a time. Do not let yourselves be carried away by your hatred and wrath against me; you will suffer if you do. Many heads do I see tottering; let each man see to it that his own remains on his shoulders!

When at last Mu'awiyah knew that his own days were numbered, he obtained *in advance* the consent of his followers to the succession of his son Yazid to the caliphate. It was this act that later earned Mu'awiyah the condemnation of Muslim historians (even though Hasan's attempt to succeed Ali must have set the precedent). From that time on up until the abolition of the caliphate in 1924, the highest political office in Islam was hereditary in fact, even if it remained elective in principle.

I wonder, though, whether Islam would have been better off if Mu'awiyah had not founded the Umayyad dynasty. True, the Arab tribesmen, if given a choice, would have gravitated to the Kharijite position, which was that any adult male Muslim could become caliph, no matter what his race or lineage, and that any caliph who sinned should be overthrown in favor of another. The Kharijite idea survived throughout Islamic history, especially among nomads in Arabia and North Africa. In fact, some modern Muslims would like to revive the caliphate without restricting the office to descendants of the Quraysh tribe. However, a popular election of the Muslim ruler, using Kharijite principles, would have caused anarchy in the seventh century. Although there were die-hard supporters of the sons of Ali (as you will soon see) and also of other companions such as Zubayr, their appeal was limited to particular cities within the *ummah.* Mu'awiyah alone could command the support of Syria and Egypt, and his henchmen could control Arabia, Iraq, and Iran. True, the Umayyads were lax Muslims. Mu'awiyah had fought against Muhammad until all Mecca capitulated to Islam, then turned around 180 degrees and became the Prophet's secretary. His descendants' drinking and sexual exploits make amusing reading but shocked the pious Muslims of their day. Nevertheless, the Umayyads continued to control the caravan trade between Syria and Yemen, and their business experience enabled them to make policy decisions, reconcile differences, and neutralize opposition. The Umayyad dynasty, although condemned by most Muslim historians, built up the great Arab empire.

Mu'awiyah's Successors

What Mu'awiyah accomplished came close to being buried with him in 680. Yazid, his designated successor, was disliked by the old Meccan companions of Muhammad and by some of the Arab tribes, despite his successes in earlier battles against Byzantium. The problem originated in Yazid's childhood. His mother, one of Mu'awiyah's favorite wives, had hated the settled life of the Umayyad court and pined for the bedouin encampments of her youth. To this effect she wrote a poem, grossly insulting to Mu'awiyah, that convinced him that she and her son, Yazid, still young at the time, belonged in the desert. Yazid grew up with his mother's tribe, Kalb, which made him a bold warrior but a heavy drinker. When he became caliph, he favored this tribe at the expense of its great rival, Qays. During the period of the early conquests, the tribes had formed two large confederations that involved most of the Arab soldiers, one "southern" (including Kalb) and the other "northern" (including Qays). During Yazid's reign their rivalries escalated into a full-scale civil war, the second *fitnah* of Islam.

Husayn's Rebellion and the Rise of Shi'ism

Before I discuss the second *fitnah,* let me say something about a small rebellion, not in itself a great threat to Yazid's power, but one that has since taken on immense significance in Islamic history. Remember that some Muslims still abhorred the very idea of an Umayyad caliphate and wanted the leadership of the *ummah* to go back to the Hashimite clan, preferably a direct descendant of the Prophet. Muhammad, as you know, had no sons. His son-in-law, Ali, had been killed, as had Hasan, leaving the Prophet's other grandson, Husayn, as the only possible claimant. Husayn was a rather pious and otherworldly man who had lived most of his fifty-four years in Medina. But when Yazid succeeded Mu'awiyah in 680, Husayn refused to recognize his ascent as legitimate. Husayn's partisans in Kufah, thus encouraged, talked him into getting up a rebellion against the Umayyads. But the Umayyad governor of Kufah (a son of Ziyad) managed to terrorize most of Husayn's would-be supporters. When the Prophet's grandson reached Iraq, he found he had only seventy-two warriors pitted against an Umayyad force numbering several thousand. Husayn's pitiful band fought bravely under the circumstances, but they all fell in battle. Husayn's severed head was brought to the feet of Yazid in Damascus.

The significance of these events was that the partisans of the "martyred" descendants of the Prophet, Ali and now Husayn, resolved never to accept the Umayyads as caliphs. They called themselves Shi'at Ali ("the Party of

Ali"), from which came the name "Shi'ites," or "Shi'is." From Iraq they spread to all parts of the empire, wherever Muslims were dissatisfied with Umayyad rule.

Nowadays we see the Shi'is as the second largest Muslim sect and contrast them with the majority group, called Sunnis, who accepted (often reluctantly) the ruling caliphs. Some religious differences exist between Sunnis and Shi'is, but most can be traced to the latter's conviction that only Ali and his descendants (diagramed in Table 2) had any right to lead the *ummah.* To Shi'i Muslims, even Abu-Bakr, Umar, and Uthman, let alone Mu'awiyah and his heirs, were usurpers; whereas Ali was the first imam ("leader") and he bequeathed special powers and esoteric knowledge to his sons, his sons' sons, and so on.

In due course, disputes arose between brothers claiming the imamate, causing splits among their Shi'i followers. Some Shi'ites managed later on to form states in opposition to the Sunni caliphate. Since about 1500, the rulers and people of Iran have been Shi'i Muslims. But to identify Shi'ism with Iranian or Persian nationalism illuminates better the mind of the twentieth century than that of the seventh. Shi'ism began as a movement of political protest couched in religious terms, appealing to Arabs as well as Persians. It found expression in pilgrimages to Najaf and Karbala (the burial sites of Ali and Husayn respectively), in the annual processions mourning the martyrdom of Husayn, and in the passion play reenacting his tragic end.

Other Challengers

Although the other challenges to the Umayyads were at the time more dangerous than Husayn's rebellion, they are not so well remembered now. Abdallah ibn al-Zubayr, son of the Zubayr killed in the Battle of the Camel, also refused allegiance to Yazid and escaped from Medina. But instead of courting the Kufans as Husayn did, Abdallah stayed in Mecca and fomented rebellions elsewhere. When Yazid died in 683, leaving the caliphate to his sickly young son, Abdallah claimed the office for himself. Muslims in all the provinces, even some in the cities of Syria, announced they would favor him. The Arab tribes supporting Qays, the northern confederation, rebelled against the Umayyads, who were linked to Kalb and hence the southern Arabs. When the teenaged caliph died, leaving the Umayyads with no plausible candidate, all Abdallah had to do was to come to Damascus and claim the caliphate there. But he linked himself with the pious descendants of Muhammad's companions living in Medina and Mecca. They hated Damascus and everything that smacked of Umayyad rule, so Abdallah stayed in Mecca. The oldest and most respected member of the Umayyad family, Marwan, reluctantly agreed to oppose Abdallah's

TABLE 2
The Hashimite Clan, showing Shi'i Imams (numbered)

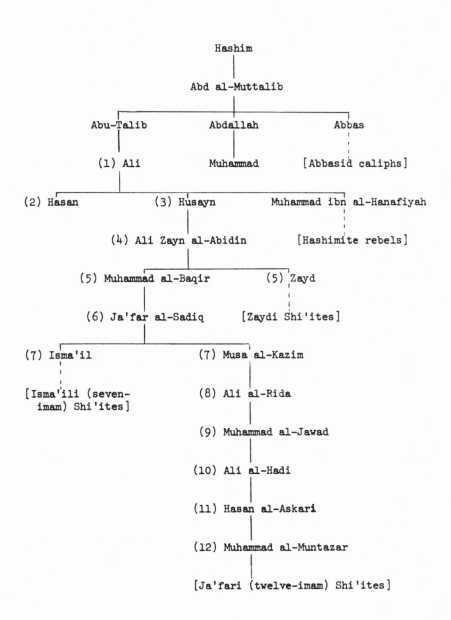

partisans, and in July 684 the supporters of the Umayyads defeated the opposing Arab tribes and drove them out of Syria.

Rebellions went on for almost a decade. In 685 a group of penitent Shi'ites, mainly Persian in origin, revolted unsuccessfully in Kufah. There were several Kharijite uprisings—you can generally count on them whenever there was trouble. It took a long time for the Umayyads to crush the caliphate of Abdallah ibn al-Zubayr, and I must leave that story for chapter 6. Never again would descendants of the emigrant companions and the *ansar* put forth their own candidate for the leadership of the *ummah.* Never again would a large group of Muslims try to make Mecca the capital city of Islam.

CONCLUSION

Between Muhammad's death and the second *fitnah,* the *ummah* had grown so large that Arabia could no longer be its political center. The Arabian tribes that had carried out the conquests had formed a powerful aristocracy spread throughout the empire, but their effectiveness as a police force was fatally weakened by their rivalries. The government of the *ummah* had ceased to be an extension of Arab tribal democracy or Muhammad's religious prestige; now it was firmly grasped by a Meccan mercantile clan based in Syria. Its administrative arm was a team of Arabs and Syrians, some of them Christian, who carried on the ruling practices of the Byzantines. Many of the Arabs, whether nomads, sedentarized Meccan traders, Medinan farmers, or tribal warriors living in garrison towns, felt alienated from this neo-Roman kingdom. Some of the non-Arab subjects had become Muslims, but these *mawali,* especially in Iraq, were second-class citizens who resented Arab claims to superiority. Shi'ite and Kharijite movements reflected these various tensions. Meanwhile, we must not forget that most of the caliphate's subjects were Jews, Christians, and Zoroastrians, not Muslims who could be counted on when the *ummah* was in danger. In sum, we should marvel that Islam survived the death of Muhammad, that it gained new lands and adherents so quickly, and that it absorbed mighty empires and civilized societies. But despite these achievements of half a century, Muslims were not yet secure.

6

The High Caliphate

For about a thousand years, history has been playing mean tricks on the Arabs. They have been wracked with internal factionalism and strife, external invasion, subordination to outside rulers, various natural disasters, and exaggerated hopes and fears. But in the bleakest moments of their history, the Arabic-speaking peoples of the Middle East have comforted themselves with the memory of a time when their ancestors ruled most of the eastern hemisphere, when the Europeans and the Chinese feared and courted them, and when theirs was the language in which humanity's highest literary and scientific achievements were expressed. In common speech, the time remembered was that of the two great caliphal dynasties, the Umayyads and the Abbasids. This chapter uses a term coined by the late Marshall Hodgson for the years from 685 to 945: the High Caliphate.

During this period, the Islamic *ummah* was initially headed by the Marwanid branch of the Umayyad family, followed by the Abbasids. Both dynasties belonged to the Quraysh tribe and were supported by the Muslims who came to be called Sunnis, a term that I will explain later. The caliphal state was militarily powerful, relative to the Byzantine Empire, Western Europe, India, and China. Territorial conquests continued up to about 750, when the Abbasids took over from the Umayyads. After that time some land was lost and the caliphal state started to break up. As long as any semblance of unity remained, though, the old Roman, Syrian, Persian, and other political and cultural traditions continued to combine in new forms. Economic prosperity, based fundamentally on agriculture, was enhanced by commerce and manufacturing. These facilitated the movement of people and the spread of ideas, and hence the growth of an Islamic civilization.

The relative position of various groups changed gradually during the High Caliphate. Under the Abbasids, if not before, Arab dominance declined, concurrent with the spread of Islam among non-Arabs and the widespread adoption of the Arabic language. It is necessary to be careful, though, with generalizations concerning Arab influence. The word "Arab" is ambiguous: it can mean "bedouin," or someone wholly or partly descended from Arabian tribesmen, someone who speaks Arabic, or a person living under Arab domination. During those time, tribal soldiers from Arabia slowly gave way to salaried troops, notably Iranians from Khurasan, and then to Turkish tribal horse soldiers paid in land.

The increasing size and complexity of the caliphal state required a growing bureaucracy. The early Umayyads had tended to borrow from Roman administrative traditions, but the Persian administrators and Sasanid practices now took over. At the same time, there grew up a class of pious Muslims who could recite and interpret the Quran, relate and record *hadith*s (authenticated accounts of Muhammad's sayings and actions), systematize Arabic grammar, and develop the science of law (called *fiqh* in Arabic). Eventually they became known as ulama, which means "those who know," or experts on Islamic law, doctrines, and history. Interest was also developing in classical philosophy, science, and medicine, aided by the large-scale translation of Greek works into Arabic. One result was the evolution of systematic Muslim theology (*kalam*). Muslims also developed some more esoteric ideas and rituals, leading to the growth of Sufism (organized Islamic mysticism), a topic I will discuss later.

The caliphal state faced ongoing opposition from Kharijites, who rejected any type of hereditary caliphate, and from Shi'ite movements supporting various descendants of Ali. Toward the end of the period, some areas of the Muslim world came under the control of pro-Shi'ite dynasties. For most of this time, the majority of the people living in the lands of the *ummah* were non-Muslims, but their relative power and importance were declining.

RESTORATION OF THE UMAYYAD ORDER

Most scholars agree that, among the early caliphs considered to be the "founding fathers" of Islamic government, the names of Umar, Mu'awiyah, and Abd al-Malik should be counted. You have already learned about Umar, who presided over the early conquests, and Mu'awiyah, who bequeathed the caliphate to his Umayyad heirs. What about this Abd al-Malik? He took over the caliphate on the death of his aged father, Marwan, who had ruled briefly during what was (from an Umayyad viewpoint) the worst period in the second *fitnah*. At the time of Abd al-Malik's accession, the northern Arab tribal confederation was rebelling against his family, in league with Abdallah ibn al-Zubayr, who was claiming the caliphate in Mecca. All provinces except Syria had turned against Umayyad rule. The martyrdom of the Prophet's grandson,

Husayn, had angered Muslims, especially the Shi'is, against the Umayyads as well. One of Abd al-Malik's first challenges came from a rebellion of Shi'i penitents at Kufah (so called because they regretted not having come to the aid of Husayn in 680). This revolt fizzled, but the Kufans rallied around an Arab adventurer named Mukhtar. His cause gained support from Persian and Aramean converts to Islam who, as *mawali,* resented being treated as inferior to the Arabs. Abd al-Malik could not stop Mukhtar's revolt, but, luckily for him, the army of Abdallah did. This was a time when Abdallah's partisans in Mecca were stronger than the Umayyads in Damascus.

The Triumph of Abd al-Malik

Although he took office in 685, Abd al-Malik waited until 691 to take Iraq from the forces of Abdallah ibn al-Zubayr. The next year Hajjaj, an Umayyad general famous for his ironhanded government in Iraq and Iran, captured Arabia. His men had to bombard Mecca (damaging the Ka'bah, by the way) before Abdallah's forces surrendered. Hajjaj spent two years wiping out Kharijite rebels in Arabia before he went into Kufah. Wearing a disguise, he entered the main mosque, mounted the pulpit, tore the veil from his face, and addressed the perfidious Kufans: "I see heads ripe for cutting. People of Iraq, I will not let myself be crushed like a soft fig. . . . The commander of the believers [Abd al-Malik] has drawn arrows from his quiver and tested the wood, and has found that I am the hardest. . . . And so, by God, I will strip you as men strip the bark from trees . . . I will beat you as stray camels are beaten." Iraq settled down after that, and Hajjaj restored prosperity to the eastern provinces of the Umayyad empire.

The New Absolutism

Abd al-Malik laid the basis for a new, absolutist caliphate, one patterned after the traditions of the divine kings of the ancient Middle East instead of the patriarchal shaykhs of the Arab tribes. The change can be seen not only in authoritarian governors like Hajjaj, but also in Abd al-Malik's decree that henceforth Arabic would be the language of administration. Before then, some parts of the empire had used Greek, others Persian, Aramaic, Coptic, depending on what the local officials and people happened to speak. Many bureaucrats, especially the Persians, resented having to give up a language rich in administrative vocabulary for one used until recently only by camel nomads and merchants. But it is those Persians whom we can thank (or curse, if you study Arabic) for having systematized Arabic grammar, since they soon realized that no Persian could get or keep a government job without learning to read and write this complicated new language.

In the old Roman imperial tradition of erecting fine buildings, Abd al-

Malik had the magnificent Dome of the Rock built atop what had been Jerusalem's Temple Mount. It was a shrine built around the rock of Abraham's attempted sacrifice and of Muhammad's departure on his miraculous night journey to Heaven, but it was also a message to the Byzantine Empire and the Christians of Jerusalem that Islam was there to stay. With the Dome of the Rock set almost directly above the Western Wall, the sole remnant of the second Jewish Temple, you can see why arguments between Arabs and Jews get heated when they discuss who should control the Old City of Jerusalem, holy to all three monotheistic faiths. Another symbolic act was the minting of coins to replace the Byzantine and Sasanid money used by earlier Arab rulers. The caliphal state was becoming an empire.

Resumption of the Conquests

As you might expect, these developments led to further territorial expansion. The Arab conquests resumed after the second *fitnah* ended. One army headed west across North Africa, while a Muslim navy drove the Byzantines from the western Mediterranean. The North African Berbers, once they had been bested by the Arabs, converted in large numbers to Islam. During the reign of Abd al-Malik's successor, a Muslim army crossed the Straits of Gibraltar and conquered most of what is now Spain and Portugal. It was not until 732—exactly a century after the Prophet's death—that a European Christian force stemmed the Muslim tide in central France. The big Arab thrust, though, was eastward from Iran. Muslim armies attacked the Turks, first in what is now Afghanistan, then in Transoxiana, the land beyond the Oxus River (Amu Darya), including Bukhara and Samarqand. They eventually reached the northwest border of China, which became the eastern limit of the Arab conquests. Another force pushed north to the Aral Sea, adding the province of Khwarizm to the lands of Islam. Another moved south, taking Baluchistan, Sind, and Punjab, roughly the area of modern Pakistan.

There was only one nut too tough to crack, the Byzantine Empire. From the time they conquered Syria, the Arabs seem to have felt that taking over all of Byzantium was their "manifest destiny" much as the United States regarded Canada and the Latin American republics in the nineteenth century. The Byzantines, though weakened by the loss of their Syrian and North African lands and of their naval supremacy in the Mediterranean, seem to have regarded the Arabs as a nuisance that, God willing, would soon pass away. They reorganized their army and the administration of Anatolia, making that mountainous area impregnable to Arab forces. Constantinople, guarded by thick walls, withstood three Umayyad sieges, the last of which involved an Arab fleet of 1800 ships and lasted from 716 to 718. Using "Greek fire," a mysterious substance (probably a petroleum derivative) that ignited upon hitting the water and with favorable winds set fire to enemy ships, the Byzantines wiped out almost the entire Arab fleet. After that the caliphs seem to have concluded that Byzantium was just too hard to take. Gradually they gave up their claim of being a new "Roman" empire and took on a neo-Persian aura instead.

Fiscal Reforms

Whatever the pretensions of the caliphs, their government was more Arab than Roman or Persian, but most of their subjects were not Arabs. It was these non-Arabs who paid the taxes. Even after they converted to Islam, the early Umayyads went on charging them the same rates as before. The major levies were the *zakat,* which Muslims paid on their land, animals, farm produce, or business earnings, as specified in the Quran; a property tax paid to the *ummah,* mainly by non-Muslims, in the conquered lands outside Arabia; and a head tax or tribute paid by Christians, Jews, and Zoroastrians in return for exemption from military service. Both the terminology and the administration of these taxes were confused and definitely biased against the *mawali,* the converts to Islam who were by now as numerous as the Arab tribesmen themselves.

This problem was tackled by Umar II (717-720), who alone among all the Umayyad caliphs, is well remembered for his piety by later Muslim historians. Umar wanted to get rid of all administrative practices based on Arab superiority and to build a new consensus around common adherence to Islam. When his advisors warned him that exempting the *mawali* from the taxes paid by non-Muslims would lead to massive conversions to Islam and the depletion of his treasury, Umar retorted that he had not become Commander of the Believers to collect taxes and proceeded to institute the reforms. Since he also cut military expenditures, the treasury did not suffer, and he did gain Muslim converts. He must have wanted this to happen, because he also put humiliating restrictions on non-Muslims: they could not ride horses or camels, only mules and donkeys; they had to wear special clothing that identified them as Jews or Christians; and they were forbidden to build new synagogues or churches without permission. These rules, often called the "Covenant of Umar," were rigorously enforced by a few of his successors and ignored by the others. We cannot generalize about the conditions of Jews and Christians under Muslim rule—they varied so greatly—but conversion to Islam was almost always socially or economically motivated, not forced. It was Hisham (724-743) who finally systematized the taxes into a pattern that would be followed for the next thousand years: Muslims paid *zakat,* all property owners (with some exceptions you need not worry about) paid a tax on their lands or buildings called *kharaj,* and Christians and Jews paid a per-capita tax called *jizyah.*

DOWNFALL OF THE UMAYYADS

Even after the fiscal reforms of Umar and Hisham, the Umayyad caliphate remained an Arab kingdom. Muslims could put up with this as long as the conquests continued. But as they were now slowing down, the Arab tribes that supplied most of the warriors became worthless because they bickered constantly among themselves. Most of the later caliphs also seemed useless, with their hunting palaces, dancing girls, and swimming pools filled with wine. Some of them sided with one or the other of the great tribal confederations, which was worse, for the slighted tribes were thus encouraged to incite Shi'ite or Kharijite revolts that were very hard to suppress.

Mawali Discontent

Meanwhile, the *mawali* were the intellectual leaders, the bureaucrats, and even the commercial elite of the *ummah,* but political and social discrimination killed their desire to preserve the existing system. The best way they could express their discontent was to back dissident Muslim movements that might overthrow the Umayyads. Especially popular among the *mawali* was a Shi'ite revolutionary movement called the Hashimites. As you can see from Table 2 (p. 61), the name simply indicates the family of Muhammad without revealing which line of imams ("leaders") this Shi'ite movement supported. The line in fact descended from a son whom Ali had had by a woman other than Muhammad's daughter. In the turbulent province of Khurasan, the Hashimites conferred their support on a branch of the clan called the Abbasids, who were descendants of Muhammad's uncle, Abbas. The Abbasids in turn gladly used these Shi'ite revolutionaries and disgruntled *mawali* in order to gain power.

The Abbasid Revolt

The Umayyads' weakness was the Abbasids' opportunity. The Arab tribes were bitterly divided, the army was demoralized, river irrigation had increased Iraq's importance relative to Syria, popular opinion was demanding Muslim equality in place of Arab supremacy, and Khurasan was a province with about 200,000 Arab colonists intermingled with the Persian landowning aristocracy. There, in 747, a Persian named Abu-Muslim unfurled the black banner of revolt on behalf of the Abbasids.

Despite the heroic resistance of the last Umayyad caliph and his governor in Khurasan, the revolt spread. The Abbasids reached Kufah in 749 and laid claim to the caliphate for one Abu al-Abbas, surnamed "al-Saffah" (the bloodshedder). Abu-Muslim's troops defeated the Umayyad army decisively in January 750, pursued their last caliph to Egypt, and killed him. Then they went on to wipe out all the living Umayyads and to scourge the corpses of the dead ones. Only one member of the family escaped. After a harrowing journey across North Africa, he safely reached Spain, where he founded a separate state at Córdoba that lasted almost three centuries.

THE ABBASID CALIPHATE

The Abbasid revolution is generally seen as a major turning point in Islamic history. People used to think the revolution was significant because the Persians threw the Arabs out of power. This is, at best, a half-truth. The Abbasids were Arabs, proud of their descent from the Prophet's uncle. Their supporters included Arabs and Persians, Sunni and Shi'i Muslims, all united by a desire to replace an Arab tribal aristocracy with a more egalitarian form of government based on the principles of Islam. Like many other revolutions that have occurred in history, the overthrow of the Umayyads reinforced certain trends that were already developing under the old regime: the shift of the power center from Syria to Iraq, the rise of Persian power and influence to displace the Byzantine-Arab synthesis of Mu'awiyah and Abd al-Malik, the declining drive to take over all the Christian lands of Europe, and the growing interest in cultivating the arts of civilization.

Even though most Westerners may not know who the Abbasids were, a reference to the caliph of Baghdad or Harun al-Rashid is apt to conjure up images of *The Arabian Nights*—a never-never land of flying carpets, genies released from magic lamps, and passwords like "open sesame." One could guess that the country was rich, that its rulers had the power of life and death over their subjects, and that the state religion was Islam. These guesses would prove true for the Abbasid empire under its fifth caliph, Harun al-Rashid (786-809), whose name means "Aaron the Wise."

The Building of Baghdad

When Abu al-Abbas, Harun's great-uncle, was acclaimed as the first Abbasid caliph by the populace at Kufah in 749, Baghdad was just a tiny Persian village a few miles up the Tigris River from the ruined Sasanid capital, Ctesiphon. The early Abbasids wanted to take the government out of Damascus, but they tried several other cities before Abu al-Abbas's brother and successor, Abu Ja'far al-Mansur, chose Baghdad in 762 as the site of his capital. It was just where the Tigris and Euphrates come closest together. A series of canals linking the rivers there made it easier to defend the site and also put Baghdad on the main trade route connecting the Mediterranean (hence Europe) with the Persian Gulf (hence Asia). It was an area where Persian culture was still strong. Finally, it was closer to the political center of gravity for an empire still stretching east toward India and China.

Mansur wanted a planned capital, not a city that had long been used for other purposes, like Damascus or Kufah. His architects gave him a round city. The caliphal palace and the main mosque fronted on an open square in the middle. Around them stood army barracks, government offices, and the homes of the chief administrators. A double wall with four gates girdled the city, and soon hundreds of houses and shops surrounded the wall. Across the Tigris rose the palace of the caliph's son, with a smaller entourage. The later caliphs built still more palaces along the Tigris, which was spanned at one point by a bridge of boats. The building of Baghdad was part of a general public works policy by which the Abbasids kept thousands employed and their immense fortune circulating. It was a popular policy, for it called for the construction of mosques, schools, and hospitals throughout the empire, but its success depended on general economic prosperity, since the people had also to pay the taxes needed to support it.

Public Piety

The Abbasids made a public display of their piety, which was their main justification for seizing power from the high-living Umayyads. To be sure, the third caliph loved wine, music, and perfumed slave girls, but he also paid for the expansion of the courtyard surrounding the Ka'bah and the establishment of guard posts and wells along the pilgrimage routes in Arabia. Harun al-Rashid went on the hajj every few years throughout his life, even going once from Medina to Mecca on foot (which he hoped would earn him God's favor). Most of the Abbasids put on a big show of generosity during the great feasts of the Muslim calendar or for family celebrations, such as the birth or the circumcision of a prince. Harun personally conducted the army in a Muslim jihad across Christian Anatolia that almost reached Constantinople before the Byzantines paid tribute to induce the Abbasids to withdraw.

Anti-Abbasid Revolts

With so much public piety, you might have expected that the Abbasids would have been spared religious uprisings of the sort that had troubled the Umayyads. Not so. The revolts became more frequent and varied than ever before. Kharijite groups rebelled in peripheral areas like Oman and North Africa, ending up with several small states of their own. The Shi'i Muslims were more dangerous, for they soon saw that the Abbasids had tricked them when using their support in the revolution against the Umayyads. Two descendants of Hasan revolted in 762, one in Mecca and the other in Basrah, and Mansur had to kill thousands of Shi'ites to crush their rebellions. In 788 another Shi'ite led a group of Berbers in a revolt that succeeded in separating Morocco permanently from Abbasid control. It would take several more pages to cover all the Shi'ite revolts that broke out in different parts of the empire.

To make matters worse, Shi'ism now had several branches, divided according to which descendant of Ali each sect believed to have been the last imam, as shown in Table 2 (p. 61). Thus the followers of Zayd were able to set up separate principalities in Tabaristan (the land just south of the Caspian Sea) and the Yemen. Some followers of Isma'il, the Qarmatians, set up a communist republic in Bahrain and also maintained a stronghold in Arabia and Syria from which they raided Abbasid caravans. In the tenth century another group of Isma'ili Shi'ites, the Fatimids, seized control of Tunis and later of Egypt and Syria. They will be covered in chapter 7.

Some of the revolts against Abbasid rule were anti-Islamic in spirit, especially those in which Persians took part. This is hard to explain if you accept the view that the Abbasids were pro-Persian Muslims rebelling against the Umayyads and their policy of Arab supremacy. But let us take up the story from the Persian side. A dark curtain fell across Iran's history after the Arab conquests extinguished the Sasanid Empire. The Persians seem to have gone into shock for a century, during which most of the landlords and peasants became Muslims, learned Arabic, and got used to the new power relationships. The decline of the Umayyads and the economic regeneration of Iraq in the middle of the eighth century encouraged the Persians to come out of their shock and to rally behind any hero who would restore their lost prestige.

Abu-Muslim won a tremendous following in Khurasan as a Persian leader of the Abbasid revolt. The first two Abbasid caliphs, Abu al-Abbas and Abu Ja'far al-Mansur, used him to defeat the Umayyads and crush the Shi'ites, but Mansur seems to have feared that Abu-Muslim might put his popularity to work against his own dynasty. The Persians claim that Mansur, acting treacherously, summoned Abu-Muslim to his court and had him put to death. Some Arabs accused him of being a Zindiq (heretic), meaning that he probably retained some of the esoteric practices of a pre-Islamic Iranian religion. I cannot judge between their claims.

At any rate, Abu-Muslim's execution brought the Abbasids no peace.

Immediately rebellions broke out in Khurasan. One of his friends, Sinbad the Magean (possibly a Zoroastrian), set out to destroy the Ka'bah. Then a "veiled prophet" claiming to be Abu-Muslim began a rebellion that lasted almost twenty years. With thousands of supporters, he robbed caravans, destroyed mosques, and virtually controlled Khurasan. Fifty years later, another reincarnation of Abu-Muslim turned up in Azerbaijan, a Persian named Babak. His rebellion also lasted twenty years. All of these uprisings carried strong undertones of the religions prevalent in Iran before Islam, such as Zoroastrianism (the faith of the Sasanid establishment) and a sort of peasant religion called Mazdakism. Indeed, the philosophical dualism of the Manichaeans seems to have survived or revived in Iran among the Zindiqs. This group is hard to characterize accurately, though, as Muslim conservatives branded almost all dissidents by that name.

The Rise of the Persians

The resurrection of Persian influence in Abbasid times did not always take dissident forms. Hundreds of Persians, especially from Iraq and Khurasan, rose to high positions within the army and the administration, displacing the Arabs and Syrians favored by the Umayyads. These men may have taken a greater interest in the Sanskrit and old Persian classics than their Arab colleagues would have liked, but they also learned Arabic as well and carefully toed the Abbasid line on religious matters. Some Persians became ulama (religious scholars) and helped to shape the laws of Islam. Loyal to their Abbasid masters, they helped them to suppress dissenting ideas and movements, but in effect they Persianized the state from within.

As the central administration grew more complex, Persian bureaucratic families rose to power. The greatest of these was the Barmakids, of whom three generations served the Abbasids from Abu-Ja'far to Harun as bursars, tax collectors, provincial governors, military commanders, tutors, companions, and chief ministers. The title they bore, *wazir* in Arabic and *vizir* in Persian, came to be applied to any high-ranking official. Originally meaning "burden bearer," it is now used to mean "cabinet minister" in most Middle Eastern languages. Harun in particular unloaded many of his burdens onto his Barmakid vizirs. Eventually he realized that he had let them get too much of his power and wealth, so he dramatically killed the one to whom he was most attached and locked up his father and brother. So sudden was the move that many people attributed it to a thwarted homosexual love affair that also involved a fictitious marriage between the murdered Barmakid and the caliph's sister. This explanation, which still turns up in popular histories, may humanize a rather pompous caliphate, but a more credible explanation is that the Barmakids' prestige and power were eclipsing Harun's own position. It was him or them. How could Harun claim to be God's representative on earth and the fountainhead of justice if everyone looked to the Barmakids for patronage?

A less spectacular ladder for upwardly mobile Persians was a literary movement called the Shu'ubiyah. Persians, especially in the bureaucratic class, used their knowledge of literature to prove their equality with (or superiority over) the Arabs. After all, they reasoned, Persians had built and managed mighty empires, prospered, and developed a high intellectual culture for centuries while the Arabs were chasing camels in the desert. The Arabs were quick to accuse the Shu'ubiyah of hostility to Islam and the Prophet, but its bureaucrats and scholars were really working for equal rights within the system, a Persian version of the NAACP.

A greater threat to the Abbasids came from those Persians who broke away to form separate dynastic states in Iran, such as the Abbasid general who founded the Tahirids (820-873) or the coppersmith who started the long-lasting Saffarids (861-1465). Indeed, the Abbasids themselves were being Persianized by their harems. So many caliphs had Persian wives or mothers that the genetic mix of the middle ninth-century Abbasids was more Persian than Arab. Harun's Persian mother pushed him into becoming caliph. The succession struggle between his two sons was intensified by the fact that the mother of Amin (809-813) was Harun's Arab wife, while Mamun (the challenger and ultimate victor) was a son by a Persian concubine.

The Caliphate of Mamun

Mamun (813-833) deserves a high rank among the Abbasid caliphs, even though his rise to power resulted from a bloody civil war that almost wiped out Baghdad. A great patron of scholarship, Mamun established the Islamic equivalent of the old Sasanid university of Jundishapur, a major intellectual center called Bayt al-Hikmah ("the House of Wisdom"). It included several schools, astronomical observatories in Baghdad and Damascus, an immense library, and facilities for the translation of scientific and philosophical works from Greek, Aramaic, and Persian into Arabic.

Mamun's penchant for philosophical and theological debate led him to espouse a set of Muslim doctrines known collectively as the Mu'tazilah. This early attempt at systematic theology was originally an effort to combat Persian Zindiqs and the Shu'ubiyah, but it came across as a rationalist formulation of Islam, stressing free will as opposed to divine predestination. The customary test of whether a Muslim was a Mu'tazilite was to ask him whether God had created all things, including the Quran. A yes answer showed he was a Mu'tazilite, opposed to the popular idea that

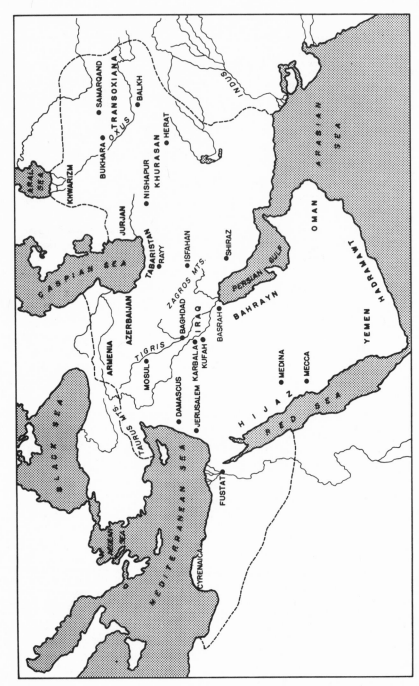

Map 3. The Abbasid Caliphate circa 800

the Quran had existed eternally before God chose to reveal it to Muhammad. Mamun and his two immediate successors had this test administered to all ulama and government officials as a requirement for keeping their posts. The extreme rationalism of the Mu'tazilah was too much for the later Abbasids, who ended the test, and for the general public, who venerated the Quran and believed that God had decreed all human acts. It was also Mamun who thought he could reconcile Sunni and Shi'i Muslims by naming the imam of the latter as his successor. The plan backfired. The people of Iraq resisted Mamun's concession to a descendant of Ali, and the imam in question died, probably of poison.

DECLINE OF ABBASID POWER

With so many dissident sects, revolts, secessions, and intellectual disputes going on between 750 and 945, you may wonder how the Abbasids ever managed to rule their empire. Well, as time went by, they no longer could. In addition to those previously mentioned Shi'ite and Kharijite states in the remoter areas of the empire, there were governors appointed by the Abbasids who managed to take over their provinces and passed them on to their heirs. An Abbasid governor, sent by Harun in 800 to Tunis, set up a dynasty called the Aghlabids, who, while paying a small annual tribute to Baghdad, ruled independently for over a century. Their attacks on nearby Sicily, Italy, and southern France gave them some prestige among Muslims, since Harun's successors were no longer taking Christian lands. In fact, the Christians of Egypt revolted on a large scale in 832, and a Byzantine navy landed in the Nile Delta some twenty years later. Ahmad ibn Tulun, sent by the Abbasids in 868 to put Egypt in order, made the country virtually independent for forty years.

The Turkish Influx

Ahmad ibn Tulun was a Turk. During the ninth century, thousands of Turkish tribesmen from central Asia moved into the Middle East, seeking grazing lands for their horses and lucrative jobs for their warriors. In addition to those whole tribes that came in, there were individual Turks who became incorporated into the Abbasid ruling system. To begin with, there were war captives who became slaves for the caliphs. During the reign of al-Mu'tasim (833-842), however, the induction of individual Turks into the service of the caliphate became much more systematic and large-scale. Hundreds of boys were purchased from their families in central Asia, taken to Baghdad, converted to Islam, and trained to be soldiers, administrators, or domestic servants for the Abbasids. Because these Turks had been taught from a tender age to view the caliphs as the source of all their material blessings, they were more trustworthy than the Persian mercenaries. Soon they had become the strongest element in the Abbasid army. Then they were able to manipulate the caliphs and murder any one they disliked. To escape the Turkish stranglehold, the caliphs moved their capital up the Tigris to Samarra; however, this attempt failed. Not only were individual Turkish slaves gaining control over their masters, but whole Turkish tribes were moving in from the northeast and seizing large areas as well, a process I will elaborate on in the next chapter. Hardy and well-disciplined, the Turks took over the caliphal state—both its capital and some of the provinces—from within.

CONCLUSION

The period of the High Caliphate was the zenith of Arab political power. The Umayyads and Abbasids have come to be viewed collectively as great Arab leaders, although only a few of these caliphs merit such a tribute. Some were brave, generous, and farsighted; most are forgotten, save by a few historians. It was a time of prosperity, brought about by improved river irrigation and by long-distance trade. The Arab conquests brought together peoples of diverse languages, religions, cultures, and ideas. The result was a flowering of artistic and intellectual creativity.

The political history, as you now know, was turbulent—a chronicle of palace coups, bureaucratic rivalries, and rural uprisings. Islam did not put an end to ethnic differences. Indeed, Muslim unity was more and more a facade, a polite fiction. No dramatic revolt overthrew the Abbasids. Even as their power ebbed away in the ninth and tenth centuries, their accumulated power and wealth enabled them to outlast most of the usurper dynasties. They went on producing caliphs in Baghdad until 1258, then in Cairo up to 1517. But dry rot had set in during the Augustan age of Harun al-Rashid and Mamun, or even earlier perhaps, for the political unity of the *ummah* had broken down when the Umayyads had held on to Spain after 750.

During the late ninth and early tenth centuries, a welter of Muslim dynasties took control of the various provinces of North Africa, Syria, and Iran. Finally the city of Baghdad was captured in 945 by a Persian Shi'ite dynasty called the Buyids (sometimes Buwayhids), and the Abbasids ceased to be masters even in their own house.

It mattered less than you might think. As the caliphate declined, other types of political leadership emerged to maintain and even increase the collective power of the Muslim world. Meanwhile, new institutions evolved to sustain the feeling of community among Muslim peoples. My next two chapters will treat these two trends at greater length.

7

Shi'ites and Turks, Crusaders and Mongols

The period of Middle East history from the tenth through the thirteenth centuries is the hardest one for us to study. There is no one dynasty or country on which we can focus our attention, so we must jump around. The Arabs were no longer dominant everywhere; they had given way to the Berbers in North Africa and to the Persians in the lands east of the Euphrates. Numerous central Asian peoples, Iranian or Turkish in culture and language, played a growing role in the various successor states to the Abbasid caliphate, which maintained a shadowy existence in Baghdad, subordinated to other dynasties. Most of the central Asian peoples came in as slaves or hired troops for the Abbasids or their successors. Gradually they adopted Islam, learned Arabic and Persian, and became assimilated into the culture of the Middle East. By the late tenth century, Turkish horse nomads from central Asia were entering the eastern regions in droves. Some, notably the Ghaznavids and the Seljuks, formed great empires.

Further complicating our study of this period is the fact that some of its greatest dynasties were Shi'ite, but not all from the same sect. We cannot ignore these sectarian splits and their effects on people's beliefs and behavior. But the relationships among Muslim dynastic states were more apt to be affected by geopolitical and economic interests, just as the United States since World War II, despite its proclaimed policy of containing Communism, has sometimes wooed such Communist countries as Yugoslavia and Poland, or lately China and Cuba. Sunni and Shi'i leaders usually gained power by appealing to the religious feelings of influential groups within a given area, but they often followed quite different policies once they were securely entrenched.

During this time, the Byzantines tried to regain Syria, Spanish Christians began to reconquer the Iberian peninsula, and (most notoriously) European Christians from various lands launched a series of crusades to recapture the "Holy Land" from the Muslims. Not all Muslim rulers responded in the same way, for some had ideological or economic reasons to withhold aid from rival Muslim states under Christian attack. The general effect of the Christian onslaught, though, was to make Islam more militant in the twelfth century than it had been in, say, the ninth. The weakening of the Byzantine Empire (a hardly surprising development, as it had now outlasted all its Arab rivals) enabled the Muslim Turks to move into Anatolia, an area of Greek-speaking and Orthodox Christian peoples up to the eleventh century. But then, during the thirteenth century, the heartland of Islam was hit by a terrible disaster, the invasion of the Mongols, who had built up a great empire under Chingis Khan and his heirs. Nearly every Muslim state in Asia was either conquered or forced to pay tribute to the Mongols. Only a surprising victory by the Mamluks of Egypt saved Muslim Africa from the same fate.

You might be tempted (as I was) to call this chapter "one damned dynasty after another," but I hope you will learn from it that Islamic civilization overcame factionalism and sectarianism, prospered in spite of Turkish infiltration and domination, and triumphed over the Christian Crusades and the Mongol vision of a universal empire. The civilization survived because a growing majority of the people wanted to preserve the coherent and comprehensive way of life that Islam had made possible. It survived because, in times of crisis, new leaders seized power and guided the governments and peoples of the various regions of the Middle East. The dynasties these leaders founded each went through a cycle of growth, flowering, and decay, usually lasting about a century. You may not be able to remember the names of all the dynasties mentioned in this chapter, but I hope you will soon recognize the most important ones.

SHI'I ISLAM IN POWER

Here is where we first encounter the problem of periodization in Islamic history. How do we decide when one period ends and another begins? Always the stars and planets move along their courses, the seasons follow their usual cycle, and people are born, grow up, carry on trades, marry, have children, and eventually die, seemingly oblivious to the eras and periods designated by historians. Earlier scholars used the dates of caliphal and dynastic reigns; now we look to broader trends, social as well as political, to find our turning points. To start this chapter, I might use the year 909, when the Fatimids seized Tunisia and established a Shi'ite anticaliphate that later moved to Cairo. Or it could be 945, when the Abbasid caliphate in Baghdad was captured by a very different Shi'ite dynasty called the Buyids. In either case, the first theme of this chapter is the rise of Shi'ism as a political force.

The Main Sects of Islam

As you know, we customarily speak of Muslims as being either Sunni, Shi'i (or Shi'ite), or Kharijite. This may be oversimplified, but we must start somewhere. Sunni Islam is often mistranslated as the "orthodox" version. True, some Muslims call a person a "Sunni" if he follows the recorded practices (sunnah) of Muhammad. But when historians identify a Muslim as a Sunni, they mean that he or she acknowledged the Rashidun, Umayyad, and Abbasid caliphs as legitimate leaders of the entire *ummah* because most other Muslims accepted their rule. The person in question might have been a mystic, a rationalist freethinker, or a rebel against the laws of Islam; the "Sunni" designation is more political than theological. It usually indicates, though, that the Muslim in question adhered to one of the four standard "rites" of Islamic law, which I will explain in chapter 8.

A Shi'i Muslim, on the other hand, is a partisan of Ali as Muhammad's successor, at least as imam ("leader") of the *ummah,* and of one of the several lines of Ali's descendants, shown in Table 2 (p. 61). He or she rejects all the other caliphs and all successors to Ali other than the "correct" line, which is often thought to have inherited from Ali a perfect knowledge of what Muslims should do and think. Given these essentially genealogical differences, Shi'is soon split into many sects. Some grew up and died out early, like the "Hashimites," who supported a son of Ali born of a wife other than Fatimah and then transferred their loyalty to the Abbasids just before they took power. Others stayed underground until the Abbasid caliphate began to weaken, then surfaced in revolutionary movements.

The three Shi'ite sects you are most apt to read about are the "Twelve-Imam" (or Ja'fari) Shi'is, the Isma'ilis (sometimes called "Seveners"), and the Zaydis. The first of these recognized a line of infallible imams extending from Ali to Muhammad al-Muntazar, who is thought to have disappeared around 878, but will someday return and restore truth and justice on earth. The Isma'ilis differ with the Twelve-Imam Shi'ites over the designation of the seventh imam, maintaining that Isma'il was wrongly passed over in favor of his brother. Soon after Isma'il died in 760, his followers founded a strong revolutionary movement, leading to the emergence of the Qarmatians in Arabia and Bahrain, the Fatimids in Tunisia, the Assassins in Syria and Iran, and (in modern times) the Agha Khan in India. The Zaydis broke off even earlier. Zayd, who rebelled against Umayyad Caliph Hisham (724-743), was to his followers the rightful imam. By 900 descendants of Zayd had independent states in the Yemen and Tabaristan, both mountainous regions. The Zaydi imams of Yemen ruled right up to 1962, when a military coup overthrew them and set off a five-year civil war, the repercussions of which have continued until the present.

Just to round out this overview, the Kharijites were the Muslims who had turned against Ali. They believed that neither he nor his descendants nor the Umayyads nor the Abbasids had any special claim on the leadership of the *ummah*. They would accept the leadership of any adult male Muslim who would uphold the laws of Islam. If, however, he strayed from the straight path, they would depose him. Even though their doctrines seemed anarchistic, some Kharijites did form dynastic states, notably in Morocco and Oman.

As a result of the disintegration of political unity during the ninth and tenth centuries, various small dynastic states emerged in the Middle East and North Africa. Most of these are now forgotten (except by scholars). However, two of the Shi'ite dynasties posed a direct threat to the Sunni Abbasid caliphate in Baghdad: the Fatimids, who challenged its legitimacy, and the Buyids, who ended its autonomy.

The Fatimid Caliphate

The Fatimids appeared first. You may notice the resemblance between their name and Fatimah, the daughter of Muhammad who married Ali and bore Hasan and Husayn. This was deliberate. The dynasty's founder, Ubaydallah (who called himself al-Mahdi, "the rightly guided"), claimed descent from Fatimah and Ali. He proposed to overthrow the Abbasid caliphate and restore the leadership of Islam to the house of Ali, for he counted on Shi'ite—specifically Isma'ili—support. Perhaps because Isma'il's surviving fifteen-year-old son had disappeared at a time when other Shi'ite sects either had living imams or had shot their bolt in unsuccessful revolts, the Isma'ilis became an underground revolutionary movement, based in Syria. During the late eighth and ninth centuries, Isma'ili Shi'ism gradually picked up support from discontented classes or clans throughout the Muslim world. To do this, it developed a network of propagandists and a set of esoteric beliefs, the gist of which had allegedly been passed down from Muhammad, via Ali and his successors, to Isma'il, who enlightened a few followers before his death.

The Isma'ilis may remind you of the early communists, with their secret cells, complicated doctrines, and widespread propaganda against the established order; and by the same analogy Sunni Islam suggests the capitalist system. One branch of the Isma'ilis, the Qarmatians, formed a protocommunist state in Bahrain and picked up supporters elsewhere in the ninth and early tenth centuries, but they deviated from the Isma'ili leadership in Syria. The Lenin of the Isma'ilis was Ubaydallah, who overthrew the Aghlabids and seized their North African empire in 909. His Red Army was the band of Berber nomads who had turned to Shi'ism as a means of expressing their opposition to their Aghlabid overlords (who were Arabs and Sunni Muslims tied to the Abbasid caliphate).

To the Fatimids, Tunisia seemed an inadequate base from which to build a new universal Muslim empire to replace the faltering Abbasids. They strengthened the corps of Isma'ili propagandists throughout the Muslim world and looked for a more centrally located province to conquer. They found Egypt, an area that had played a surprisingly minor role in early Islamic history. It had been ruled by various dynasties since Ahmad ibn Tulun had set up his autonomous state there in 868. While fighting the Byzantine navy in the Mediterranean, the Fatimid general Jawhar saw that Egypt was in political chaos and suffering from famine. In 969 Jawhar entered Fustat, where he encountered no resistance, and declared Egypt a bastion of Isma'ili Shi'ism. Then the Fatimid caliph, Mu'izz, brought his family and government from Tunis to Egypt. It is said that a welcoming deputation of ulama challenged him to prove his descent from Ali. Mu'izz pulled out a sword, exclaiming, "Here is my pedigree!" Then he scattered gold coins among the crowd and shouted, "Here is my proof!" They were easily convinced.

The Fatimids chose a site just north of Fustat for the new capital of what they hoped would be the new Islamic empire. They called their city al-Qahirah ("the conqueror," a reference to the planet Mars); we know it as Cairo. It soon eclipsed Fustat in size and prosperity, becoming a rival to Baghdad as the leading city in the Middle East. Its primacy as an intellectual center was assured by the founding of a mosque-university called al-Azhar, where the Fatimids trained Isma'ili propagandists for two centuries. Cairo and al-Azhar outlasted the Fatimids and remained respectively the largest city and the most advanced university in the Muslim world up to the Ottoman conquest in 1517. Today Cairo, with its eight million inhabitants, is again the world's largest Muslim city, and al-Azhar survives as a major university attracting Muslim scholars from many lands. Fatimid government in Egypt was highly centralized and hierarchical, favorable to long-distance trade (in which Cairo soon surpassed Iraqi centers like Basrah and Baghdad), but not to agriculture (the Fatimids neglected the irrigation works on the Nile). A strong navy helped the Fatimids to expand. They soon took over western Arabia, Palestine, and Syria, but lost interest in (and control over) their earlier North African possessions.

Surprisingly, the Fatimids did not try to convert Sunni Muslims in the lands they ruled to Isma'ili Shi'ism and gave considerable freedom to their many Christian and Jewish subjects. The one exception was the Fatimid caliph, al-Hakim (996-1021), who has been depicted as a lunatic who persecuted Christians, destroyed their churches, killed stray dogs, outlawed certain foods, and eventually proclaimed himself divine. Recent scholarship has shown that Hakim was hostile mainly to Orthodox Christians, who he thought supported Byzantium, which had taken over much of Syria just before his accession. His sumptuary laws were in fact intended to fight a famine caused by his predecessors' neglect of Nile irrigation. In addition, far from declaring himself God, Hakim was trying to play down the distinction between Isma'ilis and other Muslims.

Possibly Hakim's bad name among Muslims is due to the preaching done on his behalf by an Isma'ili propagandist, Shaykh Darazi, who persuaded some Syrian mountain folk that Hakim was divine. These Syrians built up a religion around the propaganda of Darazi, from whom they got the collective name of Duruz, hence "Druze." The Druze faith is a secret one that combines some of the esoteric aspects of Isma'ili Shi'ism with the beliefs and practices of other Middle Eastern religions. As mountainers, the Druze people could not be controlled by Muslim governments in the low-lying areas. Thus, in the eyes of Muslim historians, they were troublemakers as well as heretics. They have survived until now. The Druze are still important in the tangled politics of modern Syria and Lebanon. They own large amounts of land and often become army officers. There are also Druze in northern Israel. There they tend to support the Jewish state and even serve in the Israel Defense Force. A proud and hardy people, the Druze share the language and culture of the Arabs, but their desire to retain their religious identity has kept them distinct politically.

The Fatimids ruled Egypt for two centuries, a long time as Muslim dynasties go, but they seem to have done better at building a strong navy and a rich trading center than at spreading their empire or their doctrines. This is odd, because Sunni Islam seemed to be waning. The Abbasid caliphs were no longer credible claimants to universal sovereignty, since in fact they were captives of the Buyids, who were Persian and Shi'ite. In fact, the strongest states resisting Fatimid expansion were already Shi'ite. They were not at all impressed by these self-styled caliphs with their network of propagandists and their dubious genealogies.

The Buyid Dynasty

Best known for having captured Baghdad and the Abbasids in 945, the Buyids were one of several dynasties that played a part in the revival of Persian sovereignty. This era was the last stage in Iran's recovery from the Arab conquest, manifested earlier in the revolt of Abu-Muslim, the various sects that rebelled in his name, the Shu'ubiyah literary movement, the rise of the Barmakid vizirs, Mamun's victory over Amin, and the creation of such dynasties as the Tahirids and the Saffarids. During the tenth century, Iran came to be ruled entirely by Persian dynasties: the Shi'i Buyids in the west and the Sunni Samanids in the east. Both consciously revived the symbols and practices of Iran's pre-Islamic rulers, the Sasanids. Persian language, literature, and culture made a major comeback at this time.

The Buyid family was made up of several branches concurrently ruling different parts of Iraq and western Iran. I know of no other Muslim dynasty that was founded by three brothers, each having his own capital. All Buyid branches were Twelve-Imam Shi'i, but they tolerated other Muslim sects. They let the Abbasids go on holding the caliphate, although as prisoners in their Baghdad palace without independent means of support. One Abbasid caliph was blinded, another reduced to begging in the street; however, the institution of the caliphate was a useful fiction as it stood for the unity of the *ummah*. The Buyids' foreign policy was friendly to Christian Byzantium, to whoever was ruling Egypt, and to the Isma'ili Qarmatians; but hostile to their Twelve-Imam Shi'i neighbors, the Hamdanids of Mosul, and to their fellow Iranians, the Samanids of Khurasan. The point I want to make is that economic interests counted for more than race or ideology.

Domestically, the Buyids relied on their viziers to govern in their name, encouraged trade and manufacturing, and continued a practice begun under the Abbasids of making land grants (*iqta'*) to their chief soldiers and bureaucrats in lieu of paying them salaries. The *iqta'* was supposed to be a short-term delegation of the right to use a piece of state-owned land or other property. Under the Buyids, though, it came to include the right to collect the land tax (*kharaj*) and to bequeath the property in question to one's heirs. This has led some historians to call the *iqta'* a fief and the system feudalism. This is misleading. But, whatever it is called, the *iqta'* system often resulted in gouging the peasants and neglecting the irrigation works so important to Middle Eastern agriculture. Even more harmful to Buyid interests, though, was a shift of the trade routes away from Iraq toward Egypt and also toward central Asia.

THE TURKS

Before we can unravel the destiny of the Buyids, we must shift our attention to central Asia. The century of Shi'ism and the Iranian revival were both cut short by events taking place there, especially the rise of the Turks. The origin of the Turkic peoples has been lost in the mists of legend and may not become known until archeologists have excavated more of central Asia and Mongolia, where the Turks are supposed to have originated. They started as nomadic shepherds who rode horses and used two-humped camels as beasts of burden, although some became settled farmers and tradesmen. Their language is distantly related to Finnish,

Magyar, Mongolian, and possibly Korean. Their original religion was centered around shamans, who were wizards or soothsayers capable of healing the sick and communicating with the world beyond. The shaman's spirit was thought to be able to leave his body at will, and he seems also to have served as the guardian of tribal lore.

Early Turkish Civilization

Around 550 the Turks formed a large tribal confederation that is known to us (mainly through Chinese sources) as the T'u-chüeh. Its domains extended from Mongolia to the Ukraine. But soon the T'u-chüeh empire split into an eastern branch, which later fell under the sway of China's T'ang dynasty, and a western one, which became allied with Byzantium against the Sasanids and later fell back before the Arab conquests. This early empire exposed the Turks to the major civilized societies of the sixth and seventh centuries: Byzantium, Persia, China, and India. It also led some to espouse such religions as Nestorian Christianity, Manichaeism, and Buddhism. Somehow they adopted a runic (old Germanic) alphabet, enabling them to leave some inscriptions on the banks of the Orkhon River, the earliest known example of written Turkish.

The transmission of cultures among the various Eurasian regions seems incredible, until you stop to think that people and horses have crossed the steppes and deserts for ages, forming one of the world's oldest commercial highways, the Great Silk Route. In the eighth century a group of eastern Turks, the Uighurs, formed an empire on China's northwestern border. Its official religion was Manichaeism and its records were kept in a script similar to the Aramaic, which gives you an idea how far the Turks could take some of the ideas and customs they picked up. Meanwhile, one of the western Turkish tribes, the Khazars, adopted Judaism, probably to avoid antagonizing its Christian and Muslim trading partners.

The Islamization of the Turks

Eventually, though, most Turkic peoples became Muslim. The Islamization process was gradual and varied from one tribe to another. Once the Arab armies crossed the Oxus River (Amu Darya)—if not long before then—they encountered Turks. Even in Umayyad times some Turks became Muslims and served in the Arab armies in Transoxiana and Khurasan. As you know, under the Abbasids the Turks became numerous and powerful in the government. The earliest Turkish soldiers for Islam were probably prisoners of war who were prized for their skill as mounted archers but regarded as slaves. Most historians believe that the institution of slavery grew in the Abbasid empire to the point where some tribes would sell their boys (or turn them over as tribute) to the caliphs, who would train them to be disciplined soldiers or skilled administrators. These slaves became so imbued with Islamic culture that they no longer identified with their original tribes. In addition to these individual Turks, some of the tribes, once they had embraced Islam, were hired by the Abbasids or their successors (notably the Samanids) as *ghazis* (border warriors for Islam) to guard the northeastern boundaries against the non-Muslim Turks. A lot of nonsense has been written about how the Turks "naturally" gravitated to Sunnism or Shi'ism. Actually, those who entered into the service of a particular Muslim dynasty usually took on its political coloring. The *ghazis* cared nothing about such political or doctrinal disputes. Their Islam reflected what was taught to them by Muslim merchants, mendicants, and mystics, combined with some of their pre-Islamic beliefs and practices.

The Ghaznavids

Two Turkish dynasties, both Sunni and started by *ghazis* serving the Samanids in the late tenth century, are especially important in this period of Islamic history. They are commonly called the Ghaznavids and the Seljuks. The Ghaznavids got their name from Ghazna, a place located 90 miles or 145 kilometers southwest of Kabul (the capital of modern Afghanistan), because their leader received that region as an *iqta'* (land grant) from the Samanids in reward for his services as a general and local governor. The Ghaznavids, especially Sebuktegin (977-997) and his son Mahmud (998-1030), parlayed this *iqta'* into an immense empire, covering at its height (around 1035) what would now be eastern Iran, all of Afghanistan and Pakistan, and some parts of India. The Ghaznavids are especially noteworthy for having extended Islam into the Indian subcontinent, although their efforts at forcible conversion of Hindus gave them a bad name among some Indians.

The Seljuk Empire

The other major dynasty, the Seljuks, takes its name from a pagan Turkish chieftain, correctly Selchuk, who converted to Islam about 960. Later he enrolled his clan in the service of the Samanids. Selchuk's descendants proved to be one of the most remarkable ruling families in Islamic history. They made themselves indispensable to the Samanids and later the Ghaznavids as *ghazis* in Transoxiana against the pagan Turks. In return, they received *iqta's*, which they used to graze their horses and to attract other Islamized Turkish tribes, who would occupy the grazing lands with their sheep and goats, horses and camels. As more Turkish tribes joined the Seljuks, they increased their military strength and also their need for land. The trickle became a flood, and in 1040 the Seljuks and their fellow Turks defeated the Ghaznavids and took over all of Khurasan. The

Buyids had grown weak, leaving western Iran and Iraq open to these military adventurers, who had the encouragement of the Abbasid caliph himself, simply because they were Sunni Muslims.

When the Turks, thus encouraged, entered Baghdad in 1055, it was not to extinguish Arab sovereignty, but to restore the authority of the caliphate. The Turco-Abbasid alliance was cemented by the marriage of the Seljuk leader to the caliph's sister, and the caliph recognized him as regent of the empire and sultan ("authority") in the East and the West. Soon the title was for real, as the Seljuks proceeded to take Azerbaijan, Armenia, and finally most of Anatolia following a major victory over the Byzantines at Manzikert in 1071. You would have to go back to the ninth century, when the Aghlabids took Sicily and raided the coasts of France and Italy, to find a time when a Muslim ruler had so successfully waged a jihad against Christendom. Not since the reign of the early Abbasids had so much land been united under the rule of one dynasty. Malikshah, the sultan at the height of Seljuk power, ruled over Palestine, Syria, most of Anatolia, the Caucasus mountains, all of Iraq and Iran, plus parts of central Asia up to the Aral Sea and beyond the Oxus River. "Praise be to God the exalted," wrote a contemporary, "that the defenders of Islam are mighty and happy because the Turk carries the sword in his hand to the lands of the Arabs, Persians, Byzantines, and Russians, and fear . . . is firmly implanted in all hearts."

The Seljuk success story was too good to last. Soon after Malikshah's death in 1092, the empire started to crumble. By the end of the twelfth century nothing was left, except a part of Anatolia, ruled by a branch of the family called the Seljuks of Rum. "Rum" meant Anatolia, historically part of the Byzantine Empire, which called itself "Rome"; hence the Arabs, Persians, and Turks all called the area "Rum." The Turkish "Rome," with its capital at Konya, lasted until about 1300. Nevertheless, the Seljuk legacies had a lot of influence on the Middle East. Let me summarize them: (1) the influx of Turkish tribes from central Asia; (2) the Turkization of some of eastern Iran and northern Iraq, most of Azerbaijan, and eventually Anatolia (the land we now call Turkey); (3) the restoration of Sunni control over southwest Asia; (4) the spread of Persian institutions and culture (both greatly admired by the Seljuks); (5) the development of the mosque-school (*madrasah*) system for training ulama, especially in Islamic law; (6) the regularization of the *iqta'* (land grant) system for the payment of tribal troops; and (7) the weakening of the Byzantine Empire in Anatolia, long the center of its power.

THE CRUSADES

The last of these enumerated results of Seljuk rule opened a new chapter

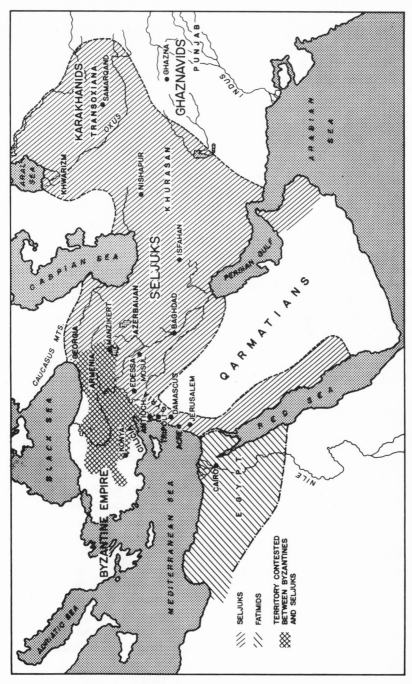

Map 4. The Fatimids and the Seljuks circa 1090

in the history of Christian-Muslim relations. The Byzantines were disturbed by the encroachment of Muslim Turkish nomads on the lands of Christian Greek peasants and alarmed by the rise of Seljuk military power early in the eleventh century. They were so alarmed, in fact, that the Byzantine emperor begged the Catholic pope, with whom the Greek Orthodox church had broken definitively forty years earlier, to save his realm from the Muslim menace. Pope Urban II, hardly a great friend of the Byzantine Empire, responded to the call for help—but for his own reasons. Eager to prove the power of the papacy in relation to the temporal rulers of Christendom, Pope Urban made a speech in 1095, inviting all Christians to join in a war to regain the Holy Sepulcher in Jerusalem from "the wicked race." This inaugurated the first of what would be a series of Christian wars, known to history as the Crusades.

Since the Crusades have inspired so many popular novels, movies, and television programs, most of you must already know a little about what seems like a romantic episode in the history of medieval Europe. Many Catholics and Protestants are apt to have picked up a positive view of the Crusaders from their religious education. Consequently, several school and college sports teams are called "the Crusaders"; none, to my knowledge, are called "Saracens" (the word used for Arabs by the Crusaders themselves). You will soon see why this early confrontation between the Middle East and the West is less favorably remembered by Muslims in general and by Syrian and Palestinian Arabs in particular.

The Beginning of the Crusades

The rise of the Turks in the Middle East was paralleled in Europe during the eleventh century by the rise of the Norsemen (or Northmen, Normans, Vikings, etc.), who breathed new life into a poor and backward corner of the world. The resulting success of Christian armies in pushing back the Muslims in Spain and Sicily gave new courage to the kings and princes of Europe. During this time, travel overland or across the Mediterranean to the Middle East for trade or pilgrimage was becoming an increasingly common experience. One of the strong points in Pope Urban's speech was his allegation that the Muslims (probably the Seljuks) were interfering with the Christian pilgrimage to Jerusalem.

From northern and southern Europe, thousands of volunteers, mighty and lowly, rich and poor, left their homes and fields in response to the papal call. Led by the ablest European commanders of the day, the soldiers of the cross joined up with the Byzantines in 1097. They took Antioch after a nine-month siege, progressed southward along the Syrian coast, and reached the walls of Jerusalem in June 1099. Only a thousand Fatimid troops were guarding the city. After six weeks of fighting, the forty thousand Crusaders managed to break through the walls. Both Muslim and Christian accounts attest to the bloodbath that followed, as thousands of noncombatant Jews, Muslims, and even native Christians were beheaded, shot with arrows, thrown from towers, tortured, or burned at the stake. Human blood was said to flow knee-deep in the streets of Jerusalem. The Dome of the Rock was stripped of hundreds of silver candelabra and dozens of gold ones, then turned into a church.

Once the Holy Sepulcher was safely back in Christian hands, some of the European and Byzantine soldiers went home, but many stayed on to colonize the conquered lands. Four Crusader states were established: the kingdom of Jerusalem, the principality of Antioch, and the counties of Tripoli and Edessa. In addition, the Crusaders shored up the principality known as "Little Armenia," formed in southwestern Anatolia by Armenian Christians fleeing from the conquering Seljuks.

Muslim Reactions

You may ask how Islam, supposedly reinvigorated by the Turkish influx stood by and let the Crusaders in. To some extent, they were lucky. By the end of the eleventh century, Seljuk rule in Syria and Palestine had broken up and the successor states were fighting one another. The Shi'i Fatimids farther south cared little about stopping an invasion that, until it reached Jerusalem, took lands from Sunni rulers. The Abbasid caliph in Baghdad was helpless; it is erroneous to suppose that he was an Islamic pope who could command all Muslims to wage a jihad against the Crusaders. Besides, the lands taken by the Crusaders were inhabited mainly by Christians of various sects, some of which did not mind Catholic rule, or by Jews, Druze, or heterodox Muslims. The Crusaders never took a city that played a major role in the political or economic life of Islam, such as Aleppo, Damascus, Mosul, Baghdad, or Cairo. If we look at the Muslim world in 1100 as a whole, the First Crusade was only a sideshow.

It is odd, though, that the Middle Eastern Muslims waited so long before driving the Crusaders out. Part of the reason is that they, like the Arabs now, were divided into many small, quarrelsome states. Some Muslim rulers actually formed alliances with the Crusaders against their own coreligionists. Relations between Fatimid Egypt and the Crusaders were usually close because of the lucrative trade that went on between Alexandria and such Italian commercial cities as Venice and Genoa.

The first turning point came in 1144, when the governor of Mosul, Zengi, who had carved himself a kingdom from the decaying Seljuk empire in eastern Syria, captured the county of Edessa from the Crusaders. The Second Crusade, led by the holy Roman emperor and the king of France, tried to take Damascus and thus the Syrian hinterland, including Edessa.

The Crusaders botched the attack, though, and Islam was back on the offensive. Zengi had meanwhile been killed by one of his slaves, but his son, Nur al-Din, proved to be a worthy successor. Soon he controlled all of Syria, except for the narrow strip of coastal land occupied by the Crusaders.

The Rise of the Salah al-Din

Then the scene shifted to Egypt, still under the Fatimid caliphs. Having become decadent, they had gradually let power fall into the hands of their vizirs, who commanded the army and directed the bureaucracy. Both Nur al-Din and the Crusader king of Jerusalem coveted the rich Nile Valley and Delta. But Nur al-Din got the upper hand through the political acumen of his best general, a Kurd named Shirkuh, seconded by his nephew, Salah al-Din, known to the West as Saladin. Acting on behalf of their patron, they fended off the Crusader threat to take over Egypt (which they reportedly planned to share with the Byzantine Empire) and obtained for themselves the Fatimid vizirate. As the last Fatimid caliph lay dying of an incurable disease, Salah al-Din quietly arranged to replace the mention of his name in the Friday congregational prayers with that of the Abbasid caliph in Baghdad. This act symbolized the passing of Egypt from Shi'i to Sunni control and was hailed as such by the country's Sunni majority. In practical terms, it meant that Egypt was now under a lieutenant of Nur al-Din, the ruler of Syria, for Salah al-Din proclaimed himself sultan of Egypt after the Fatimid caliph died in 1171.

Equally complicated is the story of Salah al-Din's seizure of power in Damascus after Nur al-Din died three years later. It took at least a decade to overcome the challenges of the Shi'ites, especially that colorful branch of the Isma'ilis known as the Assassins. But he managed to capture Jerusalem and most of Palestine from the Crusaders between 1187 and 1192. To reduce the story to a few generalities, Salah al-Din was a master at perceiving his enemies' weaknesses and his own opportunities in time to capitalize on them. If he happened to be weak while they were strong, he could become a shrewd negotiator. Both Muslim and Christian historians portray him as a master of bravery and magnanimity (what we call chivalry and the Arabs *muruwwah*) in contrast with some of his Christian foes. For example, Reynaud de Chatillon, one of the Crusader princes, raided caravans of Muslim pilgrims going to Mecca. When Salah al-Din retaliated, he stopped firing on Reynaud's castle upon learning that a wedding feast was taking place inside. On the other hand, he could be vindictive and cruel toward Muslims who disagreed with him; he had many of the Fatimid courtiers and poets publicly crucified in Cairo, and the great Muslim mystic, Suhrawardi, was executed at his command.

To most of his European contemporaries, Salah al-Din had a master plan to drive the Crusaders out of the Middle East. If so, he was not wholly successful, for he failed to dislodge them from much of what we call Lebanon. The Third Crusade, which brought France's King Philip and England's Richard the Lionhearted to Palestine, took the fortress of Acre from Salah al-Din in 1191. The late British scholar, Sir Hamilton Gibb, believed that Salah al-Din wanted to restore the unity of Islam under the Abbasid caliphate, but a more recent study by Andrew Ehrenkreuz has disproved this. Salah al-Din did manage to unite Egypt and Syria under his own family, which became the Ayyubid dynasty. The Ayyubids continued to rule, not always wisely or well, over these lands for almost two generations after the death of Salah al-Din. Even though the Abbasid caliphate did revive at this time, the lands it recovered were all in Iraq and Iran. Stranger still, in 1229 the Ayyubid sultan in Cairo actually leased Jerusalem back to the Crusaders, who also kept control of the coastal areas of Syria and Palestine. Twice they raided the Egyptian Delta. The Ayyubids in Egypt resisted the Christian raiders with the help of their Turkish ex-slave soldiers, called Mamluks, who later took over the country for themselves (see chapter 9).

In general, the Ayyubid era was one of greater Muslim militancy and intolerance in response to the Crusader challenge. Even the founder of the Ayyubid dynasty, Salah al-Din, is revered mainly as a symbol of Muslim resistance to the Christian West. Because he retook Jerusalem from the Crusaders, Muslims regained their self-confidence—just in time to face a far greater menace from the East.

THE MONGOL INVASION

The unwelcome interlopers from Asia were cousins of the Turks, the Mongols. For centuries these hardy nomads had lived on the windswept plateau north of the Gobi Desert, occasionally swooping down on China or on the caravans that plied the Great Silk Route. Most of the Mongols had kept aloof from the civilizations and religions surrounding them, worshipping their own deity, Tengri ("eternal blue sky"). But in the late twelfth century a warrior chieftain known as Chingis Khan united the eastern Mongol tribes into a great confederation. He started making forays into northern China, but then turned abruptly toward central Asia in response to a call for help from the oppressed Turkish subjects of a rival Mongol confederation called the Kara-Khitay. After he had annexed their lands, Chingis confronted the ambitious but foolhardy Muhammad, prince of the Khwarizm-Shah Turks. From 1218 to 1221 the Mongols chased Muhammad's army, laying waste to the great cities and much of the farmlands of Transoxiana, Khwarizm, and Khurasan. The atrocities committed by the Mongol armies defy description: 700,000 inhabitants of Merv were massacred; the dams near Gurganj were broken in order to flood the city *after* it had been taken; a Muslim governor had molten gold poured down his throat; thousands of Muslim artisans were carried off to Mongolia as slaves, most of them dying on the way; the heads of the men, women, and children of Nishapur were piled in pyramids, and even dogs and cats were murdered in the streets. The Mongol aim was to paralyze the Muslims with such fear that they would never dare to fight back.

Chingis Khan's death in 1227 gave Islam a respite, while his successors ravaged China, Russia, and Eastern Europe. However, one of his sons sent a large army into Azerbaijan, from which the Mongols could threaten both the Christian kingdoms of the Caucasus Mountains and the Muslims of Iraq and Anatolia. One result of this incursion was the defeat of the Seljuks of Rum in 1243. The Mongols reduced them to vassal status and let the Turkish tribes carve up Anatolia into dozens of principalities. Another result was a strange but lasting alliance between the Mongols and the kingdom of Little Armenia (which had consistently supported the Crusaders against Islam). This led many Europeans to think that a greater alliance between the Mongol East and the Christian West would crush Islam completely.

Destruction of the Caliphate

But the Mongols needed no help. In 1256 Hulegu, a grandson of Chingis, renewed the attack. He may have been encouraged to do so by the envoys whom the kings of Europe sent to the Mongol court, but he spurned their alliance offers. Hulegu was a pagan, but his wife was a Nestorian Christian who is said to have influenced his hatred of Islam. The continued existence of the Abbasid caliph, with even a shadowy claim to the obedience of millions of Muslims, offended Hulegu, who could brook no rivals. After wiping out the Assassins, who had terrorized Sunni Muslims for two centuries, the Mongols crossed the Zagros Mountains into Iraq. The caliph's army resisted bravely until the Mongols flooded its camp, drowning thousands. Hulegu's forces proceeded to bombard Baghdad with heavy rocks flung from catapults until the caliph surrendered in February 1258. Then the Mongols pillaged the city, burned its schools and libraries, destroyed its mosques and palaces, murdered possibly a million Muslims (the Christians and Jews were spared), and finally executed the whole Abbasid family by wrapping them in carpets and trampling them beneath their horses' hooves. Until the stench of the dead forced Hulegu and his men from Baghdad, they loaded their horses, packed the scabbards of their discarded swords, and even stuffed some gutted corpses with gold, pearls, and precious stones, to be hauled back to the Mongol capital. It was a melancholy end to the independent Abbasid caliphate, to the prosperity and intellectual glory of Baghdad, and, for some historians, to Arabic civilization itself.

Mamluk Resistance

The world of Islam did not vanish. Its salvation came from a group of slave soldiers, the Mamluks (their name literally means "owned men"), who had seized control of Egypt in 1250 from their Ayyubid masters, the descendants of Salah al-Din. In 1259-1260 Hulegu's forces pushed westward, supported by Georgian and Armenian Christians eager to help destroy their Muslim enemies. They besieged and took Aleppo, massacring its inhabitants. Damascus, deserted by its Ayyubid ruler, gave up without a fight. Then Hulegu sent envoys to Cairo with this summons:

> You have heard how we have conquered a vast empire and have purified the earth of the disorders that tainted it. It is for you to fly and for us to pursue, but whither will you flee, and by what road will you escape us? Our horses are swift, our arrows sharp, our swords like thunderbolts, our hearts as hard as the mountains, our soldiers as numerous as the sand. Fortresses will not detain us. We mean well by our warning, for now you are the only enemy against whom we have to march.

Then suddenly, Hulegu got word that his brother, the great khan of the Mongols, had died. Grief stricken (or maybe power hungry), he withdrew from Syria, taking most of his men with him. Meanwhile, the Mamluks murdered his envoys and marched into Palestine, where they defeated the Mongols at Ayn Jalut ("Spring of Goliath") in September 1260. The Battle of Ayn Jalut was doubtless a turning point in Middle East history, as it marked the height of Mongol expansion against Islam. Arab historians also noted that the Mamluks, who were mainly Turks at most one generation removed from the central Asian steppes, defeated the Mongols by using their own methods of cavalry fighting. Some pro-Mongol chroniclers pointed out, however, that the Mamluks had twelve times as many men on the field. Hulegu could not avenge the defeat because of a power struggle within the Mongol empire. Thus the Muslim world survived the Mongol ordeal.

CONCLUSION

To bring this long and gruesome tale to an end, Hulegu and his descendants settled down in Iraq and Iran, calling themselves the Il-Khanid dynasty. Eventually they adopted Persian culture, including the Muslim religion, and repaired some of the damage they had done. The Mamluks survived for centuries, driving the last Crusaders out of Palestine in 1293 and forming a kingdom in Egypt and Syria that became the major Muslim center of power, wealth, and learning. Both states are discussed further in chapter 9.

What should we conclude from this mournful chronicle of invasions, conquest, and destruction, or from the bewildering succession of dynasties, few of which are known outside the Middle East? The rise and fall of Shi'ite political power and the influx of the Turks probably benefited the area on the whole; however, the Crusades and the Mongol invasions did the Middle East more harm than good. Nevertheless, the religion and culture of Islam survived and in some ways grew stronger. Perhaps the secret of its resilience will be revealed in the next chapter.

8

Islamic Civilization

Now that you have been taken—or dragged—through almost seven centuries of political history, it is time to look at the civilization as a whole. But what should we call it? Scholars are divided between the terms "Islamic" and "Arabic." Some say the civilization was Islamic because the religion of Islam brought together the various peoples—mainly Arabs, Persians, and Turks—who took part in it. The religion also affected its politics, commerce, life-style, ideas, and forms of artistic expression. But, for much of the period you have studied so far, Muslims were still a minority within the lands of Islam. Since the Muslims were relatively unlettered at first, it is hardly surprising that many of the scholars and scientists active within the civilization were Jews, Christians, Zoroastrians, or recent converts to Islam whose ideas still bore the stamp of their former religions. The civilization evolving in the Middle East drew on many religious and philosophical traditions. The alternative name, "Arabic civilization," emphasizes the importance of Arabic in the development of the culture. Not only because of its prestige as the language of the Quran and of the conquering elite, but also because it could easily assimilate new things and ideas, Arabic became the almost universal language of arts, sciences, and letters between 750 and 1250. But do not assume that all the artists, scientists, and writers were Arabs. The builders of the civilization came from every ethnic group within the *ummah*. Although many were Arabized Berbers, Egyptians, Syrians, and Iraqis whose present-day descendants would call themselves Arabs, only a few were wholly descended from Arab tribesmen. Because "Islamic" is a more comprehensive term than "Arabic", I have chosen the title "Islamic Civilization" for this chapter.

ISLAMIC LAW

Islam begins with a profession of faith, but it is manifested and elaborated by what Muslims do and what they condemn. Ever mindful of the impending Judgment Day, Muslims wish to know and to obey the rules of behavior that will please God and maintain a harmonious society. These rules have been carefully compiled and organized into a law code called the Shari'ah (an Arabic word meaning "way"). It is somewhat like the Talmud for Orthodox Judaism; there is nothing comparable in Christianity. The Shari'ah tries to describe all possible human acts, classifying them as obligatory, recommended, neutral, objectionable, or forbidden in the eyes of God, the supreme legislator. The Shari'ah covers, in addition to commercial and criminal law, rules about marriage and divorce, child rearing, other interpersonal relationships, property, food and clothing, hygiene, and the manifold aspects of worship. At least up to the time of the Mongols, there was nothing a Muslim might experience or observe on which the Shari'ah was silent.

Development of Jurisprudence

The first Muslims based their ideas of right and wrong on the customary norms of the society they knew, that of western Arabia. Caravan traders had worked out elaborate rules about commercial transactions and property rights, while criminal law still held to the principles of retribution based on the tribal virtues (the *muruwwah*). Muhammad's mission broadened and strengthened the realm of rights and responsibilities. The Quran spelled out many points, and Muhammad's precepts and practices (what later Muslims would call his sunnah) fixed some of the laws of the nascent *ummah*. After the Prophet died, his survivors tried to pattern their lives on what he had said or done, and on what he had told them to do or not to do. Muhammad's companions, especially the first four caliphs, became role models to the Muslims who came later; indeed, their practices were the sunnah for the caliphs and governors who followed them. Gradually, the traditional norms of Arabia took on an Islamic pattern, as the companions inculcated the values of the Quran and the sunnah in their children and instructed the new converts to Islam. Even after the men and women who had known Muhammad died out, the dos and don'ts of Islam were passed down by word of mouth for another century.

Because of the Arab conquests, the early Muslims picked up many concepts and institutions of Roman and Persian law. Quran reciters and Muhammad's companions gradually gave way to arbiters and judges who knew the laws and procedures of more established empires. As the *ummah* grew and more arguments arose about people's rights and obligations within this hybrid system, the leaders and the public realized that the laws of Islam must be made clear, uniform, organized, acceptable to most Muslims, and thereby enforceable. By the time the Abbasids took power in

750, Muslims were starting to study the meaning of the Quran, the life of Muhammad and the sayings and actions ascribed to him by those who had known him. A specifically Islamic science of right versus wrong, or jurisprudence, thus evolved. Its Arabic name, *fiqh*, originally meant "learning," and even now a close relation exists in the Muslim mind between the *fuqaha* (experts on the Shari'ah) and the ulama (the Muslim religious scholars, or literally "those who know").

Sources of the Law

Historians of Islam see in the Shari'ah elements taken from many ancient legal systems, but Muslims customarily view their law as having four, or at most five, main sources: the Quran, the *hadith*s (documented statements about the sunnah of Muhammad), interpretation by analogy, consensus of the *ummah*, and (for some) judicial opinion. Strictly speaking, only the first two are tangible sources. The Quran, as you know, is the record of God's words to Muhammad. It contains many commandments and prohibitions, as well as value judgments on the actions of various individuals and groups in history. Let me give some examples. The Quran lays down explicit rules, obeyed by all Muslims up to modern times, for divorce (2:226-238), contracting debts (2:281-283), and inheriting property (4:11-17). When it describes the wickedness of the dwellers in Sodom (7:78-82), the message is implicit: clearly their acts are unlawful for Muslims. But the variety of human actions far exceeds what the Quran could cover. It might order people to pray, but only the example of Muhammad taught Muslims how to do so.

The sunnah of the Prophet was broader than the Quran, but Muslims had to avoid certain pitfalls in order to use it as a source for the Shari'ah. How could they be sure that an act had been committed or enjoined by the Prophet? There had to be a *hadith* (which literally means "news") that said he had done it or said it. The *hadith* had to be validated by a chain of reporters, an *isnad*. The recorder of the *hadith* would have to start by saying who had reported to him this news, and who had told his informant, and who had told him, and so on back to the person who had witnessed the action or saying in question. The *isnad* served the function of a source footnote in a term paper; it authenticated the information by linking it to an established authority. Since the *hadith*s were not written down until more than a century had gone by, the *isnad*s were needed to weed out those falsely attributed to Muhammad. What if the *isnad*, too, were fabrications? To weed out *hadith*s with false *isnad*s, the early ulama became quite expert on the lives of the Prophet, his family, and his companions. If it could be proved that one link in the chain of transmitters was weak because the person in question was a liar or could not have known the previous transmitter, then the *hadith* was suspect. After a century of dedicated labor by many scholars, there emerged several authoritative collections of *hadith*s, six for Sunni Muslims and several others for the Shi'i sects. They are still being used by Muslims today.

Meanwhile, various scholars helped to formulate the Shari'ah itself, which they did by writing books that compiled the laws of Islam for reference and guidance. Because of the numerous changes that had occurred in the *ummah* since the lifetime of the Prophet, the Quran and the *hadith* compilations could not, in the view of most ulama, cover every conceivable problem. They also adopted reasoning by analogy, comparing a new situation with one for which legislation already existed. The Quran forbids Muslims to drink wine; therefore, the ulama reasoned that all liquors having the same effect as wine should also be banned. In much of what they wrote, Muslim scholars looked to the consensus of the *ummah* to settle hard legal points. This did not mean polling every Muslim from Córdoba to Samarqand. Rather, consensus meant that which could be agreed upon by those who had studied the law. It was through this practice that many laws from older societies were incorporated into the Shari'ah. Thus the laws of Islam could cover lives far removed from conditions known to Muhammad: a sailor in the Indian Ocean, a rice farmer in the marshes of lower Iraq, or a Turkish horse nomad in Transoxiana. In addition, the early legists incorporated decisions that had been made by the wisest judges in difficult or contested cases, rather as legal precedents are used in the administration of Anglo-Saxon law. The inclusion of "judicial opinion" gave the Shari'ah added flexibility and relevance to changing needs and changing conditions. In time, however, this fifth source fell out of common use.

Sunni Legal Systems

The compilation of the Shari'ah into authoritative books was, at least for the Sunni majority, completed by the late ninth century. Several "rites" or systems of Sunni legal thought (*madhhab,* a term no English word adequately translates) resulted, of which four have survived: Hanafi, Maliki, Shafi'i, and Hanbali. The Hanafi rite is the largest of the four. It grew up in Iraq under Abbasid patronage and made considerable use of consensus and judicial reasoning (in addition, of course, to the Quran and *hadith*s) as sources. Today, the Hanafi rite predominates in Muslim India and Pakistan and in most of the lands formerly part of the Ottoman Empire. The Maliki rite developed in Medina and made heavy use of the Prophetic *hadith*s that circulated there. It now prevails in Upper Egypt and in northern and western Africa. The Shafi'i rite grew up in ninth-century Egypt as a synthesis of the Hanafi and Maliki systems, but with greater stress on analogy. It was strong in Egypt and Syria at the time of Salah al-Din; it now prevails in the Muslim lands around the Indian Ocean and in Indonesia. The fourth canonical rite, that of the great jurist and theologian Ahmad ibn Hanbal (d. 855), rejected analogy, consensus, and judicial opinion as sources. Because of its strictness, the Hanbali rite has tended to have a smaller following, though its adherents have included the thinkers who inspired the modern reform movement within Islam. It is also the official legal system in present-day Saudi Arabia. Other Sunni rites used to exist but have died out. The substantive differences among the four rites are minor except in matters of ritual, and each (except at times the Hanbali rite) has regarded the others as legitimate.

Shi'i Legal Systems

Shi'i jurisprudence also relies on the Quran, *hadith*s (with the difference that an authenticating *isnad* should include one of the legitimate imams), analogy, and consensus. Some differences do exist between Shi'i and Sunni Muslims over the authenticity of certain statements by the Prophet, especially on whether he was partial to Ali. In certain matters Shi'i law is more permissive: it allows temporary marriage, the female line receives a slightly larger share of the inheritance, and some sects let a Shi'i Muslim deny his religious identity if his safety is at stake. The major difference is that, while most Sunni rites allow no reinterpretation of the Shari'ah, in Shi'ism the imams can interpret the law and are regarded as being, in principle, alive. Among Twelve-Imam Shi'is, whose last imam is hidden, certain qualified legal experts called *mujtahid*s can interpret the Shari'ah until the twelfth imam reappears. This "interpretation" (*ijtihad*) does not mean changing the law to suit one's temporary convenience, but rather the right to go back to and examine the Quran and the *hadith* compilations without being bound by consensus. In this sense, Shi'ism has kept a flexibility long since lost by the Sunni majority, and the Shi'i ulama, especially the *mujtahid*s, have remained influential in countries like Iran right up to modern times. Indeed, the central issue among Sunni Muslim ulama committed to Islamic reform has been to regain for themselves the right of *ijtihad.*

Administration of the Law

At the dawn of Islamic history, the administration and enforcement of the law was handled by the caliphs and their provincial governors. Greater complexity of society led to more specialization, and they began to appoint Muslims who knew the Quran and the sunnah (of the caliphs as well as of Muhammad) to serve as *quadi*s or "judges." As the judicial system evolved, an aspiring *qadi* at first got his training under an experienced master jurist.

The schools were instituted in the big city mosques for the training of one (or more) of the various legal rites. The training schools for propagandists of Isma'ili Shi'ism and later the *madrasah*s founded by the Seljuks and other Sunni dynasties became centers for training judges and legal experts. Students would read the law books and commentaries under the guidance of one or several masters. When they had memorized enough of the information to function as *qadi*s, they would receive certification to practice on their own.

Various other judicial offices also evolved; the mufti ("jurisconsult"), who gives authoritative answers to technical questions about the law for a court or sometimes for individuals; the *shahid* ("witness"), who certifies that a certain act took place, such as the signing of a contract; and the *muhtasib* (market inspector), who enforces the Shari'ah in public places. It is interesting to note that the Muslim legal system had and still has no lawyers; that is, opposing parties are not represented by attorneys in court cases. Muslims felt that an advocate or attorney might well enrich himself at the expense of the litigant or the criminal defendant. There were also no prosecutors or district attorneys. In most cases the *qadi* had to decide on the basis of the evidence presented by the litigants and the witnesses, guided by relevant sections of the Shari'ah and sometimes by the advice of a mufti.

The caliph was supposed to assure that justice prevailed in the *ummah* not by interpreting the Shari'ah, but by appointing the wisest and best *qadi*s to administer it. True, many of the Umayyad caliphs flouted the Shari'ah in their personal lives, but its rules remained valid for the *ummah* as a whole. We must always distinguish between what an individual can get away with doing in his home (or palace, or dormitory room) and what he can do in public, in the possible presence of a police officer. But no Umayyad or Abbasid caliph could abolish the Shari'ah or claim that it did not apply to him as to all other Muslims. When the caliphs could no longer appoint *qadi*s and other legal officers, the various sultans and princes who took over his powers had to do so. When the caliphate could no longer serve as the symbol of Muslim unity, then everyone's common acceptance of the Shari'ah bridged the barriers of contending sects and dynasties to unite Islam. Even when the Crusaders or Mongols entered the lands of Islam and tried to enforce other codes of conduct, Muslims went on following the Shari'ah in their everyday lives. And, to a degree that may surprise some Westerners, they still do. You can go into a bazaar (covered market) in Morocco and feel that it is, in ways you can sense even if you cannot express them, like bazaars in Turkey, Pakistan, or thirty other Muslim countries. A Sudanese student greets me with the same *salam alaykum* ("peace to you") that I have heard from Iranians and Algerians. The common performance of worship, observance of the Ramadan fast, and of course the pilgrimage to Mecca are all factors unifying Muslims from every part of the world.

Applicability of the Law

But is the Shari'ah relevant today? The laws are immobile, critics claim, and cannot set the norms for human behavior in a rapidly changing world. Even in the period we have studied so far, strong rulers tried to bypass certain aspects of the Shari'ah, perhaps by a clever dodge, more often by issuing secular laws, or *qanuns*. The ulama, as guardians of the Shari'ah, had no police force with which to punish such a ruler. But they could stir up public opinion, even to the point of rebellion. No ruler would have dared to change the five pillars of Islam and, until recently, none interfered with laws governing marriage, inheritance, and other aspects of personal status. Islam today must deal with the same problem facing Orthodox Judaism: How can a religion based on adherence to a divinely sanctioned code of conduct survive in a world in which many of its nation-states and leading minds no longer believe in God—or at any rate act as if they do not? Perhaps the time will come when practicing Muslims, Christians, and Jews will settle their differences—even the Arab-Israeli conflict—in order to wage war on their common enemies: secularism, positivism, hedonism, and the various ideologies that have arisen in modern times.

What parts of the Shari'ah are irrelevant? Are the marriages contracted by young people for themselves more stable than those arranged for them by their parents? Has the growing frequency of fornication and adultery in the West strengthened or weakened the institution of the family? If the family is not to be maintained, in what environment should children be nurtured and taught how to act like men or women? Has the blurring of sex roles in modern society increased or decreased the happiness and security of men and women? Should the drinking of intoxicating beverages be allowed, let alone encouraged, when alcoholism is a major public health problem in most industrialized countries today? Does lending money at interest encourage or inhibit capital formation? Do gambling and other games of chance enrich or impoverish most of the people who engage in them? If the appeal to jihad in defense of Islam seems aggressive, in the name of what beliefs have the most destructive wars of this century been fought? Would Muslims lead better lives if they ceased to pray, fast in Ramadan, pay *zakat,* and make the hajj to Mecca? These are just some of the questions that must be answered by people who claim that Islam and its laws are anachronistic.

ISLAMIC SOCIETY

In the early period, the social structure of Islam was far more formalized than that of our society nowadays. Every class had certain rights and duties, as did each religion, sex, and age group. The rulers were expected to preserve order and promote justice among their subjects, to defend the *ummah* against non-Muslim powers, and to assure maximum production and exploitation of the wealth of their realm. Sunni Islam developed an elaborate political theory. It stated that the legitimate head of state was the caliph, who must be an adult male, sound in mind, descended from the Quraysh tribe. His appointment must be publicly approved by other Muslims. In practice, though, the assent given to a man's becoming caliph might be no more than his own. Some of the caliphs were juveniles. A few were insane. Eventually, the caliphal powers were taken over by vizirs, provincial governors, and military adventurers. The fiction, however, was maintained, and the Sunni legist might have asked whether to be governed by a usurper or a despot was worse than by no ruler at all. The common saying was that a thousand years of tyranny was preferable to one day of anarchy.

The abuse of political power was often checked by the moral authority of the ulama. The rulers were to govern with the aid of classes commonly called the "men of the pen" and the "men of the sword." The men of the pen were the administrators who collected and disbursed the state revenues and carried out the rulers' orders, plus the ulama who provided justice, education, and various welfare services to Muslims. The Christian clergy and the Jewish rabbinate had functions in their religious communities similar to those of the ulama. The men of the sword expanded and defended the borders of Islam and also, especially after the ninth century, administered land grants and maintained local order.

Social Groupings

The great majority of the people in the Muslim world belonged to the subject class, responsible for producing the wealth of the *ummah*. The most basic division of subjects was between nomads and settled peoples, with the former group further divided into countless tribes and clans, and the latter broken down into many occupational groups. Urban merchants and artisans had various trade guilds, often tied to specific religious sects or Sufi orders (brotherhoods of Muslim mystics), which looked out for their common interests. By far the largest group was the peasant population, whose status tended to be lower. There were also slaves; some served in the army or the bureaucracy, others worked for merchants or manufacturers, and still others were household servants. Plantations using slave labor were rare. Islam did not prohibit slavery, which was common in seventh-century Arabia, but it enjoined masters to treat their slaves kindly and encouraged their liberation. Slaves could be prisoners of war, children who had been sold by their parents, or captives taken by slave traders from their homes.

Crossing these horizontal social divisions were vertical ones based on ancestry, race, religion, and sex. Although various *hadith*s showed that Muhammad and his companions wanted to play down distinctions based on family origins, early Islam did nonetheless give higher status to descendants of the earliest Muslims or of Arabs generally than to later converts to the religion. As you have seen in earlier chapters, Persians and then Turks gradually rose to the same status as Arabs. Other ethnic groups, such as Berbers, Indians, and Black Africans, kept a distinct identity and often a lower status even after their conversion to Islam. Racial discrimination, however, was generally less acute than it has been in Christian countries in modern times.

The divisions based on religion, though, were deep and fundamental. Religion was a corporate experience, a community of believers bound together by adherence to a common set of laws and beliefs, rather than a private and personal relationship between each person and his maker. Religion and politics were inextricably intertwined. Christians and Jews did not have the same rights and obligations as Muslims; they were protected communities living within the realm of Islam where the Shari‘ah prevailed. Exempted from military duties, Christians and Jews were also not allowed to bear arms. If they did not have to pay *zakat,* they did have to pay a head tax *(jizyah)* plus whatever levies were needed to maintain their own religious institutions. They could not testify in a Muslim court against a Muslim, or ring bells or blow shofars ("ram's horns") or have noisy processions that might interrupt Muslim worship. Sometimes the restrictions were more humiliating, and in a few cases their lives and property were threatened. But they were able to maintain their identity as Jews or Christians and follow their own laws and religious beliefs for hundreds of years. The treatment of religious minorities in Muslim countries that upheld the Shari‘ah was better than in those that have recently watered the code down or abandoned it altogether, and much, much better than the treatment of Jews in medieval Christendom, tsarist Russia, or Nazi Germany.

As for social divisions based on sex, Islam (like most religions that grew up in the agrarian age) is patriarchal and gives certain rights and responsibilities to men that it denies to women. Muslims believe that biology has dictated different roles for the two sexes. Men are expected to govern countries, wage war, and support their families; women to bear and rear children, take care of their households, and obey their husbands. There is little women's history in early Islam; a few women took part in wars and governments, wrote poetry, or had profound mystical experiences, but most played second fiddle to their husbands, fathers, brothers, or sons.

Importance of Family Life

As you may have guessed, the family has played a primary role in Islamic society. Marriages were arranged by the parents or the oldest living relatives of the potential couple, because it was understood that a marriage would tie two families together or tighten the bonds between two branches of the same family (marriages between cousins were preferred because they helped keep the family property intact). Muslims assumed that love between a man and and a woman would develop once they were married and had to share the cares of maintaining a household and bringing up children. Romantic love did arise between unmarried persons, but it rarely led to marriage. The freedom of Muslim men to take additional wives (up to a total of four) may have caused some domestic trouble, but many an older wife rejoiced when her husband took a younger one who could better bear the strains of frequent pregnancy and heavy housework. The "harem" of the Western imagination was rare. Only the rich and powerful man could afford to take the four wives allowed him by the Quran; many poor men could not afford any, since the groom had to provide a dowry. Islamic law made divorce easy for husbands, almost impossible for wives; but in practice divorce was rare, since the wife got to keep the dowry. A Muslim marriage contract might also discourage divorce by specifying that the groom pay part of the dowry to the bride at once and the rest of it only if he later divorced her.

Another point worth making about family life is that parents expected (and received) the unquestioning obedience of their sons and daughters, even after they had grown up. Once a woman married, she had also to defer to her husband's parents. Women naturally wanted to bear sons, who would eventually give them daughters-in-law to boss around. Parents disciplined their children harshly; yet, they loved them deeply and took great pride in their achievements in later life. While a youth usually learned his father's trade, the gifted son of simple peasant or tradesman could get an education and move into the ranks of the ulama or the administrative elite. Of course, a vizir's son might also turn into a bum. Opportunities for a girl to receive an education were limited, but certain occupations were reserved for women, and wives often worked beside their husbands in the fields or in domestic industries, such as weaving. Relationships between brothers, sisters, and cousins had an intensity (usually love, sometimes hate) that is rare in Western families, perhaps because Muslim youths spent so much of their free time within the family circle.

Personal Relationships

Even social relationships outside the household were apt to be more intense than in our culture. The individual in Islamic society tended to have fewer acquaintances than in our more mobile world, but his friendships (and enmities) were apt to be stronger and more enduring. Physical as well as verbal expressions of endearment between two friends of the same sex were common and did not usually signify homosexuality (though such relationships did exist). Men's friendships were generally based on common membership in a Sufi brotherhood, trade guild, or athletic club. We know less about women's social arrangements.

Both men and women entertained their friends, segregated by sex, at home. Mutual visiting, at which food and drink were shared and news exchanged, was the most common pastime for every class in Islamic society. The usual time for this activity was in the late afternoon or early evening as the weather cooled off, or at night during the month of Ramadan. Large groups of men (or of women) liked to gather at someone's house to listen to poetry recitations or, less often, musical performances. Both sexes liked to go on picnics; Egypt and Iran even retained pre-Islamic holidays that required making an early spring trip into the countryside for a meal outdoors. The two great festivals of Islam, the Feast of (Abraham's) Sacrifice during the month of the hajj and the Feast of Fast-breaking following Ramadan, were major social occasions everywhere. People also gave lavish parties to celebrate births, circumcisions, and weddings. Funeral processions, burials, and postburial receptions also played a big part in the social life of Muslims. While a death was mourned, of course, the survivors consoled themselves with the certain belief that the deceased would soon be with God. Men also got together in mosques, bazaars, public baths, and restaurants. Women might also meet their friends at women's baths, at the public well where they drew their water, or at the streams where they did their laundry. Compared with our society, early Muslims had less freedom and privacy, but more security and less loneliness.

Food and Clothing

The foods Muslims ate, the clothing they wore, and the houses in which they lived differed according to their economic condition, locality, and the era in question, so it is hard to generalize on how they met their fundamental needs. Wheat was the basic cereal grain. It was usually ground at a mill, kneaded at home, and baked in small flattened loaves in large communal or commercial ovens. Bulgur or parched wheat was used in cooking, especially in Syria and Palestine. Wheat gruel or porridge was eaten by bedouins. Rice was less common then than now; corn and potatoes were unknown. Many fruits and vegetables were eaten, some fresh, others dried, pickled in vinegar, or preserved in sugar. Sheep, goats, camels, water buffaloes, and cows were milked, and the dairy products consumed included cheese, butter (also clarified for use in cooking), and yogurt. The meat most commonly eaten was lamb or mutton, usually roasted or baked. Various animal organs not highly prized by Westerners, such as eyes, brains, hearts, and testicles, were considered delicacies. Pork was forbidden to Muslims, and so were fermented beverages, although Hanafi Muslims were allowed a very mild date wine. Lax Muslims drank wine from grapes and other fruits, beer, and *araq* (a fermented beverage made from date palm sap, molasses, or rice). The observant majority drank fruit juices in season, sherbet (originally snow mixed with rose water or fruit syrup), and diluted yogurt. Coffee and tea did not come into widespread use until the seventeenth century. Middle Eastern food has never been highly spiced; salt, pepper, olive oil, and lemon juice are the commonest seasonings. Saffron was used for its yellow coloring more than its flavor, because Muslim cooks like to enhance the appearance of their dishes. Honey, more than sugar, served as a sweetening agent.

People's clothing had to meet stiff requirements for modesty and durability. Linen or cotton clothes were worn in hot weather and woolen ones in the winter—and at all times of the year by some mystics and nomads. Loose-fitting robes were preferred to trousers, except by horseback riders who wore baggy pants. Muslim men covered their heads in all formal situations, either with turbans or various types of brimless caps. Different colored turbans might identify a man's status; for instance, green singled out one who had made the hajj to Mecca. Arab nomads wore flowing *kufiyahs* (headcloths) bound by headbands. Hats with brims and caps with visors were never worn by Muslims, because they would have interfered with prostrations during worship. Women always wore some type of long cloth to cover their hair, if not also to veil their faces. Christians, Jews, and other minorities wore distinctive articles of clothing and headgear. If what you wore showed your religion and status, as did the attire of a stranger you might meet in the bazaar, each of you would know how to act toward the other.

Houses were constructed from whatever type of building material was locally most plentiful: stone, mud brick, or sometimes wood. High ceilings and windows helped provide ventilation in hot weather; and in the winter, only warm clothing, hot food, and an occasional charcoal brazier made indoor life bearable. Many houses were built around courtyards containing gardens and fountains. Rooms were not filled with furniture; people were used to sitting cross-legged on carpets or very low platforms. Mattresses and other bedding would be unrolled when people were ready to sleep and put away after they got up. In houses of people who were reasonably well-off, cooking facilities were often in a separate enclosure. Privies always were.

INTELLECTUAL LIFE

Limitations of time and space will not let me give the intellectual life of early Islam all the attention it deserves. Unfortunately, many Westerners still believe that the Arab conquests stifled artistic, literary, and scientific creativity in the Middle East. In reality, no area of intellectual creativity was closed to Muslim scholars. Although the Quran is not a philosophical treatise, nor Muhammad a philosopher, the Arab conquests brought Muslims into direct contact with the philosophical ideas of the Hellenistic world, including those of Plato, Aristotle, and many later thinkers. Hellenistic philosophy was alive and well in several Middle Eastern schools, including the Neoplatonist academy of Alexandria and the great Sasanid university of Jundishapur; and in ninth-century Baghdad Mamun's Bayt al-Hikmah picked up where these places left off. The encyclopedic writings of Aristotle, translated by Syrian Christians into Arabic, inspired much Muslim thinkers as al-Kindi, Ibn Sina (Avicenna), and Ibn Rushd (Averroes).

The "Philosopher of the Arabs" al-Kindi (d. 873) rated the search for truth above all other human occupations, exalted logic and mathematics and wrote or edited many works on science, psychology, medicine, and music. He was adept at taking complicated Greek concepts, paraphrasing them, and simplifying them for students, a skill any textbook writer can appreciate. Ibn Sina (d. 1037), originally from Transoxiana, also combined philosophy with medicine. His theological writings are unusually lucid and logical, although his devout contemporaries shunned them because he separated the body from the soul and conceded that the individual has free will. He argued that the highest form of human happiness was not physical, but spiritual, and that it aimed at communion with God. His scientific writings include what amounts to an encyclopedia of medical lore. Translated into Latin, his greatest book remained a text for European medical students until the seventeenth century. Like al-Kindi, he wrote on logic, mathematics, and music. The greatest Muslim writer of commentaries lived in twelfth-century Spain. Ibn Rushd (d. 1198) is best known for his works on the philosophy of Aristotle and on Muslim theologians. Because of his unorthodox religious views, many of his writings were burned, and some of his original contributions to knowledge may have been forever lost.

Theology (Kalam)

Like medieval Christianity, Islam had to come to grips with some pretty big issues: Does divine revelation take precedence over human reason? Is God the creator of all the evil as well as all the good in the universe? If God is all-powerful, why does He let people deny His existence and disobey His laws? If God has predestined all human acts, what moral responsibility do people have for what they do? Philosophical questions seemed to lead Muslims into theology, as did their disputations with their Jewish and Christian subjects, who were intellectually and theologically more sophisticated than they. Islam developed several systems of scholastic theology, starting with the Mu'tazilah (mentioned in chapter 6). The main points in the Mu'tazilite doctrine were (1) belief in the absolute oneness of God, the sole eternal being and creator of everything else, including the Quran, and (2) insistence that everyone has free will and will be rewarded or punished for what he does. Since these positions seem reasonable to most of us, it is interesting to see why some Muslims objected to them. Was the Quran really created? It must have been known to God before Gabriel revealed it to Muhammad. How could God exist without His knowledge? If He has existed eternally, then His knowledge (the Quran) must also have been around since time began, not created like all other things. It may help to point out that Muslims have always revered the Quran as the means by which they know God; it occupies a position in Islam somewhat like that of Jesus in Christianity. On the question of free will, if everyone will be rewarded or punished for what he or she does, what will happen to babies and small children who die before they have learned to obey or disobey God's will? If the innocents automatically go to Heaven, is this fair to those who struggled to obey the laws of Islam all their lives? Despite these objections, the Mu'tazilah was for a while the official ideology of the Abbasids. However, its advocates attacked dissident Muslims so zealously that a reaction set in, new theological ideas took hold, and the movement died out.

Who spearheaded the reaction of these Mu'tazilites? Ahmad ibn Hanbal, founder of the Sunni legal school that bears his name, broke with them over their application of rigid logic to the Quran and the laws of Islam. His writing influenced a major theologian named al-Ash'ari (d. 935). Trained as a Mu'tazilite, al-Ash'ari came to the conclusion that divine revelation was a better guide than human reason. The Quran, he maintained, was an attribute of God, eternally existent, yet somehow separate from God's essence. Faith was absolute. If the Quran mentioned God's hand (or other manlike features), this should be accepted as is "without specifying how" or even interpreting the words allegorically, which the Mu'tazilites and some of the later theologians tried to do. Finally, al-Ash'ari and his disciples accepted the complete omnipotence of God: everything people do is predestined, for God created all persons and all their actions; yet He assigned these actions to them in such a way that individuals remain accountable for their actions. Later theologians proved that Muhammad must have been God's messenger because the content and the style of the

Quran could not be imitated. The capstone of early Muslim theology was the work of Abu-Hamid al-Ghazali (d. 1111). One of the greatest teachers of the Shari'ah in Baghdad, his main distinction as a theologian was his use of Aristotelian logic to prove the main tenets of Islam, but he also wrote a stinging refutation of Muslim philosophers. Among Muslims he will always be remembered for bringing together theology and Sufism.

Mysticism

Sufism is a difficult subject to discuss. Any effort to define it is apt to mislead you. My attempt to do so in the Glossary ("organized Muslim mysticism") is rather like calling the oyster "a sea creature with a grey shell." While many Muslims whom I know scorn Sufism as a nonrational perversion of Islam, others make it the essence of their faith. Many Sufis regard their beliefs and practices as universal, existing in every religion, no more (or less) Islamic than they are Christian, Buddhist, or Zoroastrian. Each religion, they say, contains the germ of ultimate truth; but, when controlled by an unsympathetic and worldly hierarchy, it can degenerate into a meaningless cult. Sufism seeks to rediscover meaning that is veiled from our sense and impenetrable to human reason. In monotheistic religions like Islam, finding ultimate truth is called communion with God. This can be done by meditation or by esoteric rites, such as prolonged fasting, night vigils, controlled breathing, repetition of words, or whirling for hours on one spot.

There was always an element of Sufism in Islam, but it emerged as a distinct movement during the second century after the *hijrah.* At first it was a movement of ascetics, people who sought spiritual exaltation by denying themselves the comforts of the flesh. Their driving force was a strong fear of God, but this evolved toward a belief in the love of God. Sufism could cut through the intellectualism of theology and soften the rigid legalism of "straight" Sunni (or Shi'i) Islam. It was not—as some modern writers suppose—a negation of the Shari'ah itself. Sufism also permitted Islam to bring in some of the traditional practices of converts from other religions without damaging its own essential doctrines. This facilitated its spread to central Asia, Anatolia, southeastern Europe, India, Indonesia, and Black Africa. From the eleventh to the nineteenth century, Sufism dominated the spiritual life of most Muslims. Brotherhoods of mystic dervishes, also called Sufi orders, grew up throughout the *ummah,* providing a new basis for social cohesion. The Safavid dynasty, which ruled Iran between 1501 and 1736, began as a Sufi order. Sufism also held together the warrior *ghazi*s who founded its better-known rival, the Ottoman Empire. The Safavids were Shi'is and the Ottomans Sunnis, which goes to show that both of the main branches of Islam could accommodate Sufism.

Review of Muslim Divisions

Let me now go over with you the various bases of division within Islam. The first is political: After Muhammad died, should the leaders have been chosen by the *ummah* or taken from the male members of his household? The second, overlapping somewhat with the first, is legal: Which rite or system of jurisprudence can best guide the conduct of individual and communal Muslim life? The third raises theological issues: How much can human reason be applied to the formulation and defense of Islamic beliefs, and is God or humanity responsible for the actions of the latter? The fourth can be called spiritual: To what extent, if any, should the practice of Islam include mysticism and the search for hidden meanings not contained in outwardly tangible aspects of religion? The resulting sectarian divisions have not been watertight compartments. For instance an eleventh-century Egyptian could be a Sunni Muslim adhering to the Maliki rite and to Ash'arite theology and could practice Sufism within a particular brotherhood of mystics, even while living under the Shi'i Fatimids.

Mathematics and Science

I alluded to mathematics, science, and medicine in discussing Islamic philosophy, for early Muslims did not split up the areas of human knowledge as much as we do now. We tend to appreciate Muslim thinkers, if at all, for preserving the body of classical learning until the West could relearn it during the Renaissance. Our debt is really much greater. Muslim mathematicians made important advances in algebra, plane and spherical trigonometry, and the geometry of planes, spheres, cones, and cylinders. Our "Arabic numerals" were probably a Hindu invention, but Arabs transmitted them to Europe. Muslims used decimal fractions at least two centuries before Westerners knew about them. They applied their mathematical knowledge to business accounting, land surveying, astronomical calculations, and mechanical devices.

In medicine, the Muslims built on the work of the ancient Greeks, but they were especially indebted to Nestorian Christians. One of these was Hunayn ibn Ishaq (d. 873), who translated many Greek and Aramaic texts into Arabic but whose greatest work was in the science of optics. I have already mentioned the continuing use of Ibn Sina's work as a medical textbook in Europe. To give another example of the influence of Middle Eastern medicine, the illustrations in Vesalius's pioneering work on anatomy show many parts of the body labeled with Arabic and Hebrew terms. Physicians in early Islamic society studied both botany and chemistry in order to discover curative drugs and also antidotes to various poisons.

Rational and nonrational methods of observation were often closely tied together. For example, chemistry would be mixed with alchemy and astronomy with astrology. Knowledge of the movements of stars and planets aided navigation and overland travel by night. But Muslims, like most other peoples, thought that heavenly bodies affected the lives of people, cities, and states, and so many of the caliphs kept court astrologers as advisers. Muslims also used astrolabes (devices for measuring the height of stars in the sky) and built primitive versions of the telescope. One astronomer is said to have erected a planetarium that reproduced not only the movements of the stars but also peals of thunder and flashes of lightning. Muslim scientists, if not the public, knew that the earth was round and that it revolved around the sun, long before Copernicus or Galileo.

To come closer to earth, descriptive geography was a favorite subject. Thanks to the Arab conquests and the expansion of trade throughout the eastern hemisphere, Muslims liked to read books describing distant places and their inhabitants, especially if they were potential trading partners or converts to Islam. Much of what we know about Black Africa from the ninth to the thirteenth centuries comes from the writings of Arab travelers and geographers. History was a major discipline, too. Nearly every Muslim scientist had to write about the previous development of his specialty. Rulers demanded chronicles, either to publicize their own accomplishments, or to learn from their precursors' successes and failures. The ulama could never have developed the Shari'ah without first having biographies of Muhammad and his companions. Muslims also liked to read accounts of the early caliphs and conquests for amusement as well as instruction. Muslim historians were the first to try to structure history by looking for patterns in the rise and fall of dynasties, peoples, and civilizations. These efforts culminated in the monumental *Muqaddimah* of Ibn Khaldun (d. 1406), which linked the rise of states with the existence of a strong group feeling (*asabiyah*) between the leaders and their supporters.

Literature

Every subject mentioned so far in this survey is part of the literature of the Muslim peoples. Poetry was also an important means of artistic expression, instruction, and popular entertainment. There were poems that praised a tribe, a religion, or a potential patron; some that poked fun at the poet's rivals; others that evoked the power of God and the exaltation of a mystical experience; and still others that extolled love, wine, or sometimes both (you cannot always be sure which).

Prose works were written to guide Muslims in the performance of worship, instruct princes in the art of governing, refute the claims of rival political and theological movements, or teach any of the 1001 aspects of living from cooking to lovemaking. Animal fables scored points against despotic rulers, ambitious courtiers, naive ulama, and greedy merchants. You probably know the popular stories that we call *The Arabian Nights,* set in Harun al-Rashid's Baghdad, but actually composed by many ancient peoples, passed down by word of mouth to the Arabs, and probably set to paper only in the fourteenth century. You may not have heard of a literary figure equally beloved of the peoples of the Middle East. The Egyptians call him Goha, the Persians say he is named Mollah, and the Turks refer to him as Nasruddin Hoja. One brief story will have to suffice. A man once complained to Goha that there was no sunlight in his house. "Is there sunlight in your garden?" asked Goha. "Yes," the other replied. "Well," said Goha, "then put your house in your garden."

Art

Muslims do not neglect the visual arts. Some of the best proportioned and most lavishly decorated buildings ever erected were the great congregational mosques in Islam's largest cities. They had to be monumental to accommodate all their adult male worshippers on Fridays. Some have not survived the ravages of time or the Mongols, but the congregational mosques of Qayrawan, Cairo, Damascus, and Isfahan are impressive enough. Muslim architects also devoted some of their time and talents to palaces, schools, hospitals, caravansaries, and other buildings. Artists worked in many different media. While painting and sculpture were rare until modern times, early Muslim artists did illustrate manuscripts with abstract designs, beautiful pictures of plants and animals, and depictions of the everyday and ceremonial activities of men and women. Calligraphy (handwriting) was also an important art form, used for walls of public buildings as well as manuscripts. Many artistic creations were in areas we usually regard as crafts: glazed pottery and tile work; enameled glass; objects carved from wood or ivory; incised metal trays; elaborate jeweled rings, pendants, and daggers; embroidered silk cloths, and tooled leather bookbindings. You doubtless have seen "oriental" carpets. Most of the genuine ones were woven—or, more correctly, knotted—in Middle Eastern countries.

CONCLUSION

The social, cultural, and intellectual life of early Islam was so rich and so varied that it defies brief descriptive surveys. The Muslim peoples of the Middle East drew on their own pre-Islamic traditions, plus those of the various civilizations with which they came in contact, many of which had already flourished for centuries. They absorbed the customs and ideas that would go with their basic belief in the unity of God and the mission of Muhammad—and rejected the others.

Over many centuries and under many dynasties, the peoples of the Middle East continued to develop and to enrich this many-faceted civilization. Even the destruction of Baghdad and other great cities during the Mongol invasions did not stop these processes. Nor did centuries of Muslim-Christian warfare stop Europe from learning the arts and sciences of Islam at the beginning of the Renaissance. Indeed, I maintain that the high point of Muslim power and artistic expression was not reached until the sixteenth century, the era of the "gunpowder empires" that will be the subject of my next chapter.

9

The Gunpowder Empires

Because we tend to equate the history of the Middle East with that of the Arabs, we assume that Muslim military might, political power, and artistic elegance all peaked before the Mongol conquests. This is wrong. To be sure, the Mongols were a calamity for Muslim city dwellers in thirteenth-century Transoxiana and Khwarizm, Khurasan and Iran, Iraq and Syria. Their record for mass murder and destruction stood unbroken until the time of Hitler and Stalin. Their champion wrecker, Hulegu, hated Islam and especially its political pretensions. Yet his descendants, the Il-Khanid dynasty, converted to Islam within half a century and soon became Persian in culture. Indirectly, Hulegu and his heirs laid the groundwork for a succession of Muslim military states: the Mamluks in Egypt and Syria, the Safavids in Iran and Iraq, the Timurids in central Asia and later in India (where they were called the "Moghuls"), and most notably the Ottoman Empire, which ruled the Balkans, Anatolia, and most of the Arab lands up to modern times.

WHY "GUNPOWDER EMPIRES"?

My title may startle you. I admit that none of the states I have just listed started out as "gunpowder empires." I chose this name because all of them either learned to use gunpowder or perished because their enemies had done so. The harnessing of gunpowder, used in fireworks since ancient times, changed the nature of European and Middle Eastern government and society. Once this happened during the fourteenth and fifteenth centuries, any army or navy that failed to adapt to the use of firearms in sieges and later in battles got crushed. Cannons and muskets needed disciplined foot soldiers trained to load, fire, and maintain them. This in turn aided the rise of centralized governments at the expense of feudal lords who fought on horseback and protected themselves with plated armor and walled castles. The states that successfully made the transition to the age of gunpowder were those that strengthened their administrative and commercial classes at the expense of the landowning aristocracy. No Middle Eastern country was as successful as England or Holland; the one that came closest was the Ottoman Empire.

Because the Middle East is so central within the Afro-Eurasian land mass, the area is apt to get measured in any given time span by military yardsticks: Were its governments strong or weak? Did they win wars or lose them? Did they gain land or give it up? Did its people invade other territories or did other armies occupy their land? With this in mind, note that the date opening the chapter, 1260, was that of a Muslim victory, that of the Mamluks over the Mongols at Ayn Jalut. The terminal one, 1699, marks the general recognition of a Muslim defeat, by which the Ottoman Empire ceded Hungary to Habsburg Austria. But between these two dates the Muslims of the Middle East recovered from the Mongol shock, developed new political institutions, expanded the lands of Islam by conquest of the Balkans and parts of India and by peaceful penetration into West Africa and Southeast Asia, generated high levels of prosperity, and built some works of art—like the Taj Mahal—that still set a standard for created beauty.

THE MAMLUKS

The Mamluks who saved Egypt from the Mongol menace in 1260 were Turkish slaves who had recently seized power from the Ayyubids, the descendants of Salah al-Din. This illustrious ruler had adopted the practice of many Muslim dynasties going back to the Abbasids of importing Turkish boys (mamluks or "owned men") from central Asia and training them to be soldiers. Under Salah al-Din's descendants, these Mamluks became the largest element within the Ayyubid armies. In the thirteenth century, Egypt, not Jerusalem, bore the brunt of the Crusader attacks. The Seventh Crusade, led by France's King Louis IX (later "Saint Louis"), occupied the coastal town of Damietta in 1249-1250 and almost took Mansurah before the Ayyubids sent the Mamluks against the Crusaders. The Mamluks repulsed this threat and captured Louis and his army. Meanwhile, the aged Ayyubid sultan died. His presumed successor (a son) was far away, and so for several months his concubine, Shajar al-Durr, concealed his death and ruled in his name. When the son returned, the dominant Mamluk faction in Cairo, seeing that he preferred another faction, murdered him before he could take the throne. Soon afterwards this faction made Shajar al-Durr the new sultan—one of the few times in Islamic history when a woman has ruled in her own name—when in reality the Mamluks ruled Egypt. Their commander made this perfectly clear when he married Shajar al-Durr a few months later.

The Mamluk Ruling System

The Mamluks developed a pattern of succession almost unique in the history of the Middle East. Although a son would often succeed his father as sultan, usually his reign would be a brief one during which the leading factions would contend for power. As soon as one party of Mamluks had triumphed over the others, its leader would seize the sultanate. It should have been the worst system of government known to man; oddly enough, it worked well for more than 250 years.

For one thing, the system enabled several gifted leaders to rise to the top and stay there. My favorite example is Baybars (1260-1277), who had served his predecessor, Qutuz, as one of the generals at Ayn Jalut. Soon after the victory, he murdered Qutuz and conned the other Mamluks into accepting him as their new sultan. Ever mindful of the Mongol threat farther east, Baybars tried to bring as much of Syria as possible under Mamluk control. This meant taking over the remaining Ayyubid principalities, reducing the Crusaders to a small coastal strip (they held Acre until 1291), and ravaging the kingdom of Little Armenia, the Mongols' most faithful ally. But Baybars did not let religion or nationality stand in the way of useful alliances. He courted the Byzantines and the Catholic rulers of Aragon, Sicily, and several Italian city-states, all of which became Egypt's trading partners. He made alliances with the Mongols in Russia, the Golden Horde (which had become Muslim), against their Il-Khanid cousins in Iran. Thanks to Baybars, Egypt became the richest part of the Muslim world. He also took in a fugitive Abbasid prince from Baghdad and proclaimed him caliph. It mattered more to Muslims, though, that Baybars earned the title of "Servant of the Two Holy Cities," when Mecca and Medina accepted Mamluk sovereignty. This meant that, until they were taken by the Ottoman Empire in 1517, any Muslim who made the pilgrimage to these cities passed through the lands of the Mamluks.

It is hardly unusual for army officers to seize power in the Middle East. We therefore might picture Baybars as a thirteenth-century version of Napoleon or Nasser. But there is a difference: Baybars built a political system that lasted 250 years. Only in recent years have Muslim and Western scholars started to uncover the secrets of Mamluk power and endurance. The analysis that follows will barely scratch the surface. A mamluk, as you know, is a slave. Slavery in early Islam was not as bad as we tend to think, for it often enabled gifted young men to rise through the army or the bureaucracy to positions of power. In some of the wilder parts of the Middle East—the steppes of central Asia (home of the Turks and the

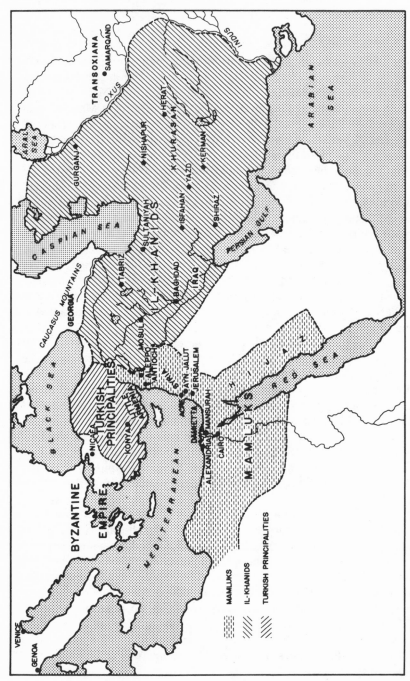

Map 5. The Mamluks and the Il-Khanids circa 1300

Mongols), the eastern shores of the Black Sea (inhabited by Circassians), the northern Zagros Mountains (Kurdistan), and even the Greek islands in the Mediterranean—lived families that gladly sold their sons into the service of Muslim rulers. In the thirteenth and fourteenth centuries, the greatest source of new mamluks was a Turkish tribe called the Kipchaks. Then, from about 1380, the Circassians took the lead, sending their sons to the barracks and their daughters to the harems of Muslim sultans and emirs (princes).

Generally speaking, a boy became a mamluk when he was between ten and twelve, not yet adolescent but old enough to take care of himself and learn to ride a horse, if indeed he had not been riding since he was old enough to walk. He would be sold into the service of the reigning sultan (if he was lucky), or to one of the emirs, and put into a barrack or dormitory with other mamluks his age. All the boys would receive basic instruction in Islam and Arabic. They would be drilled in the care and riding of horses, taught to fight with lances and swords, and trained in archery. The rigorous training lasted for eight to ten years, during which time the youths were kept under the strictest discipline (a visit to the public baths was the high point of their week), but they developed a feeling of group solidarity that lasted the rest of their lives. Upon completing his military training, each mamluk received his liberation paper, a horse, and his fighting equipment.

Even as a freed soldier of fortune, though, the Mamluk stayed loyal to the sultan or emir who had trained and liberated him, to his teachers and proctors, and to the men who had gone through training with him. Each group of trainees tended to become a faction once within the army, rather like a class in a boarding school or a group of pledges in a fraternity. If the master died or lost his position, his mamluks would often suffer demotion or exile, yet refuse to transfer their attachments to someone else. Not surprisingly, the ringleaders of Mamluk factions formed larger federations, took power, and became emirs and, from 1250 on, sultans. This meant that men who had been trained as mamluks became the owners and trainers of new mamluk boys from central Asia or Circassia. The ties between master and mamluk were almost like a family relationship. In fact, few sons of mamluks got into the system. Those who did ranked below the sultan's and even the emir's mamluks; they did better to become ulama or administrators. The succession to the sultanate was rarely hereditary. The Mamluk sultans usually rose through the ranks of the sultan's mamluks. Their success in reaching the top depended on their military skill and political acumen. This may explain why the Mamluks ruled Egypt and Syria longer than any of the other dynasties you have studied so far.

The Mamluk Decline

In time, however, favoritism took the place of advancement by ability, the rigor of the mamluks' training went down, and the quality of Mamluk rule (especially under the fifteenth-century Circassian sultans) deteriorated. The Mamluks became greedy and amassed huge rural estates. They also taxed free peasants and merchants so heavily that many ran away to become nomads. Their attempts to monopolize commerce in luxury goods so antagonized both European Christians and Asian Muslims that the lucrative trade routes began shifting away from Egypt in the fifteenth century. The Mamluks' killing of the goose that had laid their golden eggs led, by the way, to Portugal's efforts to sail around Africa and to Columbus's famous voyages to the Americas. At a time when other armies adopted cannons and muskets, the Mamluks relegated the use of firearms to minor corps of mercenary foot soldiers and continued to fight on horseback, wielding their accustomed swords and spears, and shooting with bows and arrows. This is what caused their dramatic downfall before the disciplined Ottoman army in 1516 and 1517.

THE MONGOL IL-KHANIDS

The great rivals of the Mamluks in the Middle East were the Il-Khanids, descendants of the Mongol conquerors of Iraq and Iran. Hulegu (d. 1265) established his main capital at Tabriz. Its position was important, set in the highlands of Azerbaijan, close to the Great Silk Route leading to central Asia and southeast Europe, and also near concentrations of Christians in eastern Anatolia and northern Iraq. This last point is rather interesting.

The Religious Issue

The most pressing question for Hulegu and his successors was which religion would they adopt, now that they were living among civilized peoples. They might well have become Christian. Indeed, Europeans believed that somewhere beyond the lands of Islam they might find the mighty Christian ruler whom they called "Prester John." They hoped that this potentate—mythical of course—would attack the Muslim menace from the rear and save Western Christendom. In the late thirteenth century, Prester John was thought to be a Mongol; two centuries later Europeans would seek him in Ethiopia. Driven by this strange combination of hope and fear, the popes sent missions to make contact with the Mongol emperors and, if possible, convert them to Christianity. Catholicism had little to offer the Mongols, but some did adopt a form of Christianity already common in Iraq, Iran, and central Asia, namely Nestorianism. The Mongols also allied themselves with Georgians, Armenians, and other Middle Eastern Christians during their assault on Islam. The late thirteenth century was the last golden age for such Christian sects as the Nestorians and the Jacobites (Syrian Monophysites). Afterwards their political power and level of learning declined drastically, and most of the world forgot about them.

The early Il-Khanids actually preferred Buddhism, with which the Mongols had long been familiar. Buddhist temples were erected in many Persian towns, and saffron-robed priests seemed as numerous as turbaned ulama. But the Il-Khanids remained tolerant of all faiths and made no serious attempt to convert the Muslims, clearly the majority of their subjects. In time, Mongol tribesmen intermarried with Turkish or Persian Muslims, adopted their language, and finally took on their religion. The death in 1294 of Qubilai Khan (the "Kubla Khan" of Coleridge's poem) severed the remaining ties between the Il-Khanids and the great Mongol empire, which now became just one more "Chinese" dynasty. A year later, a new Il-Khanid ruler, Ghazan Khan (1295-1304), formally converted to Islam. Iranian Buddhism, an exotic growth, soon shriveled and died. Ghazan and his successors converted temples into mosques and repaired much of the damage done to Iran by their ancestors. Ghazan's successors proved to be weaker, conflicts broke out between Sunni and Shi'i Muslims, and by 1360 Il-Khanid rule had fragmented and vanished.

Effects of Il-Khanid Rule on Iran

The Mongol period was not so tragic a chapter in Iran's history as we might imagine from the massacres and destruction caused by Chingis Khan and Hulegu. Even before they became Muslims, the Il-Khanids gave active encouragement and support to architects, artists, scholars, and poets. Some of the great mosques of Iran, such as those of Yazd and Kerman, date from the Il-Khanid period, although many of the monuments of Mongol architecture have not withstood the ravages of time, earthquakes, and later invaders. Several of the Il-Khanids commissioned great new complexes, with mosques, public baths, bazaars, hostels for travelers and Sufi mystics, schools, libraries, hospitals, and monumental tombs for themselves, in or near Tabriz. Few of these edifices still stand. One remnant is that eight-sided tomb of Ghazan's successor, Oljeitu (1304-1317), which supports a dome 250 feet (75 meters) high. The tomb once stood in the center of a new capital city called Sultaniyah, high in the mountains of Azerbaijan, but today all its other buildings have crumbled away.

The Mongol conquests exposed Persian artists and craftsmen to the achievements of Chinese civilization, resulting in some beautiful manuscript illustrations, glazed tile walls, and other ceramic creations. Hulegu, reportedly contrite at the damage he had wrought, patronized the great Persian scholar, Nasiruddin Tusi (d. 1274), who saved the lives of many other scientists and artists, accumulated a library of 400,000 volumes, and built an astronomical observatory that became the model for later observatories in both the Middle East and Europe. Some Persian Muslims became vizirs to the Il-Khanids and other Mongol dynasties. Two of these men, Ata Malik Juvaini (d. 1284) and Rashid al-Din (d. 1318), wrote universal histories—a rare achievement in any culture—chronicles from which we have learned much of what we know about the Mongol empire and its accomplishments. Two of Persia's best-loved poets, Sa'di (d. 1291) and Hafiz (d. 1389 or 1390), lived in Shiraz, a city the Mongols hardly harmed at all. In general, the late thirteenth and fourteenth centuries were a time of economic revival and intellectual brilliance for Iran. Islamic civilization east of the Tigris took on a more distinctly Persian character. Once again, as in the days of the early Arabs and the Seljuk Turks, the Mongol era proved the old adage that captive Persia always conquers its conquerors.

"Tamerlane" and the Timurids

Just as the Il-Khanid state was fading away, a new military star rose in the east. A petty princeling, Timur Leng, often called "Tamerlane," was born in 1336 in Transoxiana, a land suffering from the constant bickering among Turkish and Mongol tribes. From his childhood, Timur associated with influential emirs and generals. He started to put together an army of Muslim Turks (or Turkish-speaking descendants of the old Mongol tribes), with which he hoped to build a universal empire like that of Chingis Khan. Even before he could subdue his turbulent homeland, Timur crossed the Oxus in 1379 and proceeded to plunder and pacify Khurasan. When the Mongols of Russia, the Golden Horde, tried to organize the principalities of eastern Anatolia and western Iran against him, Timur led his troops through Azerbaijan, Georgia, Armenia, northern Iraq, and parts of southern Russia. Everywhere they went, he ordered the slaughter of thousands of men, women, and children. Cities were razed and farms destroyed. As a devout Muslim, Timur inflicted special tortures on Middle Eastern Christians.

After a brief rest, during which he embellished his capital in Samarqand, he invaded Iran a second time, crossed Iraq and Syria, and carried his empire to the eastern shore of the Mediterranean. Then, giving the Middle East a respite, he turned against India. He defeated its Muslim emirs, sacked Delhi, and filled his coffers with Indian booty, the proceeds of which enabled him to turn westward once more. Between 1400 and 1403 he took Aleppo and Damascus from the Mamluks and almost wiped out the rising Ottoman Empire at Ankara. However, even with a Middle Eastern realm as large as the Asian empire of Chingis Khan, Timur remained dissatisfied. Only his sudden death in 1405 stopped Timur's soldiers from an expedition to conquer China itself.

History buffs have often admired the ambition of an Alexander, a Napoleon, or a Chingis Khan to build by war a universal empire in which all peoples would live together in peace. There is something rather untidy about a world full of contending tribes and kingdoms, or one like ours with its close to two hundred nation-states. Besides, the conquerors I mentioned were men of vision. They appreciated scholars, artists, and craftsmen, and left legacies in the fields of political or military organization. The Mongols may even have spread the use of gunpowder. But it is hard to praise Timur, who left pyramids of human heads and smoking ruins where great cities once had stood. All the same, his legacies did include impressive mosques, some *madrasah*s ("schools"), and tombs in Samarqand and Herat. Descendants of Timur patronized scholars, manuscript illustrators, and jewelers. Eventually, his great-great-grandson, Babur (1483-1530), founded a Muslim gunpowder empire in India. We usually call it the Moghul Empire, but it was really an offshoot of the Timurid dynasty that lasted up to 1858, when Britain took full control of India.

Except for central Asia, the other parts of Timur's empire broke away after he died. The Mamluks recovered Syria, the Turkish emirs of Anatolia regained their independence, and various dynasties took over in Iran. Most memorable of these were the Shi'i Black Sheep and Sunni White Sheep Turcoman states, which fought each other for most of the fifteenth century. Out of this chaos would come a new dynasty to lead yet another Persian cultural revival, the Safavids (1501-1736). I will cover them later in this chapter.

GUNPOWDER TECHNOLOGY

In its earliest and most primitive phases, written history tends to be an account of battles and the deeds of kings. War and diplomacy were the preoccupation of most ruling classes, so this is what they paid their clerks and scholars to record. It was basically a "drum-and-trumpet" history of Europe and America that our great-grandparents learned in school. Even now, what we get in Middle East history tends to be political and military, because historians of this area have barely begun to study the literary and archeological sources that would let us branch out into economic and social history. One field we are now exploring is the history of military technology. In 1965 a European historian, Carlo M. Cipolla, published a book called *Guns, Sails, and Empires*, in which he shows that the development of gunpowder weapons and long-distance sailing ships was what enabled the Europeans to expand at the expense of the Muslim world in the sixteenth century. But he also uses Turkish sources to show that some

Muslim armies used siege cannons and field artillery as early as the Western Christians did.

The spread of gunpowder and of firearms was as momentous a technological change as the proliferation of nuclear weapons has been since 1945. Gunpowder had been used in China for fireworks since the tenth century, possibly earlier. It was being used as an incendiary device during the Mongol era, spreading quickly from northern China to Europe. By 1330 both Christian and Muslim armies in Spain were loading gunpowder into cannons in order to fire huge projectiles against enemy fortifications. The big guns were too clumsy to do much harm to an enemy soldier, but, by injuring or frightening horses, they could block a cavalry charge. During the fourteenth and fifteenth centuries, Italian and German gunsmiths were refining these weapons. Bronze (easy to cast but very costly) gave way to iron, the diameters of the barrels were slowly standardized, and the weapons were made easier to load and to move around. This meant that simultaneous improvements were being made in mining, metallurgy, designing and assembling the component parts, harnessing draft animals, and building roads.

New methods of recruitment and training were devised to produce disciplined corps of foot soldiers and sailors who could maintain and fire these gunpowder weapons. Any European ruler who wanted to keep his territory—or even to survive—had to acquire these new implements of war. And those Muslim states that fought against Europe had also to get firearms. The emir of Granada had them by 1330 and the Mamluks by 1365, but the greatest of the Muslim gunpowder states was the Ottoman Empire.

THE OTTOMAN EMPIRE

Our story begins with a humble Turkish principality centered around a mountain village called Sogut, located in northwestern Anatolia. At the end of the thirteenth century, it was one of several hundred such principalities, fragments of the once mighty Seljuk sultanate of Rum. The growth of this minuscule state into a sprawling empire, perhaps the greatest power of the sixteenth century, is an amazing success story that has been told and explained time and again. According to ancient legend, the empire's origins went back to the Kayi tribe of Turks, settled in Khurasan, who fled westward from the invading Mongols in the thirteenth century. The Seljuk sultan of Rum was fighting the Byzantine army when one of the Kayi chieftains, Ertogrul, happened to come along. Ertogrul offered 400 horse soldiers and turned the tide of battle in favor of the Seljuks, who rewarded him with an *iqta'* (land grant) at Sogut. Upon Ertogrul's death (about 1280, but possibly as late as 1299), the leadership passed to his son, Osman, who was girded by a Sufi leader with a special sword and commanded to wage ceaseless jihad against his Christian neighbors, the Byzantines. He took the title of *ghazi* (meaning "raider" or "victor" in Arabic and other Muslim languages). From that time until the end of the empire in 1922, the descendants of Osman—the Ottomans—would upon accession be girded with his sword and commanded to fight for Islam against the Christian rulers of Europe.

Now we do not know whether Ertogrul really lived. Recent studies suggest that the ancestors of Osman had lived in Anatolia ever since the Seljuks had defeated the Byzantines in 1071. But in history we are just as interested in what people believe happened as in the literal truth. The legend stresses the Ottoman opposition to the Mongols and the Byzantines (both of which were, as you know, non-Turkish and non-Muslim) and their loyalty to the Seljuks and to the tradition of Islam Militant. These attitudes are keys to your understanding the spirit of the Ottoman state.

Beginnings

In the late thirteenth century the Byzantine Empire was recovering from a terrible blow that it had received in 1204, not a Muslim raid as you might imagine, but the Fourth Crusade, a Venetian occupation of Constantinople itself. For almost sixty years the Venetians ruled this historic capital; only a rump of the Byzantine Empire survived in western Anatolia with its main city at Nicaea. Restored to Constantinople in 1262, the Byzantines' grip on Asia began to weaken. At this time, the Seljuk sultanate of Rum was a poor and enfeebled kingdom that had been humiliated by the Mongols in 1243. No longer could it control the Turkish warlords whose ancestors it had brought into Anatolia. Soon there were several hundred principalities that were practically independent of the Seljuks in Konya. The mountainous lands of western and northern Anatolia were what historians call "marches," a border region contested by two or more groups. The local settled population was Greek-speaking and Orthodox Christian. The hillside nomads were Turkish-speaking and Muslim, either Sunni or Shi'i but almost always Sufi. Raiding the settled peoples was their favorite occupation, and the traditions of jihad reinforced their militancy.

Osman's *iqta'* at Sogut may have been tiny, but it was well situated on a hill overlooking Byzantine lands. Osman I (ca. 1280-1326) was a warrior chief who led a band of pastoral nomads on raids into Byzantium to win new territories for Islam and for other Turkish tribes from the east, who always needed more grazing lands for their flocks. Although other Turkish rulers occasionally made peace with the Byzantine Empire, Osman never did. The chance for perpetual raiding attracted the land-hungry nomads to move west and fight for Osman. More sedentary Turks also came from the east, drawn by his connection with a Sufi group of *akhi*s ("mystics"), and they organized his rudimentary government. For nine years the Turks besieged the great Byzantine city of Bursa, capturing it as Osman lay dying. It became the first real capital of the Ottomans (the name used by Westerners for the descendants of Osman).

Expansion

Orhan (1326-1360) was the first Ottoman to have coins struck in his name and to take on other attributes of Islamic sovereignty as he expanded his empire northwest to the Dardanelles and east to Ankara. Twice his armies were invited to cross the Straits into Europe by Byzantine emperors courting Ottoman support against internal rivals and external enemies. In 1354 Orhan's men crossed over a third time, took Gallipoli, and refused to go back to Anatolia. Orhan's son, Murad I (1360-1389), conquered many parts of the Balkans, including Thrace, Macedonia, and Bulgaria. The Byzantine Empire was reduced to an enclave on the European side of the Bosporus, a shriveled husk that survived mainly on Ottoman goodwill. The great Christian power in southeastern Europe was Serbia. Its king, Lazar, gathered a force of Serbs, Bosnians, Bulgars, Wallachians, and Albanians (totaling possibly 100,000 men) to defend his bastion against the Ottoman menace. Murad, leading perhaps 60,000 troops, defeated Lazar's coalition at Kosovo in 1389. Both rulers lost their lives, but Serbia also lost its independence. The new Ottoman ruler, Bayezid I (1389-1402), started to besiege Constantinople in 1395. Western Europe perceived this new threat to Christendom, and the king of Hungary led English, French, German, and Balkan knights in a great crusade against the Turks. They were badly defeated at Nicopolis, though, and the Ottoman Empire emerged as master of the Balkans. This was symbolized by the transfer of their capital from Bursa (in Anatolia) to Edirne (in Thrace). However, nearby Constantinople still did not fall.

If Bayezid had stuck to his father's policy of expanding mainly against Christians in Europe, the Ottoman state would have had smoother sailing, although it might never have matched the prestige of other Muslim empires. The first Ottoman ruler to be called "sultan" (a title given to him by the Mamluks in Cairo), Bayezid began conquering the other Turkish principalities in Anatolia. This incurred the wrath of Timur, drawn to Anatolia by cries for help from dispossessed Turkish emirs. The armies of Bayezid and Timur met near Ankara in 1402. The Ottoman sultan, deserted by his Turkish vassals, was defeated and taken prisoner. His newly won Anatolian lands were restored to their former rulers. Bayezid died in captivity, and four of his sons started quarreling over what was left of the Ottoman Empire.

TABLE 3
The Sultans of the Ottoman Empire (numbered)

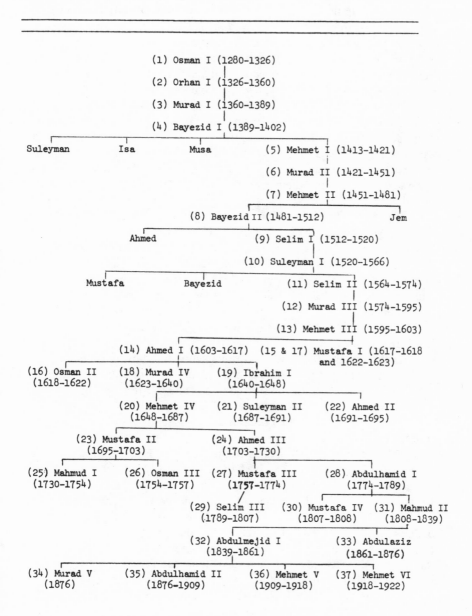

(1) Osman I (1280-1326)

(2) Orhan I (1326-1360)

(3) Murad I (1360-1389)

(4) Bayezid I (1389-1402)

Suleyman   Isa   Musa   (5) Mehmet I (1413-1421)

(6) Murad II (1421-1451)

(7) Mehmet II (1451-1481)

(8) Bayezid II (1481-1512)   Jem

Ahmed   (9) Selim I (1512-1520)

(10) Suleyman I (1520-1566)

Mustafa   Bayezid   (11) Selim II (1564-1574)

(12) Murad III (1574-1595)

(13) Mehmet III (1595-1603)

(14) Ahmed I (1603-1617)   (15 & 17) Mustafa I (1617-1618 and 1622-1623)

(16) Osman II (1618-1622)   (18) Murad IV (1623-1640)   (19) Ibrahim I (1640-1648)

(20) Mehmet IV (1648-1687)   (21) Suleyman II (1687-1691)   (22) Ahmed II (1691-1695)

(23) Mustafa II (1695-1703)   (24) Ahmed III (1703-1730)

(25) Mahmud I (1730-1754)   (26) Osman III (1754-1757)   (27) Mustafa III (1757-1774)   (28) Abdulhamid I (1774-1789)

(29) Selim III (1789-1807)   (30) Mustafa IV (1807-1808)   (31) Mahmud II (1808-1839)

(32) Abdulmejid I (1839-1861)   (33) Abdulaziz (1861-1876)

(34) Murad V (1876)   (35) Abdulhamid II (1876-1909)   (36) Mehmet V (1909-1918)   (37) Mehmet VI (1918-1922)

After an eleven-year interregnum, Mehmet I (1413-1421) overcame his brothers and started to rebuild the empire. This meant he had to fight new wars against the Turkish emirs in Anatolia, the Venetian navy in the Aegean Sea, and a Christian ex-vassal in the Balkans. He also suppressed revolts by a popular Sufi leader and by a hostage of the Byzantines who claimed to be his lost brother and hence the true sultan. Murad II (1421-1451) made further advances into Europe, but was stymied by the Hungarians. After several Ottoman setbacks between 1441 and 1444, the king of Hungary was encouraged to lead a crusade, just when Murad had turned over his throne to his twelve-year-old son Mehmet. The Christians reached the Black Sea port of Varna, whereupon Murad came out of retirement to command the Ottoman army and defeat the latter-day Crusaders. Having resumed control of the sultanate, Murad led expeditions against John Hunyadi of Transylvania and Skanderbeg of Albania, two Christian warriors whose resistance to the Turks has made them legendary among their people.

The Height of Empire

When Mehmet II "the Conqueror" (1451-1481) resumed the throne, he was under the influence of a vizir, originally a Greek, who called for the conquest of Constantinople. They soon had a castle put up on the European side of the Bosporus, facilitating Ottoman movement between Anatolia and the Balkans while cutting the Byzantines off from any aid they might have received from their Christian allies at Trebizond, a Black Sea port city. In 1453 Mehmet did what so many Muslim rulers had tried since the time of Mu'awiyah—he laid seige to the walled city of Constantinople. But this time the Ottoman guns and ships succeeded where earlier Arab and Turkish attacks had failed. Constantinople was taken, pillaged for three days, and converted into the new Ottoman capital with a new name, Istanbul. The city was repopulated with Turks, Greeks, Armenians, and Jews. Soon it became as rich as it had ever been under the Byzantines. The Greek patriarch was given civil and religious authority over all the Orthodox Christians in the Ottoman Empire. Monophysite Christians and Jews soon received similar confessional autonomy. This live-and-let-live policy was in striking contrast with the fanatical bigotry of Christian states of the day. Fearing Catholic domination, Balkan peasants in Mehmet's time used to say, "Better the turban of the Turk than the tiara of the pope." By the end of his reign, they had got what they wanted, as Mehmet's troops took the Morea (southern Greece), most of Albania, and the coast of what we now call Yugoslavia from the Venetian army. In 1480 the Turks landed on the heel of Italy and threatened to march on Rome, but Mehmet's death saved Roman Catholicism from the fate of Greek

Orthodoxy. What would our history have been like if Mehmet "the Conqueror" had lived longer?

Mehmet's son, Bayezid II (1481-1512), was relatively passive, traditionally seen as the least interesting of the first ten Ottoman sultans. His pacifist policies were due, however, to the captivity of his brother and rival, Jem, under a succession of European rulers. If Bayezid had ordered another attack on Rhodes, Italy, or Hungary, the Christians would have unleashed Jem to raise a Muslim rebellion in Anatolia, where Ottoman rule was detested. Many of the peasants and tribesmen there espoused Shi'ism to voice their hatred of Ottoman repression. In fairness to Bayezid, though, he managed to bring contending factions into balance, restore lands confiscated by his father to their rightful owners, and end the debasement of the currency. Even so, the Ottomans went to war against the Mamluks over Cilicia and against Venice for some of the Aegean islands. More dangerous was the Shi'ite challenge from the Turks of Anatolia, spurred by the rise of the Safavids in Azerbaijan. When their first shah, Isma'il I, got up a rebellion of Turkish nomads that spread as far west as Bursa by 1511, Bayezid's son, Selim, decided to seize control.

Selim I "the Inexorable" (1512-1520) transformed the Ottoman Empire from a march warrior state on the western fringe of the Muslim world into the greatest empire since the early caliphate. Equipped with firearms and highly disciplined, Selim's forces routed the Safavids at Chaldiran in 1514 and even took their capital, Tabriz, before they withdrew from Azerbaijan. Two years later they likewise defeated the Mamluks and took over their sprawling empire. As the new masters of Syria, Egypt, and the Hijaz, the Ottomans now ruled the heartland of Arab Islam. Even if we discount the story that the puppet Abbasid caliph in Cairo turned over his position to Sultan Selim, it is still true that the Ottoman capture of Cairo made Selim the most prestigious ruler in the Muslim world. Medina and Mecca also came under Ottoman rule, as did Jerusalem.

Suleyman "the Lawgiver" or "the Magnificent" (1520-1566) had no living brothers with whom to dispute the succession to Selim. Usually considered the greatest of the Ottoman sultans by Turks and Westerners alike, Suleyman commanded the forces that took Belgrade and Rhodes, defeated the Hungarians, besieged Vienna, captured most of the North African coast, drove the Portuguese navy from the Red Sea, and twice defeated the Safavids. He systematized the government and laws of the Ottoman Empire. Unfortunately, though, he delegated too many of his functions to his viziers and fell under the influence of his favorite wife, who caused him to have one of his sons (by another woman) killed and another sent into exile, thus leaving the throne to her son, Selim II "the Drunkard" (1566-1574). Few of the remaining sultans would match the quality of the first ten.

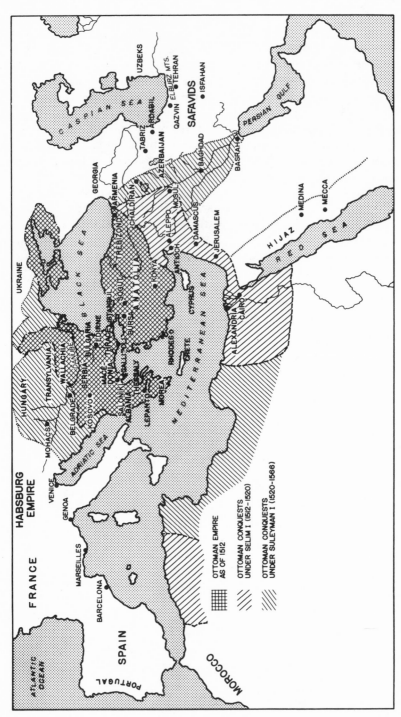

Map 6. The Ottoman Empire in the 16th and 17th Centuries

OTTOMAN EMPIRE
AS OF 1512

OTTOMAN CONQUESTS
UNDER SELIM I (1512-1520)

OTTOMAN CONQUESTS
UNDER SULEYMAN I (1520-1566)

ATLANTIC OCEAN

PORTUGAL

SPAIN

FRANCE

HABSBURG EMPIRE

MOROCCO

BARCELONA

MARSEILLES

GENOA

VENICE

HUNGARY

TRANSYLVANIA

MOHACS

BELGRADE

SERBIA

KOSOVO

WALLACHIA

ADRIATIC SEA

SALONIK

JANINA

LEPANTO

MOREA

BULGARIA

EDIRNE

ISTANBUL

MACE-
DONIA

THRACE

BURSA

GALLIPOLI

RHODES

CRETE

MEDITERRANEAN SEA

CYPRUS

BLACK SEA

UKRAINE

SOGUT

KONYA

ANATOLIA

TREBIZOND

ARMENIA

GEORGIA

CHALDIRAN

ANTIOCH

ALEPPO

MOSUL

DAMASCUS

JERUSALEM

ALEXANDRIA

CAIRO

HIJAZ

RED SEA

MEDINA

MECCA

AZERBAIJAN

TABRIZ

ARDABIL

QAZVIN

TEHRAN

ELBURZ MTS.

ISFAHAN

SAFAVIDS

BAGHDAD

BASRAH

PERSIAN GULF

CASPIAN SEA

UZBEKS

Causes of Ottoman Success

Was the power and the glory of the Ottoman Empire due to the personalities and policies of the first ten sultans? Rarely in history has one state enjoyed such a succession of just and brave rulers for close to 300 years. No doubt the Ottoman Empire owed some of its strength to these capable sultans who learned the principles of government and warfare from their fathers and their on-the-job training in the provinces. They gained power by competing against their brothers, and usually the best man won. They let no religious prejudices stop them from using the administrative (sometimes also the military and naval) skills of their Anatolian and Balkan Christian subjects to benefit the Ottoman Empire. When rival factions arose in the army and the bureaucracy, they kept them balanced and thus under control. "No distinction is attached to birth among the Turks," wrote a sixteenth-century envoy from the Habsburg Empire:

> The deference to be paid to a man is measured by the position he holds in the public service. There is no fighting for precedence; a man's place is marked out by the duties he discharges. In making his appointments the sultan pays no regard to any pretensions on the score of wealth or rank, nor does he take into consideration recommendations of popularity; he considers each case on its own merits, and looks carefully into the character, ability, and disposition of the man whose promotion is in question. . . . Among the Turks, therefore, honors, high posts, and judgeships are the rewards of great ability and good service.

Political Institutions

The strength and efficiency that awed the sixteenth-century Europeans were made possible by the Ottoman ruling class, who were called Osmanlilar ("Ottomans") or *kapi kullar* ("slaves of the gate"). In keeping with standard Muslim theory, the functions of the ruling class were to expand and defend the territory of the Ottoman Empire and to assure the maximum exploitation of its sources of wealth. The dominant groups within the ruling class were the landowning aristocracy, made up of conquered Christian princes in the Balkans and Turkish emirs in Anatolia, and a group of slaves taken from their families as boys, converted to Islam, and trained for military or administrative service. The system of recruiting and training this group was called the *devshirme* ("boy levy"). The same word was applied to the group of soldiers and bureaucrats produced by this system, which was rather like that of the Mamluks.

Any Ottoman subject could get into the ruling class if he took on the following attributes: (1) complete dedication of his life and worldly goods to the sultan's service; (2) acceptance and practice of Islam, although this rule seems not to have been enforced until the sixteenth century; and (3) learning and practicing the complicated system of customs, behavior, and language called the "Ottoman way." As in the Mamluk system, special schools were set up in the capital and the main provincial centers to train youths for Ottoman government service. Most, though not all, of these boys were taken from Christian families under the *devshirme* system. Although we may view taking preadolescent boys away from their families as theft, neither the children nor their parents seemed to mind, for the *devshirme* opened ways to climb as high in the government as their talents and aspirations might take them.

The ruling class was divided into four branches: administrative, military, scribal, and cultural. The administrative branch was the palace; it included the sultan's wives, children, and household servants (sometimes called the "inner service"), and the cabinet (*divan*), which supervised all the other branches of the Ottoman government (and hence was called the "outer service"). The chief administrator of the outer service was the grand vizir, who was authorized to take the sultan's place on military campaigns or in the divan. By Suleyman's reign, the vizirs often did both and were considered second in power and prestige to the sultan himself. The early vizirs were usually Turkish princes or administrators from older Muslim states; Christian converts to Islam began to serve as chief ministers under Mehmet the Conqueror and almost monopolized the post from the reign of Suleyman.

The military branch was very important, for the Ottoman Empire often resembled an army camp. There were many subdivisions, both administrative and functional, but for our purposes the main ones were the horse soldiers (*sipahis*), who fought with lances or bows and arrows, and the foot soldiers (notably the janissaries), who were trained to use firearms. Although the *sipaphis* played the main role in the early Ottoman conquests, it was the well-armed and highly disciplined janissary corps that enabled the Ottomans to defeat the Safavids, the Mamluks, and the Habsburgs in the sixteenth century. The janissaries, whose origins remain obscure, were by far the largest product of the *devshirme* system. Their training and their discipline were extremely strict. Confined to barracks except during campaigns, the janissaries were forbidden to marry or to own land, so that their entire loyalty was focused on the sultan and his state. The *sipahis*, on the other hand, received estates, called *timars*, which they were entitled to exploit so long as they reported for duty and outfitted a certain number of horse soldiers whenever the sultan needed them. As the use of siege cannons and field artillery increased in the sixteenth century, the *sipahis* declined in power and numbers, relative to the janissaries.

The janissaries and other foot soldiers required food, shelter, and clothing from the government, and by the sixteenth century they also received salaries, plus accession money each time a new sultan came to the throne. As a result, the Ottoman Empire needed a well-managed treasury. This function was performed by the scribal branch, which took in the revenues and paid the salaries and other government obligations. Tax collection was not usually done by salaried officials, as in our system; rather, it was farmed out to Ottomans known as *multezims*. A *multezim* ("tax farmer") was entitled to collect all the taxes he could from a given area of land (or block of houses or part of a city bazaar) on condition that a fixed amount or a specified percentage of his take was remitted to the treasury. The *multezim* pocketed the rest. On the same principle, many government officials were authorized to collect fees, called *bakhshish* (a word that has come to mean "bribe" or "handout" in the modern Middle East), for services rendered, not from the state treasury, but rather from the public. As long as the Ottoman government was strong, this delegation of the right to collect taxes or fees ensured that officials would carry out their duties efficiently. Later on, as the treasury's need for money made it necessary for a man to buy his post in the scribal branch, the system became exploitative and oppressive to the subjects of the Ottoman Empire.

The cultural branch of the ruling class was really what you have learned to call the ulama. These Muslim scholars were responsible for the administration of justice, the management of *waqf*s ("pious endowments") to support schools and hospitals, the education of most Muslim youth, and the various religious functions usually handled by ulama. Sometimes they also served as a buffer between the subject peoples and the other branches of the ruling class. What was new in the Ottoman system was that they became a recognized branch of the government, headed by an official called the shaykh al-Islam, who was appointed by the sultan.

The subject class (*re'aya*) included everyone in the Ottoman Empire who did not belong to the ruling class. Its function was to produce the wealth of the empire. Herders and peasants, miners and builders, artisans and merchants were all *re'aya*. Their cohesion was strengthened by trade guilds, Sufi orders, and athletic clubs. Their main political organization was the *millet,* which I translate as "confessional community." The Greek Orthodox church was a *millet,* headed by a patriarch who served at the pleasure of the sultan. All ecclesiastical, judicial, educational, and other benevolent activities involving Orthodox Christians in the Ottoman Empire, whether in Bosnia or Basrah, were handled by their respective *millet.* The Armenian *millet* performed similar functions for Armenians (and, in theory, other Monophysite Christians), wherever in the empire they might be. A rabbi appointed by the sultan headed the Jewish *millet,* with comparable jurisdiction over all Jewish Ottoman subjects. The Muslim *re'aya,* who made up less than half the population of the Ottoman Empire at its height, viewed themselves as part of the Islamic *ummah* (*ummet* in Turkish). They, too, could be considered a *millet,* though with the cultural branch as their equivalent of an ecclesiastical organization.

Europeans living or doing business in the Ottoman Empire, being Catholic or (from the sixteenth century on) Protestant, did not care to be a part of any of these *millets.* Nor did they have to be. The Ottoman government took over a practice, which went back to the Ayyubids, of issuing "capitulations," which gave autonomy to foreign Christians living within a Muslim territory. In effect, European nationals were freed from having to obey Ottoman laws or pay local taxes. Although older history books claim that the capitulations started with a treaty between Suleyman the Magnificent and the king of France, the system was really taken over from the Mamluks. It amounted to a series of unilateral concessions to foreign states. It may seem odd that the Ottoman sultans would agree to a system that kept them from prosecuting criminals within their empire, if they had the protection of a foreign power. Indeed, when the European states grew stronger and the Ottomans weaker in the eighteenth and nineteenth centuries, many Westerners did abuse the privileges they enjoyed under the capitulations. However, keep in mind that Muslims conceive of the law as binding on people according to their religion, not according to the place where they happen to be. The capitulations also encouraged European traders and technicians to live in the empire, while sparing the Ottomans the trouble of governing them.

Ottoman Decline: Signs and Causes

The accession of Selim the Sot in 1566 and the defeat of the Ottoman navy at Lepanto in 1571 are commonly identified as the first signs of decline. Some of its root causes went back much earlier, though, and the outward signs were not visible for quite a long time. Well into the seventeenth century, Ottoman armies went on attacking European Christians and Persian Shi'ites almost at will. True, the Ottoman princes were confined to the imperial harem and manipulated by factions of janissaries and *devshirme* administrators until they came to the throne unfit to rule. True, occasional border setbacks showed that the janissaries were no longer keeping up their high training standards of yore, or using the latest weapons and techniques of war. In fact, they were living outside their barracks, getting married, enrolling their sons in the corps, staging riots for greater privileges, and taking up trades more lucrative than soldiering. The Ottoman navy was still using oar-driven galleys when rival powers had converted to sailing ships and could blockade the Turks in the

Mediterranean, the Red Sea, and even the Persian Gulf. Vast expenses of countryside lay unpopulated and wasted by neglect.

Other aspects of Ottoman society were likewise deteriorating, but most Europeans did not see any decline until the late seventeenth century. The Ottoman army besieged Vienna in 1683. It had done so once before, only to be driven back by an unusually cold October, but in the second siege the superior arms and tactics of the Europeans saved the Habsburg capital and drove back the Turks, despite their great numbers. By 1699, when the Ottomans signed the Treaty of Karlowitz, ceding control of Hungary to the Habsburg Empire, they were clearly on the defensive. The Ottoman Empire had ceased to be the scourge of Europe; in another century it would be called the sick man of the continent.

Why did the Ottoman Empire start to decline in the sixteenth century? No state has yet found a political fountain of youth that would arrest its ultimate downfall. Will America hold up as long as the Ottoman Empire did? Perhaps we should admit that countries, like people, have life spans that, though variable in length, are never infinite. But historians have noted some other reasons for the Ottoman decline. One was its insistence on having only one army, for the experience of previous Muslim states had been that dividing their forces had resulted in breaking up their realms. Besides, the army was in principle led by the chief *ghazi*: the sultan himself or his authorized representative, the grand vizir. This meant that the army could fight only one campaign at a time, and never farther from Istanbul than it could march during the campaign season (April to October), because the *sipahi*s went home each winter to supervise their *timar*s and the janissaries wintered in Istanbul. If two states could coordinate an attack on the Ottoman Empire from two different sides, the army was in trouble. Besides, the Ottoman troops lagged behind the West in their weapons and techniques of warfare. The officers and men liked sticking to the old ways; learning new ones was too much of a nuisance.

Economic conditions were also getting worse. Europe's discovery and exploitation of the New World and of sea routes around Africa to the riches of Asia weakened the role of the Muslim countries as middlemen controlling the main trade routes. There was also a flood of cheap silver from the Americas into Europe and the Middle East, causing a general price inflation in the late sixteenth century. Some countries, like England and Holland, had ambitious merchants and manufacturers who were ready to expand their business activities; other countries, including Spain as well as the Ottoman Empire, suffered severe economic disruption because of the inflation. Indeed, many merchants and craftsmen in the Ottoman Empire were ruined by European competitors sheltered by the capitulations. In addition, rural overpopulation and extortionate tax collection by the *multezims* led peasants to leave their farms and flock to the cities. When they found no work, they became vagabonds and brigands. This impoverished the Ottoman economy even more.

There is a popular idea among Westerners that Islam engenders fatalism and discourages individual initiative. If this were universally true of Muslims, it would be hard to account for the successes of the high caliphate, the Mamluks, or the Ottomans up to 1566. But I will admit that the ulama were very conservative. As guardians of the Muslim law, the Shari'ah, they had to be wary of blameworthy innovations. But it does seem as if the ulama carried this caution to absurd lengths when they forbade the introduction of Arabic and Turkish printing presses into the Ottoman Empire until the eighteenth century, lest a printed Quran violate the principle that God's word was written, and (in a more practical vein) lest Muslim scribes be thrown out of work. The ulama also amassed considerable power as interpreters of the laws, managers of the *waqf*s, and local administrators, and would fight any threat to their position.

The most basic cause of the loss of Ottoman power, though, was the disappearance of the balance among the various forces within the ruling class. English-speaking peoples often call for a balance of power within their government, whereby an equilibrium among its branches or special interest groups helps protect the individual citizen from official tyranny. The Ottoman balance of power served a different purpose. The early sultans had encouraged competition between the traditional leaders (the landowners and ulama) and the men who had been recruited and trained under the *devshirme* system. When Suleyman the Magnificent appointed a succession of vizirs all taken from the *devshirme,* he tilted the balance in favor of that group. By the end of his reign, neither the old aristocracy nor anyone else could check the power of the *devshirme* administrators. Matters got worse under his successors. A similar imbalance occurred in the army, where the janissaries, who used gunpowder weapons, overpowered the various groups of horse soldiers, who did not. This is why the janissaries could claim all those privileges for themselves in the seventeenth century, becoming useless as defenders of the empire. In fact, the Ottoman government took no more levies of Christian boys and phased out the rigorous training schools for janissaries and administrators. Once the ruling class had called its members "slaves of the [sultan's] gate"; now the Ottoman sultan was their servant, a prisoner inside his own palace harem.

IRAN UNDER THE SAFAVIDS

I would like to compare the Ottoman Empire with a contemporary

Muslim state less known or feared in the West, Safavid Iran. The Safavid dynasty grew out of a militant Sufi order centered in Ardabil, a city in Azerbaijan. Although Sunni at first, the Safavids became ardently Shi'i after the Mongol conquest. The rapid breakup of Timur's empire after his death in 1405 created a lot of small dynastic states in Iran, most of them ruled by quarrelsome nomadic tribes like the Black Sheep and White Sheep Turcomans mentioned earlier. Under the leadership of Shaykh Junayd (d. 1460) and the protection of the Black Sheep Turcomans, the Safavids began converting large numbers of Turks in Azerbaijan and Anatolia to Shi'ism. These Shi'i Turks came to be called *kizilbash* ("redheads") because of their distinctive headgear. When the Black Sheep Turcomans turned against Junayd and expelled him from Ardabil, he made political and marital alliances with their White Sheep rivals.

The Safavids kept on growing in strength and numbers, even after Junayd's death, until they threatened the power of their new protectors. The White Sheep Turcomans proceeded to kill or to lock up almost the whole Safavid family. By 1494 no leader of the *kizilbash* revolutionaries remained free save one seven-year-old grandson of Junayd, Isma'il, who eluded his pursuers during a house-to-house search of Ardabil and escaped to another part of Iran. In the summer of 1500 Isma'il and his *kizilbash* followers were ready to declare a revolt in central Anatolia against their oppressors. Turkish Shi'i tribesmen turned out in droves, and in early 1501 the White Sheep Turcomans were decisively defeated.

Rise of Safavid Power

The Safavid state was born in Azerbaijan, when Isma'il, now thirteen, entered Tabriz, proclaimed himself shah, and declared that Twelve-Imam Shi'ism would henceforth be the sole religion of the state. This amounted to a declaration of war against the Ottoman Empire, which, as you know, was Sunni and not securely in control of the Anatolian Turks, who leaned toward Shi'ism. In fact, just about every Muslim dynasty was Sunni in 1501, which made the Safavids quite distinctive. It was even hard for them to find books expounding the fundamentals of Shi'i Islam. Nevertheless, Isma'il aspired to conquer the whole Muslim world for Shi'ism, and he enjoyed the unswerving support of his *kizilbash* warriors. Even though most of the Turkish nomads and Persian peasants living in Iran were Sunni, Isma'il was determined to unite the country both politically and religiously. Within a decade the Safavids, though Turkish by race, had taken control of all Iran and won the local inhabitants over to Shi'ism, which has been a badge of Persian identity ever since. As far as the Iranian people were concerned, the Safavids were a Persian dynasty, just as we view Eisenhower as American and George III as English in spite of their German ancestry. Indeed, the Safavid period was one of the most glorious for the history of Persian art and political power.

True, the Safavids could not match the might of the Ottoman Empire. You may remember that in the Battle of Chaldiran (1514) the janissaries with their muskets and cannon defeated the *kizilbash* fighting on horseback. The Ottomans entered Tabriz, but left after eight days, for the janissaries would only spend the winter in Istanbul. The Safavids lost some of their lands in Anatolia and Armenia, but Iran was saved from Ottoman rule. However, the fanatical loyalty of the *kizilbash* Turks to Isma'il Shah was shaken by the Chaldiran defeat, and the impetus to extend Safavid rule to other lands controlled by Sunni Islam was lost. So shaken was Isma'il that he became a recluse and spent the last decade of his life hunting and drinking. An unanswered question in Middle East history is why the Safavids were so much slower than the Ottomans to adopt gunpowder weapons. Like the Mamluks, the *kizilbash* knew about them but seem to have considered them unmanly. Also, the Safavids' other opponents, the central Asian Uzbeks, did not use firearms either.

The Safavid Zenith

At least some of the effort that the Safavids did not put into conquering the rest of the Muslim world must have gone into creating a good life for themselves. Tabriz, Qazvin, and finally Isfahan became the capitals of their empire. Each in turn became a center for artists, craftsmen, and (most conspicuously) architects. Isfahan was an especially dazzling and beautiful city. Even today its mosques, bazaars, *madrasah*s, and palaces are eloquent testimony to the opulent life-style of the Safavid shahs. But Isfahan is better seen, even in slides, than read about in a textbook. See it. As the Persians say, "*Isfahan nisf-i-jehan,*" or "Isfahan is half the world."

The reign of Shah Abbas I (1587-1629) was the high point of Safavid wealth and power. His predecessors had usually been controlled by the *kizilbash* tribal chiefs, but Abbas brought them to heel by executing anyone he suspected of plotting against his life and by taking away a lot of their agricultural land. Like the Ottomans and many earlier Muslim dynasties, Abbas imported slave boys (called *ghulam*s in Persian) to be indoctrinated and trained as salaried warriors and administrators. In the Safavid case they were mainly Armenian and Georgian Christians, not all of whom converted to Shi'ism. Abbas hoped to set up a balance between his aristocracy (the *kizilbash*) and this new corps of *ghulam*s, each competing to serve the Safavid state. Like the Ottoman sultans, the Safavids divided their government into branches: the royal household, the state administration, the military corps, and the religious-judicial system. Each branch contained two or more dignitaries competing for the shah's favor, giving him more leverage. This system of government, which social scientists call "patrimonial," was not unique to the age; it can be traced back to the early caliphs, the Sasanids, and even the Achaemenids of ancient Persia.

The Europeans took a great interest in Abbas. English advisers came in to train his *ghulam*s in the use of cannons and handguns, which strengthened the Safavid army against the Ottomans. Because of the rivalry between the Christian West and the Ottoman Empire, every European country that hoped to be a naval and commercial power sent envoys and merchants to Isfahan, seeking Abbas's help against Istanbul. Spain, Portugal, France, England, and Holland all had representatives at his court. Even Catholic missionaries went into Safavid Iran. Was Abbas a new Prester John?

Certainly not. He was a great Muslim ruler like Suleyman the Magnificent or Harun al-Rashid. His reign marked a turning point in the history of his dynasty (as had theirs). Because of his early troubles with the *kizilbash,* Abbas had come to suspect anyone else who had power. This included his own sons, all of whom he had blinded or put to death, so that his ultimate successor was a grandson of little account. Abbas's successors continued his policy of putting more and more land under the control of the state administration at the expense of the *kizilbash* chieftains. To some extent, they needed to raise money to pay the *ghulam*s, but the Safavids overdid the practice, for their administration of the crown lands never matched the quality of *kizilbash* management. Like the *devshirme* groups in the Ottoman Empire, the *ghulam*s kept increasing their numbers and internal power—though not their strength as a fighting force—until they manipulated and strangled the Safavid government.

The Aftermath of the Safavids

By the eighteenth century, Safavid Iran was ripe for the plucking. Both the Ottoman sultans and the Russian tsars hoped to move in, but in 1722 a group of Afghan tribesmen seized control of Isfahan, and the Safavids took to the hills of Azerbaijan, their first home. The Ottoman Empire, breaking a ninety-year truce, invaded the region. No match for the janissaries on the field, the Afghans skillfully undermined the loyalty of the Ottoman auxiliaries and negotiated a peace, ceding large areas of western Iran. This was more than the Iranian people could stand. Under the inspiring leadership of a warrior named Nader Afshar, Persian and Turkish tribes joined forces to wipe out the Afghan usurpers and then, more gradually, the dissolute Safavids. The victorious leader had himself crowned as Nader Shah in 1736. His reign was the "last hurrah" for traditional Iran. Within a decade he had driven back the Ottomans and conquered most of India. Had Nader Shah not been so intent on converting the Iranians from Shi'i to

Sunni Islam, he might have founded another great Muslim state. Upon his assassination in 1747, Nader Shah's empire collapsed. A succession of minor dynasties led Iran into a long night of political breakdown and social decay from which it is recovering only now.

CONCLUSION

In this chapter, or perhaps earlier, you may have seen a pattern emerging. An area is divided among many states or nomadic tribes. Then a ruler emerges with a mission, probably related somehow to Islam, that inspires his followers and enables them to motivate others like themselves to overcome rival states. Lower taxes or improved public order win peasant support and help to promote economic well-being. As the empire expands, it builds up a large army and bureaucracy that it must then support, increasing the burden on its subjects. The quality of leadership also declines. Finally the empire breaks up and the cycle repeats itself. All of the empires you have studied here—the Mamluks and the Il-Khanids, the Timurids and their "Moghul" descendants (whom I have slighted, since India is not in the Middle East), the Ottomans and the Safavids—were Muslim military states in an era when possession and mastery of gunpowder weapons became prevalent, then essential for survival. But some of these states lasted a long time because they also set up institutions that assured the best use of their subjects' talents as soldiers and bureaucrats while keeping a power balance between their competing factions. Even when this was lost, the Ottoman Empire and other Muslim states found another type of equilibrium that saved their independence: the European balance of power.

10

European Interests and Imperialism

Since the early eighteenth century, the West has achieved and maintained military, political, and economic superiority over the Middle East. This had not been the usual power relationship before. It may not be so in the future. Neither the rulers nor the subjects of the Ottoman Empire—or of any other Muslim country—wanted this subordination to the European Christians, whom they used to look down upon. But what could they do? Whereas once the Muslims had controlled the commercial routes between Europe and Asia and had dictated the terms of trade to both, now Europeans were selling their manufactures to the Middle East in exchange for raw materials and agricultural products. In addition, Europeans living or trading in Muslim lands lived in special quarters of the big cities and were exempt from paying local taxes and obeying local laws and regulations. Whereas once the Mediterranean Sea and the Indian Ocean had been dominated by Muslim navies (or pirates), now European sailing ships—military and merchant—controlled the high seas. Earlier, the Ottoman sultan could choose the time and place for any attack on Christian Europe and then dictate the terms of peace; now his armies were at the mercy of the stronger forces of the Austrian Habsburgs and the tsars of Russia. To Muslims, accustomed to victory on the field of battle, these changes seemed to be a cosmic error. There is no power and no strength save in God, the ulama would say; yet they realized the might of the Western world was overwhelming them.

OTTOMAN WEAKNESS

We can trace the changing relationship between the Middle East and the West by a series of dated events: in 1683 the Ottomans failed to take Vienna, the capital of the Habsburg Empire (or Austria); in 1699 they signed the Treaty of Karlowitz, ceding Hungary to the Habsburgs and the Aegean coast to the Venetians; in 1718 they signed away more of their

141

European lands; in 1774 they lost the Crimea and allowed Russia to speak on behalf of *their* Orthodox Christian subjects; and in 1798 Napoleon Bonaparte occupied Egypt and marched into Palestine. Meanwhile, other Muslim dynasties, such as the Timurids ("Moghuls") of India, the Safavids and their successors in Iran, and the Sharifian rulers of Morocco, were also weakening before the rising might of eighteenth-century Europe. But the Ottomans were closest to the new powers, had traditionally fought as *ghazis* for Islam, and stood to lose the most if the Europeans could partition their lands. Our focus will therefore be on the Ottoman Empire.

Some Symptoms and Causes

Some popular histories would have you believe that the Ottoman rulers cared nothing for their empire's fate. Enchanted by the charms of the harem, dulled by wine or hashish, hamstrung by janissary revolts or quarreling court factions, the sultans (so the story goes) lost interest in maintaining their government or defending their lands. By the same token, the venal vizirs tried to keep the sultans out of their way, in order to profit from the corruption of the system. Administrators bought their offices and sold subordinate posts to others, while everyone in power gouged the poor peasants and workers on taxes and fees (which were really assessed bribes). The janissaries, who should have been the backbone of the Ottoman army, became a hereditary caste of urban merchants and artisans who failed to keep in training or to learn how to use muskets, bayonets, and other modern weapons. Worse, they overturned their soup pots and went on a rampage if anyone dared to call for reforms. The ulama became ever more like *juhala* ("ignoramuses"), steeped in superstition and untouched by the expansion of knowledge taking place in Europe. Landowners and merchants were being robbed by brigands, from which there was no protection. Peasants suffered from rapacious landlords and tax farmers; many ran away to become brigands themselves. So the mournful cycle turned. The easy answer is to blame incompetent or impotent sultans. As the Turks used to say, "*Balik basdan kokar*" (The fish stinks from the head).

Reforming Sultans and Vizirs

There is, as usual in such popular accounts, some truth in all this. Conditions were getting worse. No one denies the insanity of Sultan Ibrahim (1640-1648), who had his 280 concubines tied up in sacks and drowned in the Bosporus. Mustafa II (1695-1703) should never have been allowed to command his troops in battle. His catastrophic defeat at the hands of Prince Eugene of Savoy, the military genius of the age, cost the Ottomans an army, the province of Hungary, and much of their military prestige. Drinking problems and harem intrigues were clearly more common among the later sultans than the first ten. In addition, there were members of the ruling class who milked the Ottoman system to enrich themselves or who failed to perform their duties. But one of the secrets of Ottoman longevity was that the system went on producing capable sultans and vizirs who saw the corruption and brought in reforms. Among the reforming sultans were Osman II (1618-1622), who tried to create a new Turkish militia and was killed by the janissaries for his pains; Murad IV (1623-1640), a powerful wrestler and champion archer who executed 25,000 of his subjects within a single year; Mahmud I (1730-1754), the first to bring in Europeans to teach new military techniques; and Selim III (1789-1807), who introduced a comprehensive reform scheme, the *Nizam-i-Jedid*, which I will cover in the next chapter.

Equally interesting are the reforming vizirs. For example, the Koprulu family produced six grand vizirs who strengthened Ottoman security abroad and implemented political, social, and aesthetic reforms at home. The first, Mehmet (d. 1661), was taken from his Albanian Christian parents by the *devshirme* and began his career working in the imperial kitchen. As grand vizir to Sultan Mehmet IV (1648-1687), he defeated the Venetians and quashed revolts in Transylvania and Anatolia, executing thousands in the process. His son, Ahmad, strengthened the vizirate, checked the Habsburgs, and conquered Crete as well as parts of Poland. His brother led the Ottoman troops to the gates of Vienna in 1683. A nephew of Mehmet Koprulu, serving Mustafa II, reduced taxes on consumer goods, tried to set up factories, and hoped to restore agricultural production.

Another important vizir was Damad Ibrahim, best known for diverting Sultan Ahmed III (1703-1730) into building pleasure palaces and tulip gardens; but he also brought in European artists, commissioned Turkish translations of Western scientific works, and introduced the first printing press. Mehmet Ragib tried in the mid-eighteenth century to better the lot of his subjects through fiscal and legal reforms, while keeping the empire at peace. In short, even in this dark age of Ottoman history, there were sultans and vizirs who tried to bring in some light. There would be some westernizing reformers in the nineteenth century; I will write on them later. The point I want to make clear now is that reforms alone could not save the Ottoman Empire.

THE EUROPEAN POWERS AND THE EASTERN QUESTION

Most historians think that the key to the Ottomans' predicament—but also, paradoxically, their salvation—lay in Christian Europe. Had it not been for the Renaissance, the Reformation, the age of exploration and discovery, the expansion of trade, the Enlightenment, and the Industrial Revolution, Europe would not have surpassed the Muslim world by the eighteenth century. The Ottoman Empire had not experienced all of the changes these movements brought to Western culture. But then neither had such traditional Ottoman foes as Venice, Poland, and Spain; by 1750 they no longer threatened Ottoman security. Habsburg Austria still played its customary role as chief defender of Christendom against the Muslim menace. But Austria's leadership was paling before a new star rising in the north, tsarist Russia. Many English-speaking people, before and since the rise of Communism, have believed that Russia would have taken over all Ottoman lands, but for the determined opposition of the other European states. To test this belief, let us now look at the policies of the most important European countries (the "Great Powers") toward the Ottoman Empire.

Tsarist Russia

Unlike the other Great Powers involved in the Ottoman Empire during the nineteenth century, Russia had once known Muslim rule under the Mongol "Golden Horde." It had emerged in the fifteenth century as a small but independent state, centered on Moscow and close to the headwaters of the main rivers and to the portage routes of central Eurasia. According to historian Robert Kerner, the expansionist policy of Muscovite rulers was made possible by their control of these rivers and dictated by their ceaseless quest for outlets to the high seas. Rivers flowing into the Baltic Sea or the Arctic Ocean are apt to be icebound for half the year; therefore, Russia needed the Black Sea as a warm water outlet for trade. In the seventeenth century this body of water was just about surrounded by Ottoman lands. As a result, Peter the Great and his successors fought several wars against the empire in the eighteenth century in order to assure Russian access to the Black Sea. Even when it almost seemed to be a Russian lake in the nineteenth century, ships still had to pass through the Ottoman-ruled Bosporus and Dardanelles (the Straits) in order to reach the Aegean and hence the Mediterranean. So Russia sought control of the Straits, or at least assurances that the Ottomans would not bar passage to its warships and merchant vessels. Russia also wanted the Straits in order to keep out its enemies' navies.

There was another reason behind Russia's drive to the Straits: it wanted to rule that great city on the Bosporus, Istanbul. Remember that, up to the Ottoman conquest, it had been Constantinople, capital of the Byzantine Empire, hence the "Second Rome," and chief jewel of the Greek Orthodox Christian religion. When Constantinople fell, Russia became the greatest Greek Orthodox country, and Moscow was declared to be the "Third

Rome." A Muscovite prince, Ivan II, married a niece of the last Byzantine emperor. Their descendants, Russia's tsars, wanted to regain control of Constantinople (which they called "Tsargrad") and restore the power and prestige of Greek Orthodoxy to the level of Roman Catholicism. Besides, many Orthodox Christians lived under Ottoman rule, especially in the Balkans. True, Austria had captured some of them early in the eighteenth century, but the Habsburgs were Catholic and hence unsympathetic. Mother Russia would be a better protector for the Serbs, Bulgars, Rumanians, Greeks, and Albanians seeking freedom from Muslim rule, for they were nearly all Orthodox. So, when Catherine the Great defeated the Ottomans in 1769-1774 and could dictate the terms of the peace treaty, she secured Ottoman recognition of Russia's right to intervene diplomatically on behalf of Orthodox Christians living *within* the Ottoman Empire. This treaty set a precedent for many later pacts between Russia and Turkey (as the Ottoman Empire now came to be called by the Europeans).

Later on, Russia's rulers stressed something else they had in common with many of the sultan's Balkan subjects, namely that they were Slavs. Once thought to be a race, the term "Slav" really denotes membership in a language group. Russian and Ukrainian are Slavic languages; so, too, are Bulgarian, Serbian, and Croatian. During the nineteenth century, many Balkan peoples adopted a kind of nationalism called "pan-Slavism" that would unite all peoples speaking Slavic languages within a single state. Russia, the largest Slavic country, would be its leader. The Ottoman Empire feared the divisive effect of pan-Slavism as much as it had Russia's earlier sponsorship of Orthodox Christians. But keep in mind that there were other European states opposed to pan-Slavism, such as Prussia and Austria with their many Polish subjects, which often caused Russia to play down the movement.

In the nineteenth century, Russia's drive toward the sea, leadership of the Orthodox Christians, and encouragement of pan-Slavism combined at times to produce an aggressive Middle East policy. Russian troops went into the Balkans during the 1806-1812 conflict with Turkey, the Greek struggle for independence in the 1820s, the Rumanian uprising of 1848, the Crimean War of 1853-1856, and the Russo-Turkish War of 1877-1878. In the last of these struggles, Russian troops came to within ten miles (fifteen kilometers) of Istanbul and dictated the peace terms at San Stefano in February 1878. Because all the other Great Powers opposed Russia's military and political gains from that war, some of the Balkan lands were given back to the sultan in the comprehensive Treaty of Berlin, signed later in the same year. Russian encouragement of pan-Slavism even helped cause the Balkan Wars of 1912-1913 and the outbreak of World War I in 1914. You may feel overwhelmed (as I often do) by all the twists and turns of the "Eastern Question" between 1774 and 1917. If so, you can safely assume that the Ottomans viewed Russia as their main enemy for nearly all of that time. I will mention an exception later.

The Eastern Question centered on whether Russia would gobble up Turkey's European possessions, especially the Straits, or be prevented from doing so by the other Great Powers. Although other countries might sometimes accept or even welcome the growing might of Russia (for example, when Russian forces helped defeat Napoleon in 1812-1814—or Hitler in 1942-1945, if I may jump ahead a bit), their usual policy was to head off a Russian capture of the Balkans and the Straits lest it endanger the European balance of power. Now this is a concept that you may want me to explain. Included among the Great Powers of nineteenth-century Europe were Britain, France, the Habsburg Empire, Prussia (Germany after 1871), and of course Russia. There was no way they could decree that each was to have the same power as the other. After all, England had industrialized first, built up the strongest navy, and acquired a large overseas empire. France derived more of its wealth from farming, but it also had a big empire and a very strategic location. Austria and Russia each ruled over vast areas with large and diverse populations, necessitating big standing armies. Prussia's army was unusually well armed and disciplined. Therefore, the balance of power did not assure that each state had equal power; but no one state or coalition became so strong that it could dominate all the other countries of Europe. Failure to keep that equilibrium enabled Louis XIV and later Napoleon to impose French power over the rest of the continent, hardly an experience that the English or the Germans (or the Dutch, Belgians, Swiss, Italians, etc.) cared to relive. On the same logic, many feared in the nineteenth century that, if Russia ruled the Balkans and controlled the Straits, all Europe would be at the mercy of the tsars. We have seen a similar dread of Soviet influence in Turkey during the cold war after World War II, so perhaps this desire to maintain a power balance will not seem strange to you.

Habsburg Austria

Of course, Russia's rivals had also more positive reasons to get involved in the Ottoman Empire. The Habsburg Empire, for instance, bordered directly on Turkish-held lands in southeastern Europe. Having whetted its appetite by taking Hungary in 1699, Austria naturally hoped to move down the Danube River toward the Black Sea. It also wanted to control lands south of the Danube, especially Bosnia and Serbia, parts of what we now call Yugoslavia. The interests of the Habsburg emperors seem to have been mainly economic, but they also saw themselves as carrying on the old crusading traditions against the Muslim Turks. As various Balkan states wrested their independence from the Ottoman Empire, Austria would often step forward as their patron, protector, and trading partner. In a few cases, they seem to have traded one master for another. Bosnia and Herzegovina, two regions that were culturally and geographically close to Serbia, were placed under Habsburg military occupation as part of the 1878 Berlin Treaty. Thirty years later, with no prior permission from the Ottoman Empire (and to the discomfiture of Russia), Austria annexed Bosnia and Herzegovina. However, Serbian agitation kept many of their inhabitants stirred up against Habsburg rule, resulting in the assassination in 1914 of the heir to the Austrian throne in Sarajevo. You probably know that this was the spark that set off World War I. This takes us far ahead of where we should be, but some historians see Austria's Near Eastern (or Balkan) policy as a cause of that great conflagration once facetiously called "the War of the Turkish Succession."

Britain and the Middle East

The British government, suspicious of Russia's aims during the nineteenth century, tended to back Austria in the Balkans. This suspicion led to a general British policy aimed at preserving the Ottoman Empire against all outside attempts to divide or control its territory. The overriding reason for this policy was that Britain wanted to ensure a safe route to India for its navy and merchant ships. As long as most maritime transport had gone around South Africa, the Ottoman Empire had not been a major British concern. From about 1820, though, the beginning of steamship travel and better overland communications made it faster and safer to transship goods and people across Egypt or the Fertile Crescent, both of which were (at least in name) Ottoman lands. Britain believed that Ottoman Turkey was the best guardian of the routes to India and soon committed itself firmly to its defense. By 1850 the empire had become a leading customer of British manufactured goods (thanks to low Ottoman import tariffs) and a major supplier of foodstuffs and raw materials to Britain.

When Britain led the West European countries in the Crimean War of 1853-1856, it was clear that it would go to great trouble and expense to defend Turkey against Russian expansionism. On the same logic, Britain also sent part of its fleet into the Dardanelles in 1878 as a warning, after Russia had occupied most of the Balkan lands. In chapter 11 you will see how Britain's commitment extended to pushing westernizing reforms within the Ottoman government during these times of crisis. In a further attempt to secure its shipping routes to India, Britain also took Aden in 1839 and Cyprus in 1878, occupied Egypt in 1882, and made treaties with most of the Arab rulers along the Persian Gulf from Oman to Kuwait.

Several times Britain sent troops into Iran or Afghanistan to drive back the Russians, whose desire to reach the Gulf nearly equaled their drive to the Straits. These nineteenth-century events foreshadowed Britain's dominance over the Middle East in the first half of the twentieth.

France: Protector and Civilizer

The best friend of the Ottoman Turks was usually France. Its strategic location, with major ports on both the Atlantic and the Mediterranean, made France a frequent contender for the mastery of Europe. Up to the nineteenth century its greatest rival in the Mediterranean was the Habsburg Empire, which tended to bring France into alliance with the Ottomans. France claimed to have the oldest capitulatory treaty, and French merchants and investors were almost always foremost among Europeans doing business in the Ottoman Empire. When Turkey needed military or naval experts, engineers, or teachers, it usually sought French ones. Young Ottomans going abroad were more apt to choose France than any other country for higher education or advanced vocational training.

Religion, too, furthered the French connection. When Russia tried to protect Orthodox Christians under Ottoman rule, France advanced similar claims on behalf of the Catholics. Because these were relatively few, the Turks minded them less. One fateful result was the special relationship between France and Syria. One key to this binding tie was a Christian sect, the Maronites, who predominated in what is now northern Lebanon. In the seventh century, the Maronites had taken the compromise position between Orthodox and Monophysite Christianity, which gave them a special identity. They later entered into communion with Rome, possibly during the Crusades but definitely by the eighteenth century. They were allowed to keep their traditional practices (such as prayers in Syriac and married priests), but now gained access to the knowledge of the West through a papal seminary for Maronites in Rome. When France emerged as the leading Catholic power, the Maronites welcomed French missionaries and merchants to Syria, where they built up a network of schools, churches, factories, and trading posts. France's primacy in Syria rested on ties with other Christians as well. Various Christian groups were breaking away from their native churches, usually Orthodox but also Jacobite (Monophysite) and Nestorian, and entered into communion with Rome as Uniates. These converts to Catholicism, like the Maronites, studied in the French schools and traded with French businessmen. Not surprisingly, some adopted other aspects of French culture too.

Strategically speaking, Egypt mattered more to France than Syria. This was not widely understood in the eighteenth century, when Egypt's economy and society reached their lowest point in recorded history, owing to Ottoman neglect and Mamluk misrule (about which I will say more in the next chapter). But Napoleon Bonaparte, who once called Egypt the world's most important country, occupied it in 1798. For three years Britain and Turkey went through a most complicated series of military and diplomatic maneuvers to get the French troops out of Egypt. In the wake of the French departure, a military adventurer named Mehmet Ali rose to power in Cairo. Aided by French advisers, he instituted an ambitious reform program, built up a strong army and navy, and took Syria from the Ottoman Empire in 1832. France supported and applauded Mehmet Ali's triumphs. Not so the other Great Powers, which saw them as a threat to the European balance of power. Mehmet Ali was viewed as a French agent. It took Britain's military intervention to get his troops out of Syria in 1840, but Mehmet Ali retained his power in Egypt and founded a dynasty that reigned there until 1952.

France played the lead role in yet another Egyptian drama. Mehmet Ali's son, Sa'id, granted a concession to a French engineer in 1854 to build a ship canal across the Isthmus of Suez. The British tried to block the project, fearing that it would give the French control over a major route to India. However, once the Suez Canal was opened in 1869, Britain became its main user. Soon it bought the Egyptian government's shares in the controlling company and then occupied Egypt when France failed to act during a nationalist uprising in 1882. French economic and cultural ties with Egypt remained strong, but by the end of the nineteenth century, in spite of French opposition, Britain dominated the Valley of the Nile. France did, however, control most of the rest of North Africa. During World War I, it would seek further compensation in Syria.

CONCLUSION

This brings to a close my rapid survey of the Middle Eastern interests and policies of the major European powers. I went beyond the eighteenth century, hoping to give you a bigger picture. You may have wondered why I focused on Russia, Austria, England, and France, to the exclusion of all other countries. This is a bit oversimplified. The complete cast of characters in the Eastern Question would include Swiss archeologists, Belgian investors, German military advisers, American Protestant and Italian Catholic missionaries, Greek grocers, and Armenian carpet sellers. By 1900 the German, Italian, and American governments started to play parts in the political drama as well. Iran was also becoming more important.

This chapter has also tended to view the Middle East, not as an area acting, but as one acted upon. This, too, is a distortion. Even if it did lose lands in the Balkans and North Africa, the Ottoman Empire stayed independent throughout this time. Even if Western ambassadors and advisers might overdirect sultans and vizirs, the scope of their actions was limited by Muslim conservatism and anxiety to prevent another country's intervention. Likewise, Iran staved off the Russians and the British until they agreed to split the country into zones of influence in 1907. Most Middle Easterners lived as if Europe were on another planet. The changes affecting them were political reforms started by their own rulers, and it is to these that we now must turn.

11

Westernizing Reform in the Nineteenth Century

Europe's power rose so dramatically between the sixteenth and nineteenth centuries that every other part of the world had to adapt or go under. Some human groups, like the Fuegian Indians at the southern tip of South America and the natives of Tasmania, actually were wiped out by white people's diseases, alcohol, or deportation. Others, like the North American Indians and the Australian aborigines, lost nearly all their lands and liberties to the English colonists. Some peoples mixed with the European settlers, creating a hybrid culture, as in Brazil. Many West Africans were uprooted, enslaved, and shipped to strange and distant lands. Such ancient countries as India, Java, and Vietnam were incorporated into European empires. Japan kept its independence, but aped Western ways on a large scale. Several other Asian countries tried to stay independent by grafting onto their traditional societies those Western customs and institutions that seemed to be a source of strength. China, Thailand, Iran, and the Ottoman Empire followed this path, which seemed moderate, logical, and appropriate for countries with deeply ingrained cultural norms and values. Islam, for instance, was both a faith and a way of life. Thus Muslim countries wanted to strengthen their armies and navies, their governments and economies, but not to discard a life-style they had developed and followed for centuries. Reformers had to select with care the institutions and practices they borrowed from Europe, but they soon learned that a westernizing program in, say, defense could not be blocked off from the rest of society. Military, political, and economic reforms sparked reactions in seemingly remote areas, often catching the reformers off guard.

You may run into problems defining "reform." In Western countries, the reformer often comes from outside the power elite, challenges the system, and, if successful, changes it. He or she may resort to violent revolution, but most successful reforms are achieved through the ballot box, the legislature, or the forum of public opinion. They may well reflect economic or social changes that have already taken place. When we speak of the "Reform Bills" in English history, we mean the acts of Parliament that extended voting rights to more classes of people during the nineteenth century. When we speak of a "reform party" in American politics, we usually refer to an out-group wanting to stop corrupt or unjust practices within a city, state, or national government.

We commonly assume that reformers come from below. In a few cases they have, even in the Middle East. You learned earlier about the Kharijites and the Hashimites under the Umayyad caliphate. In the seventeenth and eighteenth centuries there were peasant revolts in Anatolia and the Balkans, but they were usually separatist, not reformist. A better example would be the Wahhabis. They were a group of highly puritanical Muslims, growing out of the Hanbali rite of Sunni Islam, who seized power in central Arabia during the eighteenth century. Led by a family named Saud (hence the modern political term "Saudi Arabia"), these Wahhabis wanted to conquer the whole Arabian peninsula (if not more) and to purify Islam from practices they deemed corrupt. They built up a fairly strong state in the late eighteenth century, then were checked by the Ottomans and Mehmet Ali in the nineteenth. They made a strong comeback, however, early in this century. Many of their ideas have gained acceptance from Muslim thinkers outside Saudi Arabia. I suppose you could call them reformers. There have been many other movements within Islam during the past two centuries that aim to restore the greatness of Islamic civilization or to reconcile Islamic institutions with the demands of modernity. They come not from below, but from the intellectual elite. Sometimes they are encouraged by the rulers themselves.

For purposes of Middle East history, I think you should assume that significant and effective reforms have usually come from above. Generally speaking, they have been instituted by the rulers, their viziers, generals, or local governors. They have seldom been demanded by the poor, or done this class much good once in effect. In particular, we will be concerned with those that involved westernization, often at the expense of traditional Islam as the people understood it. Our focus in this chapter will be on westernizing reform in Egypt, the rest of the Ottoman Empire, and Iran.

EGYPT

If Rip Van Winkle had nodded off in Cairo around 1795 and had been aroused seventy-five years later, he would have been astounded—if not bewildered—by the changes that had taken place during his nap. Egypt made the fastest and most dramatic change of any Middle Eastern country during the nineteenth century. Since 1517 the country had been ruled by the

Ottoman Empire, but an early uprising had taught Istanbul to leave most local control in the hands of the Mamluks. You probably remember this aristocracy of ex-slave soldiers that had ruled Egypt since 1250. Under the Ottomans, the Mamluks continued to bring in Circassian boy slaves and to train them as soldiers and administrators. It might have been a good system once upon a time, but no longer; the Mamluks by the eighteenth century had turned into rapacious tax farmers and cruel governors. Caught up in factional struggles, they neglected to provide the irrigation works and security needed by the peasants, whose prosperity and population plummeted to a new low. Starved for revenue, the intellectual caliber of the *madrasahs*, including the ancient university of al-Azhar, also fell. The ulama became incompetent, lazy, and corrupt. Their Christian and Jewish counterparts were not much better. The Ottoman governors could do nothing to ameliorate the situation. Although soldiers and peasants revolted, sometimes successfully, they too could not reform the system. Egypt was running down. In the end, it took two extraordinary foreigners to get the country moving again: Napoleon Bonaparte and Mehmet Ali.

Napoleon's Occupation of Egypt

Napoleon was sent by the French revolutionary government in 1798 to capture Egypt and, if possible, Syria and Iraq. The government seems to have wanted to get the ambitious young general out of Paris and to move on India, parts of which France had lost to the British in 1763. Napoleon was fired with a desire to emulate the conquests of Alexander the Great, which would have meant leading his army from Egypt through the Fertile Crescent to Iran, Afghanistan, and what is now Pakistan. It was a fantastic dream never realized, but Napoleon did manage to defeat the Mamluks and occupy Cairo. Seeking to win the Egyptians over to his side, he posted manifestos, of which a portion read:

> Peoples of Egypt, you will be told that I have come to destroy your religion. This is an obvious lie; do not believe it! Tell the slanderers that I have come to you to restore your rights from the hands of the oppressors and that I, more than the Mamluks, serve God . . . and revere His Prophet Muhammad and the glorious Quran. . . . Formerly in the land of Egypt there were great cities, wide canals, and a prosperous trade. What has ruined all this, if not the greed and tyranny of the Mamluks? . . . Tell your nation that the French are also faithful Muslims. The truth is that they invaded Rome and have destroyed the throne of the pope, who always incited the Christians to make war on the Muslims. . . . Furthermore, the French have at all times declared themselves to be the most sincere friends of the Ottoman sultan and the enemy of his enemies. The Mamluks, on the contrary, have always refused to obey him. . . . Blessing upon blessing to the Egyptians who side with us. They shall prosper

in fortune and rank. Happy, too, are those who stay in their dwellings, not siding with either of the parties now at war; when they know us better, they will hasten to join us. . . . But woe upon woe to those who side with the Mamluks and help them to make war on us. They will find no escape, and their memory shall be wiped out.

The Egyptians loved the Mamluks little, but they soon loved the French even less. Napoleon and his men were not Muslims, nor did they restore Ottoman sovereignty. The French occupation of Egypt was harsh, heavy-handed, and hated. Taxes and government fees, high but sporadic under the Mamluks, were now collected regularly from everyone, which made them seem more oppressive. Ignorant of local mores and customs, the French troops shocked pious Muslims by their lewd conduct, public drinking, and blasphemous behavior, which included the shelling of al-Azhar in response to a local insurrection. When the British navy sank most of Napoleon's ships in the Battle of Abu-Kir, then when the French army marched into Palestine but failed to take Acre from the Turks, and finally when Napoleon himself escaped through the British blockade to return to France, the Egyptians became even more hostile. Yet the French occupation lasted until 1801. The Egyptian people were sullen but unarmed. Their Mamluk ex-rulers were divided and weakened. It took a joint Anglo-Ottoman landing at Alexandria, followed by a general European treaty, to get the French out of Egypt.

The French occupation tends to get played up because Napoleon was so colorful, or because France held cultural ties with Egypt later on. Still, the French expeditionary force did include a large staff of scholars, scientists, and artists, who went around Cairo and the countryside studying almost every aspect of Egypt. The published results of their studies, with ten volumes of text and fourteen of illustrations, give us a surprisingly thorough and fairly accurate description of the country's condition and the life of its people. The French also introduced the first Arabic printing press and established a research institute, which attracted the notice of a few inquisitive ulama. Few historians now think (as we once did) that these events caused the intellectual awakening of Egypt. What did help was that Napoleon's invasion (1) led to ongoing competition for Egypt between England and France, (2) destroyed whatever notions Ottoman Muslims still cherished about their superiority over Europe, and (3) weakened the Mamluks, creating a leadership vacuum once the last British troops pulled out in 1802.

Mehmet Ali and His Reforms

The man who eventually filled that vacuum was a Turkish soldier of fortune, Mehmet Ali. He had come to Egypt as second in command of the Albanian regiment in the Ottoman expeditionary force that tried, unsuccessfully in 1799 but victoriously two years later, to dislodge the French. Mehmet Ali used to underscore his personal ambitions with the remark, "I was born in the same year as Napoleon in the land of Alexander." He may have patterned his career after both men: by 1805 he had emerged from the pack of contenders for power and secured recognition from a group of ulama and local notables. The next year he incited a revolt against the Ottoman governor and secured the sultan's consent to take his place. Like many of the Ottoman reformers, Mehmet Ali realized that losses on the field of battle showed the glaring weakness of the existing army and the political system behind it. Unlike the others, though, he realized that the adoption of European uniforms, weapons, and tactics, or even the importation of foreign instructors and technicians, could not solve their military problems. Wholehearted and comprehensive reforms were a must. If Western ways did not appeal to Muslims, then Mehmet Ali would have to be ruthless and dictatorial.

Fortunately for him, the Nile Valley made Egypt a proverbially easy country to govern, once all rival power centers were wiped out. The Mamluks were the major obstacle; thus in 1811 Mehmet Ali had them all massacred. Because the ulama enjoyed great power and prestige, Mehmet Ali first exploited their internecine rivalries, then weakened them by taking away most of the land they had managed as *waqf*s (Muslim endowments). He also put most privately owned land under state control, thus wiping out the tax farmers and the old rural aristocracy. This gave his government a monopoly over Egypt's most valuable resource, its agricultural land. The state now decided what crops the peasants might grow; supplied them with seeds, tools, and fertilizer; purchased all their crops; and sold them at a profit. To make it easier to move goods from one part of the country to another, Mehmet Ali conscripted peasants to build roads for carts and canals for barges. New irrigation works made it possible to raise three crops a year in fields that used to produce just one. Egypt became the first Middle Eastern country to make the transition from subsistence agriculture (in which peasants raised essentially the crops they consumed, plus what they had to pay in rent and taxes) to cash crop farming (in which peasants raised crops to sell on the market). Tobacco, sugar, indigo, and long-staple cotton became major Egyptian crops. Using the revenues they produced, Mehmet Ali paid for his ambitious schemes for industrial and military development.

Mehmet Ali was the first non-Western ruler to grasp the significance of the Industrial Revolution. He realized that a modernized army would need textile factories to make its tents and uniforms, food processing mills, and munitions plants. French advisers helped the Egyptian government build and equip them. Hundreds of Turkish- and Arabic-speaking Egyptians were sent to Europe for technical and military training. In addition, Western instructors were imported to establish schools in Egypt for medicine, engineering, and military training. A new Arabic printing press was set up as well to publish translated textbooks and an official government journal.

Mehmet Ali's Military Empire

Mehmet Ali was also the first ruler since the pharaohs to use Egyptian peasants as soldiers. The peasants hated it. They regarded military service as tantamount to death, for few of the conscripts ever saw their homes again. Despite their ingenious attempts at draft dodging, they got dragged into the army all the same. Turkish, Circassian, and European officers whipped this new Egyptian army into a potent fighting force. It served Mehmet Ali (at the request of the Ottoman sultan) against the Wahhabis who had taken over Mecca and Medina. He also put together an Egyptian navy, with which he helped the Ottomans against the Greeks, who were fighting for their independence. When the Great Powers stepped in to help the Greeks defeat the Turks, however, Mehmet Ali decided to turn against the sultan himself. He put his son, Ibrahim, in charge of a large expeditionary force that marched into Palestine and Syria. By the end of 1832 he held most of the Fertile Crescent and the Hijaz. Ibrahim proceeded to carry out this father's westernizing reforms in Syria, but the Syrians proved less docile than the Egyptians. Revolts broke out in the mountains, as peasants protested against agricultural controls and the confiscation of their weapons. In an attempt to exploit Ibrahim's troubles the Ottoman government took back some of his land. However, Mehmet Ali and Ibrahim struck back, moving deep into Anatolia. By 1839 it looked as if Cairo would take over the whole Ottoman Empire, as the imperial fleet deserted en masse to Alexandria and a sixteen-year-old was girded with the sword of Osman. Only the intervention of the Great Powers, mainly British, forced Mehmet Ali to pull his troops out of Syria and settle for autonomy within Egypt.

The stature of Mehmet Ali is somewhat diminished when we learn that he cared little for the Egyptian people; after his diplomatic defeat he lost interest in his economic and military reforms. Most of the schools and nearly all the state-run factories were closed. The state monopolies and other controls on agriculture lapsed. Most of the lands were parceled out to his friends and relatives. Nevertheless, upon his death Mehmet Ali could bequeath to his children and grandchildren a nearly independent Egypt with recent memories of military might. Also, his empire had been based on agricultural and industrial development, without any money owed to Western governments, banks, or investors. Few of his heirs ever matched this final boast.

WESTERNIZATION OF THE OTTOMAN EMPIRE

Less impressive results came from the efforts of Mehmet Ali's contemporaries to reform the Ottoman Empire. The first was Sultan Selim III (1789-1807), whom America's leading historian of Ottoman Turkey, Stanford Shaw, has shown to be a transitional figure among the westernizing reformers. Shaw divides the Ottoman government's attempt at internal reform into three phases. In the first, such reformers as the Koprulu vizirs of the late seventeenth century tried to restore the administrative and military system to what it had been when the empire was at its height in the sixteenth. When this failed, some of the eighteenth-century sultans and vizirs tried a selective westernizing policy, primarily in the army; but this second phase did not check Russia's advance into the Balkans or Napoleon's occupation of Egypt. In the third phase of Ottoman reform, mainly in the nineteenth century, the government tried to Westernize many parts of the empire, in an effort (only partly successful) to halt the secession or annexation of its territories.

The Nizam-i-Jedid

Selim III was acutely aware of the European designs on his country, as well as its internal problems, with some provinces in open revolt and a serious shortfall in tax revenues. He planned a full-scale housecleaning, a *nizam-i-jedid* ("new order") that would reform the whole Ottoman government. But with the military threat so imminent, Selim concentrated on creating the westernized elite army to which that name is usually applied. The training of the *nizam* soldiers (most of whom were recruited from Istanbul street gangs) had to be carried out secretly. Selim knew that the janissaries—and their friends—would react violently once they found out. He was right. The janissaries feared that an effective fighting force, trained by European instructors and using modern weapons, would show them up as useless parasites of the state. They also were not about to let their privileges be jeopardized by military reform, however necessary. As a result, they revolted, slaughtered the new troops, locked up Selim, and touched off a bloody civil war. The tragedy is that Selim could have built up his new army and stopped the Russians if he had put into effect the comprehensive reform scheme he had originally proposed. But it was too bold a plan. Selim therefore seemed to stand between the phase of selective westernization and the nineteenth-century effort to reshape the Ottoman

Empire along European lines.

Mahmud II

An ill-starred attempt by Selim's successor to revive the *nizam* sent the janissaries on such a rampage that they killed all the male members of the Ottoman dynasty but one, a cousin of Selim named Mahmud II (1808-1839). Understandably, Mahmud came to the throne in fear and trembling. Not only could the janissaries stir up the city mobs, trade guilds, and *madrasah* students to defend their privileges, but the whole empire was in trouble. Several of the Balkan provinces had become independent in all but name under local warlords. A nationalist uprising of the Serbs threatened to affect other subject peoples. Local landowners in parts of Anatolia were taking the government into their own hands, and the garrisons in such Arab cities as Aleppo and Mosul were held by dissident mamluk or janissary factions. Worse yet, Russia was at war with the empire and had invaded its Danubian principalities (what we now call Rumania), while Napoleon's forces were battling the British navy for mastery of the eastern Mediterranean. The future of the empire looked bleak, but Mahmud surprised everyone. Like his late cousin, he wanted to reform and strengthen the Ottoman state. However, as Shaw points out, Mahmud also realized that (1) westernizing reforms must include all aspects of Ottoman government and society, not just the military, (2) reformed institutions would work only if the ones they replaced were wiped out, and (3) any reform program must be preceded by careful planning and mobilization of support.

At first Mahmud kept a low profile, quietly cultivated groups that favored centralization of Ottoman power, and slowly built up a loyal and well-trained palace guard to be used against the janissaries and their supporters when it was strong enough. Only in 1826 did Mahmud feel he was ready to strike. In a move reminiscent of Mehmet Ali's treatment of the Mamluks fifteen years earlier, he ordered a general attack on the janissaries. This time the sultan had a strong army, the ulama, the students, and most of the people on his side. The janissaries were massacred, their supporting groups (including the Bektashi Sufi order) abolished, and their properties seized for redistribution among Mahmud's backers. So glad were the people to be rid of the janissaries that the massacre has come down in Turkish hisory as the "auspicious event." It cleared the way for a large-scale reform program that took up the last thirteen years of Mahmud's reign.

Predictably, highest priority went to developing a new military organization to replace the janissaries and other outmoded units, for the Greeks, backed by the Great Powers, were rebelling against Ottoman rule.

Mahmud gathered soldiers from all parts of the old military system into his new army, to be issued European uniforms and weapons and subjected to Western drillmasters and instructors. Ottoman youths had also to be trained in technical fields closely tied to the military. Existing schools of military and naval engineering were expanded, a new medical college was founded, and new institutions were later set up to teach marching music and military sciences. In addition, a system of secondary schools was started to help boys bridge the transition from the mosques that handled nearly all primary education to these new technical colleges and military academies.

It was hard to create schools in Istanbul based on French, German, or Italian models. The first teachers were all Europeans. So, too, were the books they assigned, which forced the boys to master French or German before they could study medicine, engineering, or science. Even now this is a problem in the Middle East, due to the rapid growth of human knowledge. University students in Turkey, Iran, Israel, and (though to a lesser extent) the Arab countries must still use American or European textbooks for specialized courses in engineering, business, social work, and even the humanities. But the problem was more acute 150 years ago in the Ottoman Empire. Printed books in any language were rare, and Turkish texts on the European sciences still had to be written. Some French and German textbooks got translated, but never enough. Special programs were set up to train Turkish Muslims to be translators and interpreters for the Ottoman government, replacing the Greeks who could no longer be trusted. Like Mehmet Ali, Mahmud set up a newspaper to print government announcements. He also sent some of his subjects to study in European universities, military academies, and technical institutes.

The general aim of the Ottoman reforms was to concentrate power in the hands of the sultan and his cabinet. The ministries of the government were organized more tightly to eliminate overlapping jurisdictions and superfluous posts. In addition, Mahmud abolished the system of military land grants (*timars*) that had sustained the *sipahis* since the beginning of the Ottoman Empire. He could not follow Mehmet Ali's example by putting all farmland under state control—the Ottoman Empire was larger and more diverse than Egypt—but he could at least tax the rural landlords. Improved roads furthered the centralization of power. Mahmud also had to overcome opposition from most local and provincial officials, the feudal *sipahis*, the traditional government scribes, and the ulama. Often he failed. There were too many members of the Ottoman ruling class who had a vested interest in the good old ways. There were too few who shared Mahmud's vision of an empire reformed and reinvigorated, comparable perhaps to Russia under Peter the Great.

Military Defeat and European Protection

Westernizing reform in the Ottoman Empire had another serious fault: it did not stop the army from losing wars. By 1829 the Greeks had won their independence, although their little kingdom in the Morea held only a minority of the Near East's Greek-speaking people. Their success was due mainly to intervention by Russia, which fought another war against Turkey between 1827 and 1829 and gained a lot of territory east of the Black Sea. Ibrahim's advances into Syria were another blow to the Ottoman Empire, especially when Mahmud's new army failed to dislodge them. Outside help would be needed if the empire was to survive. The first choice should have been France, but it was backing Mehmet Ali and Ibrahim, so Mahmud turned instead to his powerful northern neighbor. In a treaty bearing the euphonious (if forgettable) name of Hunkar-Iskelesi, Russia agreed in 1833 to defend the territorial integrity of the Ottoman Empire. In other words, the fox would guard the hen house!

This pact between two states that had fought four wars over a sixty-year span hit the West like a bombshell. Britain believed the Treaty of Hunkar-Iskelesi gave Russian warships the right to use the Straits, from which Western navies were excluded, and it campaigned vehemently against the threat of Russian domination in Istanbul. How could the British outbid the Russians? Luckily, the Ottomans wanted to expand their trade with Britain. In a commercial treaty signed in 1838, the Ottoman government increased Britain's capitulatory privileges and limited to 9 percent its import tariffs on British manufactures. This relatively low rate stimulated British exports to the empire, thus wiping out many Ottoman merchants and artisans who could not compete against the more mechanized factories of the West. One unexpected result of the 1838 treaty was to increase Britain's economic interest in the Ottoman Empire and hence its desire to keep it alive. This soon came in handy.

The Tanzimat Era

Mahmud II died while Mehmet Ali's army was invading Anatolia, whereupon the sultan's navy, laboriously rebuilt with British and American help after the Greek war for independence, defected to Alexandria. Mahmud's successor was his teenaged son, Abdulmejid (1839-1861). Seemingly ill-prepared to take on the duties of government, Abdulmejid actually reigned during the greatest period of Ottoman reform, the era of the Tanzimat ("reorganizations"). The guiding genius of the early Tanzimat was Mahmud's foreign minister, Mustafa Reshid, who happened to be in London seeking British aid against Mehmet Ali at the time Abdulmejid took over. On the advice of both the British and Reshid, the new sultan issued a proclamation called the Noble Rescript of the Rose Chamber (Hatt-i-Sherif of Gulhane), authorizing the creation of new institutions guaranteeing his subjects' fundamental rights, assessing and levying taxes fairly, and conscripting and training soldiers. No more tax farming, bribery, and unequal justice would take place. But how could these promises, revolutionary for the Ottoman Empire, be carried out? Luckily, Mustafa Reshid had an entourage of young and able officials who believed that liberal reforms would save the Ottoman Empire. Almost all aspects of Ottoman public life were restructured. This meant creating a system of state schools to produce government clerks; reorganizing the provinces so that each governor would have specified duties and an advisory council; extending the network of roads, canals, and now also rail lines; and developing a modern financial system with a central bank, treasury bonds, and a decimal currency.

The Tanzimat was not a total success. Many an Ottoman's ox was gored. The subject nationalities expected too much from the 1839 rescript and were disappointed by the actual reforms. Balkan Christians did not want centralization of power; they wanted autonomy. Some now sought independence. The Rumanians were among the many European peoples who rebelled in 1848; it took a Russian invasion to quell their revolt. Without firm British backing, the Ottoman reform movement would have collapsed. Unfortunately, Britain's insistence on upholding Ottoman territorial integrity was on a collision course with Russia's attempt to increase its influence in the Balkans. The crash was the Crimean War of 1853-1856. The Ottoman Empire, aided by British and French troops, defeated Russia and regained some territory.

But the price for Western support was a new official proclamation, Sultan Abdulmejid's Imperial Rescript (Hatt-i-Humayun) of 1856. Its gist was that all Ottoman subjects whether Muslim or not, were now to enjoy the same rights and status under the law. This was a revolutionary statement. Predictably, many Ottoman Muslims objected to giving Jews and Christians the same rights and status as themselves, an act contrary to the basic principles of the Shari'ah. Some of the *millet* leaders, used to being Uncle Toms, feared they would lose their communal autonomy. Rebellions of discontented Christian subjects continued, but now there were also uprisings of Muslim conservatives opposed to the Ottoman government's new policies. However, the Tanzimat reforms contined in such areas as land ownership, codification of the laws, and reorganization of the *millet*s (or at least those of the Armenians and the Jews, who did not yet seek separate states). After the Crimean War, the Ottoman Empire was admitted to full membership in the European Concert of Powers, and no one dared to speak of its collapse or partition. Not for a while anyway.

IRAN

Iran was the only Middle Eastern country outside the Arabian peninsula that was never fully absorbed by the Ottoman Empire. Even if the Safavid shahs had sometimes fallen back before the might of the janissaries in the sixteenth and seventeenth centuries, they had always retained control at home. After the Safavids' fall in the early eighteenth century, a succession of dynasties (most of them Turkish in race, but Persian in culture) ruled over that sprawling and heterogeneous country, either in uneasy alliance or in open contention with the nomadic tribes, rural landlords, urban merchants, and Shi'ite ulama. After the meteoric career of Nader Shah (d. 1747), the country went into a long decline. The Qajar dynasty (1794-1925) halfheartedly resisted dissolution from within and encroachments from without. Russia was pushing southward into the Caucasus region and into such central Asian lands as Transoxiana, Khwarizm, and Khurasan. The tsars' ultimate goal seems to have been the Persian Gulf. Britain, concerned with the defense of India, vacillated between a policy of supporting the Qajar government in Tehran and one of seizing parts of southern Iran. The Qajars rarely ruled the countryside, which was dominated by the rural landlords or the nomadic tribes. For the most part, the shahs seemed intent on enriching themselves and enlarging their families. My favorite example is Fath Ali Shah (1797-1834), who was survived by 158 wives, 57 sons, 46 daughters, and almost 600 grandchildren.

Iran had no Mehmet Ali, no Mahmud II, and precious little Tanzimat. We could make a grudging exception for Nasiruddin Shah (1848-1896), who opened his reign with a program of military, financial, and educational reforms. But the credit for them goes to his energetic prime minister, whom he suddenly executed in 1851. After that Iran became embroiled in war with Britain, accompanied by various tribal and religious uprisings. There was never enough money in the treasury to pay for the things Nasiruddin wanted to do, such as building palaces and traveling to Europe, so he began selling concessions to British and other European investors. He also hired Russian cossack officers to train his army. Instead of using reform to protect Iran from foreigners, the shah encouraged them to take control of his country.

SOME AFTERTHOUGHTS

Westernizing reforms seemed to be the obvious remedy to the problems of the nineteenth-century Middle East. Yet they rarely worked as well in practice as they had looked on paper. What went wrong? One problem was that the reforms were costly and had to be paid for. New armies and westernized bureaucracies could not subsist on the traditional Islamic taxes: the *kharaj* paid on land and other fixed property, the *jizyah* paid by Jewish and Christian subjects, and the canonical *zakat*. Each of the countries we have studied would in the years following stub its toes on finance, having run up a foreign debt so high (by nineteenth-century standards) that it had to accept European control over its governmental receipts and expenditures.

A related problem they shared was a shortage of trained personnel to run the westernized institutions they set up. True, Europeans were often around to do the work. Some were talented, dedicated to their jobs, and cooperative with native officials. Others were incompetents who could not have held a job back home, fugitives from an unhappy past, alcoholics, or snobs who hated the local leaders. Turks, Arabs, and Persians could also be trained to administer the reforms. If they were sent abroad for their training, though, they were apt to pick up some of the less desirable aspects of Western civilization. If they got their education at the newly founded local schools, remaining accessible to steadying influences from home and mosque, they could turn into half-baked Europeans unable to grasp either the values of the West or the real needs of their own societies. Such "Levantines" should have been a bridge between Europe and the Middle East. Most were not.

Results of the Westernizing Reforms

The best members of the generation that got its education from the reforms of Mehmet Ali, the Tanzimat, or Nasiruddin's vizir were apt to become imbued with ideas that were in one sense directly opposed to those of the early reformers themselves. Instead of hoping to centralize power in the hands of the ruler, they called for constitutions that would protect the rights of the individual against a strong government. Even some rulers encouraged these ideas. Mehmet Ali's grandson, Isma'il, ruling as khedive ("viceroy") of Egypt from 1863 to 1879, was almost as ambitious a reformer as his illustrious ancestor. During his reign, parts of Alexandria and Cairo were turned into copies of Paris; railroads crisscrossed the valley and delta of the Nile; and Egypt took on such attributes of modernity as schools, factories, law codes, and even an African empire. But Isma'il also set up a representative assembly and a newspaper press, both of which started out tame but later turned into noisy critics of his government. He may even have encouraged the rise of a nationalist party in the army, but let me save that story for the next chapter.

The Ottoman reaction to the reforms was more complex. Some officials and ulama reacted against them. They were encouraged in this by Sultan Abdulaziz (1861-1876), who patronized pan-Islam, an ideology that called on all Muslims, no matter where they lived, to unite behind the sultan's leadership and to uphold their traditional institutions and culture against Western influences. There were also bureaucrats, army officers, and intellectuals who reacted against the Tanzimat in the opposite direction, demanding more individual freedom, local autonomy, and decentralization of power. They called themselves New Ottomans (*yeni osmanlilar*), which we must be careful not to confuse with the nationalistic Young Turks of the next generation.

Great Power policies, which I started to discuss in the last chapter, often hindered reforms more than they helped. Britain and France stepped up their competition for control of Egypt when the new Suez Canal became a major waterway. After Khedive Isma'il ran up a debt of almost a hundred million pounds, Britain and France established a financial commission in 1876. In addition, they made him appoint foreigners to key posts in his cabinet, then ordered the sultan to depose him, and finally threatened to suppress the Egyptian nationalist movement, all in order to guard their financial interests. Russia's zeal for protecting Orthodox Christians, gaining control of the Straits, and promoting pan-Slavism led in 1875 to peasant revolts against Ottoman rule in several parts of the Balkans. In 1876 the New Ottomans seized control of the government, drew up a liberal constitution for the empire, and tried to persuade the powers to let them settle their internal affairs in peace. Some countries agreed, but Russia distrusted the Ottoman provinces, invaded the Balkans, and set off the Russo-Turkish War. Turkey's humiliating defeat put an end to the Tanzimat, the New Ottomans, and their constitution.

Iran also suffered from the effects of foreign imperialism. Its northern part, especially the key province of Azerbaijan, was under Russian military occupation much of the time. European businessmen (usually backed by their governments) went around obtaining concessions to operate Iran's mines, banks, railroads, and public utilities, for which they paid Nasiruddin Shah handsomely. The sale of Iran's assets reached the point where a concession to process and market all the tobacco in the country was sold to a British firm. This touched off a nationwide tobacco boycott in 1892. It worked so well that the shah himself could not smoke his water pipe in the palace! Its success was a warning to the West that Middle Easterners' patience had limits. Someday they would strike back. But this brings us to the rise of nationalism, a subject that deserves a chapter of its own.

12

The Rise of Nationalism

Of all the ideas that the Middle East has imported from the West, none has been more popular and durable than nationalism. Often called the religion of the modern world, this ideology or belief system is hard to pin down. Drawing on the Western historical experience, I define nationalism as the desire of a large group of people to create or to maintain a common statehood, to have their own rulers, laws, and other governmental institutions. This desired political community, or nation, is that object of that group's supreme loyalty. In the Middle East, shared characteristics among Egyptians and also among the peoples of Iran gave positive cause for the early growth of nationalism in both areas. Other nationalist movements have grown up around shared feelings of opposition to governments, institutions, and even individuals regarded as foreign.

Nationalism was itself foreign to the world of Islam. In traditional Islamic thought, the *ummah,* or "community of believers," was the sole object of political loyalty for Muslims. Loyalty meant defending the land of Islam against rulers or peoples of other faiths. All true Muslims were supposed to be brothers and sisters, regardless of race, language, or culture. Although there were differences between Arabs and Persians, or between them and the Turks, common adherence to Islam was supposed to transcend these divergences. Nationalism was not meant to exist in Islam.

Yet it does, and it is interesting to note how religion has influenced nationalism in the Middle East. Arab nationalism has indeed included Christians and even Jews, and yet its most conspicuous manifestations lately have been resistance to Christian domination in Lebanon and to Jewish colonization in Palestine (Israel since 1948). The rhetoric of nationalism often confuses the Arab nation with the Islamic *ummah,* as when an Arab nationalist cause is called a jihad. Other Middle Eastern nationalist movements have been based even more strongly on religion and have called on their people to resist oppression by others having a different faith. These include Greeks and Armenians among the Christians of the

Middle East, as well as Turks and Persians among the Muslims. Political Zionism, which worked for Israel's creation as the Jewish state, drew its inspiration from Judaism, even if many of its advocates were not very religious themselves. In all three monotheistic faiths, the rise of nationalism has meant the substitution of collective self-love for the love of God, enhancing life on this earth rather than preparing for what is to come after death, and promoting the community's welfare instead of obeying God's revealed laws.

During roughly the last forty years before World War I, the peoples of the Arab world, Turkey, and Iran began to develop feelings of nationalism. Since this era was also the heyday of European imperialism, it is natural to see rising nationalism as a reaction against the West. But it was also the end result of a century of westernizing reform, with its enlarged armies and bureaucracies, new schools, printing presses, roads and rail lines, and centralized government power. The techniques of Europe, usually taught in French, could not be learned without absorbing some of the ideas of Europe. A Middle Eastern student at a French or German university had plenty of chances to get exposed to Western ideas, even if he never attended lectures in political theory. There were newspapers and magazines being hawked in the streets, lively student discussions in cafes, demonstrations (or riots), and occasional encounters with Western orientalists (the nineteenth-century equivalent of our Middle East historians and linguists), who could explain what was happening in Europe to a Turkish, Egyptian, or Iranian newcomer. Even the students who acquired all their technical skills in Istanbul, Cairo, or Tehran were apt to be exposed to Western ideas through some of their European instructors. Besides, their schools usually had reading rooms. A Middle Easterner studying engineering from French textbooks could also read works by Rousseau or other Western writers.

In short, as Middle Easterners learned how to work like Europeans, they also learned how to think like them. They learned that bad governments did not have to be endured, that individuals had rights and freedoms that should be protected against arbitrary official coercion, and that people could belong to political communities based on race, language, culture, and shared historical experience—in short, to nations. During the 1870s these liberal and nationalist ideas became current among many of the educated young Muslims of the Middle East, especially in the capital cities. As they faced the frustrations of these years and the ones that followed, their ideas crystallized into nationalist movements.

I started to mention some of the religious and ethnic groups that formed nationalist movements in the Middle East before World War I. All are worth studying, but I will limit this chapter to three that grew up within existing states that had governments with at least some experience with westernizing reform. I plan to cover those of the Egyptians, the Turks in the Ottoman Empire, and the Persians within Qajar Iran. Arab nationalism and Zionism will be covered later. Nationalism among such Christian peoples of the Ottoman Empire as the Greeks and the Armenians will be discussed only when they affected the rise of Turkish nationalism.

EGYPTIAN NATIONALISM

Egypt used to be described by Western writers as the "land of paradox." Almost all its inhabitants were crowded into the valley and delta of the great River Nile, without which Egypt would have been only a desert supporting a few bedouin nomads. To European visitors of a century ago, Egypt was filled with relics of antiquity—temples, obelisks, pyramids, sphinxes, and buried treasures—and haunted by pharaohs whose tombs had been violated by bedouin robbers or Western archeologists. To most Muslims, however, Egypt was the very heart and soul of Islam, with its great mosque-university of al-Azhar, its festive observance of Muslim holy days and saints' birthdays, and its annual procession bearing a new cloth that would be sent to cover the Ka'bah in Mecca. Egypt meant Cairo, with its hundreds of mosques and *madrasahs*, ornate houses and bazaars, survivals of a time when the Mamluks really ruled and the city was unsurpassed as an economic and intellectual center. To a student who has just been exposed to Mehmet Ali's reforms and to the building of the Suez Canal, Egypt was the most westernized country in the nineteenth-century Middle East.

Picture then, if you will, one of the newer sections of Alexandria or Cairo in 1875, or the all-new cities of Port Said and Ismailia, their wide straight avenues lined with European-style houses, hotels, banks, shops, schools, and churches. Horse-drawn carriages whiz past the donkeys and camels of a more leisurely age. Restaurants serve *coq au vin* or veal scallopini instead of *kuftah* (ground meat) or kebab, and their customers smoke cigars in place of water pipes. The signs are in French, not Arabic. The passersby converse in Italian, Greek, Armenian, Turkish, Yiddish, Ladino (a language derived from Spanish and spoken by Sephardic Jews), or several dialects of Arabic. Top hats have replaced turbans and frock coats the caftans of yore. Each of these images fits a part of Egypt a century ago—but not all of it.

Khedive Isma'il

The man who ruled over this land of paradox was Mehmet Ali's grandson, Isma'il (1863-1879), a complex and controversial figure. Was he a man of vision, as his admirers claimed, or a spendthrift who brought Egypt into British bondage? His admirers could tick off the railroads, bridges, docks, canals, and sugar refineries built during his reign. It was also the period when the Egyptian government paid explorers and military expeditions to penetrate the Sudan and East Africa and worked to abolish slavery and slave trading within its empire. The Egyptian mixed courts were established to hear civil cases involving Europeans protected by the capitulations. Public and missionary schools—for girls as well as boys— proliferated in the cities. The Egyptian museum, national library, observatory, geographical society, and many of the professional schools first saw life under Isma'il.

But Isma'il's detractors point out that he spent money wildly in an effort to impress Europe with his munificence and power. Building the Suez Canal had been costly to the Egyptian government, for it had to reimburse the Suez Canal Company when the latter was forced to pay wages to the peasant construction workers (the company had planned on paying them nothing). This was really the fault of Isma'il's predecessor, Sa'id. But it was Isma'il who turned the canal's inauguration into an extravaganza, inviting the crowned heads and leaders of Europe to come—at Egypt's expense. Costing at least £2 million (worth $100 million in today's prices), it must have been the bash of the century, with enormous receptions, evening parties, balls, parades, fireworks displays, horse races, excursions to the ancient monuments, and cities festooned with flags and decorated with lanterns. Villas and palaces sprouted up, streets were widened and straightened, old neighborhoods were demolished, and even an opera house was erected in Cairo. Giuseppe Verdi, the Italian composer, was commissioned to write *Aida* for the occasion (as often happens, he turned it in two years late). Isma'il also spent huge sums in Istanbul to increase his independence from the Ottoman government, changing his title from pasha ("governor") to khedive ("viceroy") of Egypt and obtaining the right to pass down his position to his sons in Cairo rather than to brothers living in Istanbul. He also won a fateful privilege: contracting foreign debts without Ottoman permission.

Financial Problems

But where could the money come from? The Egyptian taxpayer could hardly cover Isma'il's extravagance. The start of his reign had coincided with the American Civil War, which caused a cotton boom in Egypt. The British, cut off by the northern blockade from their usual cotton supply, were willing to pay any price for other countries' crops in order to feed the textile mills of Lancashire. The high demand for Egypt's cotton stimulated output and greatly increased the revenues to both the Egyptian growers and their government. During this cotton boom, European investment bankers offered Isma'il loans on very attractive terms. When the boom ended after the Civil War, Egypt's need for money was greater than ever, but now credit could be had only at high interest rates. In 1866 Isma'il convoked a representative assembly of landowners, seeking their consent to raise taxes. Soon there were taxes on date palms, flour mills, oil presses, boats, shops, houses, and even burials.

Still other stratagems were needed to put off the day of reckoning. Isma'il promised substantial tax abatements to landowners who could pay three years' taxes in advance. He sold Egypt's shares in the Suez Canal Company—15 percent of the stock—to the British government in 1875. When a British commission came to check into rumors of Egypt's impending bankruptcy, the khedive agreed to appoint a European commission to manage the public debt. But a low Nile in 1877, high military expenses incurred in the Russo-Turkish War, and an invasion of Ethiopia put the Egyptian government into worse trouble. In August 1878, pressed by European creditors, Isma'il agreed to put an Englishman and a Frenchman into his cabinet, inaugurating what is called the Dual Control, and agreed to leave the government of Egypt to his ministers. Meanwhile, he secretly stirred up antiforeign elements in his army. This was easy, for the Dual Control had put the Egyptian officers on half-pay. A military riot in February 1879 enabled Isma'il to dismiss the foreign ministers and later to appoint a cabinet of liberals, who started to draw up an Egyptian constitution, much as the Ottoman Empire had done in 1876. Britain and France, guarding their investors' interests, called on the Ottoman sultan to dismiss Isma'il. He did. When Isma'il turned the khedivate over to his son, Tawfiq, and left Egypt in July 1879, the state debt stood at £93 million. It had been £3 million when he came to power in 1863.

Beginnings of Egyptian Nationalism

Isma'il's successes and failures made him the father of Egypt's first nationalist movement. His new schools, law courts, railroads, and telegraph lines drew Egyptians closer together and helped to foster nationalist feeling. So did the newspapers he patronized in the hope of building up favorable public opinion. The Suez Canal and related projects drew thousands of Europeans into Egypt; they became models for modernization and at the same time objects of native resentment.

Muslim feeling, always strong but usually quiescent, was aroused at this time under the influence of a fiery agitator, Jamal al-Din "al-Afghani" (I use quotation marks because his claim to be an Afghan was false; he was really from Iran), who came from Istanbul to teach at al-Azhar. He soon clashed with the conservative ulama and was out running a sort of "free university" that attracted many Egyptians who would later become political leaders or Islamic reformers. Two of them were Muhammad Abduh

(d. 1905), the greatest Muslim thinker modern Egypt has produced, and Sa'd Zaghlul (d. 1927), leader of Egypt's struggle for independence after World War I. Afghani, like Isma'il, encouraged journalists, but bolder ones, often Jews or Christians who readily espoused secular nationalism.

Isma'il's financial troubles, which tied Egypt to Western creditors and to their governments, shamed Egyptians, especially his representative assembly. Once a subservient assemblage of frightened rural landlords, it now turned into a vociferous body of government critics. But the key institution for the development of nationalism was the army. Sa'id had started admitting Egyptian peasants' sons into the officer corps and had promoted some of them rapidly; however, Isma'il held back their promotions and pay raises in favor of the traditional elite, the Turkish and Circassian officers. Frustrated, the Egyptian officers formed a secret society to plot against their oppressors. It later became the nucleus of the first National party.

During Isma'il's last months in power, the Egyptian army officers joined forces with government workers, assembly representatives, journalists, and ulama to back the drafters of a constitution that would give to Egyptians some of the rights and freedoms enjoyed by Europeans in their own countries. However, the khedive's deposition set back the progress of this alliance. Tawfiq, his successor, thought it safer to side with the European creditors than with the Egyptian nationalists. He dismissed the liberal cabinet, restored the Dual Control, suppressed some of the newspapers, and exiled Afghani and other agitators.

Ahmad Urabi

Thus, under Tawfiq nationalism seemed to go into eclipse, but Sa'd Zaghlul and Muhammad Abduh could still express constitutionalist views in the official newspaper that they edited. Disgruntled, the Egyptian officers still remained together also. In February 1881 these officers, led by a Colonel Ahmad Urabi, mutinied and forced Tawfiq to replace his Circassian war minister with a nationalist, Mahmud Sami al-Barudi. In September of that year, 2500 Egyptian officers and soldiers surrounded the khedive's palace in Cairo and made him appoint a more liberal cabinet. They also demanded a constitution, parliamentary government, and an enlarged army. All these demands were also sought by the civilian nationalists and detested by the European creditors, who wondered how Tawfiq or Urabi would ever find money to pay for these reforms.

During the following year, Egypt came as close as it ever would to either democratic government (if you take the Egyptian nationalist view of history) or political chaos (if you buy the European—especially British—interpretation of what happened). A liberal cabinet drew up a constitution and held parliamentary elections as Egypt's finances got worse. Britain and France sent a joint note in January 1882, threatening to intervene in support of Khedive Tawfiq (meaning, in effect, to restore the Dual Control). The nationalists called their bluff, declaring that Egypt's Parliament, not the British and French debt commissioners, would control the government budget. Mahmud Sami al-Barudi took over the premiership and Urabi became war minister—bad news for Turkish and Circassian officers in the Egyptian army. The nationalists even toyed with the idea of ousting Tawfiq and declaring Egypt a republic. More likely, though, they would have replaced him with one of his relatives.

Since nationalism was fairly new in Egypt, we may ask who was behind these moves. A few English liberals helped Urabi, and the French consul in Cairo may have given encouragement; however, the chief supporters seem to have been the Ottoman sultan and a dispossessed uncle of Tawfiq living in Istanbul. This may make the movement seem less than wholly nationalist. A recent book by a German scholar has shown that what we usually call the National party was really a constellation of several groups with various political, economic, or religious interests. All the same, the movement was very popular in Egypt by June 1882. But its downfall was Britain's determination to move in, by force if need be, to protect the investments and lives of Europeans in Egypt and (perhaps secondarily) to safeguard the Suez Canal, which had become so important to British shipping.

Riots in Alexandria caused a general exodus of Europeans, and both British and French gunboats dropped anchor just outside the harbor. Then the British fired on Alexandria's fortifications, somehow much of the city caught on fire, and British marines landed to restore order (as the French ships sailed away). When Urabi declared war on Britain, Khedive Tawfiq declared him a traitor and threw in his lot with the British in Alexandria. Other British imperial troops occupied the canal and landed at Ismailia. Defeating Urabi's army was short work, and the British occupied Cairo in September 1882. The Barudi cabinet was dismissed, the nationalists were locked up and tried for rebellion, Urabi was sent into exile, the constitution was suspended, the nationalist newspapers were banned, and even the army was dissolved by Tawfiq. The early nationalists had proved a weak force. Their party was divided among Egyptian officers resenting Turkish and Circassian privileges, civilians who wanted parliamentary government, and Islamic reformers like Jamal al-Din al-Afghani and Muhammad Abduh.

Lord Cromer and the British Occupation

The British government that sent troops into Egypt in 1882 expected the military occupation to be brief. As soon as order was restored, Britain's troops would pull out, and Egypt would go back to being an autonomous Ottoman province. But the longer the British stayed in Egypt, the more disorder they found to set straight, and the less they wanted to get out. In particular, the financial situation required major economic and administrative reforms. The British agent and consul general in Cairo from 1883 to 1907, Lord Cromer, was a brilliant financial administrator. With a small (but growing) staff of British advisers to the various Egyptian government ministries, Cromer managed to expand the Nile irrigation system to raise agricultural output, raise government revenues, lower taxes, and reduce the burden of the public debt. The Englishmen around him were generally competent, dedicated to the Egyptians' welfare, and scrupulously honest. When (much later) Cromer died and was buried in Westminster Abbey, his epitaph called him the "regenerator of modern Egypt."

Maybe so, but Cromer is not well remembered in Egypt today. Many Egyptians living under Cromer felt that their own advancement in government posts or the professions was blocked by the numerous foreigners holding high positions in Cairo. In addition, they objected to Cromer's policy of limiting the growth of public education. Some resented the fact that the Egyptian army, despite its British imperial officers, lost the Sudan in 1885 in a rebellion led by the self-styled Mahdi ("rightly guided one"). After the British and Egyptian armies won back the Sudan in 1898, it was put under a condominium, with Britain effectively in control. Opposition to the continuing British occupation of Egypt came from a few British antiimperialists, the French, who (despite their greater economic interest in Egypt) had failed to intervene in 1882, and the Ottoman Turks, who resented losing another province of their empire. As long as there was no internal opposition, though, these groups could do little against the British presence.

The Revival of Egyptian Nationalism

Major opposition began when Abbas, Khedive Tawfiq's seventeen-year-old son, succeeded him in 1892. High-spirited, jealously guarding what he felt were his khedivial prerogatives, Abbas fought with Cromer over the right to appoint and dismiss his ministers and over control of the Egyptian army. Although the British proconsul won the battles by bullying the ministers and having his government send more troops to Egypt, he lost the friendship of the young khedive. Seeking to undermine Cromer, Abbas built up an entourage of European and native supporters. Among the latter was an articulate law student named Mustafa Kamil, who emerged in 1895 as an effective palace propagandist in both Europe and Egypt. In the ensuing years, he gradually turned what had been a secret society headed by Abbas into a large-scale popular movement, the (revived) National party. He founded a boys' school and a daily newspaper, the better to spread the idea of Egyptian nationalism. As his popularity grew, Mustafa Kamil became more interested in obtaining a democratic constitution and less concerned about the khedive's prerogatives. Of course, he and his followers always viewed the evacuation of British troops as their main goal.

In 1906 an incident occurred that helped to spread his fame. A group of British officers went to shoot pigeons in a village called Dinshaway. Owing to some misunderstandings between the villagers and the officers, a fracas started. A gun went off, accidentally setting fire to a barn. Another wounded a peasant woman. The peasants began beating the officers with heavy sticks. One of the latter got away, but collapsed after running several miles and died of sunstroke. The British authorities, suspecting a premeditated assault, tried the villagers before a special military court. Many peasants were found guilty of murder. Four were hanged and several others flogged in the presence of their families as an object lesson to the Dinshaway villagers. These barbarous sentences shocked Mustafa Kamil, most Egyptians, and even many Europeans. Then people were shocked by atrocities that now, after Hitler and Stalin, seem tame. Mustafa capitalized on these sentiments to increase his following and to hasten Cromer's retirement, but he died less than two years later before his thirty-fourth birthday.

Mustafa Kamil's successors became divided over their tactics and aims. Was the National party for Muslims against Christian rulers or for all Egyptians against the British occupation? If the latter, could Egypt still expect support from the Ottoman Empire? Should the party seek independence by peaceful or revolutionary means? If the latter, would it oppose Khedive Abbas and other large landowners? Should it seek general economic and social reforms, or should it concentrate on getting the British out of Egypt? How could a party consisting mainly of lawyers and students, with little or no support in the Egyptian army, persuade Britain to leave? New and more moderate Egyptian leaders, like Ahmad Lutfi al-Sayyid, argued that constitutional government and education should come before independence. In addition, the British consul who replaced Cromer in 1907 proved adept at neutralizing the Nationalist threat by wooing Khedive Abbas and the more conservative landowners to Britain's side. By 1914 the Nationalist leaders were in exile. Only after World War I would the Egyptians build up enough resentment against British rule to form a truly national and revolutionary movement.

OTTOMANISM, PAN-ISLAM, AND TURKISM

The rise of Turkish nationalism was somewhat complicated by the fact that, up to the twentieth century, no educated Ottoman cared to be called a Turk, even if Turkish was his native language. The Ottoman Empire, though Europeans called it Turkey, was definitely not a Turkish nation-state. It contained many ethnic and linguistic groups: Turks, Arabs, Greeks, Armenians, Serbs, Croats, Bulgarians, Syrians, Albanians, and Kurds, just to name a few. Its rulers were Sunni Muslims, but it contained Greek Orthodox, Armenian, and Jewish subjects organized into *millets* (which functioned almost like nations within the state) and many smaller religious groups. Traditionally, its inhabitants were either *osmanlilar* ("members of the ruling class") or *re'aya* ("members of the subject class"), with nothing in between.

Early Nationalism in the Ottoman Empire

Nationalism in the modern sense first appeared among such Christian subjects as the Greeks and the Serbs, who were closer to Western or Russian influences. As nationalist movements proliferated in the Balkans, the Ottoman rulers grew ever more worried over how to hold the empire together. Westernizing reforms were their first answer, but these raised more hopes than they could meet and did not create a new basis of loyalty. The reformers began pushing the idea of Ottomanism (loyalty to the Ottoman state) as a framework within which racial, linguistic, and religious groups could develop autonomously but harmoniously. To this the New Ottomans of the 1870s had added the idea of an Ottoman constitution that would set up an assembly representing all peoples of the empire. The constitution was drawn up in 1876—the worst possible time, with several nationalist rebellions going on in the Balkans, war raging with Serbia and Montenegro (two Balkan states that had already won their independence), Russia threatening to send in troops, and Britain preparing to fight against the Turks to protect the Balkan Christians and against the Russians to defend the Ottoman Empire (a policy as weird to people then as it sounds now). Besides, the New Ottomans had seized power in a coup, put on the throne a sultan who turned out to be crazy, and had to replace him with his brother, Abdulhamid II (1876-1909), whose promises to uphold the new constitution were suspect.

Well, they should have been. The ensuing Russo-Turkish War put the empire in such peril that almost no one could have governed under the Ottoman constitution. Sultan Abdulhamid soon suspended it and dissolved Parliament. For thirty years he ruled as a dictator, appointing and dismissing his own ministers, holding his creditors at bay, keeping the Great Powers sufficiently at odds with one another so that they would not carve up the Ottoman Empire, and suppressing all dissident movements within his realm. People now look back on him as a cruel sultan, reactionary in his attitudes toward westernizing reforms, and devoted to the doctrine of pan-Islam. This gave much trouble to Russia, Britain, and France with their millions of Muslim subjects in Asia and Africa. (It is interesting to note that Istanbul, seat of the sultan-caliph, became the final home of that wandering pan-Islamic agitator, Jamal al-Din al-Afghani.)

Abdulhamid is remembered for his censors and spies, his morbid fear of assassination, and his massacres of Armenians (though it is only fair to point out that some of them plotted against his regime). Even though scholars trying to rehabilitate him have shown how he continued the centralizing tendencies of the earlier Tanzimat reformers, even though the Ottoman Empire lost no European lands between 1878 and 1908, and Muslims at home and abroad hailed him as their caliph, still I must say that he was incompetent, paranoid, and cruel. The finances of the empire were controlled by a European debt commission, freedom of speech and assembly vanished, the army was standing still, and the navy was deteriorating. The ablest reformers went into exile. Midhat, leader of the New Ottomans, was lured back with false promises, tried for attempted murder, imprisoned in the Arabian town of Taif, and secretly strangled. It is said that Midhat's head was shipped back to Istanbul in a box marked "Japanese ivories, to be opened only by the sultan."

Many Ottomans, especially if they had been educated in Western schools, thought that the only way to save the Ottoman Empire was to restore the 1876 constitution, even if it meant overthrowing Abdulhamid. Many opposition groups were formed. All of them tend to get lumped together as the "Young Turks," a term borrowed from Mazzini's "Young Italy," or perhaps from the "New Ottomans." Many were not Turks, and some not even young, but the term has stuck. The key society was a secret one started at the military medical college in 1889 by four cadets—all Muslims but of several nationalities. It came to be known as the Committee of Union and Progress (or CUP). Its history was long and tortuous, with moments of hope interspersed with years of gloom and despair, centering at times on exiled Turkish writers living in Paris or Geneva, at others on cells of Ottoman army officers in Salonika or Damascus. Gradually the ideas of the CUP spread to many groups within Ottoman society: the empire must be strengthened militarily and morally, all religious and ethnic groups must be put on an equal footing, the constitution must be restored, and Sultan Abdulhamid must be shorn of power. Unless these things happened, Russia would move in and take what was left of the empire in Europe, including Istanbul and the Straits. Then the other Western powers would carve up the empire in Asia, just as they had partitioned Africa and divided China into spheres of influence.

The Young Turks in Power

The CUP was Ottomanist, not Turkish nationalist, as long as it was out of power. In July 1908 it inspired a military coup that forced Abdulhamid to restore the Ottoman constitution. Every religious and national group in the empire rejoiced; the committee, even if most of its leaders were Turks, had the support of many loyal Arabs, Armenians, Balkan Christians, and Jews. Most wanted to go on being Ottoman citizens under the 1876 constitution. Many Western well-wishers thought that Turkey was about to revive. Elections were held for a new parliament, the tide of democracy seemed to be sweeping into Istanbul, and the CUP started so many changes that even now we call vigorous reformers "Young Turks." Indeed, their coming to power was a harbinger of the many revolutions that have changed the face of Middle Eastern politics since 1908.

However, if we look at what really happened to the Ottoman Empire under the Young Turks, we must give them lower marks for their achievements than for their stated intentions. They did not ward off disintegration, as Austria annexed Bosnia, Bulgaria declared its independence, and Crete rebelled, all in late 1908. Their hopes for rapid economic development were dashed when a French loan deal fell through in 1910. The next year Italy attacked the Ottoman Empire in an attempt to seize Libya. Its success was assured when Bulgaria and Serbia joined forces in 1912 (with Russia's blessing) and attacked the empire in the Balkans. In a few months the Turks lost almost all their European lands. Even Albania, a mainly Muslim part of the Balkans, rebelled in 1910 and later won Great Power recognition as an independent state. The Arabs, as you will see in chapter 13, were getting restless.

How could Istanbul's democratic government, as set up under the restored 1876 constitution, weather all these problems? Soon after the CUP won the 1912 election through massive use of bribery and intimidation, the army forced its ministers to resign in favor of a rival bloc called the Liberal Entente. It took another military coup and a timely assassination in 1913 to bring the CUP back into power. By the outbreak of World War I, the government of the Ottoman Empire was in the hands of a triumvirate: Enver as war minister, Talat as minister of the interior, and Jemal in charge of the navy. Democracy was a dead letter in the Ottoman Empire.

Turkish Nationalism

Amid these crises, the Young Turks became more and more Turkish in their political orientation. Their initial hopes that the Great Powers and the minority groups within the empire would support their attempts at Ottomanism had been dashed. The powers grabbed territory and withheld aid. The minorities revolted, plotted, or grumbled. What could the Young Turks do? Some stuck to their Ottomanist guns. Others argued for pan-Islam, which would have held the loyalty of most Arabs and also gained needed support from Egypt, India, and possibly other parts of the Muslim world. But the new wave was pan-Turanism. This was the attempt to bring together all speakers of Turkic languages under Ottoman leadership, just as pan-Slavism meant uniting all speakers of Slavic languages under Russia. Indeed, since most speakers of Turkic languages were then living under tsarist rule or military occupation, pan-Turanism seemed a good way to pay back the Russians for all the grief they had given the Ottoman Empire. Several of the leading spokesmen for pan-Turanism were refugees from Russian Turkistan or Azerbaijan, but it was hard for Ottoman Turks to renounce their traditional sentiments toward Islam and the Ottoman Empire. Few believed that there really was a distinct Turanian culture. The CUP efforts to impose Turkish in the schools and offices of their Arabic-speaking provinces helped give rise to Arab nationalism. The committee's influence on central Asian Turks was almost nil. The Turks' ethnic and linguistic nationalism raised more problems for them than it solved, until they learned to limit their national idea to fellow Turks within the Ottoman Empire. The idea was not unknown. A sociologist named Ziya Gokalp was writing newspaper articles in support of what he called Turkism, but this idea would only become popular after World War I. By then it was too late to save the Ottoman Empire.

NATIONALISM IN IRAN

Iran, as you know, lagged far behind Egypt and the Ottoman Empire in its westernizing reforms. However, it had a compensating advantage when it came to the development of Persian or Iranian nationalism. Consider what historians and political scientists usually cite as components of nationalism: (1) a previously existing state, (2) religion, (3) language, (4) race, and (5) life-style, (6) shared economic interests, (7) common enemies, and (8) shared historical consciousness. If you test Egyptian and Turkish nationalism against these criteria, you will find them falling short on several counts. Not so Persian nationalism. The Qajar dynasty may have been a weak government, but it was heir to a Persian political tradition traceable to the ancient Achaemenids, with slight interruptions due to Greek, Arab, Turkish, and Mongol invasions. Iran was predominantly Muslim; but its uniqueness was assured by its general adherence to Twelve-Imam Shi'ism, while its Muslim neighbors were mainly Sunni. Its chief written and spoken language, Persian or Farsi, was widely associated with Iran, even though many of the country's inhabitants spoke Turkish and there were numerous Muslims in India and the Ottoman Empire who could read and write Persian well. "Race" is a tricky term to use in an area so often invaded and settled by outsiders, but certainly the Persians considered their physical appearance to be distinctive. Their life-style or culture had stood the tests of time, invasion, and political change. Both visitors and natives hailed the Persian way of life: its cuisine, architecture, costumes, social relationships, poetry, and even its jokes. The economic interests of nineteenth-century Iran seem to have been, if not homogeneous, at least complementary among city dwellers, peasants, and nomads. Russia was clearly Iran's "common enemy number one," with Britain a close second. No other Middle Eastern people could match the Persians' strong historical consciousness, which found expression in their monumental architecture, painting, epic poetry, written history, and music, glorifying twenty-five centuries of distinction.

Early Resistance to Foreign Power

Therefore, it should not surprise you to learn that a Persian nationalist movement arose during the period between 1870 and 1914. Fundamentally, it was a reaction against the threat of a Russian military takeover, against the growing subservience to the West, and against the divisive effects of tribalism in the rural areas. It was facilitated by the spread of roads, rail lines, telegraphs, and both public and mission schools. Nasiruddin Shah's policy of selling concessions to foreign investors particularly antagonized the people. In 1872 he sold a concession to one Baron de Reuter, a naturalized British subject, to set up a monopoly that would build railways, operate mines, and form a national bank within Iran. Russian objections and domestic opposition forced the shah to cancel the concession, though the baron was later authorized to found the Imperial Bank of Persia. In 1890 Nasiruddin sold a concession to an English company to control the production, sale, and export of all tobacco in Iran. A nationwide tobacco boycott, inspired by Jamal al-Din al-Afghani, forced the cancellation of this concession. This successful action gave both westernized Iranians and Shi'ite ulama enough confidence in their political power to spur the growth of a constitutionalist movement in the ensuing years. Many people looked at the mounting problems of the Qajar shahs, their economic concessions to foreigners, the widening disparities between rich landowners and poor peasants, and Iran's growing dependence on Russian military advisers, and wondered how soon it would be before Russia occupied Iran. Iranians also noted the British occupation of Egypt, the weakness of Abdulhamid's regime, the foreign penetration of China, and questioned how long their country could remain free of Western rule. The shah, surrounded by fawning and corrupt courtiers, had sold most of his inherited treasures and was spending the proceeds of his foreign loans on trips to Europe and gifts to his family and friends.

The Constitutionalist Movement

Patriotic Iranians felt the remedy for all this was a constitution that would limit the arbitrary acts of their rulers. The idea spread among merchants, landlords, ulama, army officers, and even some government officials and tribal leaders. Secret societies sprang up in various cities, notably Tabriz (the main city in Azerbaijan) and Tehran (the capital of the country. The spark that set off the revolution was an arbitrary act by the shah's prime minister, Ayn ud-Dowleh, who ordered some merchants flogged for allegedly plotting to drive up the price of sugar in the Tehran bazaar. The merchants took refuge in the royal mosque (which, by a time-honored Persian custom called *bast* gave them sanctuary from arrest), but Ayn ud-Dowleh had them expelled. This angered the Shi'i ulama of Tehran and swelled the number of protestors, who moved on to another mosque. Desiring peace, the shah offered to dismiss his minister and to convene a "house of justice" to redress their grievances. But he failed to act on his promises. While the shah was incapacitated by a stroke, Ayn ud-Dowleh moved against the protestors, who then staged a larger *bast* in Tehran. Meanwhile, the *mujtahids*, the leading Shi'i legal officials, sought *bast* in nearby Qum and threatened to leave Iran in a body (which would have paralyzed the administration of the country) unless their demands were met. Shops throughout Tehran closed. When Ayn ud-Dowleh tried to force them to open, 15,000 Persians sought refuge in the British Legation, camping on its lawn for several weeks during July 1906. Finally the shah bowed to popular pressure. He dismissed Ayn ud-Dowleh and accepted a Western-style constitution in which the government would be controlled by a representative assembly. So great was his aversion to the Iranian nationalists, though, that only pressure from Britain and Russia (plus his failing health) kept him from blocking the constitution before it could take effect. He died soon afterwards.

The Iranian nationalists achieved too much too soon. In 1907 Britain and Russia reached an agreement recognizing each other's spheres of influence in Iran. Britain was to have primary influence over the southeast, the part of the country closest to its Indian empire. Russia got the right to send troops and advisers to the heavily populated north, including the key provinces of Azerbaijan and Khurasan, plus Tehran itself. Russia then gave enough support to the new shah to enable him to close the new representative assembly, or Majlis, in June 1908. Even though an alliance between one of the larger tribes and the constitutionalists managed to regain military control of Tehran and to reopen the Majlis in 1909, the Iranian nationalist movement could no longer summon the fervent support it had enjoyed from the people three years earlier.

Oil Discoveries

Meanwhile, a more hopeful trend was taking place in the province of Khuzistan, located in the Zagros Mountains of southwestern Iran, where a

British company had begun exploring for oil in 1901. In 1908 it made its
first strike, and by 1914 thousands of barrels were being piped to a refinery
on the Persian Gulf island port of Abadan. When the British navy switched
from coal to petroleum just before World War I, the future of Iranian oil
looked even brighter. But this was cold comfort to nationalists or
constitutionalists. It was taking place far from Tehran, in lands
traditionally controlled by tribal shaykhs. The revenues were going mainly
to British stockholders, not to the Iranian government, let alone its
impoverished subjects. In the last years before World War I, Iran as a
whole seemed to be drifting toward becoming a Russian protectorate.

CONCLUSION

Speaking in general terms, nationalist movements in the Middle East
fared badly in those times. They surely did not increase the power, the
lands, or the freedom of the Muslim states in which they arose. Except
during a few moments of success, which now seem like lightning flashes
within a general gloom, these movements did not win any wide popular
support. There is no nationalism in Islam, said the critics, so these
movements could only appeal to young men who had lost their religion
because of Western education. Even when they reached a wider public,
their success was due to popular misunderstandings. Simple folk often
mistook the nationalist triumphs for Muslim victories. And these were few
indeed. "Roll up the map of Islam," wrote a leading British sympathizer in
his diary in 1911. Soon the European Christians would divide up what little
was left of the independent Muslim world. Perhaps, the writer mused, only
in Arabia, its birthplace, would Islam survive as an independent political
force.

You may wonder why I have spent so much time telling you about these
unsuccessful nationalist movements. Why learn about them? History is not
just the story of winners; sometimes we study losers whose grandchildren
could be winners. History is more than just facts, names, and dates; we also
look at the ways in which the peoples we care about view their own past.
Ahmad Urabi and Mustafa Kamil are heroes to the Egyptian people and
their leaders today. When I visited Istanbul, I found postcards for sale that
bore pictures of some of the leading New Ottomans. Every Turkish student
sees the Young Turks as a link in the chain of national regenerators going
from Selim III to Kemal Ataturk. Iran's rulers still pay lip service to the
1906 constitution; for the Iranian people, it is the written guarantee (often
violated, to be sure) of their fundamental rights. For the peoples of the
Middle East, these early nationalist movements were the prologue for the
revolutionary changes that were to come.

13

The Roots of Arab Bitterness

Few topics of study have generated as much heat as Arab nationalism. Few peoples are as poorly understood as today's Arabs. Even deciding who is an Arab or defining what is meant by Arab nationalism can easily get scholars and students into trouble, with both the Arabs and their detractors. Nevertheless, Arab nationalism seems to be a growing phenomenon in the late twentieth century. In our analysis we may find that what is called Arab nationalism is now dissolving into many different movements, whose main common feature is that they pertain to various Arabic-speaking peoples who wish to control their own political destinies. Thus, it is necessary to study these various manifestations of Arab feeling. And let us not fool ourselves: Arab feeling is strong, and it is likely to grow stronger in the years ahead. It is also sometimes bitter, due to some of the unhappy experiences of the Arabs in the early twentieth century. Let us see what did happen, and why.

ARAB NATIONALISM

What is Arab nationalism? Simply put, it is the belief that Arabs constitute a single political community (or nation) and ought to have a common government. Right away we can see problems. There is no general agreement on who is an Arab. The current definition is that an Arab is anyone who speaks Arabic as his or her native language. This is not enough. Many Arabic-speaking peoples do not typically think of themselves as Arabs, nor do other Arabs so regard them, i.e., the Maronites of Lebanon, possibly the Egyptian Copts, and almost certainly the Jews born in Arab countries who went to live in Israel. Until I hear a better definition, I lean toward one adopted by a conference of Arab leaders many years ago: "Whoever lives in our country, speaks our language, is reared in our culture, and takes pride in our glory is one of us."

Up to the twentieth century, the term "Arab" was applied mainly to the camel-raising nomads of Arabia, the bedouin. To the settled peoples of, say, Egypt or Syria, to be called an Arab was almost an insult. Turks used to call them *pis arabler* ("dirty Arabs"), which they naturally resented. The idea of Syrians and Egyptians glorifying in being Arabs, let alone uniting their countries in the name of Arab nationalism, as happened in 1958 and almost recurred several times since then, would have been taken as a joke. The question "What are you?" might have rated such answers as "I am a Syrian," "I am a Damascene," "I am a Muslim of the Shafi'i legal rite," or "I am a carpenter." Even a tribal affiliation might have been mentioned, but never "I am an Arab," at least not before the twentieth century. Even nowadays, we must remember that there are some twenty countries that see themselves as part of the Arab world, each with its own government, flag, currency, stamps, passport or identity card, and seat on the Council of the Arab League. None would deny its loyalty to the ideal of Arab unity, yet they go their separate ways. Even common opposition to the state of Israel has not brought the Arabs together; rather, it has divided them even more.

Historical Background

As we review the history of the Arabic-speaking peoples, we should remember that they have not been united since the era of the High Caliphate, if indeed then. Furthermore, they have not ruled themselves (except for the bedouin) from the time the Turks came in until quite recently. The very idea of people ruling themselves would not have made much sense to Middle Easterners before the rise of nationalism. What the settled peoples cared about was that a Muslim government ruled over them, defended them from nomads and other invaders, preserved order, and promoted justice in accordance with the Shari'ah. It did not matter whether the head of that Muslim government was an Arab like the Umayyad caliphs, a Persian like the Buyid emirs, a Turk like the Seljuk and Ottoman sultans, or a Kurd like Salah al-Din and his Ayyubid heirs. Almost all rulers succeeded either by heredity or by nomination; no one thought of letting the people elect them.

The Arabs under Ottoman Rule

From the sixteenth to the twentieth century most Arabs—all of them, really, except in parts of Arabia and Morocco—were part of the Ottoman Empire. Even in periods of Ottoman weakness, the local officials and landlords were apt to be Turks, Circassians, or other non-Arabs. Lately it has been fashionable for Arab nationalists and their sympathizers to denounce the horrors of Ottoman rule, blaming the Turks for the Arabs' backwardness, political ineptitude, disunity, or whatever else was wrong in their society. What went wrong? How did the state of the Arabs under

Ottoman rule compare with what it had been earlier? We have found that there was little deterioration that could be blamed directly on Istanbul. It could even be argued that early Ottoman rule benefited the Arabs by promoting local security and bringing their merchants into closer relations with Anatolia and the Balkans. If the Ottoman decline of the eighteenth century and the overzealous reforms of the nineteenth hurt the Arabs, the Turks within the empire suffered too. If Ottoman rule was so oppressive, why did the Arabs not revolt?

Well, at times they did. I have already mentioned the Wahhabi revolt in eighteenth-century Arabia, but that group wanted to purify Islam rather than set up an Arab state. Peasant and military revolts sometimes broke out in Egypt, but for economic rather than national reasons. Some people have seen an anti-Ottoman angle in the policies of Mehmet Ali and Ibrahim. The latter, as governor of Syria, is supposed to have said: "I am not a Turk. I came to Egypt as a child, and since that time, the sun of Egypt has changed my blood and made it all Arab." But Mehmet Ali and his heirs spoke Turkish, considered themselves members of the Ottoman ruling class, and treated the Egyptians like servants. Urabi's name implied some Arab identity (Egyptian peasants often trace their lineage to Arab tribes) and he did rebel against Turks and Circassians in the Egyptian army, but his revolt was mainly an Egyptian one directed against the Anglo-French Dual Control. Uprisings in Syria were frequent, but their cause was usually religious. Tribes might rebel against an Ottoman governor or garrison in Iraq or the Hijaz, but over local grievances.

In weighing these facts, historians have come to feel that Arab identity played no great part in Middle East politics up to the twentieth century. Muslim Arabs felt that any attempt to weaken the Ottoman Empire was likely to harm Islam. Even under Sultan Abdulhamid, for all his faults, the Arabs went on upholding the status quo. Many served in the army or the civil administration and some were among his leading advisers. They might take pride in being from the same "race" as Muhammad and his companions, but this did not make them want to rebel against the Turks, who were Muslims too.

Christian Arab Nationalists

Not all Arabs are Muslim. In the nineteenth century, perhaps as many as one fourth of the Arabs under Ottoman rule belonged to protected minorities. Most of these were Christians, who were less likely than the Muslims to feel a strong loyalty to the empire. But we must pin down each particular time, place, and sect before we can discuss the politics of the Arabic-speaking Christians. Those whose rule mattered most in the birth of Arab nationalism lived in Syria, which then included most of what we now call Israel, Jordan, Lebanon, the republic of Syria, and even parts of southern Turkey. Until they came under the rule of Ibrahim (1832-1840) or the Tanzimat reformers, there was little reason for Arabic-speaking Christians in Syria to worry about who ruled over them. The *millet* system gave considerable autonomy to both Orthodox and Monophysite Christians. As for the others, they were usually so well protected by deserts, mountains, or river gorges that they hardly felt the Ottoman yoke. The Maronites (and other Catholics) enjoyed French protection by the nineteenth century, whereas Russia took a growing interest in the welfare of the Greek Orthodox Syrians. From the 1820s on, American and French missionaries founded schools in Syria, as did the British, Russians, and other Westerners, though to a lesser extent. Since Syrian Christians naturally sent their children to mission schools closest to their own religious affiliation, Maronites and Uniat Catholics tended to go to French Catholic schools and to identify with France. This created problems for the Orthodox. Some were converting to Catholicism or Protestantism (out of dissatisfaction with their largely uneducated clergy), and hence sent their children to the relevant mission schools. But even those who stayed in their ancestral faith rarely wanted to go into the priesthood, since all higher clerical positions were held by Greeks, or to attend Russian schools, when few aspired to go to Russian universities.

The Americans provided the answer to their problem, but quite by accident they contributed to the rise of Arab nationalism. The American mission schools, especially their crowning institution, the Syrian Protestant College (now the American University of Beirut), tried to serve students of every religion. However, most of them hoped also to convert young people to Protestant Christianity. Since, as many of you know, Protestantism has traditionally stressed reading and understanding its sacred scriptures, the Bible was soon translated into Arabic for local converts. Many of the early American missionaries learned the language well enough to teach in it and even to translate some English language textbooks into Arabic. Until it became clear that they could not go on recruiting teachers and finding textbooks under this system, the American mission schools and colleges used Arabic as their language of instruction. Very reluctantly, they switched to English in the late nineteenth century. Many Arabs were therefore willing to send their children to the American schools, despite their Protestant orientation. The Orthodox Christians especially did so. This raised the standard of Arabic reading and writing among the Syrian Orthodox youth, many of whom went into journalism, law, and teaching. Some also became scholars and writers. Before long they were leading the Arabic literary revival, which (as so often happened in Europe) became politicized into a nationalist movement. Perhaps the growth of nationalism was also fostered by such American ideas as using the schools to develop moral character, stressing social and benevolent activities, and teaching students to find new institutions to fit changing conditions.

Legend has it that the first Arab nationalist party was a secret society in Beirut, founded around 1875 by five early graduates of the American University. More recently, careful research by a professor at that institution, Zeine N. Zeine, has shown that these students, all Christians, were probably seeking the independence of what we now call Lebanon—not the whole Arab world—from the Ottoman Empire. Anyway, the secret society did not last long. But the commitment of students and alumni of the American University of Beirut, whether nineteenth or twentieth century, has nurtured the ideas of Arab nationalism and spread them among both Muslim and Christian speakers of Arabic. The American missionaries hoped to convert the young Arabs to Protestantism through exposure to the Arabic Bible; the unintended outcome was to make them cherish more their heritage of Arabic literature and history. Their secular colleagues may also have taught them to respect the Western ideals of liberalism and democracy, but the students applied them to the building of an Arab nationalist ideology. Teachers sow their seed in unknown soil; their students decide what they will cultivate and determine what posterity will reap.

Muslim Arab Nationalists

But Arab nationalism could not have become popular among Muslims if all its advocates had been westernized Christians. The earliest example of a truly Muslim strain within Arab nationalism was a campaign during the 1890s, popularized by a writer named Abd al-Rahman al-Kawakibi (d. 1902), to revive the Arab caliphate, preferably in Mecca. Pan-Islam, strong among Muslims since the 1860s, had called on them to unite behind the leadership of the Ottoman sultans. By juggling a few historical facts, their supporters had proved that the caliphate, maintained by the Mamluks in Cairo from the fall of Baghdad in 1258, had been transferred to the Ottoman sultans upon their conquest of Egypt in 1517. This claim must have bothered some Muslims, since Sunni political theory specifies that the caliph must come from Muhammad's tribe, the Quraysh of Mecca. The Ottomans were not Arabs, let alone members of the Quraysh tribe. They had in fact rarely used the title of caliph before the late nineteenth century. Sultan Abdulaziz (1861-1876) had been the first to do so as part of his campaign to strengthen his position among Ottoman Muslims and to counter the harmful effects of Russian pan-Slavism. Sultan Abdulhamid exploited the caliphate even more, trying to win the backing of Egyptian and Indian Muslims ruled by Britain—one of the reasons for his bad reputation in Western history books. Britain's rising hostility to the Ottoman sultan probably affected Kawakibi's nationalism. At any rate, his idea of an Arab caliphate did gain support from the non-Ottoman emirs in Arabia and even Khedive Abbas in Egypt. Although the khedives were descendants of Mehmet Ali, a Turk, they often tried to win Arab support away from the Ottoman sultans. In short, Kawakibi's campaign to free the Arabs from Turkish rule mattered more as a power ploy for diplomats, khedives, and emirs than for its popular following at the time.

The Arabs and the Young Turks

The first breakthrough for Arab nationalism was the 1908 "Young Turk" revolution, which led to the restoration of the long-suspended Ottoman constitution. Suddenly, men living in Beirut and Damascus, Baghdad and Aleppo, Jaffa and Jerusalem were choosing representatives to an assembly in Istanbul. High hopes were raised for an era of union between Arabs and Turks and for progress toward liberal democracy in the Ottoman state. An Arab-Ottoman "Friendship Society" opened branches in many cities of the empire. Even some of the Syrian intellectuals who had fled from Abdulhamid's tyranny to Egypt or America began packing their bags to return home.

Arab hopes soon faded, however. The Arabic-Ottoman Friendship Society was closed down by the Committee of Union and Progress in 1909, although an Arabic literary society was allowed to function in Istanbul as long as it steered clear of politics. Representation in Parliament tended to favor Turks against the various ethnic, linguistic, and religious minorities of the empire; furthermore, the elections were fixed to ensure that most of the deputies would belong to the CUP. The Young Turk government, imperiled by European imperialism and Balkan nationalism, resumed the centralizing policies of earlier Ottoman reformers. This made the Arabs feel that their liberties, preserved by the weakness or indifference of earlier governments, would now be in danger. The imposition of Turkish as the language of administration and education (plus the apparent shift from pan-Islam to pan-Turanism) especially angered the Arabs.

How could they react? Not since the time of Muhammad had large numbers of Arabic-speaking peoples mobilized politically to gain unity and freedom for Arabs. How could they oppose a government headed, at least in name, by a sultan-caliph? What good would it do the Arabs of Syria to overthrow Turkish rule, only to become, like Egypt, a dependency of a Christian Great Power? Few Syrians (except some Maronites) wanted French rule. Neither did Arabs in Basrah (now in Iraq) want to be regarded (like Suez) as a vital link in Britain's imperial communications.

The result of these considerations was a low-profile movement of a few educated Arabs aimed not at separation, but at greater local autonomy. It included three different groups: (1) the Ottoman Decentralization party, formed in 1912 by Syrians living in Cairo and aimed at winning Arab support for greater local autonomy at the expense of strong central control by the Ottoman government; (2) al-Fatat ("youth"), a secret society of young Arab, mainly Muslim, students in European universities, who convoked an Arab Congress, held in Paris in 1913, to demand equal rights and cultural autonomy for Arabs within the Ottoman Empire; and (3) al-Ahd ("covenant"), a secret society of Arab officers within the Ottoman army, who proposed to turn the Ottoman Empire into an Arab-Turkish dual monarchy on the pattern of Austria-Hungary since 1867. Each of these groups found backers among educated Arabs living in Istanbul, other Ottoman cities (notably Damascus), and abroad.

But do not let the strength of Arab nationalism today fool you into rewriting the early history of the movement. Most Arabs were not yet Arab nationalists; they stuck by the CUP, the Ottoman constitution that gave them parliamentary representation, and a government in which some Arabs served as ministers and ambassadors, petty officials, or army officers. If Arab nationalism was to mean separation from the Ottoman Empire, this might do more for the Egyptian khedive or the British than for the Arabs of Syria or Iraq. Even though Egypt was prospering, Arabs elsewhere did not crave British rule, let alone a French imperialism comparable to what already existed in Algeria. The Jewish settlers in Palestine, hardly large enough yet to threaten the Arab majority, might later aspire to separate statehood (see chapter 16), and Arab nationalists opposed this even more than Turkish rule.

WORLD WAR I

The next turning point in the rise of Arab nationalism occurred when the Ottoman Empire decided in August 1914 to enter World War I on the German side. The Young Turks, especially War Minister Enver, may have been influenced by their exposure to German military advisers, but their main motive was to reconquer Egypt from the British and the Caucasus mountain area from tsarist Russia. Muslim Arabs might well have applauded these aims.

Although later writers have castigated the Young Turks for committing the empire, shaken already by defeats in Libya and the Balkans, to war against the Western Allies, I must point out that the decision was highly popular in 1914, when Germany was respected for its economic and military might. The Germans were building a railway from Istanbul to

Baghdad that would help hold together what was left of the Ottoman Empire. In addition, a German military mission was in Istanbul, training officers and soldiers to use modern weapons. Two German warships, caught in the Mediterranean when the war started and pursued by the British navy, took refuge in the Straits, whereupon they were handed over by the German ambassador as gifts to the Ottoman government (complete with their German crews, who donned fezzes and claimed to be "instructors"). They replaced two ships under construction for the Ottoman navy in British shipyards, already paid for by public subscription, that had been commandeered by the British navy when the war broke out. So strongly did the Ottoman government and people support the German cause that, after the new "Turkish" ships had pulled the empire into the war by bombarding the Russian port of Odessa, the sultan officially proclaimed a jihad (Muslim holy war) against Britain, France, and Russia. All three had millions of Muslim subjects who, if they got the message, would have to rebel on behalf of their Ottoman sultan-caliph.

Britain and the Arabs

The British, especially those serving in Egypt and the Sudan, were worried about how to counter this pan-Islamic proclamation on behalf of the Turco-German war machine, which launched a well-publicized invasion of Sinai in late 1914, just as Britain declared an official protectorate over Egypt. Some units of the Ottoman army did reach the Suez Canal in February 1915. One actually crossed to the Western side under cover of darkness. For several years, Britain had to keep over a hundred thousand imperial troops stationed in Egypt, partly to intimidate the Egyptian Nationalists, but mainly to stop any new Ottoman effort to take the canal, which the British now viewed as their imperial lifeline.

Britain's response was to make contact with an Arab leader in the Hijaz (western Arabia), namely Husayn, the sharif and emir of Mecca. You may want me to explain these grand titles. A sharif is a descendant of Muhammad, of which there were many in the Hijaz, especially in the Muslim holy cities. Protection of Mecca and Medina mattered greatly to the Ottoman sultans; they lavished honors on the sharifs but also played on their rivalries to keep them in line. The various clans of sharifs fought one another for the position of emir (prince), which carried considerable temporal authority.

From the Tanzimat era, though, the Ottoman government was also trying to strengthen its direct rule over the Hijaz, using an appointed local governor. Sharif Husayn, the leader of one of the contending clans (which he called the Hashimites, the clan of the Prophet himself), had long struggled with the Ottoman sultan and his governors, enduring almost sixteen years of house arrest in Istanbul. Even though he remained loyal to the Ottomanist ideal after he became emir in 1908, Husayn disliked the CUP's centralizing policies. One of his sons, Abdallah, had close ties with the Arab nationalist societies in Syria even before World War I. Abdallah went to Cairo, seeking support from the British consul-general, Lord Kitchener, a few months before the war started. The British were not yet ready to plot against the Ottoman Empire, which they had earlier tried to preserve, but Kitchener did not forget the meeting. When he returned home to help in the central planning of Britain's war effort, London became interested in a possible Arab alliance against the Ottoman Empire, using these Hashimite sharifs in Mecca. The British government instructed its representatives in Cairo to contact Emir Husayn, hoping to dissuade him from endorsing the jihad or, better yet, persuade him to lead an Arab rebellion against Ottoman rule.

The Husayn-McMahon Correspondence

In Cairo, Britain's high commissioner (the new title resulted from the declaration of the British protectorate over Egypt), Sir Henry McMahon, wrote to the sharif of Mecca. The British wanted him to start a revolt against Ottoman rule in the Hijaz. Husayn in turn asked for a pledge that the British would support the rebellion financially and politically against his Arab rivals as well as the Ottoman Empire. If he called for an Arab revolt, it was not merely for the sake of changing masters. The British in Egypt and the Sudan knew from talking with Arab nationalists living there that the Hashimites could not rally other Arabs to their cause—especially given the power and prestige of rival families living in other parts of Arabia—unless the Arabs were sure of gaining their independence in the lands in which they predominated: Arabia, Iraq, and Syria, including Palestine and Lebanon. The Arab nationalists did not yet worry much about Egypt and the rest of North Africa.

Keeping these considerations in mind, the emir of Mecca and the British high commissioner for Egypt and the Sudan exchanged some letters in 1915-1916 that have since become famous and highly controversial. In the course of what we now call the Husayn-McMahon correspondence, Britain pledged that, if Husayn proclaimed an Arab revolt against Ottoman rule, it would provide military and financial aid during the war and would support the creation of independent Arab governments in the Arabian peninsula and most parts of the Fertile Crescent.

Britain did exclude some parts, though. These included the port areas of Mersin and Alexandretta (now part of southern Turkey), also Basrah (now in Iraq) and "portions of Syria lying to the west of the areas [districts] of Damascus, Homs, Hama, and Aleppo." One of the toughest issues in modern Middle East history is to figure out whether McMahon meant to exclude only Lebanon, a largely Christian region coveted by France, or also Palestine, in which some Jews hoped to rebuild their ancient homeland. Map 7 (p. 192) indicates that Lebanon is more clearly west of Damascus and those other Syrian cities than is what we now call Israel. This view would support the Arab case that Britain promised Palestine to them. But if the *province* of Syria (of which Damascus was the capital) was intended, what is now Israel and then partly under a governor in Jerusalem may have been what McMahon meant to exclude from Arab rule. Not only the Zionists, but also the British government after 1918, and even McMahon himself believed that he had never promised Palestine to the Arabs. My judgment of the issue is that, since Britain cared more in 1915 about preserving its French connection than about reserving Palestine for the Jews, the area excluded from Arab rule in the Husayn-McMahon correspondence must have been Lebanon. Only later would Jewish claims to Palestine become a moot issue.

The exclusion of these ambiguously described lands displeased Husayn, he refused to accept the deal, and his correspondence with the British in Cairo ended inconclusively in early 1916. The Ottomans could have headed off any major Arab revolt, but for the stupidity of the governor in Syria, Jemal, who needlessly antagonized the Arabs there. As former naval minister and one of the three Young Turks who really ruled the Ottoman Empire when it entered World War I, Jemal had taken charge of the Turkish expedition to seize the Suez Canal and liberate Egypt from British rule. Although his first attempt failed, Jemal planned to try again. He settled down as governor of Syria while he rebuilt his forces, but did little for the province. Many areas were struck by famine; fuel shortages prevented trains from carrying food to the stricken areas. Meanwhile, the Arab nationalist societies had come together and were wondering what to do next. One of Emir Husayn's sons, Faysal, came to Syria to parley with both the Arab nationalists and Jemal in 1915, but he accomplished nothing. In April and May 1916 Jemal's police swept down on the Arab leaders, including some scholars who were not even nationalists, arrested them for treason, and had twenty-two of them publicly hanged in Beirut and Damascus. The executions aroused so much anger in Syria—and among Arabs generally—that Faysal hastened back to Mecca, a convert to the nationalist cause, and persuaded his father that the time for revolt had come.

The Arab Revolt

On 5 June 1916 Husayn declared the independence of the Arabs and unfurled the standard of their revolt against Turkish rule. The Ottoman

Empire did not topple over at once, but large numbers of Arabs in the Hijaz, plus some in Palestine and Syria, began to fight the Turks. Historians still ask whether most Arabs in these areas were truly nationalists. Most probably did not care whether they were ruled from Istanbul or Mecca as long as the outcome of World War I was in doubt.

The Arab Revolt would have many ups and downs over the course of the next two years, but let me keep the story short. Guided by European advisers, of whom T. E. Lawrence is deservedly the best known, the Arab supporters of Emir Husayn and his sons, Abdallah and Faysal (among others), fought on the side of the Allies against the Ottoman Empire. Working in tandem with British imperial troops advancing from the Suez Canal, namely the Egyptian Expeditionary Force, they moved north into Palestine. While the British forces took Jaffa and Jerusalem, the Arabs were blowing up railways and capturing Aqaba and Amman. When the British troops drew near Damascus in late September 1918, they held back to let Lawrence and the Arabs occupy the city, which then became the headquarters for a provisional Arab government headed by Faysal. Meanwhile, the Ottoman army, now led by Mustafa Kemal ("Ataturk"), retreated from Syria. The Turks were also giving way in Iraq before an Anglo-Indian army. Late in October the Ottoman Empire signed an armistice with the Allies on the island of Mudros. The Arabs, promised the right of self-determination by the British and the French, were jubilant. Surely their independence was at hand.

The Sykes-Picot Agreement

But this was not to be. Fighting for the survival of its empire, the British government had promised parts of the Arab world to other interested parties during the war. To backtrack a little, Russia had demanded Allied recognition of its right to control the Turkish Straits. In a secret treaty signed in London in 1915, Britain and France promised to back Russia's claim. For its entry into the war on the Allied side in 1915, Italy later demanded large portions of southwestern Anatolia. The Greeks, too, wanted a piece of Turkey, the area around Izmir, which had many Greek inhabitants. France, heavily involved in the war against Germany on the western front (keep in mind that German troops held much of northeastern France between 1914 and 1918), could not give up all its claims to the Middle East. Given its historic ties with the Maronites, it was natural for France to want Syria, including Lebanon and Palestine. So Britain, France, and Russia drew up a secret treaty known as the Sykes-Picot Agreement. Signed in May 1916, it provided for direct French rule in much of northern and western Syria, plus a sphere of influence in the Syrian hinterland, including Damascus, Aleppo, and Mosul. Britain would rule

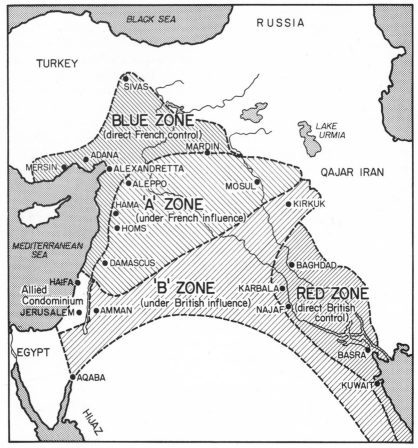

Map 7. The Sykes-Picot Agreement, 1916

lower Iraq directly, and would also advise an Arab government controlling
a stretch of land between the Egyptian border and eastern Arabia, thus
providing indirect British control from the Mediterranean to the Persian
Gulf. A small area around Jaffa and Jerusalem would be under international government because Russia wanted to share in the administration
of the Christian holy places. The only area left for the Arabs to live in
without foreign rulers or advisers was the Arabian desert.

Arab apologists have claimed that Emir Husayn knew nothing about the
Sykes-Picot Agreement until after World War I. T. E. Lawrence was
wracked by guilt because he had worked with the Arabs on behalf of
Britain, thinking that they would get their independence after the war,
while in fact they were being manipulated by British diplomacy, if not

duplicity. Now I will not deny that Lawrence's *Seven Pillars of Wisdom* is a book well worth reading, or that *Lawrence of Arabia* is one of my favorite movies. But they are not history. Emir Husayn did know about the Sykes-Picot Agreement not only from the publication of the Allied secret treaties by the Communists after they had seized control of Russia in 1917, but also from Turkish agents trying to draw him out of the war, and indeed from the British and the French themselves. To Husayn, the advantages of heading an Arab revolt against the Ottomans, who had kept him locked up for so long, outweighed the perils of Sykes-Picot, which the British assured him would not involve the lands he wanted to rule. But to many Arab nationalists, this Anglo-French agreement was a betrayal of their cause, worse because it was not made public until after the war.

The Balfour Declaration

More publicity surrounded a decision of the British cabinet to support the establishment of a Jewish national home in Palestine, formally announced on 2 November 1917. This was the famous Balfour Declaration, so called because it came out as a letter written by the foreign secretary, Lord Balfour, to Lord (Walter) Rothschild, honorary president of the Zionist Federation of Britain and Ireland. I plan to analyze the letter in chapter 16, but its salient points were that (1) the British government would help set up a national home for the Jewish people; (2) it would not undermine the rights or status of Jews choosing to remain outside Palestine, nor (3) harm the civil and religious rights of Palestine's "existing non-Jewish communities." The Arabs' main objection to the Balfour Declaration was that they made up over nine-tenths of what would later become Palestine. How could anyone create a home for one group of people in a land inhabited by another? Worse still, the inhabitants had never been asked whether they wanted to have their area become the national home for a people who would be coming from far away. In addition, the Balfour Declaration expressed no concern for the *political* rights of non-Jewish Palestinians, a point that still causes deep Arab resentment. If Britain tried to realize the Zionist dream of a Jewish state, what would be the political status of the Arabic-speaking Christians and Muslims of Palestine? Did not this declaration contradict the Husayn-McMahon correspondence and other statements meant to reassure Arabs who had thrown themselves into the revolt against the Turks?

THE POSTWAR PEACE SETTLEMENT

How would these conflicting commitments be reconciled, once the war was over? In November 1918 the guns in Europe fell silent, and everyone hoped that the diplomats would make a lasting peace. During the war,

America's President Wilson, one of the finest statesmen of the day, had laid down a set of principles called the Fourteen Points, on which he wanted the Allies to build the peace once the war was won. He denounced secret treaties, proposed self-determination for all peoples (specifically including those who had been under Ottoman rule), and called for the creation of a League of Nations to avert the threat of war in the future. When he came to Europe to represent the United States at the Paris Peace Conference, Wilson was hailed everywhere as a hero and savior.

But Britain and France, the Allies who had borne the brunt of the fighting and the casualties, were determined to dictate the peace. The defeated countries, Germany, Austria-Hungary, and the Ottoman Empire, could not attend the conference until it was time to sign the treaties. Russia (now a Communist state that had signed a separate peace with Germany) was also left out. Georges Clemenceau, who headed the French delegation, expressed a popular mood when he insisted that Germany must be punished and that France must get control over all of geographical Syria. David Lloyd George, heading the British delegation, agreed that Germany should be punished, but he also sought a formula to bring peace to the Middle East without harming the British Empire. The Zionist (or Jewish nationalist) movement was ably represented by Dr. Chaim Weizmann (about whom I intend to write more in chapter 16), while the Arab nationalists had Faysal, assisted by T. E. Lawrence.

The King-Crane Commission

It was almost impossible to reconcile the Middle Eastern claims of the Arabs, the Zionists, the British, and the French, but the conferees did try. Wilson wanted to send a commission of inquiry to Syria and Palestine to find out what the people there really wanted. Lloyd George went along with the idea, until the French insisted that, unless the commission also went to Iraq (where Britain's military occupation was already unpopular), they would boycott it. The British then lost interest, and only the Amerian team went out. This was the King-Crane Commission. It found that the local people desired complete independence under Faysal, who had already set up a provisional Arab government in Damascus. If they had to accept foreign tutelage, they wanted it to come from the Americans, who had no history of imperialism in the Middle East, or at least from the British, whose army was already there, but never from the French.

The King-Crane Commission also looked into the Zionist claims, which its members had initially supported, and concluded that their realization would lead to serious Jewish-Arab conflict. The commission urged that the Zionist program be greatly reduced, Jewish immigration into Palestine be restricted, and the project for turning the country into a Jewish national home abandoned. Faysal and his backers hoped that the King-Crane Commission would persuade Wilson to step in on behalf of the Arabs. Instead, Wilson became preoccupied with gaining American support for his League of Nations. He suffered his paralytic stroke before he could find time to read the commissioners' report, which was not even published for several years.

Allied Arrangements: San Remo and Sèvres

What happened instead was that Britain and France came together to settle their differences. France gave up its claim to Mosul and to Palestine in exchange for a free hand in the rest of Syria. As a sop to Wilsonian idealism, the Allies set up a mandate system, under which Asian and African territories taken from Turkey and Germany were put under a tutelary relationship to a Great Power (called the "mandatory"), which would train them in the art of self-government. Each mandatory would have to report periodically to a body in the League of Nations called the Permanent Mandates Commission, as a check against exploitation. Meeting in San Remo in 1920, Britain and France agreed to divide the Middle Eastern mandates: Syria (and Lebanon) to France, Iraq and Palestine (including what is now Jordan) to Britain. The Hijaz would be independent. The Ottoman government had to accept these arrangements when it signed the Treaty of Sèvres in August 1920. By this time, the French army had already marched eastward from Beirut, defeated the Arabs easily and driven Faysal's provisional government out of Damascus. The Arab dream had been shattered.

The End Result: Four Mandates and an Emirate

What happened then to the Arabs of the Fertile Crescent? The French had absolutely no sympathy for Arab nationalism and ruled their Syrian mandate as if it were a colony. In order to weaken the nationalists, France tried to break up Syria into smaller units, including what would eventually become the republic of Lebanon, plus Alexandretta (which was handed over to Turkey in 1939), states for the Alawis in the north and the Druze in the south, and even Aleppo and Damascus as city-states. The separation of Lebanon from Syria lasted (at least up to 1976) because it had a Christian majority (as of 1921) that was determined to keep its dominant position. The other divisions of Syria soon ended, but the Syrian Arabs chafed under French rule, which seemed to become permanent.

The British, on the other hand, sometimes encouraged Arab nationalism, working with the Hashimite family. Husayn still had his government in the Hijaz, but the experience of leading the Arab revolt seems to have gone to his head. He proclaimed himself "King of the Arabs" and later laid

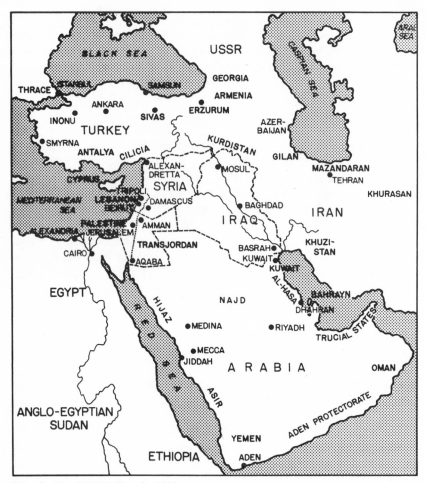

Map 8. The Middle East in 1922

claim to the caliphate of Islam. This so offended the British that, as the
Saud family rose to power in eastern Arabia, they stood by with folded
arms as the Saudis marched into the Hijaz in 1924 and toppled his regime.
As for Iraq, British control was threatened by a general Arab insurrection
in 1920. Needing a strong personality to calm the country down, the British
brought in Faysal, who was approved in a plebiscite as the new king of Iraq.
Soon peace was restored. The British worked harmoniously with Faysal's
government to speed Iraq toward independence. It is ironic that Iraq, once
seen as the most backward Arab region in the Ottoman Empire, should in

1932 have been the first new state to gain its formal independence.

What was to be done with Abdallah, whom the Hashimites had hoped would rule in Baghdad? After Faysal was ousted from Syria in 1920, Abdallah gathered a small force of Arab tribesmen, occupied Amman, and threatened to attack the French in Syria. Although he could not have driven them out, the British wanted to keep him out of trouble. Thus Winston Churchill, then the colonial secretary, met Abdallah in Jerusalem and persuaded him to accept—temporarily—that part of Palestine that lay east of the Jordan River, until the French should leave Syria. This provisional arrangement was opposed by the Zionists, who wanted all of Palestine as defined by the 1920 peace treaties to be open to Jewish settlement and eventual statehood. The French feared that Abdallah's new principality would become a staging area for Hashimite raids into Syria. No one expected this "Emirate of Transjordan" to last long, but it did. While the rest of the Palestine mandate was seething with Jewish-Arab turmoil, Transjordan became an oasis of tranquil politics and economic development. The sad story of Britain's mandate in the rest of Palestine must be saved for chapter 16.

CONCLUSION AND SUMMARY

The Arabs had been roused from centuries of political lethargy, first by American teachers and missionaries, then by the revolution of the Young Turks, and finally by the blandishments of Britain and France during World War I. They remembered their ancient greatness and longed to recapture it. From the West they learned about rights and freedoms, democratic governments, and national self-determination. Led by members of the family of the Prophet Muhammad, a few Arabs had dared to rebel against the greatest Muslim state left in the world, the Ottoman Empire. In its place they hoped to set up one or more independent Arab states ruled by members of the Hashimite family. Thus motivated, they helped the British and French defeat the Ottoman Empire in World War I, but afterwards the Allies failed to keep the pledges they had made to the Arabs. In the lands of the Fertile Crescent, where Arabs were clearly in the majority, where they hoped to form independent states, where someday the Arab nation might revive its former power and glory, the victorious Allies set up mandates that were merely colonies in disguise. Instead of coming together, the Arabs found themselves being pulled farther apart. One area, Palestine, was even declared to be the Jewish national home, leaving in doubt the future of its Arab inhabitants. Theses were the roots of Arab bitterness put down over half a century ago. In the chapters to come, we shall see the ways in which bitter feelings flourished.

14

Modernizing Rulers in the Independent States

In the last four chapters I have written about Middle Eastern peoples and countries that fell under European control. Actually, it is hard to think of any region, except for the inaccessible deserts of Arabia and the highest mountains of Anatolia and Iran, that did not feel the impact of the West by 1914. As you have seen, Egypt and the Fertile Crescent region came under Western rule, direct or indirect, before or during World War I. Even those areas that escaped—Anatolia, central Iran, and most of Arabia—were being eyed as potential colonies. The Allied secret agreements during the war would have awarded Istanbul and the Straits to tsarist Russia and parts of western and southern Anatolia to Italy and France. Meanwhile, British agents were lining up the tribes of Arabia and Iran. Treaties were drafted that would have made their lands virtual protectorates of the British Empire, as indeed Kuwait, Bahrain, the Trucial States (now called the United Arab Emirates), and Oman had already become by 1914. Aden was still technically a settlement of the Indian government; it would not formally become a crown colony until 1937. In 1917 the Bolshevik Revolution pulled Russia out of the war and out of the contest for influence over its Middle Eastern neighbors, at least for a while. Once Germany and the Ottoman Empire conceded defeat in 1918, there seemed to be no one left to stem the spread of Western—especially British—influence throughout the whole Middle East.

But the tide did turn. At least three areas of the Middle East did manage to salvage their independence after World War I. The Turks in Anatolia drove off the Western invaders, terminated the moribund Ottoman Empire, and established the republic of Turkey. In a remote part of east-central Arabia called Najd, a young man from an old ruling family combined a Muslim reform movement with a group of militant tribesmen to unite most of the peninsula in what we now call the Kingdom of Saudi Arabia. A few soldiers and civilian nationalists blocked British and Bolshevik attempts to take over Iran and then replaced the weak Qajar shah with a more dynamic ruler.

Since most Middle East maps we see in classrooms and in the news media are political, we tend to think of "Turkey," "Saudi Arabia," and "Iran" as entities that have always been what they are today. In reality, Turkey and Saudi Arabia got their present names and boundaries only between the two world wars. Iran, while its modern borders differ only slightly from those of the last Qajars, is a far cry from the "Persia" that was divided in 1907 into Russian and British spheres of influence. In each of these countries, these changes were due to the inspiration, the ingenuity, and the industry of a military commander who became a great leader: Mustafa Kemal "Ataturk," Ibn Saud, and Reza Shah Pahlavi.

TURKEY: PHOENIX FROM THE ASHES

When the Ottoman naval minister signed the Mudros Armistice in October 1918, ending his country's active role in World War I, the empire was nearly prostrate. Its armed forces had suffered about 325,000 deaths (more than the total number of American casualties), 400,000 wounded, and 250,000 taken prisoner or missing in action. Heavy government spending had led to higher taxes, deficit financing, and a general price inflation that brought great hardship to the people. The country's commerce and finance had been further disrupted by the deportation of the Armenians, a wartime policy of the Ottoman government that was executed so cruelly as to amount to genocide. Over half a million Armenians perished as they were driven from eastern Anatolia, and those who remained were bitter and vengeful toward the Ottoman government. Large-scale conscription and prolonged fighting had robbed many areas of the country of their young men. Farms and villages fell into neglect, and weeds choked once fertile fields. Whole forests had been cut down to fuel the trains and the factories when coal grew scarce.

Demoralized by defeats, disease, arrears in pay, and poor food, many of the soldiers deserted their units and roamed the countryside as armed brigands. As you know, the forces of the British Empire, aided by the Arab Revolt, had pushed the Ottomans out of the Fertile Crescent. Meanwhile, in the last year of the war the Young Turk triumvirs, Enver, Talat, and Jemal, sent troops deep into the Caucasus. They may have hoped to build a new Turanian empire among the Muslims of what had been tsarist Russia, now torn by civil war between the "Whites" (anti-Communists) and the "Reds" (Bolsheviks). It is one of the ironies of World War I that Turkey and Germany surrendered while some of their troops still occupied foreign lands.

Challenges to the Nationalists

The Mudros Armistice put an end to the government of the Young Turks. Enver, Talat, and Jemal fled from Istanbul on a German warship a few days before the British and the French occupied the Straits. So anxious was the Ottoman sultan to keep his power that he allied himself completely with the Western powers and was ready to do whatever they demanded. Soon his brother-in-law, Damad Ferid, took charge of the government, started dismantling the Ottoman army, and tried to pacify the country. French troops entered the area of southern Anatolia known as Cilicia (as specified in the Sykes-Picot Agreement), while the Italians laid claim in Antalya in the southwest. Although the Bolsheviks renounced claims made on Istanbul and the Straits by previous Russian governments, Britain and France now occupied these areas on the pretext of helping the White Russians against the Communists. The winter of 1918-1919 was a nightmare for the Turks of Istanbul: influenza was rife, coal and wood were scarce, youth gangs roamed the darkened streets and robbed shopkeepers and passersby, food prices skyrocketed, and the Greek inhabitants flew their national flag openly and even provided the French commander with a white horse, on which he triumphantly entered the city (just as Mehmet the Conqueror had done in 1453).

By the time the Allies opened their postwar conference in Paris, they were prepared to divide Thrace and Anatolia—as well as the Arab lands covered in the previous chapter—into spheres of influence. Some spoke of an American mandate over Anatolia and Armenia. The Turkish people, tired of wars that had taken their young men and drained their treasure steadily since the Libyan War of 1911, might have accepted foreign tutelage and military occupation, but for an unforeseen challenge. Venizelos, the Greek prime minister, went before the Paris Peace Conference to argue that the west Anatolian city of Smyrna (now Izmir) should be awarded to Greece. Greek nationalists in Athens spoke of a reconstituted Byzantine Empire that would include Istanbul, Thrace, and western Anatolia, areas where many Greek Christians still lived under Ottoman rule. Encouraged by Lloyd George, Wilson, and Clemenceau, Venizelos acted to realize these ambitions. On 15 May 1919 some 25,000 Greek troops landed at Smyrna, welcomed by its mainly Greek and foreign inhabitants. There was no resistance by the Ottoman government, which was trying to bring order and restore peace in a country close to anarchy. Yet this landing of the Greeks, long the most rebellious subjects of the Ottoman Empire, was the spark that lit the fires of Turkish nationalism in Anatolia. Four days later another landing, equally fateful for Turkey's history, took place at the

Black Sea port of Samsun.

Mustafa Kemal "Ataturk": Leader of the Resistance

Commanding the force that landed at Samsun was Mustafa Kemal, a general who had been sent by the sultan's government to disarm the population and restore order to the turbulent provinces of eastern Anatolia. Mustafa Kemal, later known to the world as "Ataturk," had already won fame for his military triumphs in World War I. He had commanded the Turks' successful defense of the Dardanelles against the Western Allies in 1915. The following year his troops had driven back the Russians in the east. He also directed the Turks' orderly retreat from Syria in 1918, gaining the respect of his British adversaries. His outspoken hostility toward the Young Turks had kept him from getting the positions or the perquisites of power that he deserved. His ambitions thwarted by the sultan's clique, Kemal had personal as well as patriotic reasons to resist the Ottoman government's subservience toward the Allies.

A myth has grown up that Kemal alone blew the breath of life into Turkish nationalism in May 1919. The truth is more complicated. There were many groups in Thrace and Anatolia that were resisting the Greeks, the Armenians, their foreign backers, and the hapless Ottoman government. The driving spirit was Muslim at least as much as it was Turkish; ulama and Sufi leaders commanded great respect in the countryside. What Kemal did was to galvanize these "defense of rights associations" by publicly resigning from the Ottoman army and convoking a national congress in the central Anatolian town of Sivas. However, the leaders of the Eastern Provinces Society for the Defense of National Rights had already called a congress at Erzurum. Invited to the Erzurum Congress, Kemal was elected its chairman. It was here that the Turks first drafted their National Pact, calling for the preservation of Turkey's existing borders (the Ottoman Empire minus its Arab lands lost in the war), opposition to any changes in those borders, formation of an elected government, and denial of special privileges to non-Turkish minorities. This set the stage for the September 1919 Sivas Congress, which rejected any form of foreign protectorate or mandate over Turkey and demanded that the weak government in Istanbul be replaced by an elected one prepared to uphold Turkish interests.

Such was the national mood that the grand vizir did resign—pushed perhaps by a nationwide telegraph operators' strike. A coalition cabinet including several of Kemal's supporters took over. New parliamentary elections gave the Turkish nationalists a whopping majority, but the popular government proved short-lived. In ratifying the National Pact, the Ottoman deputies antagonized the Allies, who formally occupied Istanbul and forced the coalition ministry to resign. Damad Ferid resumed power, and the shaykh al-Islam declared the nationalists to be rebels against the sultan. Parliament was dissolved; many of its deputies escaped (not without hardship) to Ankara, safely beyond the range of Allied gunboats and occupation forces. There, in central Anatolia, Mustafa Kemal convoked the Grand National Assembly of Turkey in April 1920.

The Kemalist movement now found itself at war with the Ottoman government in Istanbul, the Greek invaders (backed by the British) around Smyrna, the republic of Armenia in the east, and the French in the south. Poorly armed and half-starved Turkish irregulars had to fight against the well-supplied forces of the Allies and their Christian protégés. The Allies underestimated the will of Kemal's nationalist following, however, when they forced the Ottoman government to sign in August 1920 what would later become its death warrant, the Treaty of Sèvres.

Let me enumerate some of its provisions: (1) the Straits would be managed by a permanent Allied commission, (2) Istanbul could be taken away from Turkish administration if minority rights were infringed upon, (3) eastern Anatolia would be controlled by an independent Armenia and an autonomous Kurdistan, (4) Greece would have Smyrna and also Thrace, (5) Italy and France would each get parts of southwestern Anatolia, (6) the Arab lands would be divided into British and French mandates (as described in chapter 13), and (7) the capitulations, abolished by the Turks in September 1914, would be restored and extended. To the Turkish nationalists, the whole Sèvres treaty was a slap in the face. Even these humiliations did not satisfy Venizelos, whose forces (encouraged by Lloyd George) pushed eastward into Turkey, taking lands never awarded by Sèvres to the Greeks.

What saved the Turks was the aid they received from Soviet Russia. Both countries were embroiled in civil war and fending off foreign attackers. Together they wiped out the independent republic of Armenia in late 1920. Freed from any challenge from the east, Kemal's forces managed to slow down the Greek advance early in 1921. It gradually became clear that certain Western countries were not backing the Greeks either, that is, not when they claimed lands beyond what they were promised by the Sèvres treaty. After the Turks had fought the Greeks to a standstill in a bitter, three-week battle close to Ankara in August and September 1921, France decided to come to terms with the Kemalists. As a result, both France and Italy gave up their territorial claims in Anatolia. Britain alone continued to occupy the Straits, control the sultan, and egg on the Greeks. In the summer of 1922 the Turks launched a strong offensive that drove the Greek armies completely out of Anatolia. Soon afterwards the British government decided to cut its losses, calling for a new Allied peace conference to negotiate a new treaty with Turkey. The Ottoman sultan, shorn of all his foreign support, fled from Istanbul, whereupon the Grand National Assembly in Ankara abolished the sultanate altogether. On 29 October 1922 Turkey became the first republic in the modern Middle East.

The Turkish nationalists may have shown the world that they could wear down their opponents militarily, but the British still had to learn that they could also withstand diplomatic pressure. The British expected the new peace conference in Lausanne to be quick, allowing them to retain by diplomacy part of what their protégés had lost by war. General Ismet (Inonu), chosen by Kemal to represent the Turkish republic, stood firm and wore down his distinguished British counterpart, Lord Curzon, by feigning deafness and delaying the proceedings to get instructions on various issues from Ankara. When the Lausanne peacemakers finished replacing the Treaty of Sèvres, the Turks had freed their country of the hated capitulations, all forms of military occupation, and any threat of an Armenian state or an autonomous Kurdistan. Nearly all Greek Orthodox Christians living in Anatolia were deported to Greece as part of a population exchange that sent many Muslims from Greek Macedonia and Bulgaria to a Turkey that they had never known. The only setbacks for the Kemalists in the Treaty of Lausanne were the formation of an international commission to supervise shipping through the Straits (which were demilitarized) and the failure to obtain Mosul (which the League of Nations later awarded to Iraq). Thanks to the Lausanne Conference of 1923, Turkey became the only country defeated in World War I that was able to negotiate its own peace terms. Except for the 1936 Montreux Conference, which gave Turkey more control over the Straits, and the annexation of Alexandretta in 1939, the Lausanne treaty remains the basis of Turkey's place among the nations of the world. By contrast, the Versailles treaty and all other postwar peace arrangements have been scrapped long ago. Well might the Arabs, who rebelled against the Turks to support the victors in World War I, envy their erstwhile masters, who had tied their fate to that of the vanquished!

Kemal's Domestic Reforms

Mustafa Kemal devoted the last fifteen years of his life to changing Turkey from the bastion of Islam into a secular nation state. Islam, the way of life and basis of government for the Turks since their conversion a thousand years ago, was now to be replaced by Western ways of civilization, justice, and administration. If persuasion did not work, then the changes would be executed by force. Twice opposition parties arose within the Grand National Assembly, but in neither case did Kemal allow them to last. A Kurdish uprising in 1925 was severely repressed, and an attempt on Kemal's life led to the public hanging of many political dissidents. As president of the republic, Kemal was highly authoritarian; yet he also detested fascism, opposed the Marxian aspects of Communism (although he utilized Soviet aid and was the first Middle Eastern leader to adopt state economic planning), and allowed free debate in the popularly elected assembly. Kemal admired democracy in the abstract, but he ruled as a stern father and teacher to his people, who he felt were not yet ready to govern themselves democratically.

Was Kemal a Muslim? He certainly flouted the rules of Islam in his drinking, card playing, and sexual escapades. Yet he also relied on Islamic symbols and allied himself with Muslim leaders in his struggle against the Greeks. Even if he still kept some of the attitudes and practices of his Muslim forebears, he was nevertheless determined to destroy Islam's power to block the modernization of Turkey. Although he allowed a member of the Ottoman dynasty to retain the caliphate for a while, he abolished the position in 1924. Angry protests from Muslims in Egypt and India, where Britain still ruled, could not save the caliphate, and the Turks themselves were indifferent. After all, the caliphs had been powerless for a thousand years.

From 1924 on, the Grand National Assembly passed legislation closing down the Sufi orders and *madrasah*s, abolishing the *waqf*s and the position of the shaykh al-Islam, and replacing the Shari‘ah, even in the hitherto untouchable realm of family law, with a modified version of the Swiss Civil Code. Women, assured of equal rights with men in marriage, divorce, and the inheritance of property, also started to enter the higher schools and the professions, as well as shops, offices, and factories. Given the vote for the first time in 1934, Turkish women elected seventeen of their sex to the assembly the next year. The veil, which had begun to disappear in Istanbul and Smyrna before and during the war, was discarded (with Kemal's strong encouragement) during the 1920s.

Of great symbolic significance was a law prohibiting Turkish men from wearing fezzes or other brimless headgear. Muslim males had always worn turbans, skullcaps, *kufiyah*s, or other head coverings that would not interfere with prostrations during the performance of worship. In common speech, "putting on a hat" meant apostasy from Islam. But Kemal, addressing a crowd in one of the most conservative towns in Anatolia, wore a panama hat, poked fun at the traditional clothing of Turkish men and women, and announced that all males would henceforth have to wear the costumes of "civilized" peoples, including the hat. It is ironic that Turkish men fought harder to go on wearing the fez, imposed by Sultan Mahmud a mere century earlier, than to save the caliphate, started by Abu-Bakr in 632! However, what people wear often reflects how they live, the way they think, and what they value most highly. Within a few years, though, Turkish men and women dressed pretty much like Europeans.

Turkey faced west in other ways. The Ottoman financial calendar was replaced by the Gregorian, and clocks were set to European time, a change from the Muslim system by which the date advanced at sunset. Metric weights and measures replaced the customary Turkish ones, and the adoption of a formal day of rest (initially Friday, later Sunday) showed how Western the country had become. The call to worship and even Quran recitations were given in Turkish instead of Arabic. Even the reference in the constitution to Islam as Turkey's national religion was expunged in 1928.

One of the most drastic changes in Turkish culture was instituted at about the same time. Kemal announced that the Turkish language, hitherto written in an Arabic script ill-suited to its sounds and syntax, would henceforth use a modified Roman alphabet. Within three months all books, newspapers, street signs, school papers, and public documents had to be written in the new alphabet. Only 10 percent of the people had been literate under the old system; now it was their national duty to learn the new one and to teach it to their children, their neighbors, even to porters and boatmen (to use Kemal's own expression). Easier to learn and more nearly phonetic, the new alphabet speeded up the education of the Turks. The number of school pupils doubled between 1923 and 1938; and by 1970 the literacy rate climbed to 55 percent. Now it was easier for Turks to learn English, French, or other Western languages, but considerably harder to study Arabic or Persian, or even to read classics of Ottoman Turkish literature and poetry. The new Turkish Language Academy began replacing Arabic and Persian loanwords with neologisms based on Turkish roots. As in other Middle Eastern countries, English and French words came into the language, producing such terms as *dizel* ("diesel"), *frak* ("frock coat"), *gol* ("goal," as in soccer), *gazöz* ("soda," from the French *limonade gaseuse*), *kuvafür* ("coiffeur"), *otobüs* ("bus"), and *taksi* ("taxi").

Another symbol of westernization, which has since proved to be a convenience, was the law passed by the Assembly in 1934 requiring all Turks to take family names. As society became more mobile and the need for accurate record keeping increased, the customary use of given names, sometimes but not always combined with a patronymic ("Mehmet son of Ali"), military titles, physical characteristics, occupations, or places of origin, produced widespread confusion. Under the new law Ismet, Kemal's representative at Lausanne, took the surname Inonu, the site of two of his victories over the Greeks. Mustafa Kemal became Ataturk ("Father Turk"). Old titles, such as pasha, bey, and efendi, were dropped. Kemal

Ataturk even gave up the title of *ghazi* once used by Ottoman sultans and bestowed on him by a grateful Assembly following his victory over the Greeks. Henceforth men had to prefix their names with Bay, comparable to "Mr." Women were to use Bayan in place of the traditional *hanum*. But old practices die hard, and it was many years before the Istanbul telephone directory went over to alphabetizing by the new family names.

Since Kemal Ataturk launched a comprehensive program of westernization, we would expect some emphasis on economic development. Actually, he seems to have been less interested in economic reform than, say, Mehmet Ali or some of his successors. But Turkey did move toward industrialization, as factories sprang up in the large cities and around the coal-mining region where the Black Sea meets the Bosporus. Kemal was among the first non-Communist leaders of Asia to call for state ownership and control of the major means of production. Hoping to speed up modernization, he brought in Soviet economists to draft Turkey's first five-year plan. During the 1930s the Turkish government set up a textile manufacturing complex, a steel mill, and various factories for the production of cement, glass, and paper. Agricultural reforms limped in a land of 50,000 villages, some of them linked by a single donkey path to the rest of the world; but agricultural training institutes, extension agents, rural centers for health and adult education, and model farms did lead to some improvement.

Ataturk once summed up his program in six principles, which were later incorporated into the constitution of the republic. Often called the "six arrows" (from the symbol of Ataturk's Republican People's party), they are republicanism, nationalism, populism, statism, secularism, and reformism. Republicanism means selection of the leadership by and from the citizenry, as opposed to the hereditary system of the Ottoman Empire and other dynastic states. Nationalism calls on the Turks to devote themselves to the needs and interests of the Turkish nation, rejecting special ties to other Muslims or to foreign ideologies. Populism means that the government belongs to the Turkish people, working together for the common good, without distinction of rank, class, or sex. Statism, or state capitalism, requires the government to direct and take part in the country's economic development. Secularism amounts to the removal of religious controls over Turkey's politics, society, and culture. Reformism (originally "revolutionism") is the ongoing commitment of the Turkish government and people to rapid but peaceful modernization.

Kemal Ataturk was a westernizing reformer, but above all he was a Turkish nationalist. The linguistic reforms simplified Turkish, bringing the written language closer to what the Turkish people spoke. Moving the capital from Istanbul to Ankara was a rejection of the cosmopolitan

Byzantine and Ottoman past in favor of an Anatolian Turkish future. The study of history now stressed the Turks, from their misty origins on the Asiatic steppes up to their triumph over the Greeks, instead of the Islamic caliphate rooted in the Arabic and Persian cultures. Even westernization could be justified in terms of Turkish nationalism; look at what Western civilization owed to the Turks. According to the "sun language theory," an idea popular in the 1930s but since discredited, all languages went back to Turkish, whose word for "sun" was supposed to have been the sound uttered in awe by the first articulate cave dweller. If the Turks had developed the earliest language, anything they now took from other cultures was only a fair exchange. In addition, the schools, armed forces, rail and motor roads, newspapers, and radio broadcasting all reinforced the Turkish sense of nationhood.

Assessment of Kemalism

The greatest tribute that the Turkish nation has paid to Kemal Ataturk since his death in November 1938 is its continuation of the Kemalist program. To be sure, some of the extremes have been moderated. The Quran and the call to worship may now be chanted in Arabic, the Sufi orders have been allowed to resume their activities, and many Turks flock to the mosques on Fridays. But industrial and agricultural growth have gone ahead at a rate even faster than during Kemal's lifetime. To many Turks, their country is European, not Middle Eastern. Turkey has joined the Western alliance systems (such as NATO), the Organization for Economic Cooperation and Development, and the Council of Europe. It hopes to become a full-fledged member of the European Common Market by 1995, at which time its per-capita income should equal that of Italy in 1970. Although Turkey stayed out of World War II, it has built up its military might under U.S. tutelage since then and acquitted itself well fighting against the Communists in Korea. Because of communal strife between Greeks and Turks living in Cyprus, the Turkish armed forces also intervened there in 1974, and since then the Turks have controlled the northern third of the island. Military experts rate Turkey's armed might second only to Israel's among the countries of the Middle East.

Perhaps because Ataturk's methods and accomplishments have been so highly praised, we should put them into a broader perspective. First of all, Ataturk's program was a link in the chain of westernizing reforms from Selim's Nizam-i-Jedid, to Mahmud II, the Tanzimat era, Abdulhamid, and finally the CUP. His ideas can also be traced back to Ziya Gokalp, the Young Turks, and the New Ottomans. His ambivalent position between dictatorship and democracy is reminiscent of earlier experiments in constitutional government. After his death, Turkey's politics evolved toward a two-party system, as the Demokrat party rose to challenge the Republican People's party and took over power peacefully after a free election in 1950. Basing its power on the support of peasants, small businessmen, and pious Muslims, the Demokrat party grew so strong that it alarmed the army officers, who overthrew the government in 1960. Turkey's politics in recent years have been quite turbulent. No party has commanded a majority in most of the quadrennial parliamentary elections, and the army has frequently threatened to intervene. Marxist and neo-Muslim parties have gained in strength, although power continues to pass between the Republican People's party, now headed by Bulent Ecevit, and the Justice party (successor to the outlawed Demokrat party), led by Suleyman Demirel.

Ataturk's legacy has one main problem. His westernizing program has split the mind of Turkey between acceptance of modern secularism and a desire to return to the principles and institutions of Islam. Turkey is a land of two cultures that clash occasionally and coexist uneasily: trucks and oxcarts, factories and mosques, technical schools and Sufi orders, scientists and ulama. Extremist parties of the Marxist Left and the Muslim Right compete so violently that some Turkish universities have been paralyzed by student demonstrations. In time, perhaps, the two sides will come together on a moderate position. Until then, Turkey's politics will remain troubled.

THE RISE OF SAUDI ARABIA

Nowadays most people think of Saudi Arabia as a big, rich, and very influential country. This may be true today, but up to around 1945 it was poor and, in Western terms, "backward." The homeland of Islam and Arabism had been a backwater of history since the days of the High Caliphate. If Istanbul was in the vanguard of westernizing reform movements up to this century, few parts of the Middle East could have opposed them more than central Arabia, especially the area known as Najd. Its location helped. Situated among desert hills, with no outlet to any sea, Najd offered no attractions to foreign traders or Western imperialism. Most of its people were bedouin; a few small towns contained Arab merchants and ulama. So far in this book, I have hardly mentioned the area, except in connection with the rise of a puritanical Muslim sect known as the Wahhabis, whose beliefs still prevail in today's Kingdom of Saudi Arabia.

Historical Background

The story begins in the mid-eighteenth century, when a wandering young scholar, Muhammad ibn Abd al-Wahhab (d. 1787), became a Hanbali, or a supporter of the strictest of the four canonical rites of Sunni Muslim law. The Hanbalis had long attacked practices that had crept into Islam (often from older Middle Eastern religions), such as worshipping saints, visiting their tombs, and venerating trees and wells. When this Muhammad began preaching and writing in his hometown about cleansing Islam of these practices, his own relatives drove him out. He fled to a nearby village and converted his protector, Muhammad ibn Saud, to his puritanical doctrines. Thus leagued together, the two Muhammads set out to convert the neighboring Arab tribes, with the son of Abd al-Wahhab as spiritual guide (hence our use of "Wahhabi" for the sect) and the son of Saud as political and military leader (which is why we speak of the Saudi dynasty). In the late eighteenth and early nineteenth centuries, the Saudis managed to spread their rule and the Wahhabi doctrines to most of northern Arabia. They even took Mecca and Medina, destroying or damaging many of the tombs and other shrines associated with the Muslim hajj. You may remember how the Ottoman sultan sent Mehmet Ali's army to the Hijaz to drive away these Wahhabis, whose threat to the Ottomans in this sensitive area could undermine their legitimacy in other Muslim lands as well. Eventually, the Saudi-Wahhabi combine was defeated, and the Turks garrisoned the Hijaz. While Wahhabi doctrines continued to spread to the Persian Gulf and even to India, the Saudi family was confined during the nineteenth century to central and eastern Arabia. Even there it contended for power with the Rashid dynasty, which enjoyed Ottoman backing and seemed by 1900 to have gained the upper hand.

The man commonly called Ibn Saud (properly Abd al-Aziz ibn Abd al-Rahman) was born in Riyadh, the Saudis' home base, in 1880. When he was ten, the Rashids drove his family out, and it took refuge near the Empty Quarter among the Bani Murrah, a tribe so poor and primitive that they are called the bedouin's bedouin. From these desert desperadoes Ibn Saud learned to ride and shoot expertly and to deal with other Arab tribesmen. Later the Saudis were given asylum by the shaykh of Kuwait, a fishing port near the head of the Persian Gulf. There Ibn Saud started learning about the outsiders who now coveted the Arabian peninsula, one of the few areas not already carved up by the great European empires. Actually, Arabia in 1900 had a patchwork of local and foreign rulers, too many to be listed in a concise history. Suffice it to say that Sultan Abdulhamid was extending Ottoman rule into lands hitherto autonomous, such as the coastal region east of Najd called al-Hasa. Some of the Arab shaykhs along the gulf had made treaties with the British, giving them control over their defense and foreign relations. But young Ibn Saud craved neither protection by foreign Christians nor dependency on the

Ottomans who, to the Wahhabis, were backsliders from Islam; he wanted to retake Riyadh from the Rashid tribe. Heading a small band of loyal Wahhabis, he successfully recaptured his ancestral capital in 1902. This was the first episode in an epic that has been told time and again by Saudi and foreign chroniclers.

The Emergence of Saudi Arabia

This epic describes the unification of most of the tribes and petty states ("emirates") of the Arabian peninsula under Ibn Saud. This process involved numerous bedouin raids, battles, and wars between the Saudi-Wahhabi combine and other contenders for power. At first, it meant defeating the Ottoman-backed Rashid dynasty; after 1906 the Saudis started winning control over the tribes of central and eastern Arabia. Few outsiders noticed these struggles until Ibn Saud's followers challenged the kingdom of the Hijaz, the state headed by Emir Husayn and discussed in the preceding chapter. When he conquered the Hijaz and took control of Islam's holy cities between 1924 and 1926, Ibn Saud became the most respected leader in Arabia, or indeed the whole Arab world. How different Arab history would have been if Britain had heeded its India Office during World War I and backed Ibn Saud of Riyadh instead of the Hashimites of Mecca!

What caused his victory? First, Ibn Saud believed in Wahhabi Islam and enforced its rules strictly among his followers. Thus religious belief supplemented his bedouins' love of battle and booty. His own convictions, combined with his physical courage and personal magnetism, led thousands to love and obey him. His skills were marital as well as martial; both his victories and his marriages were more than you could count. Most of Ibn Saud's nuptials served to cement peace with the tribes he had subdued. In case you wonder how he stayed within the Quranic limit of four, he divorced most of the wives he married and returned them, loaded with gifts, to their guardians. Yet it was said that any woman who married Ibn Saud, however briefly, loved him for the rest of her life. I am not sure who could verify this—or how!

Another way Ibn Saud controlled the tribes was to weld them into a religious organization called the Ikhwan ("brothers"). These Ikhwan were persuaded to give up camel nomadism for settled agriculture. Although many of these bedouin proved ill-suited for pushing a plow, their settlement in farming villages made them easier to control, more willing to heed the teachings of Wahhabi ulama from Riyadh, and better disciplined when Ibn Saud needed their military services. Without the Ikhwan, the Saudis could not have united most of Arabia within a generation.

But some parts of Arabia never came under their control. Like Kemal

Ataturk, Ibn Saud knew his political limits. Once he had taken Asir, the little kingdom between the Hijaz and the Yemen, thus creating the kingdom of Saudi Arabia in 1932, there were no further conquests. After a brief war two years later, Ibn Saud relinquished all claims to the imamate of Yemen. This magnanimity made sense, for the Yemeni highlanders were Zaydi Shi'ites who would have fought against Wahhabi (i.e., Hanbali Sunni) rule by the Saudis. He also disbanded the Ikhwan in 1930 after they took to raiding tribes in Iraq. Generally speaking, the Saudis did not tamper with Arab rulers under British protection, such as Abdallah of Transjordan, the shaykh (later emir) of Kuwait, other shaykhs along the gulf coast, the sultan of Muscat and Oman, or the rulers of southern Arabia east of the colony of Aden. By the 1940s Ibn Saud had become the Arabs' elder statesman. Even his Hashimite rivals in Transjordan and Iraq, while they resented his having expelled their father from the Hijaz, came to respect Ibn Saud as a leader.

Oil Discoveries and Their Effects on the Saudi Kingdom

Because of the present state of the world, it is easy to forget that Ibn Saud and his kingdom were extremely poor for most of his life. Najd was a sun-parched, mountainous land far from any sea, while the Persian Gulf provided only pearls and a little trade to al-Hasa, Asir had some upland areas suitable for farming, and the Hijaz provided a little income from the annual Muslim pilgrimage. The economy of Saudi Arabia as a whole depended mostly on the date palm and the camel up to the late 1930s. Several British companies had tried unsuccessfully to prospect for oil in various parts of the kingdom. There were some abandoned gold mines, and it was widely thought that Arabia contained other valuable minerals; but its harsh climate, rapacious bedouin, and Wahhabi fanaticism all daunted outside prospectors. So desperately poor was Ibn Saud that he once reportedly said, "If anyone were to offer a million pounds, he would be welcome to all the concessions he wanted in my country."

The man of the hour was an American whose surname you may recall from chapter 13, Charles Crane, the plumbing manufacturer and philanthropist who had been in the 1919 King-Crane Commission. After a sojourn in the Yemen, where he financed a successful search for minerals, Crane visited Ibn Saud in 1931. They discussed a similar quest in the Hijaz, hoping to find enough underground water to pipe it into Jiddah (the port town of Mecca). But Crane's mining engineer, Karl Twitchell, soon realized that neither water nor oil existed in economic quantities beneath the largely barren Hijaz. Two years later, though, Twitchell came back, this time to the eastern part of Saudi Arabia, in the service of an American firm, Standard Oil of California, which outbid a British representative of the

Iraq Petroleum Company for exploration rights. For a cash loan amounting to 50,000 gold sovereigns (about $250,000), plus an annual rent of 5,000 more, Ibn Saud gave the Americans a sixty-year concession to search for oil in al-Hasa, with preferential exploration rights in other parts of his kingdom. More loans would be made if oil were found in marketable quantities, plus a royalty of one gold sovereign ($5) for every five long tons (a "long ton" is roughly equal to 2240 pounds, or slightly more than one metric ton) of oil extracted from Saudi territory.

Five years of exploration and drilling followed before the Americans struck oil in 1938 at Jabal Dhahran and started sending barrels to the British refinery on the nearby island of Bahrain, already an oil-exporting country. Soon they were building their own refinery, storage tanks, and a loading dock on the Persian Gulf. Petroleum technicians, construction foremen, and equipment poured into Dhahran, which became a "Little America" complete with lawns, swimming pools, air-conditioned buildings, and a commissary where the Americans could buy the canned goods, chewing gum, and cigarettes they had known back home. By this time, the Texas Oil Company had joined Standard Oil of California in forming a subsidiary officially called the Arabian American Oil Company but almost always nicknamed "Aramco." Tanker shortages during World War II halted its operations for a time, but eventually Aramco started selling oil to American forces in the Pacific. Once the war was over, new oil exploration and discoveries raised Saudi output by leaps and bounds to 1.3 million barrels per day in 1960, 3.8 million in 1970, and 8.5 million in 1976. By then, the kingdom's annual oil revenues had topped $33 billion, and over a quarter of the world's proven reserves were thought to lie within Saudi territory.

When this century has ended and our children can write a more objective and synoptic account of these years, I hope they will see the development of Middle East oil as the most revolutionary change of our time. Karl Twitchell was surely no Karl Marx, but the result of his labors—amplified by Aramco's later geologists and explorers—drastically changed the economic, social, cultural, and moral life of the Saudi Arabs. No Middle Eastern people or country has been untouched by the shower of Saudi wealth. Its effects on the world economy will be discussed later, but let me say now that the Saudi government has become the most influential in the Arab world.

What is less well known is that Saudi Arabia had hardly any government in the modern sense during the reign of Ibn Saud. For most of this period, Saudi Arabia was "governed" in the sense that Ibn Saud had the personal charm and, if needed, the force to subdue (and collect tribute from) the bedouin tribes within his realm. Any money he received from the tribal shaykhs, the pilgrims, or Aramco went into his private treasury. It was used to maintain his palace, support his harem, increase his herds of Arabian horses and camels, or to make sumptuous gifts to his foreign visitors or to his subjects, each of whom had the right to go directly to Ibn Saud to vent his grievances and obtain justice. There was no formal cabinet; Ibn Saud talked matters over with his relatives and a few foreign advisers, but made his own decisions. There was no banking system; the gold sovereigns were stored in wooden chests. The laws were those of the Quran and of the *hadith*s approved by Hanbali ulama. Thieves had their hands chopped off. Murderers were beheaded. Disobedient tribes were fined or banished from their grazing lands. The Wahhabis forced all Saudi Muslims to pray five times a day, going from house to house to ensure compliance. Alcohol and tobacco were strictly forbidden to Muslims, as were Western clothes, movies, music, dancing, and even (for a while) radios and telephones.

Imagine, then, the effect of Little America in Dhahran, where foreign Aramco employees lived in ranch houses with their wives (who did not wear the veil), threw parties, did not pray five times daily, and opened their clinic and hospital to Saudi Arabs, many of whom had never seen a doctor before. How could God bless these alien Christians more than the Muslims who feared and worshipped Him? Imagine, too, what must have happened when Ibn Saud's sons and grandsons started going abroad on diplomatic or educational missions. Palaces sprang up around Riyadh in crude imitation of what the Saudis had seen in Paris, London, and New York. Camels gave way to Cadillacs, although it took time to develop a cadre of local mechanics to maintain and repair them.

Ibn Saud was totally unprepared for the sudden wealth that oil brought to his kingdom. Aging, lame, blind in one eye, he lived to see corruption and licentiousness spread among his courtiers and even some of his sons, deeply wounding his conscience and affronting his morals. He did not understand economics. When told that the price of food had outstripped the means of his subjects, he ordered Aramco to double the wages it paid to Saudi employees, only to see the inflation get worse. Politics also bewildered him. He was troubled by the divisions among his fellow Arab rulers during and after World War II. He felt betrayed by the Palestine policies of the countries he had trusted, Britain and America. When he met U.S. President Franklin Roosevelt in 1945, Ibn Saud asked why the Allies could not take away the homes and lands of the Germans in order to house the Jewish survivors of Hitler's atrocities, instead of punishing the Arabs of Palestine by calling for a Jewish state. Roosevelt promised not to act on the Palestine question (which I will discuss in chapter 16) without first consulting both Arabs and Jews. Six weeks later he died, and Truman ignored the promise. But Ibn Saud could not really punish the Americans for helping to create Israel when their company was pumping his oil, filling his coffers, training his subjects, and even building a railroad from Riyadh to the gulf. Besides, the Saudis loathed Soviet Communism even more.

Ibn Saud's Successors

Ibn Saud died quietly in his sleep in November 1953. The ablest of his sons was probably Faysal, but the princes and the ulama agreed that the succession should go to the oldest surviving son, Saud, a weaker figure. Within a few years Saud had managed to run up a debt of $300 million despite his government's rising income. The last straw was a sensational press story that Saud had bribed a Syrian minister to kill Gamal Abdel Nasser, at a time when Egypt's president was at the peak of his popularity in the Arab world. In 1958, a turbulent year in Arab politics, the Saudi princes agreed to turn all executive powers over to Faysal as prime minister. Six years later Saud was deposed and Faysal became king. Under Faysal the Saudi government became much better organized, with regular ministries, an annual budget, development plans, new roads, schools, and hospitals. As Saudi Arabia plunged headlong into modernity, King Faysal became as influential among Arab rulers and Muslim conservatives as ever his father had been. His oil politics and eventual fate will be covered later.

THE REGENERATION OF IRAN

Among the countries or culture areas we have studied so far, Iran is unique. Deserts and mountain ranges give Iran distinct boundaries, and yet it has been invaded many times. Usually it has absorbed its invaders, but the absorption process has led to a mosaic of tribal nomads and sedentary peasants with distinctive folkways. Persian is recognized as the national language, but many of the people speak variants of Turkish, Kurdish, or Arabic. Its religion is Islam, but Iranians (unlike their neighbors) have adhered to its Twelve-Imam Shi'ite branch since the sixteenth century. More often than not throughout history, Iran (or Persia) has been a distinct political entity, but we commonly describe it by the name of its ruling family during the time in question—and the dynasties that have ruled Iran are numerous indeed.

Historical Recapitulation

You probably remember that Iran's ruling family from the late eighteenth century was the Qajar dynasty. It was under the Qajars that the country shrank to what are now its recognized borders, losing the Caucasus mountains and parts of central Asia to Russia and giving up all claims to Afghanistan and what is now Pakistan. Tehran, a small town near the

Elburz mountains, became Iran's capital under the Qajars, and so it has remained ever since. Iranians do not have fond memories of the Qajar dynasty. Its Westernizing reforms lagged behind those of the Ottomans or Mehmet Ali. Its resistance to Russian imperialism was feeble. It encouraged commercial penetration and exploitation by British and other foreign entrepreneurs. Its Iranian subjects, led by their ulama (whom they call *mollah*s) and bazaar merchants, resisted political and economic subjection to these outsiders. This resistance has been called Muslim fanaticism (by nineteenth-century imperialists) or nationalism (by twentieth-century writers, including myself); no doubt religious and political feelings were mixed together. One result was the 1906 constitution, still (with some amendments) the legal basis of Iran's government, that set up a representative assembly, the Majlis, to limit the shah's power. It now can claim to be the oldest parliament in the Middle East.

Constitutionalism alone could not build a great nation. Unable to weld the various military units into one army, hamstrung by powerful and lawless tribes, lacking the means to collect enough taxes to support its expenses, Qajar government remained weak. Besides, Britain and Russia agreed in 1907 to create spheres of influence in Iran. Russian troops occupied the northern third of the country before and during World War I. Several armies controlled or influenced by the British held parts of the south, protecting the new wells, pipelines, and refinery of the Anglo-Persian Oil Company. During the war, a German officer named Wassmuss organized a rebel army in the area just north of the Persian Gulf. Elsewhere in central Iran, German agents incited acts of murder and sabotage against British or Russian consuls and businessmen. The 1917 Bolshevik Revolution reduced Russia's pressure for a while, as the new Communist regime gave up all the tsarist claims. After Germany's defeat in 1918, Britain remained the sole foreign power with imperialist designs on Iran.

The Apogee of British Power

In 1919 Britain seemed ready to take over Iran as it had most of the Arab countries. British imperial troops occupied Iraq; guarded most of the Arab shaykhdoms, emirates, and sultanates along the gulf; entered some of the Caucasus republics formed when the Turks pulled out; and were aiding White Russian forces against the Bolsheviks. Britain offered the Qajars an Anglo-Persian treaty that would have turned Iran into a veiled British protectorate (rather like Egypt under the last khedives). But popular opposition to the treaty was so strong that the Majlis never ratified it, and it eventually became a dead letter.

As I have tried to show elsewhere, 1919-1920 now seems to have been the high tide of British power in the Muslim world. The Kemalist revolt in Turkey, nationalist uprisings in Egypt and Iraq, Arab riots in Palestine, Britain's reluctance to protect the new Caucasian republics (Azerbaijan, Armenia, and Georgia), and the failure of various Allied efforts to crush the Bolsheviks elsewhere, all taken together, mark a turning point in British policy. Unwilling to spend large sums or to commit masses of soldiers (who were impatient for demobilization anyway), London started cutting back its foreign commitments.

But Iran's integrity was still threatened. Separatist revolts broke out in 1920 in the northern provinces of Gilan and Azerbaijan, and the Bolsheviks landed troops to help them. British troops remained in many areas as instructors for various Iranian army units, but they were widely disliked. In an attempt to make both sides withdraw, the Iranian government negotiated a friendship treaty with the USSR early in 1921. The Soviets pulled out their troops, renounced all extraterritorial privileges, cancelled debts, and turned over all Russian properties in Iran. However, there was one fateful article that allowed the USSR to send in troops whenever it felt threatened by the presence of another foreign army on Iranian soil. Although the Soviets would invoke this clause on later occasions, it helped Iran at the time to ease out the British.

The Rise of Reza Shah

Five days before the signing of the Soviet-Iranian pact, an officer in the Persian Cossack Brigade (an Iranian force created and largely led by Russians) helped to overthrow the government in Tehran. This officer, Reza Khan, born in 1878 in the mountainous province of Mazandaran, had risen to prominence within the brigade during the tumultuous period after the war. Having helped to overthrow the brigade's pro-Bolshevik commander, Reza had taken charge of its infantry regiment and organized a secret society of Iranian officers opposed to both British and Russian control. A general mutiny of the Iranian cossacks resulted in the dismissal of all remaining Russian officers in the brigade. Reza, seeing how easily he had gained control of Iran's strongest military force, was encouraged to enter the wider arena. Working for an idealistic young journalist, Sayyid Ziya ud-Din Tabatabai, Reza led his cossacks into Tehran and overthrew the ministry on 21 February 1921. Sayyid Ziya became the new prime minister and Reza the commander-in-chief of the Iranian army. A vigorous and comprehensive reform program began, but Ziya stayed in power for only three months. Opposed by many of his own ministers and probably by Reza himself, he resigned and left the country.

Iran's politics lapsed into their usual state of disorder. A new session of the Majlis opened with demands for financial and administrative reform.

The last of the Qajars, Ahmad Shah, kept trying to leave the country. The old politicians were divided and dispirited. Reza Khan, who now became war minister, seemed to be the real power behind the throne, but he concentrated on bringing Iran together by reestablishing public security, consolidating the various armies, and suppressing rebel tribesmen, Communists, and other dissidents. Following an attempt on his life in 1923, Reza arrested the prime minister and forced Ahmad Shah to appoint him instead. The shah then left for Europe, never to return.

At this point, Reza Khan intended to declare Iran a republic, following Kemal's example in Turkey, but the Shi'ite ulama mobilized opposition throughout the country. After threatening to resign, Reza finally gave in. He also evened the score by replacing the cabinet, putting in ministers who were both more competent and also more compliant with his own wishes. He then went off on an expedition to suppress a tribal rebellion in Khuzistan, followed by a pilgrimage to the Shi'ite shrines at Najaf and Karbala to placate the ulama. He returned to Tehran determined to strengthen his hold on the government. While the Majlis equivocated, Reza acted on his own to start some major reforms. One of these now stands as his greatest achievement—the Trans-Iranian Railway, which connects the Caspian Sea with the Persian Gulf. Aside from being an engineering marvel, this rail line is remarkable for having been financed without any foreign loans. The costs of construction were met by special taxes on sugar and tea, two staples of the Iranian diet.

In a spirit of nationalism, the Majlis in 1925 adopted the old Persian solar calendar in place of the Muslim lunar one, and Reza took the surname "Pahlavi," the name of the pre-Islamic Persian language. The next step was for the Majlis to depose Ahmad Shah Qajar, abolishing his dynasty, and to proclaim Reza Khan as Iran's new ruler. He officially became Reza Shah in December 1925 and placed the new Pahlavi crown on his own head in a formal ceremony a few months later.

The Reforms of Reza Shah

Reza Shah was the regenerator of Iran just as Kemal, whom he greatly admired, was the father of modern Turkey. Because of this, the two leaders have often been compared, usually to Reza's disadvantage. But conditions facing the two nationalist reformers were not quite the same. Kemal had become famous as a successful general within a defeated army, while Reza was known to just a handful of officers when he led the 1921 coup. Turkey was heir to over a century of reform efforts; it had a cadre of educated officials and officers to carry out Kemal's programs. Iran had been cut off from the West, except for the dubious blessing of having Russia as a neighbor. Kemal expressed the disillusionment toward Islam felt by many

Turks and could equate westernization with civilization. Few Turks felt any affinity toward their pre-Islamic heritage in the far-off Asian steppes. Reza could make no such break with the Persian past. The popular influence of the Shi'i *mujtahid*s and *mollah*s was strong. Even when he could fight this Muslim clerical influence, Reza also knew that Iran's pre-Islamic heritage was alive and meaningful to his subjects. This tie to the past could help his reform program, as Sasanid monuments were spruced up, the Zoroastrian religion won official toleration, and the Persian language was purged of some of its Arabic words. These symbolic changes strengthened national pride and widened the gap between Iran and the Arab world.

One of Reza Shah's ablest subordinates, General Hassan Arfa, summarized his reforms under four convenient headings: (1) liberation from foreign political and economic domination, (2) establishment of internal security and centralized government, (3) administrative reforms and economic progress, and (4) social reforms and cultural progress.

Liberation from foreign domination entailed more than getting rid of British and Russian troops; it also meant replacing British with Iranian control along the gulf coast, taking charge of the banking and currency system and the telegraph lines, and gaining the right to try foreigners accused of crimes and to fix and collect the customs duties on imports. Reza Shah succeeded in implementing almost every reform, but when he cancelled the Anglo-Persian Oil Company's concession, Britain took the issue to the League of Nations. As a result, the company finally agreed to pay higher royalties to the Iranian government in exchange for a thirty-year extension of its concession. Many Iranians later criticized Reza Shah for this extension; some even accused him (without proof) of having been persuaded by British bribes.

The strengthening of Iran's national government could only be achieved at the expense of the nomadic tribes. Many were forced to settle down, their chiefs in some cases being put under house arrest. Those allowed to stay nomadic often transported their flocks under police escort. The armed forces were extensively reorganized, with vastly improved munitions, weapons, training, barracks, and health care facilities. All security forces were placed under central control, and a rudimentary political police—the precursor of SAVAK—was set up.

Iran gradually acquired a civil service, European-style law codes and courts, a state budget, and a national system for registering births, marriages, land-transfers, and deaths. Roads suitable for cars and trucks, almost nonexistent in 1921, crisscrossed the country by 1941. Often accused of stealing the peasants' lands to increase his own holdings, Reza Shah claimed that he wanted his estates to serve as model farms to discover and teach new agricultural methods. Iran also acquired some modern factories and imposing public buildings during his reign, but their effect on morale probably outweighed their material benefit to the nation.

Social reform to Reza Shah meant education. Schooling increased drastically at all levels. Although most histories mention among his major achievements the opening of the University of Tehran in 1935, Reza Shah was most interested in the basic education of peasants and workers. Night schools became common, and the army turned into a vast training program. The officers were held responsible for teaching their soldiers to read, write, and do basic arithmetic. If any soldier did not gain these skills by the end of his two-year stint, then his unit commander would not get promoted. Sports and games had existed in traditional Iran, though many *mollah*s frowned on them, but Reza Shah made cults out of physical fitness and athletic contests. He did not, like Ataturk, attack organized Islam directly, but he sometimes nettled the *mollah*s by drinking beer or wine in public, and he did insist that all men who wore the garb of ulama prove their right to do so by passing examinations. He followed Ataturk's example by imposing an "international" costume on all Iranian men and surpassed him by forbidding women to veil their faces. This reform deeply offended Muslim feelings, just as some Westerners would be shocked if women of all ages were forced to go topless in public. Muslim opposition barred what I think would have been a sounder and more lasting reform: the romanization of the Persian alphabet.

The Downfall of Reza Shah

Although Reza Shah really tried to reform Iran, he was often disappointed by the results. An impatient man, he never could delegate work. Trying to reduce Iran's dependence on Britain, he brought in advisers from other countries. When an American mission improved Iran's fiscal administration but failed to attract U.S. investors, Reza made the director resign, then phased out his subordinates. The U.S. government did not step in, much to the Iranians' amazement. Germany was more active. An able German director built up the National Bank of Iran in the early 1930s. After Hitler took power, German businessmen and advisers flocked to Iran. Reza and many of his subjects were flattered by Nazi racial theories, which considered Iran the original Aryan nation. After World War II began and Nazi forces overran most of Europe, the British came to distrust Germany's presence in Iran. In neighboring Iraq some Arab nationalist officers seized control in 1941. Suspecting them of favoring the Nazis, Britain moved in to install a pro-British cabinet. So, when Hitler turned suddenly on the USSR that June, both British and Russian troops occupied Iran. Once again Iran's independence was violated. Unwilling to rule under a military occupation that threatened to undo twenty years' work, Reza Shah abdicated in favor of his son, Mohammad, and went into exile. He died three years later.

Modern Iran

When he succeeded his father, Mohammad Reza Shah Pahlavi seemed to be no more than a Western protégé. After World War II, the USSR tried to set up Communist republics in northern Iran, but withdrew its troops in 1946 under United Nations pressure. The Communists then played on the rising dissatisfaction of the workers with the Anglo-Iranian Oil Company. Iranian nationalists won control of the Majlis, electing Mohammad Mosaddiq as prime minister. Because it nationalized the AIOC, Mosaddiq's government became highly popular at home, but it was overthrown in 1953 by a military coup. For the next quarter century, the shah ruled Iran as a dictator. Skyrocketing oil revenues enabled the government to build up its schools, industries, and armed forces. The shah's "White Revolution" promised changes in landownership, rural development, education, and women's rights beyond his father's wildest dreams.

The shah also inherited his father's authoritarianism. When his reforms failed to meet his subjects' expectations, he fell back on propaganda, censorship, and his secret police to stay in power. Although successive U.S. governments backed him as a bulwark against Communism, many Americans questioned the shah's commitment to human rights. Meanwhile, Iranian students abroad and ulama at home got up a strong opposition. They decried the erosion of Muslim values, the widening gap between rich and poor, the billions spent on arms, the failure of agrarian reform, and especially the oppressive regime. The shah's authority waned during 1978. When he finally left Iran in January 1979, his caretaker government soon disintegrated in the face of mass demonstrations and army defections. The revolution had been inspired by a leading Shi'i *mujtahid*, Ayatollah Ruhollah Khomeini, long exiled for his consistent opposition to the shah. Khomeini returned to Tehran and received huge demonstrations of popular support, but many feared that the army would seize the government and set off a civil war. Even after the ayatollah's forces took over, clashes between Muslims and Marxists continued. It was easier to destroy the old regime than to build an Islamic republic.

CONCLUSION

Three Middle eastern countries weathered the period between the two world wars—the high point of Western control over the area—without becoming colonies, protectorates, or mandates. Each country established the borders that it has had ever since. Each government tightened its hold over groups that had checked the power of previous rulers. Personal income increased, schools proliferated, and public health improved.

These were not democratic regimes. In each case, the agent for change was a military leader whose successes in war won him the respect and obedience of his subjects. Other Middle Eastern countries were quick to learn from them. Army officers have become the greatest force for modernization throughout the Middle East. Since efficiency is essential in military operations, it is natural for commanders to apply the same standards and employ the same methods to modernize their countries. Nationalistic leaders can persuade usually recalcitrant subjects to make sacrifices for the common good. But how far will they go? And what if conditions change, as has happened (thanks to oil) in Saudi Arabia and Iran?

The men we have studied raise other questions. Can modernization be sustained without a set of shared values between those who order and those who obey? Kemal Ataturk saw Islam as a barrier to progress and tried to reduce its influence, but Turkish nationalism has not yet replaced Islam in the hearts and minds of many Turks. Divided almost evenly between westernizers and Muslim traditionalists, modern Turkey drifts without the rudder of an ideological consensus. Ibn Saud's devotion to Islam united a disparate band of tribes under his rule, but his puritanical values did not help him cope with the innovations that flooded his country as a result of the oil revenues, and he died a bitterly disillusioned man. Reza Shah was ambivalent about Islam, but his reform program built up a westernized elite at the expense of Iran's Muslim leadership. Rampant individualism remains part of Iran's political culture; and so, having developed neither a new Muslim nor a strong nationalist consensus, an authoritarian shah stifled democracy and freedom in order to impose his revolution from above.

Some day, I hope, a synthesis will be achieved between Islam as a system of beliefs and behavioral norms and the values of a technical or industrialized society. Until this happens, I believe that authoritarian leaders will be, as they have been, the main agents of change in independent Middle Eastern countries.

15

Egypt: The Struggle for Independence

For at least the past century, Egypt has loomed large in any discussion about Middle Eastern politics, whether that country was acting or acted upon. One reason for this is the Suez Canal, so important strategically and economically to anyone who has wanted to be a great power. Another is Egypt's position in the vanguard of westernizing reform, going back to the time of Napoleon and Mehmet Ali. In modern times Egypt has also been, though not always willingly, the political and cultural bellwether of the Arab countries. The Egyptian struggle for independence was the longest and the most complicated of any country in the Arab world. This could be because, as Napoleon once said, "Egypt is the world's most important country." For centuries, Egypt was valued by foreign powers, as an object to be seized and held, as a symbol of imperial might, as a means of influencing the rest of the Arab world, or as a stepping-stone to Asia or the Mediterranean Sea; but never as Egypt.

What about the Egyptians themselves? Rather than actors, they had long been people acted upon. With centuries of experience as a doormat for outside invaders, oppressors, and exploiters, it is small wonder that some Egyptians distrusted all foreigners living or traveling within the country. After all, no Egyptian ruled Egypt from the time of the pharaohs to the fall of Faruq in 1952. Even the ruling aristocracy was mostly foreign, as expressed in a popular proverb: *"Bilad Misr khayruha li-ghayriha"* (In the land of Egypt what is good belongs to others).

BRITAIN'S ROLE IN EGYPT

Heroes come and go, villains appear and disappear in most political dramas. But in Egypt's struggle for independence the main antagonist for seventy-five years was Britain. By rights, Egypt was an autonomous province of the Ottoman Empire from 1841 to 1914. In reality, as a land under military occupation from 1882 on, Egypt was a British colony or protectorate in all but name. Important decisions about Egypt's administration were being made in London, not Istanbul, or (if locally) in the British Agency on the banks of the Nile, not in the khedive's palace a mile (actually about two kilometers) east in downtown Cairo. The ministers were puppets in the hands of their British advisers. Both the occupier and the occupied knew that theirs was a power relationship, with Britain dominant and Egypt either passive or protesting, although diplomatic niceties were maintained up to World War I.

Then, when the Ottoman Empire went to war against the Allies in November 1914, Britain had to bite the bullet. If holding Egypt was essential to the survival of the British Empire (as it surely was in 1914, with hundreds of troop ships carrying Indians, Australians, and New Zealanders through the Suez Canal to European war theaters), then the Turkish tie was an anomaly. Britain cut it decisively in December. No longer an Ottoman province, Egypt became a British protectorate. The change was no more legal than Germany's occupation of Belgium that August. It was certainly not approved by the Ottoman government, ratified by the Egyptian ministers, or accepted by the newly formed Legislative Assembly, which was adjourned indefinitely. Khedive Abbas, already barred from returning to Egypt by Britain's ambassador in Istanbul, was now accused of having thrown in his lot with the Turks. In reality he had fled to neutral Switzerland to get away from them, but the British deposed him anyway. In Abbas's place they appointed a pliable uncle, Husayn Kamil (1914-1917), who was given the title of "sultan" to underscore the break with the Ottoman Empire. The prime minister, Husayn Rushdi, stayed in office, believing Egypt would get its independence once the war ended. Britain's chief representative became "high commissioner for Egypt and the Sudan," and his office came to be called the "Residency." The Egyptian people accepted the changes passively, if a bit sullenly. Many hoped the Turks and Germans would win the war anyway.

Anglo-Egyptian Relations: An Overview

As you know, they lost. The period from 1914 to 1956 has been called by modern historian Elizabeth Monroe "Britain's moment in the Middle East." Since that period still looms large in the memories of most older Egyptians and Europeans, it seems like a long time span. Actually it was shorter than, say, that of Mongol domination in Iran. As long as the British were the top power in the area, the main drama was their relationship with Egypt, which was rarely an easy one. "Egypt and England are like an old married couple," wrote a Frenchman in the 1930s. "They may quarrel from time to time, but they always make up in the end." Well, eventually they would get a divorce, but the comparison is still apt. A marriage can be built on many forces besides love. One common basis is power. One partner makes the decisions; the other goes along, either out of self-abnegation or stark necessity. Think of the domineering husband and the submissive wife in Ibsen's play *A Doll's House*. Britain, like Torvald, managed everything; while Egypt, in Nora's role, cajoled and intrigued to get its way. Eventually Britain's power declined, and Egypt, never willingly obedient, found ways to topple its authority. The protectorate gave way in 1922 to a unilateral declaration of Egypt's independence, limited by four reserved points. Then the two sides agreed in 1936 to formalize their relationship in a treaty, of which Egypt soon repented. Finally, after a very bitter quarrel, they made a new agreement in 1954 terminating Britain's occupation of Egypt in 1956. Even this chapter had a sad sequel in the Anglo-French invasion of Suez in late October of that year. Throughout this period, each British concession was hedged with restrictions; each Egyptian demand went far beyond what any British government would accept. It must have been a very unhappy marriage.

I can offer several explanations for this sad state of affairs. First of all, the British stayed in Egypt not out of interest in the country or its people, but because it was a stepping-stone to India, or to the oil fields of Arabia and Iran, or a base in the struggle against the kaiser, the Nazis, or the Communists. The Egyptians knew this and felt it deeply. Besides, the British mostly disliked them. It is hard to prove this feeling objectively, but it shows through the diplomatic reports, the social arrangements, and even the fiction of the age. As seen through British eyes, the Egyptian was a portly parody of a petty French official, a boastful coward, a turbaned Muslim fanatic, a noisy agitator incapable of appreciating all the British had done for his country, or a "wog" (for "wily Oriental gentleman") selling dirty postcards in the bazaar. The Egyptians saw the British as coldhearted, exclusive (it was a sore point that, for many years, the only Egyptians who could get into the posh Gezira Sporting Club in Cairo were servants), mercenary, and power mad. Egyptians tended to prefer the French or, for that matter, the Americans but not (as is so often alleged) the Germans or the Russians. Curiously, the British could relate well to almost any other people within the Arab world, especially the bedouin. Perhaps France's influence on Egyptian schools and culture made the difference, or the greater skill of desert Arabs at horseback riding, shooting, and other sports of interest to upper class Englishmen. I do suspect, though, that it was the fact that the English were masters, while the Egyptians (unlike other Arabs) were used to being servants, that initially set the relationship between the two peoples. Neither side adjusted easily to the way the other was changing.

Conditions during World War I

The quality of British administration in Egypt, top-notch up to 1914, declined during World War I. Many of the best Englishmen either left or were called home for military service, never to return. Hordes of new officials and officers poured into Egypt, as the country turned into a vast army camp for the Allies, but the new men governed less ably. Because they were less well educated and sensitive as to how to deal with Muslims, the new men often gave offense and failed to notice the real needs of the country. So much attention had to be paid to the war against Ottoman Turkey, especially the unsuccessful Dardanelles campaign of 1915 and the Egyptian Expeditionary Force that conquered Palestine and coastal Syria in 1917-1918, that critical problems were neglected within Egypt, which had been put under martial law for the duration of the war.

Cairo and Alexandria were becoming overcrowded. Food scarcities drove up prices in the cities and other places of troop concentration, so the Egyptian government restricted the acreage that could be used to grow cotton, a very lucrative wartime crop for rural landlords and peasants. After having promised not to demand any sacrifices from the Egyptian people during the war, the British found it necessary to requisition food supplies, draft animals, and even recruit peasant labor during the Palestine campaign. "Woe on us, Wingate," sang the peasants in 1918, referring to McMahon's replacement as British high commissioner,

> who has carried off corn,
> carried off cotton,
> carried off camels,
> carried off children,
> leaving only our lives.
> For the love of God, now let us alone.

As the British grew in numbers, they lost contact with the country. The judicial adviser, an able and usually sympathetic Englishman, drew up a note on constitutional reform that would have given Egypt a bicameral legislature, with a powerful upper house made up of Egyptian ministers, British advisers, and representatives of the foreign communities, who already dominated the country's economic life. Even though it would have got rid of the capitulations, no patriotic Egyptian could have supported such a constitution, which would have tightened the foreign grip on his own country. When the plan got out in November 1918, it fueled the flames of discontent among the upper class Egyptians. Better to rule ourselves badly, was the nationalist sentiment, than to be governed well by foreigners.

The Anti-British Revolution of 1919

It was symptomatic of this loss of contact that no Englishman foresaw a revival of Egyptian nationalism once the war ended. As you may recall, the National party had declined. The followers of Ahmad Lutfi al-Sayyid, mostly landowners and intellectuals, were few in number, though influential in the Legislative Assembly that met for the first time in 1914. One of these followers was Sa'd Zaghlul, the elected vice-president of that representative body, who then emerged as a prominent critic of the government and its British advisers. Sa'd Zaghlul had an interesting background. Son of a prosperous peasant, he was educated in the 1870s at al-Azhar University, where he fell under the influence of Jamal al-Din al-Afghani. He then edited the government journal and supported the Urabi revolution of 1881-1882. Shortly after the British suppressed it, he got arrested for having joined a terrorist group plotting to kill Khedive Tawfiq. After his release from jail, Sa'd studied law in France, became a judge, and married the prime minister's daughter. This brought him into contact with Lord Cromer, who appointed him as minister of education during the strong nationalist reaction against the 1906 Dinshaway incident. In a public speech just before he left Egypt in 1907, Cromer described Sa'd Zaghlul in the following terms: "He possesses all the qualities necessary to serve his country. He is honest, he is capable, he has the courage of his convictions, he has been abused by many of the less worthy of his own countrymen. These are high qualifications. He should go far."

Sa'd Zaghlul did go far, but not in the way Cromer had hoped. His progress through the Egyptian cabinet was thwarted by his quarrels with both Khedive Abbas and Lord Kitchener, so he quit the government in 1912. Many Englishmen would later regret not having continued to co-opt Sa'd to serve their side, instead of the opposition. During the war, with the legislature not meeting, Sa'd had plenty of time to intrigue against the government. He was secretly encouraged by Husayn Kamil's successor, Sultan Fuad I (1917-1936), who hoped to increase his power, relative to that of the British in Egypt, as soon as the war ended. Fuad's ambitions were matched by those of many Egyptian politicians, who wanted a parliamentary government, liberal democracy, and Egyptian control over the Sudan, untrammeled by the British protectorate. Most of these men had also been disciples of Lutfi al-Sayyid before the war. High-minded and devoid of religious fanaticism, they looked to Sa'd as their chief spokesman, as he had been in the 1914 assembly.

On 13 November 1918, two days after the European armistice, Sa'd Zaghlul and two of his friends called on the British high commissioner, Sir Reginald Wingate, a man who had lived in the Nile Valley for twenty years, spoke Arabic, and knew the Egyptians well. In a friendly conversation, they announced their intention to form a delegation (Arabic: *wafd*) to go to London to argue for Egypt's independence. Wingate counseled patience, but agreed to cable home for instructions. The British Foreign Office, busy getting ready for the projected Paris Peace Conference, refused to talk to this delegation of "disappointed and disgraced" politicians, or even to receive Husayn Rushdi, who had stayed on as premier through the war in the hope that Britain would end its protectorate as soon as peace returned.

During the winter months Sa'd announced that he would head a six-man delegation to present Egypt's case for independence before the Paris Peace Conference. Although made up of landowning moderates, this delegation, the Wafd, enlisted the aid of the Nationalists (remnants of Mustafa Kamil's National party) to circulate throughout Egypt copies of a petition whose signers wanted the Wafd to represent them in demanding complete independence, meaning the end to the British protectorate and evacuation of all foreign troops from Egypt and the Sudan. In March 1919 the Rushdi cabinet resigned and the British exiled Sa'd and his companions to Malta, whereupon the movement to support the Wafd turned into a popular revolution, the largest of all that have occurred in modern Egypt. Students and teachers, lawyers and judges, government employees and transportation workers went out on strike. Riots broke out in the villages, railroad stations were attacked, and telegraph lines were cut. Every social class demonstrated against the British protectorate; even women from wealthy families (some of them unveiled for the first time) took to the streets. Muslim ulama preached in Coptic churches, Christian priests gave Friday mosque sermons, while Copts and Muslims marched hand in hand, demanding "Egypt for the Egyptians." A new national flag appeared, with the Christian cross replacing the star within the Muslim crescent. Only when the British government replaced Wingate with Allenby (a war hero who had commanded the Egyptian Expeditionary Force that took Palestine) and let Sa'd leave Malta to go to Paris, did a semblance of normality return to Egyptian life.

When the Wafd went to Paris to present its case before the peace conference, nearly all Egyptians had high hopes. Would President Wilson, well known for upholding the political rights of subject nations, neglect those of the world's oldest one? Was Egypt not as entitled as the Arabs of the Hijaz to a hearing in Paris? Did it not have as much a right to independence as, say, Albania or Yugoslavia? Apparently not. On the day the Wafd arrived in Paris, the United States government officially recognized what the Egyptian nationalists were fighting to terminate, the British protectorate. The Wafd was never invited to speak at the peace conference. Sa'd Zaghlul and his companions could only make speeches that were unheeded and churn out letters that were unanswered by those with the power to redraw the political maps of Europe and the Middle East.

British Attempts to Find a Solution

Eventually, though, the British government decided to send a commission, headed by Lord Milner, to "inquire into the causes of the late disorders, and to report on the existing situation in the country, and on the form of constitution which, under the protectorate, will be best calculated to promote its peace and prosperity, the progressive development of self-governing institutions, and the protection of foreign interests." Egyptian supporters of the Wafd, now well organized back home as well as in Paris, might desire peace, prosperity, and the progressive development of self-rule, but they did not want the protectorate. They organized a general boycott of the Milner mission, which led (probably against the organizers' wishes) to various terrorist acts against British soldiers and Egyptian ministers. The Milner mission saw that Britain must somehow come to terms with Egyptian nationalism, but its spokesmen were in Paris, not Cairo. The Egyptian government managed to persuade Sa'd to enter into informal talks with Lord Milner, but neither could make big enough concessions to gain the other's support. The British said that Sa'd was a demagogue, a prisoner of his own propaganda for complete independence. The Wafd believed that Britain, concerned for its imperial communications, would never really give the Egyptians a chance to rule themselves. A Zaghlul-Milner memorandum, which would have substituted an Anglo-Egyptian treaty for the British protectorate, failed to gain the support of the Egyptian government or people when Sa'd himself declined to endorse it. However, it did make it seem inevitable that Britain would give up its protectorate. An official Egyptian delegation, headed by the new prime minister, Adli Yakan, went to London in 1921 to negotiate the terms, but Sa'd was able to use his popularity in Egypt to undermine support for Adli's negotiations with the Foreign Office.

Having thus failed to negotiate a new relationship with the Egyptians, either officially with Adli or unofficially with Sa'd, Britain seemed to be stymied on the Egyptian question. New waves of strikes and assassinations made some action imperative. Continued control over the Suez Canal and the port of Alexandria, the radio and telegraph stations, the railroads and the airfields, all communication links vital to the British Empire, could be endangered by a large-scale revolution backed by Sultan Fuad and his ministers and led by Sa'd Zaghlul and the Wafd. In some ways, Britain's dilemma in 1921-1922 was like that faced by the United States over the Panama Canal in 1977: How much should one give way to national pride in order to preserve one's essential interests? The British high commissioner, General Allenby, came up with the solution. He jawboned the British government into declaring unilaterally an end to the protectorate over Egypt on 28 February 1922. However, the declaration did restrict this independence by reserving to British authority, pending future Anglo-Egyptian agreement, the following operations: (1) protection of British imperial communications in Egypt, (2) management of Egypt's defense against foreign aggression, (3) protection of foreign interests and minorities in the country, and (4) control of the Sudan.

EGYPT'S DEMOCRATIC EXPERIMENT

Despite these infringements on Egypt's sovereignty, which became known as the "Four Reserved Points," the Egyptians accepted the declaration and began to organize their new government. Fuad changed his title from "sultan" to "king" and watched nervously while a committee of Egyptian lawyers (almost none of whom supported the Wafd) drew up a constitution modeled on that of Belgium, and the British residency (Allenby kept his title) seemed to encourage this "democratic experiment." This was a time when Britain, weary of war and especially of dickering over postwar arrangements in the Middle East, was following a more accommodating policy. Elsewhere, this meant giving way to nationalist movements in Turkey and Iran and trying to move toward self-government in Iraq and Palestine. Late in 1923 Egypt finally held free elections. The Wafd, reorganized as a political party, won an overwhelming majority of the seats in the new Egyptian Parliament. King Fuad accordingly called on Sa'd Zaghlul to set up a cabinet made up of Wafdist ministers.

The Short Reign of the Wafd

The high hopes of Egypt's liberal nationalists lasted less than a year. The 1919 revolution had unleashed forces of violence that its leaders could no longer contain. Even Sa'd himself was wounded by a would-be assassin in the summer of 1924. The attempt presaged a more successful political murder that November: the assassination of the British commander of the Egyptian army. Later investigation showed that these and many other terrorist acts were being perpetrated by a secret society that had been encouraged by some of Egypt's leading politicians. Meanwhile, Allenby had presented an angry ultimatum to the Egyptian government, claiming that the murder "holds up Egypt as at present governed to the contempt of civilized peoples," demanding a £500,000 indemnity to the British government, the withdrawal of all Egyptian officers from the Sudan, and an indefinite increase in the amount of Nile River waters to be used in irrigating the Sudan (and hence to be taken away from Egypt). The Wafd could not have accepted such an ultimatum, and Sa'd's cabinet resigned. King Fuad appointed a caretaker cabinet of palace politicians. The government called for new parliamentary elections and tried to fix their outcome, but when this failed to keep the Wafd out of power, the king disbanded the Parliament and suspended the constitution. Allenby then resigned as high commissioner, to be replaced in 1925 by Lord Lloyd, an arch imperialist.

The Power Triangle

As the battle lines were drawn, three sides rather than two emerged. For the sake of brevity, let me summarize the events of the next decade of Anglo-Egyptian relations by describing the evolution of this power triangle. On one corner stood the British, anxious to protect their position in Egypt with respect to India and the rest of the Middle East, but less and less interested in reforming Egypt's internal affairs. Several times the British government, especially in 1924 and 1929 when the Labor party was in power, tried to negotiate with Egypt for a treaty that would take the place of the Four Reserved Points. These attempts foundered on the intransigence of the second party to the struggle, the Wafd party. This was *the* popular nationalist movement of Egypt, led by Sa'd Zaghlul until his death in 1927, then somewhat less ably by Mustafa al-Nahhas until the 1952 revolution.

"The Wafd," in the words of Jean and Simone Lacouture, two French writers,

> was the expression of the entire people, of which in the fullest sense it was the *delegate*. Any attempt at defining it would involve a complete description of Egypt. It contained all the generosity, intellectual muddle, good nature, contradictions, and mythomania of its millions of supporters. It united the unlimited poverty of some and the insultingly bloated fortunes of others, the demand for change and the demand for conservatism, reaction, and movement. There was something spongy, lax, and warm about it which is typical of Egypt.

It insistence on Egypt's complete independence made the Wafd the most popular political party by far. It could win any free election in which it chose to run candidates for Parliament. The few cabinets it managed to form included Coptic Christians and even, for a while, a Jewish finance minister. It might have held power longer if it had not antagonized the third party in the power triangle, King Fuad, who wanted to increase the power of the palace at the expense of constitutional government. He could count on cooperation from parties and politicians that were rivals of the Wafd in order to form governments more amenable to his wishes. Fuad also controlled a lot of patronage within the Egyptian army, civil administration, and ulama. When the contest between the Wafd and the British became too intense, Fuad and his chief minister declared a state of emergency in 1930, replaced the 1923 constitution with a more authoritarian one, and proceeded to run the country as a royal dictatorship for five years.

The Anglo-Egyptian Treaty

A series of fortuitous events in 1935-1936 altered the nature of the power struggle in Egypt. The Italians under Mussolini, already having control of Libya, threatened both Egyptian and British interests by occupying Ethiopia. This helped to bring the two sides together. The mounting frequency of student riots in Cairo showed the unpopularity of the existing regime. The British, anxious to put their relationship with Egypt on a more solid footing, came out for a return to the 1923 constitution and free elections. The sudden death of King Fuad in April 1936 and the succession of his sixteen-year-old son Faruq (under a regency), gave new hope to believers in Egyptian democracy. New elections were held in 1936, and the Wafd party predictably won. Mustafa al-Nahhas formed a Wafdist government, which successfully negotiated a treaty with Britain's foreign secretary, Sir Anthony Eden. Because it took the place of the reserved points that had left Egypt's independence in doubt for fourteen years, this new Anglo-Egyptian Treaty was immensely popular in both countries. For Britain it guaranteed for at least twenty years a large military base from which to defend the Suez Canal, plus bases in Cairo and Alexandria, and possibly many other parts of Egypt in case a war broke out. The question of the Sudan, effectively controlled by Britain, was put on the back burner. For Egypt it meant a constitutional monarchy, with ministers responsible to Parliament, ambassadors in foreign capitals, membership in the League of Nations, and all the trappings of independence so long deferred. Young Faruq was received with wild ovations wherever he went, and Sir Anthony Eden became the first foreigner ever to get his picture on an Egyptian postage stamp!

Disillusionment with Nationalism and Democracy

Again the high hopes of Egypt's liberal nationalists were dashed. The Nahhas government lasted only eighteen months. King Faruq proved as adept as his father in finding anti-Wafd politicians willing to form governments he liked better. Indeed, some of the leading Wafdists found Nahhas so objectionable that they bolted the party in 1937 and formed a strong rival movement. Meanwhile, the government did nothing to solve Egypt's pressing economic and social problems. The extremes of wealth and poverty were simply grotesque, all the more so in a country where nearly all the people (almost sixteen million in 1937) lived on 3 percent of the land, in an area roughly equal to the entire state of New Jersey. The country was becoming much more urbanized and somewhat industrialized. While foreigners remained predominant in the ranks of the owner and managerial classes, Egyptian industrial capitalists were moving up, and of course there was a growing middle class of Egyptian shopkeepers, clerks, professionals, and civil servants. The capitulations, long a drag on Egypt's independence, were abolished in 1937. Even the mixed courts started to pass slowly from the scene. No longer would the large foreign (and minority) communities of Egypt receive special privileges and protection. Still, the great majority of the Egyptian people were no better off after independence than they had been under the British, for the landowners and capitalists who dominated Egypt's Parliament were not interested in social reform. Poverty, illiteracy, and disease stalked the lives of most Egyptian workers and peasants to an extent unparalleled in Europe or elsewhere in the Middle East.

The failure of nationalism and liberal democracy to solve these problems led many Egyptians to turn to other ideologies. A few intellectuals embraced Marxist Communism, even though the USSR seemed remote and—in that era of Stalin's purge trials and liquidation of the free peasants—unappealing as a model for Egypt to follow. Besides, the Communists' militant atheism made their doctrine abhorrent to the Muslim masses. Mussolini's Italy and Hitler's Germany provided alternative models more attractive to Egyptians disillusioned with liberal democracy, and an authoritarian party of the right, "Young Egypt," did arise. But the most popular Egyptian movement in the 1930s was one wholly indigenous to the country, the Society of the Muslim Brothers (al-Ikhwan al-Muslimun). The Muslim Brotherhood (to use its common English name) called for a return to the institutions and customs of Islam as practiced by Muhammad and his followers. Although best known for its attacks against Christians and Jews, as well as its demonstrations against motion pictures, bars, modern female fashions, and other "Western innovations," the Muslim Brothers had a valid point. They were reacting against a century (or more) of westernizing reforms imposed by the rulers and the ruling classes that had brought little benefit and much harm to the average Egyptian. In terms of the culture and values of most Egyptians, the brotherhood slogan, "The Quran is our constitution," made more sense than the demands for national independence and democratic government set forth by the Wafd and the other parties. The parliamentary system, unable to solve Egypt's social problems or to meet the challenges posed by Young Egypt and the Muslim Brothers, stumbled from one cabinet to another, usually coalitions of independents or politicians from minor parties, as King Faruq kept the Wafd out of power.

World War II

Then World War II broke out in 1939. Again Egypt became a vast army camp for the Western Allies, even though popular feeling was anti-British and hence pro-German. Even the king and his ministers seemed to be trying to wriggle out of the 1936 Anglo-Egyptian Treaty, as General Rommel's crack Afrikakorps swept across Libya into Egypt's Western Desert in early 1942. With crowds of demonstrators shouting in the streets of Cairo for a German victory, the British ambassador, Sir Miles Lampson, sent British tanks to surround the royal palace and delivered an ultimatum to King Faruq: he must either appoint a Wafdist government that would uphold the Anglo-Egyptian Treaty, or sign his own abdication. After some hesitation, Faruq, caved in. Mustafa al-Nahhas, leader of the Wafd party and hence the standard-bearer of Egypt's struggle for independence, was brought to power at the point of British bayonets.

Neither Nahhas nor the king ever recovered from Britain's action, taken in the darkest hour of World War II to help save the Western democracies from the Nazi menace. Faruq, a handsome and much beloved youth with high political ideals and moral courage, started to become the gargantuan monster and dissolute playboy remembered by the West today. Perhaps, as many Egyptians said after he was deposed in 1952, Faruq was ruined by the people who surrounded him, after he realized that the British would not let him rule Egypt. For the rest of the war, thousands of soldiers, sailors, and airmen from all parts of the British Commonwealth (and also the United States) poured into Egypt, as did visiting statesmen like Roosevelt and Churchill. All major economic activity throughout the Arab world (and Iran) was coordinated in Cairo by the British-run Middle East Supply Center. Industrial and agricultural employment and output boomed. So did price inflation, urban congestion, crime, and disruption. Everyone wondered if the end of World War II would bring popular uprisings as massive as the great 1919 revolution.

THE EGYPTIAN REVOLUTION

Egypt in 1945 seemed on the brink of a precipice, but there was no revolution. I can think of several explanations. First, Britain seemed less potent as a foreign oppressor than it had in 1919. Second, the prestige of the Western democracies was high following their decisive victory over Germany, Japan, and Italy. Many people hoped that the new United Nations Organization, of which Egypt was one of the original members, would rid the world of war and colonialism. Third, the Communists, who might have had the influence to bring off a revolution, were not nearly as strong in Egypt as their counterparts in most parts of Europe. Besides, there were no Red Army soldiers in Cairo as there were in Warsaw and Budapest. Fourth, the Egyptian government managed to distract public opinion with a newfound enthusiasm for Arab nationalism.

Although Egyptians had hardly ever thought of themselves as Arabs before, both King Faruq and the Wafd began to identify Egypt more closely with the rest of the Arab world. The main reason was that Nuri al-Sa'id, the Iraqi prime minister, had proposed in 1942 an organic union of all the Arabic-speaking countries of the Fertile Crescent: Iraq, Transjordan, Syria, Lebanon, and Palestine. This would have created a huge Arab state, probably ruled by a Hashimite king in Baghdad, which would soon outshine Egypt as the leading light in the Arab world. Egypt, backed by Saudi Arabia and Yemen (which would also have been excluded from Nuri al-Sa'id's proposed union), countered with the idea of the League of Arab States. This Arab League, which came into being in 1945, would preserve the sovereignty of each Arab country while coordinating their policies on key Arab issues. Britain encouraged this trend toward greater Arab cooperation. The only trouble was that the Arab states could agree on only one issue: they did not want to see a Jewish state created in Palestine.

Frustration in the Sudan

Thus Egypt, which had plenty of domestic problems to worry about, plus the unresolved issues of British rule in the Sudan (which almost all Egyptians felt should be given back to Egypt) and British troops within Egypt itself, found its attention and energies being diverted into the Palestine issue. To be sure, Anglo-Egyptian negotiations about the continued presence of British troops in the Nile Valley did continue in 1946. The greatest of Egypt's "palace" politicians, Isma'il Sidqi, actually managed to negotiate a treaty with Britain that would have evacuated British troops from all parts of Egypt but the canal zone. However, Wafdist opponents brought out differences between Britain and Egypt over the status of the Sudan, so the treaty was never ratified. In 1947 the Egyptian government took the issue to the UN Security Council, claiming that the 1936 Anglo-Egyptian Treaty had been negotiated under duress and that it was contrary to the UN Charter. The Security Council, unimpressed by these arguments, called on the two parties to resume their long and fruitless negotiations.

Failure in Palestine

In the meantime, Egypt was being drawn into the web of Palestine. This is not the place to discuss the Jewish and Arab claims to the Holy Land, but it is worth mentioning that Egypt's policies were determined not so much by any Zionist threat to Arab interests, but rather by concern over what the other Arab governments might be doing. If Egypt totally ignored the Palestine question, then Emir Abdallah of Transjordan might well take the lead role among the Arab rulers. If he decided to fight against any Jewish attempt to form a state in Palestine, he just might succeed in taking control of much (or all) of the country, annexing it to his desert kingdom. If he chose to make peace with the Zionists, they might divide Palestine between them. Either outcome would strengthen Emir Abdallah at King Faruq's expense.

The UN General Assembly voted late in 1947 to partition Palestine into a Jewish state and an Arab one. Neither Egypt nor Transjordan seriously considered letting the Palestinian Arabs form a state in the areas allotted to them by the 1947 partition plan; instead, they resolved to fight the plan and to throttle the Jewish state as soon as it came into being. This is not to say that there were no valid objections to a partition plan that (as we shall soon see) assigned over half of Palestine to a third of its 1947 population, but simply that the Egyptian government's policy was based on Arab power politics. But it is also fair to point out that many Egyptians, especially the Muslim Brothers, strongly favored an Arab jihad to free Palestine from the threat of Zionist colonialism. King Faruq, sensing an easy victory in a popular war, made the fateful decision to commit the Egyptian army to fight in Palestine in May 1948.

But, as you might have guessed, the army was unprepared for the Palestine war. Inept commanders, crooked politicians who cheated the government on the sale of arms, an inconvenient UN cease-fire, and general demoralization of the Egyptian troops led to a crushing defeat. Some Egyptian units fought bravely in Palestine, but the victories heralded in the Egyptian newspapers and radio broadcasts were imaginary. Early in 1949 Egypt had to sign an armistice agreement with the new state of Israel. But even then there was no peace.

The Fall of the Old Regime

Defeat in Palestine discredited Egypt's old regime: the king, the ministers, the high-ranking army officers, and the democratic experiment itself. The government clamped down on the Muslim Brotherhood after it assassinated the prime minister, but the unrest continued in 1949. Free elections in 1950 brought the Wafd party back into power, this time with an ambitious program of economic and social reforms, plus a commitment to drive the remaining British troops from the Nile Valley. The latter took precedence over the former, as Prime Minister Nahhas publicly repudiated the 1936 Anglo-Egyptian Treaty he himself had signed and began sending Egyptian commandos (Arabic: *fidaiyin*) to fight against British troops in the Suez Canal zone. Not surprisingly, the British struck back, killing many Egyptians in January 1952. At this point the rumble of popular anger became an explosion. On a Saturday morning hundreds of Egyptians, better organized than any mob of demonstrators had ever been before, fanned out across downtown Cairo and set fire to such European landmarks as Shepheard's Hotel, Groppi's Restaurant, the Turf Club, Rivoli Cinema, and many bars and nightclubs. Only after much of the city had burned to the ground did either Faruq or Nahhas try to stop the rioting, looting, and killing. "Black Saturday" proved that the old regime could no longer govern Egypt. Who would? Some people thought the Muslim Brothers had set the fire and were about the seize power. Others looked to the Communists. Few suspected that the army, humiliated in Palestine and generally supposed to be controlled by the palace, would take over Egypt.

The Military Revolution of 1952

However, on 23 July, the army did just that. An officers' secret society, using a popular general named Muhammad Nagib as its front man, seized control of the government in a bloodless coup d'etat. Neither Britain nor America intervened to stop them. Three days later Faruq abdicated and went into exile. Sweeping reforms followed, as the nationalistic young officers, like their counterparts in Turkey a generation earlier, took the places and powers (though not the perquisites) of the rich leaders of the old regime. Political parties were abolished and the Parliament dissolved. The military junta would have to rule until a new political system, which the officers said would be more truly democratic, could replace the discredited 1923 constitution. A land reform decree limited the total acreage any Egyptian might own to about 200 acres. All excess lands were bought from their owners by the new regime with government bonds and redistributed (along with the royal estates) to the landless peasants of rural Egypt. Many schools and factories were opened. Foreign supporters began to claim that Egypt's new rulers, the first real Egyptians to govern the country in over two thousand years, were also the best Egypt had ever had. However, early in 1954, the figurehead leader, General Nagib, widely regarded as a moderate, was eased from power by the real mastermind of the young officers, Colonel Gamal Abd al-Nasir (generally known as "Nasser"). This dampened some foreigners' enthusiasm.

Settlement of the Suez Canal Issue

The early Nasser regime was determined to settle the Egyptian question for once and for all. With considerable pressure placed on Britain by the United States, which wanted to bring Egypt into a Middle Eastern anti-Communist alliance comparable to NATO, Anglo-Egyptian negotiations resumed. Britain finally agreed to evacuate its Suez Canal base (the largest military installation in the non-Communist world), but on terms that would allow British troops to reoccupy the canal in the event of an attack on any Arab League country or on Turkey, presumably by the USSR. British civilian technicians might also remain the canal zone. Extreme Egyptian nationalists were distressed at these conditions, as well as at Egypt's concession that the Sudanese people might decide by a plebiscite between union with Egypt and complete independence. They chose independence, despite the blandishments of the Egyptian officers. Nasser was widely accused of being a fascist or an imperialist lackey. The Communists even called him Gamal Abdel Dulles (referring to the U.S. secretary of state), but, on 18 June 1956, the last British soldier departed from the Suez Canal base. For the first time since 1882, there were no British troops in Egypt.

A STRANGE ENDING

Egypt's struggle for independence should have ended at this point, but it did not. In October 1956 British and French paratroops landed at Port Said and reoccupied the Suez Canal, as Israel's army pushed westward across the Sinai Peninsula. The full story of this sequel will be told later but a few points cannot wait. The British government that ordered the invasion was headed by the same man who had negotiated the 1936 Anglo-Egyptian Treaty and its 1954 replacement—Sir Anthony Eden. He decided to attack Egypt because Nasser in July 1956 had nationalized the Suez Canal Company, the greatest symbol of Egypt's subjection to foreign powers, but also the lifeline of the British Commonwealth and of European oil-consuming nations. The world's emerging superpowers, the United States and the Soviet Union, joined forces to pressure the British, the French, and the Israelis to stop their attack and then to withdraw from Egyptian territory. Meanwhile, the Nasser government expelled thousands of British subjects and French citizens from Egypt and seized their property, thus ending much of what remained of Western economic power within the country. Nasser had finished the struggle for Egypt's independence, but at a cost of much Western bitterness against his regime and his country.

16

The Contest for Palestine

Palestine, the "twice-promised land" as British wags called it after World War I, has probably caused the spilling of more ink than any other political issue in the twentieth century. I would say even more ink than blood. Many of you began your study of Middle East history on the assumption that the contest for Palestine, which became the Arab-Israeli conflict in 1948, has been the main cause of the troubles throughout the area. Strictly speaking, Palestine or Israel has been only one of the trouble spots in the Middle East in recent years. Civil wars, airplane hijackings, political assassinations, revolutions, and even refugee problems have occurred in many different Middle Eastern countries. Yet it is hard to think of any political problem in the Middle East today, except in Turkey and Iran, that has not somehow been affected by the Arab-Israeli conflict. Certainly the attention paid to the conflict by the leaders of the superpowers, by the United Nations, and by legions of propagandists for both sides should suggest how important the conflict has become in the world today.

ORIGINS

How did the Arab-Israeli conflict begin? Can it be traced back to Abraham's two sons, Isaac (the ancestor of the Jews) and Ishmael (progenitor of the Arabs)? Did the wars between the Hebrews and the Canaanites start it? What about Muhammad's quarrel with the Jews of Medina? Is it a religious war between Judaism and Islam? The Arabs say that it is not, for the Jews were always welcome to settle and to prosper in Muslim lands. Zionists reply that the Jews under Muslim rule were usually second-class citizens (as were all other non-Muslims). Both sides agree that Christian anti-Semitism in Europe was worse, but that is a poor standard for tolerance.

Jews and Arabs do have certain traits in common, aside from the fact that they are both Semites and often resemble each other. Both look back to a golden age early in their history, to an era of political power, economic prosperity, and cultural flowering. For each people, that era was followed by a long span of time in which their political destinies were controlled by outsiders. Owing to their long subjection, the birth of nationalism (which began in the late nineteenth century for both Jews and Arabs) was slow, painful, and uncertain. Neither people felt good about leaving its revealed religion for a modern ideology of collective self-love. Both suspected outsiders of exploiting them. Both feared that, when the chips were down, the whole world would turn against them. On the strength of the Bible and two thousand years of religious tradition, Zionist Jews believed that the land of Israel (as they called Palestine) would be restored to them someday and that the Temple would be rebuilt in Jerusalem. Muslim Arabs believed that Palestine, a territory so long within the confines of the *ummah,* containing Jerusalem, a city holy to them as well as to Jews and Christians, could not be alienated from the lands ruled by Islam. Besides, how could Christian and Muslim Arabs who had lived in Palestine for 1300 years— indeed even longer, for the seventh-century Arab conquest had not displaced the earlier inhabitants—relinquish their claim? Was the right of the Palestinian Arabs to self-determination any less than the national rights of the Egyptians, the Turks, the Iranians, or the Arabs living elsewhere?

Arguments like these have occurred so frequently during our generation that we naturally think they always did. This really is not true. While Jews and Arabs have claims to Palestine going back hundreds of years, the contest was just starting when World War I broke out. Few then foresaw how long or how strong it would be. The duration and the intensity of what we now call the Arab-Israeli conflict were largely due to the rise of nationalism in modern times. We have already covered the Arab nationalist movement in chapter 13, with some additional glances in the intervening chapters; now it is time to look at the history of Zionism. This chapter will carry the contest for Palestine up to the creation of Israel as the Jewish state. I hope you will see why I stress the struggle between Arab nationalism and political Zionism. As in later chapters we move into the various phases of the Arab-Israeli conflict, I hope you will also see why it is so intense and so hard to resolve.

Prefatory Remarks

Let me first define "political Zionism." The meaning of "Zionism" itself has become controversial lately, owing to a 1975 UN General Assembly resolution condemning Zionism as "a form of racism." Almost no one nowadays wants to have his or her beliefs associated with racism—the idea that one racial group is better than some other group and should therefore rule over it—so Zionists naturally opposed the resolution, as did most Western countries (see chapter 20). I define "Zionism" as the belief that the Jews constitute a nation (or to use a less loaded term, a people) and that they deserve the liberties of other such groups, including the right to return to their ancestral homeland, the land of Israel (or Palestine). Political Zionism is the belief that the Jews should establish and maintain a state for themselves there.

Not every Jew is a Zionist. Some Jews identify solely with the countries in which they are citizens, or reject the idea of nationalism entirely, or believe that the only meaningful affirmation of Jewishness is through observance of their religion, its laws and traditions. Not every Zionist is a Jew. Some Christians believe that the restoration of the Jews to Palestine or the creation of Israel must precede the second coming of Christ. Many Gentiles (non-Jews) support Israel out of admiration for Jews or Israelis or out of guilt for past wrongs committed to Jews by tsarist Russia or Nazi Germany. Even some Gentiles who are unfriendly to Jews support Israel, perhaps because Zionism stresses the uniqueness of Jews, just as anti-Semites (opponents of Jews) do, and aims to prevent the assimilation of Jews into gentile society. Likewise, anti-Zionists are not necessarily anti-Semites. Some may be pro-Arab out of genuine conviction, while some people with the best of intentions toward Jews or Judaism think that Zionism and the creation of Israel have done them more harm than good. This is a point many Jews ought to keep in mind. On the other hand, non-Jews should realize that their expressions of opposition (or even skepticism) toward Zionism and Israel are apt to seem anti-Semitic to many Jews. The UN resolution has increased this sensitivity and clouded discussion on the pros and cons of Zionism, a critical problem if Jews and Gentiles (or Arabs and non-Arabs) are to understand each other.

To return to my definition, Zionism is a nationalist movement rather like Arab nationalism and other Middle Eastern nationalism we have already studied. It may seem odd to Americans that the Jews should be called a "nation." We never speak of a Catholic or a Presbyterian nation in America. American Jews rarely consider themselves Israelis, nor are Israelis apt to regard them as such. Nevertheless, there is a very strong belief among almost all Jews—Orthodox, Conservative, Reconstructionist, Reform, or nonobservant—that they do constitute one people and that their collective survival depends on mutual support and cooperation. Even a person of Jewish ancestry who does not practice Judaism, indeed even if he has converted to another faith, is still likely to be regarded as a Jew unless he makes a strenuous effort to prove he is not one. Most Gentiles realize these facts, at least dimly.

The idea that the Jews are a nation is deeply rooted in the Bible: a nomadic tribe called the Habiru (or Hebrews) came to think that their deity was in fact the one true God, Y-hw-h ("Jehovah" in English); He had chosen them for His love and protection because they had chosen Him; He had commanded them to keep His covenant and obey His laws from generation to generation; He had led them out of Egyptian bondage and brought them safely to Palestine, called "the land of Israel" because He had promised it to the Israelites, or descendants of Jacob. Even though the Israelites at times married outside their tribe and even though other people or tribes converted to their faith, still they regarded all as being, at least in principle, children of Israel. Their identification with the land of Israel was a big part of their religion. Their festive holidays were—and are—tied to the agricultural seasons of that land. Many of their laws and customs cannot be understood without reference to the land of Israel in which they were first practiced. Jerusalem is featured in prayers and common expressions and is a symbol of the Jewish people's hopes and fears. "Jew" originally meant "one from Judea," the region in which Jerusalem is the main city; only later on did it indicate a religious allegiance.

The Jews in Dispersion

For at least two millennia most Jews have not been Judeans, nor until recently could it be said that they possessed Jerusalem or even that they spoke Hebrew. Jews kept their identity as a people by their observance of the faith and laws of Judaism and by their wish to remain as a people, even without a piece of territory, a common language, a government, or most of the other attributes of nationhood. However tenuous the ties might seem between Jews and their ancestral land, they never forgot them. More in good times and fewer in bad, Jews went back to Jerusalem to devote portions of their lives to study and contemplation and to be buried just outside its walls. There were always some Jews living in Palestine, and many felt that only by living there could one feel wholly Jewish. The prevalent anti-Semitism of European Christians enhanced Jewish solidarity and identification with the land.

The European Enlightenment and the rise of liberal democracy freed many Western Jews from discrimination and isolation. Some reacted against the idea of Jewish solidarity, which they associated with ghetto poverty, and against identification with a land of Israel that most would never see. A Jewish enlightenment (Hebrew: *haskalah*) took place in the eighteenth and nineteenth centuries, leading in Germany and America to what is called "Reform Judaism" and to greater Jewish assimilation into Western society. In some cases this even encouraged individuals to deny their Jewishness and convert to Christianity, like the parents of such figures in European history as Heinrich Heine, Karl Marx, Felix Mendelssohn, and Benjamin Disraeli. If the enlightenment of Western Europe had been stronger and more pervasive, would the Jews have been assimilated? Then we might never have heard of Zionism. But most Jews did not live in America, England, or even Germany; the majority could be found in tsarist Russia (especially Poland) and in various parts of the declining multinational empires of the Habsburgs and the Ottomans. When the peoples of Eastern Europe began to embrace nationalist ideas, they had to fight against desperate autocrats to gain their freedom. The local Jews got caught in the middle. Law-abiding and usually loyal to their rulers, they might well have seemed to the nationalists as enemies in their midst. Some rulers also tried to deflect nationalist anger from themselves by using the Jews as scapegoats, stirring up pogroms (organized attacks) against Jewish ghettos and villages.

How did Jews react to this new persecution from governments they had long obeyed? Some retreated into piety and mysticism. Some escaped to Western Europe or America. A few converted and tried to be assimilated into the culture and society of the majority. Some tried to revive Hebrew as a literary language (just as Arab nationalism began as a literary revival). A few Jews—and more than a few Christians—said that the only way to end persecution of Jews was for them to emigrate to Palestine to live and re-build their state in the land of Israel. The idea that Jews constitute a nation—Zionism by my definition—is nothing new, but the idea that the Jewish nation should revive its ancient state in Palestine—which I call "political Zionism"—was revolutionary for the nineteenth century.

Beginnings of Political Zionism

Like most revolutionary doctrines, political Zionism started with very few supporters. Most rabbis said that the restoration of the Jews to Palestine could only take place after God had sent the Messiah. Jews must be careful. Many false messiahs had led people astray by their extravagant claims, thereby increasing Jewish suffering. Nationalism was a form of collective self-love that ran counter to the basic commitment of Judaism: "You shall love the Lord your God with all your heart, and with all your soul, and with all your might" (Deut. 6:5). Nevertheless, some nineteenth-century rabbis began thinking along other lines. One wrote that the Jews should return to the land of Israel to await the Messiah. As early as 1843 another rabbi called on rich Jews to form a corporation to colonize the country, train young Jews in self-defense, and teach farming and other practical subjects. Some *haskalah* thinkers in Germany believed that this rebuilding of the Jewish homeland would bring young people closer to nature and make them more "normal" (like Gentiles). Moses Hess, one of the first German socialists, argued in *Rome and Jerusalem* (1862) that Jews could build a truly socialistic nation-state in the land of Israel.

His book was little read (until much later), but another book by an early political Zionist, Leo Pinsker's *Auto-Emancipation* (1882), had enormous influence in Russia. Official anti-Semitism was reaching new heights at this time, as the tsarist regime enacted a series of "May Laws" that restricted areas in Russia where Jews might live and put artificially low quotas on the admission of Jews to universities and to the professions. Pinsker's book was the first systematic attempt to prove that the Jews were vulnerable to anti-Semitism because they lacked a country of their own. It inspired the formation of Zionist clubs and study groups in Russia. Their federation, Chovevei Tzion ("Lovers of Zion") spread from Russia to other countries where Jews lived. There was also a more activist movement, BILU (Hebrew: *Beit Ya'cov lchu vnelcha* or "To the House of Jacob go and we will follow"), which sent groups of Russian Jewish student to Palestine. Immigrants in these two organizations made up what Zionist historians call the "first aliyah." "Aliyah" really means "going up," for Jews had long used the term to mean going up to Jerusalem, a city set in the hills of Judea, but it now means "going to the land of Israel." Jewish immigrants were called *olim* ("ascenders").

Early Jewish Settlers

The Zionist *olim* found other Jewish newcomers in Palestine. There were always mystics and scholars going to Jerusalem and the other main Jewish cultural centers in the land: Tiberias, Safed, and Hebron. In addition, there were already immigrants buying land and trying to farm it. These people got some help from an important Jewish educational organization, the Alliance Israelite Universelle. The alliance set up modern French-speaking schools for Jews throughout North Africa and the Middle East, doing much to upgrade their standard of education in the late nineteenth century. It founded an agricultural school near Jaffa in 1870, which did much to help the settlers, though the alliance opposed the idea of having a Jewish state. At this time the total number of Jewish settlers in Palestine could not have exceeded ten or twenty thousand; the vast majority of the population spoke Arabic. The government of the land was under the Ottoman Empire, inefficient, corrupt, and very suspicious of the Zionists (curiously, because so many had come from Russia, the enemy of the Turks). Not a few quit in disgust and went home—or to America.

Theodor Herzl

Zionism based solely on Russian resources—mainly youthful enthusiasm—probably would not have lasted. What gave the movement endurance and popularity was an assimilated Jewish journalist-playwright living in Vienna, Theodor Herzl, who in 1896 wrote *Der Judenstaat* ("The Jews' State"), an eloquent plea for political Zionism. Because Herzl was a gifted and popular writer, his book carried the ideas of Pinsker and other early Zionists to an enormous number of German-speaking Jews. Their conversion to Zionism enabled Herzl to call the first International Zionist Congress in Basle (Switzerland) in 1897. At its conclusion, the conferees adopted the following resolution:

> The goal of Zionism is the establishment for the Jewish people of a home in Palestine guaranteed by public law. The Congress anticipates the following means to reach that goal:
> 1. The promotion, in suitable ways, of the colonization of Palestine by Jewish agricultural and industrial workers,
> 2. The organizing and uniting of all Jews by means of suitable institutions, local and international, in compliance with the laws of all countries,
> 3. The strengthening and encouraging of Jewish national sentiment and awareness,
> 4. Introducing moves towards receiving governmental approval where needed for the realization of Zionism's goal.

Herzl proceeded to work unremittingly toward the formation of the Jewish state by writing more books, delivering speeches, and courting the support of rich Jews and various European governments, as well as from Jewish workers and the middle class. At one time he even got an offer from the British government that would have let the Zionists settle in what would later become the "White Highlands" of Kenya. But most of Herzl's followers, especially the Russian Jews, emphatically refused to form a state anywhere outside the land of Israel. As they put it, "There can be no Zionism without Zion." The movement became divided over this and other issues. When Herzl died in 1904, it looked as though the high hopes of early Zionism might never be realized.

The Second Aliyah

If the life and teachings of Theodor Herzl constituted the first event that saved the Zionist movement, the second was the large-scale emigration of Jews from Russia following its abortive 1905 revolution. Although most decided to seek freedom and equal opportunity in that Eldorado across the seas, the United States, some of the most idealistic men and women chose Palestine instead. With incredible fervor and dedication, these Jewish settlers of the "second aliyah" (1905-1914) built up the fledgling institutions of their community in Palestine: schools, newspapers, theaters, sports clubs, trade unions, labor-owned factories, and political parties. Because the Jews in Palestine had spoken so many different languages in the countries from which they had come, the *olim* made a concerted effort to revive Hebrew as a spoken and written language.

Actually, their best-known achievement was a novel experiment in agricultural settlement called the kibbutz (collective farm), where all houses, animals, and farming equipment were owned by the group as a whole, all decisions were made democratically, and all jobs (including cooking, cleaning, and child rearing) were handled collectively. Not all kibbutzim succeeded, but the best ones survived because their members were totally committed to rebuilding the Jewish national home and to redeeming the land by their own labor. Though most *olim* went to live in the cities, including what became the first all-Jewish city in modern history, Tel Aviv, those who chose the kibbutzim have come to typify the pioneer spirit of Israel: idealistic, self-reliant, and somewhat contemptuous of outsiders. The kibbutzniks worked incredibly long hours for what at first were pitiful material benefits, but they were determined to develop their lands (purchased for them by the Jewish National Fund at high prices from absentee Arab and Turkish landlords) without resort to cheap Arab peasant labor.

Because the best-known pioneers of the second aliyah were brave and resourceful people, the founders of what is now the state of Israel, we tend to forget that most of the *olim* soon lost their enthusiasm for this risky and unrewarding adventure. Hot summers, windy and rainy winters, malarial swamps, rocky hills or sandy desert soil, and frequent crop failures dimmed the fervor of many young pioneers. Arab nomads and peasants raided the kibbutzim. Their cousins in Jaffa and Jerusalem eyed Zionism with suspicion. As their own feelings of nationalism grew, the Arabs naturally opposed a colonization scheme that seemed likely to dispossess them, reduce them to second-class status, or break up Syria. Already they were protesting in their press and in the Ottoman Parliament against the Jewish settlers and their plans to built a Jewish state in Palestine. The Ottoman government, both before and after the 1908 Young Turk revolution, obstructed Jewish colonization for fear of adding another nationality problem to those in the Balkans and the Arab lands that were already tearing the empire apart. No European government cared to risk offending Istanbul by championing the Zionist movement in Palestine, at least before World War I.

BRITAIN AND THE PALESTINE PROBLEM

World War I was really the third event that saved political Zionism. Both sides needed Jewish support. In 1914 Berlin was the main center of the

Zionist movement, and most politically articulate Jews lived in (and supported) the countries that made up the Central Powers: Germany, Austria-Hungary, and the Ottoman Empire. Up to 1917 when the United States went into World War I on the side of the Allies, American Jews tended to favor the Central Powers because they hated the tyranny of tsarist Russia, from which so many Jews had barely managed to escape. The overthrow of the regime a little earlier in 1917 made Russia easier to support, but now the problem facing the new democratic government (which most Russian Jews favored) was how to keep Russia in the war at all. That year became crucial for both sides. They needed strong Jewish support, but Germany was inhibited from supporting Zionism by its ties with the Ottoman Empire. This is where Britain stepped in.

The Balfour Declaration

Britain, though it had relatively few Jewish subjects, could speak out more forcefully for Zionism. There the leading Zionist spokesman was Dr. Chaim Weizmann, a chemist who achieved fame early in the war by synthesizing acetone, a chemical used in making explosives that Britain had earlier been able to import from Germany. Weizmann's discoveries made him known to leading journalists and eventually to cabinet ministers. The prime minister, David Lloyd George, had developed a sympathy for Zionism from reading the Bible, and Weizmann also won the backing of the foreign secretary, Lord Balfour. It was this man who communicated to the British Zionists the cabinet's decision to support their movement in what has come to be known as the Balfour Declaration. The letter stated:

> His Majesty's Government view with favor the establishment in Palestine of a national home for the Jewish people, and will use their best endeavors to facilitate the achievement of this object, it being clearly understood that nothing shall be done which may prejudice the civil and religious rights of the existing non-Jewish communities in Palestine, or the rights and political status enjoyed by Jews in any other country.

Since this declaration has come to be seen as the Magna Charta of political Zionism, it deserves our careful scrutiny. It does not say that Britain would turn Palestine into a Jewish state. In fact, it does not say what the borders of Palestine, which the British were then in the process of conquering from the Turks, were going to be. The British government was committed only to work for the creation of a Jewish national home *in* Palestine. It also pledged not to harm the civil and religious rights of Palestine's "existing non-Jewish communities"—namely the 93 percent of the inhabitants, Muslim and Christian, who spoke Arabic and did not want to be separated from other Arabs as second-class citizens within a Jewish national home, let alone state. Both Britain and the Zionist movement would have to find a way to assuage these people's fears and to guarantee their rights. Here, in a nutshell, is what Arabs see as the nub of the contest for Palestine. Even now the hottest issue in the Arab-Israeli conflict is that of defining the legitimate rights of the Palestinian Arabs. The Balfour Declaration also had to take into account the fears of Jews who chose to remain outside Palestine and who would not want to lose what rights and status they had gained in liberal democracies like England, France, and the United States. Up to the rise of Hitler, Zionism had the backing of only a minority of these Jews. What the Balfour Declaration seemed to assure was that the British government would take over Palestine after the war with a commitment to build the Jewish national home there. Let us see what really happened.

The British Occupation of Palestine

When World War I ended, Britain's Egyptian Expeditionary Force and Faysal's Arab army occupied between them the area that would become Palestine. The British set up a provisional military government in Jerusalem and soon got embroiled in the contest between Jewish settlers, who poured into Palestine and began working to form their state as fast as they could, and the Arabs, who resisted their efforts. Zionist writers often accuse British officers and officials of stirring up Arab resentment. It is probably true that many of these Englishmen had learned how to get along with Arabs in Egypt and the Sudan, but knew little about the Jewish settlers from Russia, who were often abrasive and intransigent because they had suffered so much under tsars and sultans. Some Englishmen seem to have assumed that, because of the Communist takeover in Russia, the Jews from that country had Bolshevik tendencies.

But Arabs were capable of drawing their own conclusions about Jewish immigration, the Balfour Declaration, the cover-up of the King-Crane Commission's report criticizing Zionism, and British suppression of revolutions in Egypt and Iraq. When Weizmann proposed to make Palestine "as Jewish as England is English," the Palestinian Arabs revolted in 1920, killing many Jews and damaging a lot of property. Although it may have been the opening chapter in the Arab nationalist revolution in Palestine, the Zionists were right to complain that Britain punished the rebels too lightly and protected the Jewish settlers too little. Also at this time the Allies agreed in San Remo on the assignment of the mandates in the Arab world, putting Palestine definitely under British control. The Colonial Office took over the administration of Palestine from the army, and it seemed as if a more coherent British policy would be formulated. However, this was never to be.

The Palestine Mandate

In the years that followed, Britain's formulation of Palestine policy seemed to go in two different directions. In the international arena it tended to back Zionist aims, because of Jewish political pressure on London and indeed on the League of Nations headquarters in Geneva. On the spot, however, British officials tended to lean toward the Arab side. Remember that these were general tendencies, not hard-and-fast rules. When the League of Nations awarded the Palestine mandate in July 1922, it specifically charged Britain with carrying out the Balfour Declaration. This meant it must encourage Jews to immigrate to Palestine and settle there, help create the Jewish "national home," and even set up a "Jewish agency" to advise and assist the British authorities in developing the national home.

The Palestine mandate could not be a carbon copy of the League of Nations mandates for Syria and Iraq, which were to facilitate the progressive development of these countries as independent states to be granted constitutions within a three-year period. In Syria and Iraq it was obvious that the mandates were supposed to prepare their inhabitants to rule themselves. In Palestine, however, while most of the present inhabitants were Arabs, it was the Jewish national home that was to be created. The Palestine mandate simply called for "self-governing institutions" with no definite deadline for their creation. The Arabs naturally suspected that the British mandate would hold them in colonial bondage until the Jews achieved a majority in Palestine and could set up their state.

Beginnings of the Anglo-Zionist Rift

In reality, though, Britain started chipping away at the pro-Zionist features of the mandate before the ink was even dry. The Churchill memorandum issued in 1922, denied that the British government had any intention of letting Palestine become as Jewish as England was English or of giving preferential treatment to Jews over Arabs. The fateful provision was a statement that Jewish immigration would be limited to the absorptive capacity of Palestine. In the 1920s this caused no problems in Anglo-Zionist relations, as there were rarely enough Jewish immigrants to fill the quotas, but after the rise of Hitler this issue became a major one indeed.

Another British action that seemed to violate the mandate was the creation of the Emirate of Transjordan, which effectively removed the two-thirds of Palestine that lay east of the Jordan River from the area in which the Jews could develop their national home. Actually, the number of Jews wanting to settle in what had once been Moab or Gilead must have been minuscule, but the Zionists saw in the British attempt to give Abdallah a kingdom an unnecessary appeasement of Arab nationalism. The British claimed that this first partition of Palestine was only temporary. But, as the French did not get out of Syria and Abdallah began building up a bureaucracy and an army (the British-officered Arab Legion) out in Amman, the separation of Transjordan became more and more permanent. Most Jewish leaders in Palestine thought it best to cooperate with Britain all the same, but some turned to terrorist methods of opposition, specifically a group known as the "Revisionists." They were led by Vladimir Jabotinsky, who had organized a Jewish legion in World War I and the first self-defense group, Haganah, during the 1920 Arab riots. Jabotinsky occupied the nationalistic Right in the Zionist political spectrum and influenced greatly the present prime minister of Israel, Menachem Begin.

Sir Herbert Samuel and Hajj Amin al-Husayni

Britain's first civilian governor in Palestine was Sir Herbert Samuel. Although he had been a prominent Zionist, Samuel made a sincere and concerted effort to be fair to all sides, so that Palestine Arabs as well as Jews would accept him. He leaned so far over backwards that he appointed a hotheaded young nationalist, Hajj Amin al-Husayni, to be chief mufti ("Muslim legal officer") of Jerusalem, even though other candidates for the post enjoyed more support among the Muslim notables. Samuel probably hoped to tame him with a small taste of power, but Hajj Amin used his control of the waqfs ("pious endowments") and appointments to key Muslim positions to become the leader of Palestinian Arab nationalism. Although his flamboyant personality won him enemies as well as friends among the Arabs of Palestine, he became so influential as a spokesman that the British finally deported him in 1937, and he played a major role in Hitler's propaganda machine during World War II.

Samuel encouraged both Jews and Arabs to form their own institutions. The Jews continued to develop national organizations covering nearly every aspect of their lives in Palestine, including the Jewish Agency as an executive body and a consultative national council. Political parties mushroomed, each with its unique blend of socialism, nationalism, and religion. The general labor federation, called Histadrut, began setting up factories, food-processing plants, and even a construction company. The Arabs, divided by family and religious loyalties, failed to create comparable organizations or even a united nationalist party. Instead they went in for a sort of negativism that seriously damaged their case outside the country. Britain tried to set up a Palestinian legislature in 1923 that would have given the Arabs a plurality if not a majority of the seats, but they refused because the representation offered to the Jews was higher in proportion to their numbers. The Palestinian Arabs are supposed to have sought out Sa'd Zaghlul, leader of the Wafd party in Cairo, hoping for Egyptian support. After hearing their tale of woe, Sa'd bluntly told their delegation to go back and make their peace with the Jewish settlers who were developing the country. Other Arab and Muslim leaders did more to encourage the Palestinian Arabs to be intransigent, but as they were all outside Palestine and had problems of their own, they gave little or no material assistance to combat Zionism.

In the days of Samuel and his immediate successor, it looked as if differences between Jews and Arabs could be resolved. The number of Jewish *olim* was small; in some years more Jews left Palestine than entered it. There was also a complementary relationship between Jewish brains and Arab brawn, between Jewish technical expertise and Arab knowledge of local conditions, and between Jewish capital and Arab labor that the rhetoric of the two competing sides failed to conceal. Wise British administration might dampen down their differences. There had always been some Jews who favored keeping on friendly terms with the Arabs, and some Arabs who welcomed Jewish immigration and investment; perhaps they could emerge as leaders if both sides toned down their most extreme nationalist claims.

The Wailing Wall Incident

These hopes were dashed by the "Wailing Wall Incident" of 1929. The issue was a complicated one. The Wailing Wall (more properly called the Western Wall) is a remnant of the second Jewish Temple and an object of veneration to pious Jews. To some it symbolizes the hope that some day the Temple will be rebuilt and the ancient Jewish rituals revived. However, the Western Wall also forms part of the Muslim sacred enclosure surrounding the historic Temple Mount on which stand the Dome of the Rock and al-Aqsa mosque, centers of Muslim pilgrimage almost as important as Mecca and Medina. Muslims were sensitive about what the Jews did before the Western Wall, fearing they might try to establish a stronger claim to the Temple Mount.

In 1929 Jewish worshippers brought some benches to sit on and a screen to separate men from women. The police took them away several times, but the Jews kept putting them back. To Muslims this looked like a Jewish attempt to strengthen their claim, and several fights broke out between Arabs and Jews. These escalated into a small civil war that left hundreds of casualties on both sides. The Arabs perpetrated massacres elsewhere in Palestine, notably in Hebron, where they practically wiped out the whole Jewish population. British police protection was clearly inadequate. When the Jews complained, Britain sent out a commission of inquiry, headed by

Sidney Webb (Lord Passfield), who later issued a white paper blaming the Jewish Agency and Jewish land purchases from Arabs (which had rendered some peasants landless) for the 1929 disturbances. This report seemed so biased to Weizmann that he resigned his post as head of the Jewish Agency in protest. Chagrined, the British government issued a letter that explained away the Passfield White Paper, an action that angered the Arabs. It showed them that Zionist influence was strong enough to sway the British government whenever it acted in favor of Arab interests. The letter did little to mollify the Zionists either. The whole incident just shows how ineffective Britain's policies in Palestine had become.

Jewish Immigration Pressure and Arab Nationalist Resistance

During the 1930s Jewish-Arab relations got worse. The rise of Hitler and his Nazi party to power in Germany put the Jews in that country—almost a million—into dire peril. Many of these people stayed in Germany despite discriminatory laws, official harassment, and hooliganism directed against Jews caused by Hitler's inflammatory speeches, while other German Jews began trying to get out. The Nazis even tried, for a while anyway, to help them leave. The problem was to find a country that would take them. Most European countries were already pretty crowded and had unemployment problems due to the depression of the 1930s, so they did not want to let in large numbers of German Jews. Neither did the United States, which had set strict limits on foreign immigration since 1924. This left Palestine. From 1933 on, the trickle of Jewish immigrants into that country turned into a flood, straining the limits set by Britain out of concern for Palestine's absorptive capacity—or indeed for the extent of Arab forbearance. It was natural for the Arabs to wonder how long it would be before they were transformed into a minority. They had not brought Hitler to power. Why should their political rights be sacrificed for the sins of the Germans? On the other hand, the Zionists noticed swarms of Arab workers coming into Palestine to take jobs, yet the British seemed indifferent to this strain on the country's economy!

The Peel Commission and the White Paper

As Arab feelings of anger and impotence mounted, Hajj Amin al-Husayni was able to set up an Arab Higher Committee, representing nearly all Palestinian Christian and Muslim factions in the country. It in turn called a general Arab strike in 1936. The strike turned into a large-scale Arab rebellion that almost paralyzed Palestine for several months. Again the British government sent out a commission of inquiry, this one headed by Lord Peel. The Arabs tried to impress the Peel Commission with their power by boycotting it. The result was that the Zionists got a better hearing, and the Peel Commission report, issued late in 1937, recommended partition, giving a small portion of northern and coastal Palestine to the Jews to form their own state, but leaving most of it to the Arabs. The small allotment for the Jews would hardly have given them much space to grow in, but perhaps the foothold would later have enabled the Zionists to rescue far more European Jews from persecution and death under the Nazis. The Palestine Arabs, backed by other Arab states including Faruq's Egypt, opposed partition, fearing Britain's acceptance of the Peel Commission's plan would be a step toward their loss of Palestine. But, as often happened in the contest for Palestine, the British government later scaled down the offer and finally retracted it.

Seeking a peace formula that would satisfy everyone, the government called a round-table conference of Arab and Jewish leaders in London in early 1939, but many stayed away. By then the differences had become so great that there could be no agreement, and the meeting ended inconclusively. A new war with Germany was imminent, and Britain had to court Arab support. It issued a statement known as the Palestine White Paper of 1939, which announced that the mandate would end in ten years, whereupon Palestine would become fully independent. Meanwhile, to assure a continuing Arab majority in Palestine, Jewish immigration would be limited to 15,000 each year until 1944, after which it could continue only with Arab consent (which hardly seemed forthcoming!)

Now it was the Jews' turn to feel angry but powerless. The White Paper seemed to sell out Britain's commitment to help build the Jewish national home as given in the Balfour Declaration and the mandate itself. Remember that at this time Hitler's soldiers had already marched into Austria, the Western democracies had consented to the dismemberment of Czechoslovakia at the Munich conference, and Poland was threatened with imminent German invasion. European Jews were in peril. They had nowhere to go but Palestine, and now Britain, bowing to Arab pressure, had slammed shut the gates of immigration. Even the Arabs disliked the White Paper, but mainly because it did not give them independence soon enough or stop Jewish immigration and land purchases altogether.

During World War II most of the Arab countries remained neutral. Some of their leaders flirted with the Nazis, hoping they would free the Arab world from British imperialism and Zionism both. But the Jews in Palestine had no freedom to choose their side. The threat of Nazi annihilation outweighed the evils of British appeasement to the Arabs, so they committed themselves to the Allied cause. Following the advice of the chairman of the Jewish Agency, David Ben Gurion, the Jews agreed that "We must assist the British in the war as if there were no White Paper and we must resist the White Paper as if there were no war." Thousands of

Palestinian Jews volunteered to serve in the British army, taking high risk assignments in various war theaters. Some also undertook dangerous missions to rescue Jews from parts of Europe controlled by Hitler and his allies. A few frustrated Zionists turned to acts of terrorism, such as assassinating the British minister-resident in Cairo in 1944.

The Growing American Role

As it became clear that Britain would not lift its restrictions on Jewish immigration into Palestine or relent in its opposition to a Jewish state, the Zionists increasingly looked to the United States for support. Zionism had not made a strong appeal to American Jews earlier, but the rise of Hitler alerted them to the dangers of anti-Semitism running rampant. Most American Jews still had friends or relatives in lands falling under Nazi control. Although they could not have foreseen that Hitler would try to wipe them out, they did worry about their safety. If Germany, long one of the safest countries for Jews, now persecuted them, was there any country where Jews could always live as a minority? Maybe a Jewish state would not be such a bad idea after all, even if few American Jews went to live there.

In 1942 the American Zionists adopted what was called the Biltmore Program, calling on Britain to rescind the Palestine White Paper and make Palestine a Jewish state. Soon the World Zionist Organization endorsed this resolution. American politicians, knowing the feelings of their voters but ignorant of the Arab majority living in Palestine, began clamoring for a Jewish state. This was not just a knee-jerk response to the "Jewish vote," for many Christians hoped that creating a Jewish state would atone for Hitler's horrible deeds (their full extent was not yet widely known) and for past anti-Semitism by nearly everyone. Why did they not admit more Jewish survivors into the United States? Although this would have alleviated the Palestine problem, to do so would have undermined what the Zionists wanted. Besides, there was still anti-Semitism in America; some Jews and many Christians did not want to raise the immigration quotas for these European Jews.

Civil War in Palestine

As World War II was winding down, violence in Palestine increased. Zionist terrorist groups, like the Irgun Tzvei Leumi and the Stern Gang, blew up buildings and British installations in Palestine. In response, the U.S. government stepped up its pressure on Britain to end restrictions on Jewish immigration and to accommodate demands for Jewish statehood. An Anglo-American Commission of Inquiry went out in 1946 and interviewed various officials and nationalist leaders. It called for a continuation of the mandate, but its most publicized recommendation was to admit 100,000 European Jewish refugees at once into Palestine and to remove all the restrictions on the Jews' right to buy land. The new Labor party government in Britain turned down the Anglo-American report and advocated instead a federated Arab-Jewish Palestine. This satisfied no one. The fighting got worse. Finally Britain went before the United Nations General Assembly in February 1947 and said that it could no longer afford to keep the Palestine mandate. Britain's Palestine policy was bankrupt.

The United Nations Partition Plan

It was up to the world organization to resolve the issue. The General Assembly responded to the challenge by creating yet another investigatory body, the UN Special Commission on Palestine. This group of ten member states toured Palestine during the summer of 1947, but could not come up with a policy on which all of them could agree. Some still preferred a binational Palestine of Arabs and Jews. With the Arabs still making up two-thirds of the country's population, though, it was unlikely they would admit many Jewish refugees from Europe. The majority of the commission recommended partition of Palestine into seven sections, of which three would be controlled by Arabs, three controlled by Jews, and one (including Jerusalem and Bethlehem) administered by the United Nations. If you look at Map 9, you can appreciate how hard it would have been to enforce the plan, with borders crisscrossing in a crazy quilt pattern designed to assure that nearly all Jewish settlements would be in lands allotted to the Jews (56 percent of Palestine). However, even their area would contain almost as many Arabs as Jews. Perhaps the Arabs could be transferred, but understandably neither the Palestine Arabs nor the governments of neighboring Arab countries welcomed a proposal that would establish a Jewish state in their midst, against the wishes of the Arab inhabitants of the land. However, the Communist countries, the United States, and most of the Latin American republics favored it, and it passed in the UN General Assembly by a thirty-three to thirteen vote despite the opposition of all five Arab member states. The Zionists were not thrilled by the partition plan, but they took it as a step toward creating the Jewish state for which they had waited and worked so long. The Arabs said that they would go to war, if necessary, to block the implementation of the plan. However, words and deeds were not always the same. Jewish paramilitary groups in Palestine soon moved into lands not allotted to their side, while Arab commandos often struck back at Jewish targets. Emir Abdallah contemplated annexing Arab Palestine. When Egypt's cabinet opposed intervention, King Faruq overrode their objections.

The Creation of Israel

The partition plan was certainly not a peaceful resolution to the contest for Palestine. Both Arab and Jewish armies started recruiting volunteers and arming themselves as well as they could. Each committed brutal acts of

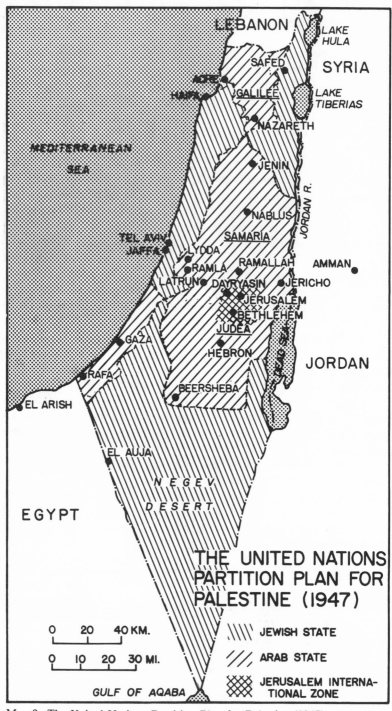

Map 9. The United Nations Partition Plan for Palestine (1947)

terrorism against innocent civilians. For example, the Irgun raided an Arab village near Jerusalem called Dayr Yasin and massacred 254 men, women, and children. A few days later, an Arab group ambushed a bus going to the Hadassah Medical Center on Mount Scopus, killing 75 Jewish professors, doctors, and nurses. The British folded their arms and did little to stop the escalating violence, as they were getting ready to pull completely out of Palestine. Some hoped they would be invited back in by whichever side was losing the contest.

The U.S. government sent the United Nations into a dither when its representative proposed in March 1948 to put off implementing the partition plan for a ten-year cooling-off period under a UN trusteeship. This plan might have satisfied the Arabs, but certainly not the Zionists, with the Jewish state almost within their grasp. Immense pressure was brought to bear on President Truman, who finally came out in favor of a Jewish state. That spring the diplomats argued at the United Nations, Arab and Jewish terrorist groups in Palestine murdered civilians and sniped at each other, large numbers of Palestinian Arabs panicked and fled for safety to neighboring countries, and finally the British pulled out.

On 14 May the Jewish Agency Executive Committee, meeting in Tel Aviv, formally declared that those parts of Palestine under Jewish control were now the independent state of Israel. The provisions of the 1939 white paper restricting Jewish immigration and land purchases were declared null and void. The Zionists urged the Arab inhabitants of the new state of Israel "to preserve the ways of peace and play their part in the development of the state, on the basis of full and equal citizenship and due representation in all its bodies and institutions." They also called on the neighboring Arab states to cooperate with them for the common good of all. Even if these statements were sincere, they came too late. Many Palestinian Arabs, having fled from their homes during the early stages of the fighting, distrusted the Zionists and looked to their Arab neighbors for help. The next day five Arab governments sent their armies into Palestine to fight against the new state of Israel.

CONCLUSION

The contest for Palestine had now entered a new phase. Arab nationalists and political Zionists had enflamed each other's worse fears under the bungling British mandate for years. Now they could fight each other openly. The Arab-Israeli conflict, as now it must be called, would become one of the most intractable problems of modern diplomacy.

Someone said that, if God is dead, He died trying to solve the Arab-Israeli conflict. Before 1948 a compromise might have been found between the extremes of Arab nationalism and political Zionism. But no attempt at accommodation worked, and the world is continuing to pay a high price for that failure.

17

Israel's Rebirth and the Arabs' Reaction

The 1948-1949 war between the new state of Israel and its Arab neighbors was a revolutionary event, setting in motion many drastic changes in the Middle East. To the Israelis and their admirers, the war was a struggle for Jewish independence, fought first against British imperialism and later against the armies of the Arab states. They saw Israel's victory as revolutionary because, for the first time in the modern history of the Middle East, the people of a country managed to overthrow a colonial regime and set up a democratic government. From the Arab point of view, their defeat in Palestine was revolutionary because it discredited the existing rulers and their regimes. In the ensuing years many Arab governments would be toppled by military coups and many kings and prime ministers assassinated. The Palestine disaster uprooted more than half a million Arabs, who sought refuge in the Gaza Strip (a small part of Palestine taken over by Egypt in 1948), Jordan, Syria, or Lebanon. These Palestinian Arab refugees soon emerged as a potent force. Some became ardent Arab nationalists. Indeed, they would espouse any ideology or back any leader that would give them back their dignity and their homes. The Palestinians' bitter opposition to Israel (and its Western supporters) was matched only by their hostility to Arab governments that might want to make peace with the Jewish state. In short, they became the greatest revolutionaries of the Arab world. On both sides, the period from 1948 to 1956 was one of readjustment to the new conditions brought about by the war.

ISRAEL'S WAR FOR INDEPENDENCE

How and why did the Israelis win the war for independence? The Arab states were larger and more populous by far than Israel. Some had large standing armies and lots of military equipment. On 14 May 1948, the day that the leaders of the Jewish Agency declared the independent existence of

Israel, the odds seemed to favor an Arab victory. Armies of Egypt, Jordan, and several other Arab countries went into Palestine the next day. If for them the war was just starting, for the Israelis (as the Jews in Palestine now called themselves), it had been going on for several years. As we saw in the last chapter, it had been building up since World War II, chiefly against the British. This meant there were already many experienced Jewish soldiers. But they had not all belonged to the same force. Aside from Haganah, the military arm of the Jewish Agency, several of the political parties had their own armies. The best known was the right-wing Irgun Tzvei Leumi (National Military Organization), which belonged to the party that hoped to set up the Jewish state on both sides of the River Jordan. Headed by Menachem Begin, the Irgun was famous for its commando attacks, most notorious of which were the bombing of Jerusalem's King David Hotel in 1946 and the night raid on the Arab village of Dayr Yasin in April 1948. The Israelis were divided at first, for the Irgun and the more extreme Stern Gang resisted being absorbed into Haganah, but the Arab invasion and what they viewed as the dire consequences of an Arab victory welded the people together. As the weeks went by, the new Israel Defense Force grew in numbers, equipment, and experience.

The Contending Forces

The opposing Arab armies proved to be smaller than expected. Countries like Egypt held back most of their troops to preserve order at home. Saudi Arabia once promised to send 40,000 men, but as of 1 October 1948 only 700 were on the field. Lebanon's 2000 soldiers were little more than a glorified police force. The best equipped and trained army proved to be Transjordan's Arab Legion, but its field strength of 10,000 could hardly match an Israeli army of over 100,000 men and women in October. Even some pro-Israel accounts like Nadav Safran's *From War to War* state that the Jews had more troops committed to battle than all of the Arab countries combined. This probably was not true in May 1948, when the reported successes of several Arab guerrilla groups in Palestine against the Jews drew flocks of volunteers to join the regular armies of Egypt, Syria, Lebanon, Transjordan, and Iraq.

In the early days of the war small bands of poorly armed Israelis had to ward off large Arab armies. In the northern Negev kibbutz of Yad Mordechai, for example, an Egyptian brigade heading toward Tel Aviv was held up for six days—long enough for Israel to strengthen its defenses farther north—by a group of less than eighty men and teenagers. In the Galilee the poorly armed defenders of the Jewish quarter of Safed put together a makeshift "cannon," whose loud (but harmless) reports are said to have fooled the enemy into fleeing without a fight. Really, it mattered less that Jewish soldiers outnumbered Arab ones in Palestine than that the Arabs came to think they did. Knowing little about the character and abilities of the Jews in Palestine, Arab military leaders tended at first to underestimate them. When the Israelis managed after a while to counter their early advances, the Arabs overreacted and started to overestimate the Jews' strength. Poor morale was a major reason for the Arab defeat.

The Policies of the Outside Powers

I should add that the attitudes and policies of the Great Powers confused both sides, but the Arabs were hurt more as a result than the Israelis. America and the USSR clearly favored Israel; both rushed to give it diplomatic recognition. Although most countries banned arms sales to both sides, Communist Czechoslovakia shipped large quantities of weapons to Israel. Considering their recent policies, why did the USSR and its satellites support Israel in 1948? No doubt their memories of the recent struggle against Nazi Germany and the destruction of European Jewry had some effect on the Russians, but the pragmatic reasons for their policy were (1) their desire to weaken Britain's influence in the Middle East, (2) their hope that the new Jewish state would adopt socialism or even Communism, and (3) their interest in discrediting "feudal" and "bourgeois" regimes in the Arab countries. The United States seemed to equivocate. Public opinion clearly favored the Jewish state. With a presidential election approaching, Truman, an incumbent in deep trouble, vied with his Republican opponents in support of Israel. However, high officials in the State Department and the military feared that an anti-Arab policy would jeopardize America's growing oil interests in the Middle East. American businessmen, missionaries, and educators who had spent years in the area argued cogently against policies that would antagonize the whole Arab world. But Israel had a much stronger body of supporters, especially in Congress.

The Arabs expected more support from Britain, which had been at odds with the Zionists since the 1939 white paper and had treaties with Iraq and Egypt permitting British troops to guard airfields and strategic waterways. The commander of Transjordan's Arab Legion, Sir John Bagot Glubb, and many of his officers were British subjects. Britain also had major oil interests in Iraq and Kuwait. But, while the Foreign Office and many senior diplomats did strongly favor the Arabs, the British government depended too much on America's economic and military support to clash openly with its policies in the Middle East. Continental Europe was still recovering from the ravages of World War II, and most liberals sympathized with the Jewish state. Europeans who volunteered to help the Arab armies often turned out to be unrepentant Nazis. Meanwhile, many Americans and Europeans rallied to Israel's cause as an act of atonement for the Holocaust.

United Nations Mediation Attempts

Overtaken by events in May 1948, the United Nations tried to settle the Arab-Israeli conflict in ways that irritated first one side, then the other, and sometimes both. It promptly sent a mediator, Count Folke Bernadotte of Sweden, who managed to get both sides to accept a month-long cease-fire in early June. Both the Arabs and Israelis were exhausted from four weeks' intense fighting, but only the latter used this respite to obtain and distribute arms to its soldiers. Count Bernadotte published a plan that would have given the Negev Desert (mostly assigned to the Jews in the 1947 Partition Plan for Palestine) and Jerusalem to Transjordan. Israel would get in return those parts of western Galilee that had been assigned to the Arabs. Egypt (whose troops had occupied most of southern Israel) would get nothing. On 8 July it broke the cease-fire, and fighting resumed on all fronts. During the next ten days the Israelis took part of Galilee and the strategic towns of Lydda and Ramleh, expelling their Arab inhabitants, as the Arab Legion drew back without a fight. However, before the Jewish forces could capture the Old City of Jerusalem (containing the revered Western Wall), the United Nations secured another cease-fire and on 18 July another uneasy truce descended on Palestine.

As both sides prepared for yet another round of fighting, the UN mediator made a new effort to gain Arab support. Bernadotte added to his plan a stipulation that the Arab refugees must be allowed to go back to their homes in cities and villages now under Israeli control. How, with the winter cold and rain approaching, could these people wait in makeshift camps for a chance to return? Who could have known that Palestinian Arabs (and their descendants) would wait and wait and wait, as pawns or perpetuators of the Arab-Israeli conflict the United Nations was supposed to settle in 1948! But the Israelis definitely did not want to let these Arabs back. Bernadotte was assassinated, predictably by the Stern Gang, in mid-September.

Ralph Bunche, an American, became the new UN mediator. His big problem area was the northern Negev, occupied mainly by Egyptian troops. Because Israel needed to supply some isolated Jewish settlements, Dr. Bunche arranged for Egyptian and Israeli truck convoys to take turns using the main roads. Egypt violated the agreement, giving Israel the pretext it wanted to resume the fighting. Pushing back the Egyptians, the Israelis captured much of the northern Negev, including Beersheba. What they most wanted, though, was Judea, where Brigadier General Moshe

Dayan attacked Arab Legion positions around Hebron and Bethlehem until the United Nations obtained a new cease-fire. Meanwhile, Israeli forces in Galilee drove the Palestinian Liberation Army northward into Lebanon. While the UN members continued to debate the Bernadotte Plan in late 1948, Israel tried to push Egyptian and Arab Legion forces out of the Gaza region and the southern Negev. Another brigadier general, Yigal Allon, attacked the Egyptians at Auja, and by the year's end the main fighting front had crossed the old Palestine border into Egyptian Sinai. When Egypt still would not sue for peace, Britain invoked the 1936 Anglo-Egyptian Treaty to intervene against Israel. Cairo hardly wanted London's help at this point, but no Arab country was willing to come to Egypt's rescue.

The Rhodes Proximity Talks

The United Nations now began a bizarre exercise in diplomacy. Since no Arab state was willing to confer directly with Israel (and thus give de facto recognition to the Jewish state), in January 1949 Ralph Bunche opened what were called "proximity talks" on the island of Rhodes. Meeting at first in separate suites in the same hotel, delegations from Egypt and Israel haggled over terms, with Dr. Bunche carrying proposals from one side to the other, finally securing an armistice agreement. Three months later, after the Arab Legion had lost what parts of the Negev it had occupied, Transjordan signed at Rhodes a separate agreement, one that in fact ratified a secret pact King (formerly Emir) Abdallah had already made with the Israeli military commanders. Israel now gained access to the Gulf of Aqaba, a fateful accomplishment that deprived Egypt and Transjordan of direct overland contact and enabled Israel to build a port at Eilat. Lebanon signed an armistice with Israel in March 1949, and Syria finally followed suit in July. Iraq, which had also sent forces into Palestine, never signed an armistice (since it had no common border with Israel, this hardly mattered at the time) and continued vigorously to oppose any Arab accommodation with Israel. It still does.

THE AFTERMATH OF THE WAR

Most people hoped these armistice agreements would lead to a comprehensive peace between Israel and the Arabs. The UN Conciliation Commission for Palestine set up a conference in Lausanne (Switzerland) where Israeli and Arab delegations were to settle their outstanding differences. However, the negotiations broke down before the two sides could meet. Israel insisted on a comprehensive settlement, while the Arabs demanded that Israel withdraw from the lands not allotted to the Jewish state by the 1947 partition plan. They also refused to negotiate with Israel until the Palestinian refugees were allowed to return to their homes. The Arab countries argued that these stipulations were contained in UN General Assembly resolutions and that Israel's admission to the United Nations had been predicated on its compliance with them. Of course Israel replied that the Arabs themselves had defied the General Assembly resolution calling for the partition of Palestine in the first place. As such arguments went on and on, hopes for a settlement dissipated. As most UN members recognized the Jewish state, Western observers thought the Arab governments would soon admit that Israel was in the Middle East to stay. Later on I hope to show why they did not.

Arab Divisions

I believe the main reason why the Arabs failed to defeat Israel in 1948, or in any of the later wars, and why (up to early 1979) they have equally failed to make peace, is that they are politically divided. In principle, all the Arab countries were united in their opposition in 1947-1948 to the UN partition plan and to the creation of a Jewish state in Palestine. As members of the Arab League, they had pledged to fight against it, putting their armies under the command of an Iraqi general. Some had refused to appropriate funds or commit troops as long as the British had stayed in Palestine. Abdallah, "king" of Transjordan, still wanted to create a "Greater Syria." Even in 1948, he was willing to make a deal with the Jews in order to annex parts of Palestine to his own kingdom, a first step to his taking over Lebanon and Syria, where some citizens still backed the Greater Syria idea. You may remember from chapter 13 how the Hashimite family of Mecca had hoped to unite the whole Arab world after World War I, but the French had taken over in Syria and Lebanon. Abdallah was a Hashimite. So was the ruling family in Iraq, which supported his Greater Syria plan and Arab nationalism generally, provided of course that the Baghdad government became the senior partner. But Kings Faruq and Ibn Saud had no use for the Hashimites or their claim to unite the Arab world. Egypt now aspired to be the leading Arab country, since it had the largest population, universities, newspapers, and broadcasting stations in the Arab world. The Arab League headquarters was in Cairo, and its energetic secretary-general was an Egyptian. And Egypt certainly did not want to have a Hashimite king ruling in Palestine and seeking to take over Syria and Lebanon. Ibn Saud, having driven the Hashimites out of Arabia, emphatically agreed with Faruq.

In other words, while the Arabs had put on a show of unity and had threatened the Jews with defeat and even extermination if they dared to set up a state in Palestine, their leaders were really trying to outbluff one another. Up to May 1948 most Egyptian generals and even cabinet ministers had hoped to stay out of the expected Palestine war. It was the enthusiasm of the Muslim Brothers, King Faruq's vanity, and the momentum of Egypt's own threats that sent the army in to fight a war for which they were unprepared. Emir Abdallah had assured such Jewish emissaries as Golda Meir that his Arab Legion would not fight, but finally sent them in so that Egypt and other Arabs could not hog the glory if they won. I said earlier that 40,000 Saudis were expected to fight on the Arab side, but in fact Ibn Saud held back his troops. Once the fighting started, the Egyptian army and the Arab Legion worked at cross purposes. The Palestinian Arabs had a "liberation army," commanded by a Syrian, but it would not cooperate with the British-officered Arab Legion. Emir Abdallah also had no use for the best-known Palestinian Arab nationalist, Hajj Amin al-Husayni, the former mufti of Jerusalem. The mufti had been expelled from Palestine by the British, taken refuge in Syria and Iraq, and found his way to Berlin, where he became an adviser and propagandist for Hitler during World War II. In 1945 he had escaped to Cairo and was now working for Faruq. As long as the Arabs had a chance of defeating Israel in 1948, the various leaders and armies maneuvered to see who could pick up the most land and glory in Palestine. Once Israel was driving the Arabs back, they began bickering over who was to blame.

The Palestinian Arabs

Who looked out for the Palestinian Arabs? No Arab government heeded the needs or interests of those people who, up to 1948, had been the majority of Palestine's population. About 150,000 managed, by chance or by choice, to stay in their homes within lands controlled by Israel. They became Israeli citizens, an Arabic-speaking Muslim and Christian minority within a Jewish state, subject for years to harsh restrictions, but also enjoying political rights, economic benefits, and educational advantages unmatched by most of their Arab neighbors. The 400,000 Arabs living in the Old City of Jerusalem and in those parts of Judea and Samaria not taken by Israel remained under the military occupation of Transjordan's Arab Legion. Abdallah promptly annexed this Palestinian region, now usually called the "West Bank," to his emirate, which he renamed the "Hashimite Kingdom of Jordan." Most other Arab countries protested, but they could no more restrain Abdallah than they could defeat Israel. Although Israel naturally resented "Jordanian" rule over the Old City of Jerusalem, its emissaries had secretly agreed to let Abdallah keep the West Bank as they hoped to make a comprehensive peace settlement with Jordan later on. Anyway, the Israelis held the western part of Jerusalem plus strategic chunks of Palestine not allotted to them by either the 1947 partition plan or the modifications later proposed by Bernadotte. There were also 200,000 Palestinians (many of them refugees) in the region of Gaza, where Egypt set up an "all-Palestine government" under the former mufti. This political ploy against Abdallah soon fell apart, leaving the Gaza Strip under Egypt's military administration, which did the local Palestinians no good at all.

The Palestinian Arab refugees, whose numbers are disputed by polemicists and historians, suffered the worst. I would place the figure at the end of 1948 somewhere between 550,000 and 700,000. Some had left their homes voluntarily before the struggle really started, while others had fled (or been forced to flee) during the fighting. Who forced their flight? Israel and its supporters claim that the Arab governments broadcast orders to Palestinian civilians to move out so that their armies could more easily move in against the Israelis. The Arabs point out that Jewish extremists used terror tactics against the Palestinians in April and May 1948 and that the Israel Defense Force drove other Arabs out during the later phases of the war. It is very hard to determine who is right, but there has never been any proof of the alleged Arab broadcasts, and both sides committed terrorist acts. Conditions varied from time to time and from place to place, but the end result was that most Palestinians ended up in camps near Israel's borders in Egyptian-held Gaza, the Jordanian-ruled West Bank, Syria, and Lebanon.

The Arab countries would not absorb them (mainly for political reasons, although economic factors also hampered their absorption). The Palestinians themselves refused assimilation because they wanted to go back to their homes. Israel, absorbing European Jewish survivors and unwilling to take in a "fifth column" of implacable foes, refused to readmit the Palestinian refugees. The United Nations realized that something must be done to help these unfortunate people. It set up the United Nations Relief and Works Agency (UNRWA), but all it could do, in 1949 or even recently, was to house them in camps, give them enough food and clothing to survive, and educate or train their children, hoping all along that the problem would someday and somehow be solved. A few Arab refugees did manage to return to Israel, many younger Palestinians gradually got assimilated in the Arab countries economically, but many others stayed in the camps, filled with bitterness against Israel, its Western backers, and indeed the Arab leaders who had betrayed them. I will have more to say about them later.

THE ARAB COUNTRIES

Let us now look at the Arab world in the wake of what soon was called the "Palestine disaster." In some cases, I have to go back to the mandate era between the two world wars. If you sometimes become confused by the details, the main point to keep in mind is that, whatever the claims made by Arab nationalists, there were several Arab states, many leaders, and various policies. Some Arab governments were stable, some were popular, and many were neither.

Jordan

The country most clearly affected by the war was Jordan. What had been a desert emirate called Transjordan was now the Hashimite Kingdom of Jordan. A half million Transjordanians, mostly of bedouin origin, were now joined by a million Palestinians, half of them local farmers or city dwellers in the annexed West Bank, the other half being refugees housed in temporary camps. The Palestinians, all of whom were offered Jordanian nationality, tended to be more westernized and politically articulate than the Transjordanians over whom Abdallah had ruled for years like a father figure. Even if most of the Palestinians were (or, in the case of the refugees, had been) subsistence farmers, some were lawyers, teachers, businessmen, or bureaucrats. Few were monarchists. For Abdallah, control of Jerusalem's Old City, with its Muslim shrines like the Dome of the Rock, was compensation for his father's loss of Mecca and Medina to the Saudis a generation earlier. He was content to rule his new lands and his tripled population. He even negotiated secretly with Israel for rail access to Haifa in exchange for diplomatic recognition. Disgruntled Palestinians, especially Arab supporters of the ex-mufti, denounced Abdallah as a traitor. In July 1951 a young Palestinian murdered him in Jerusalem. His son and successor, Talal, soon had be eased out because of mental instability (or, some say, his opposition to British influence in his country). He abdicated in favor of his seventeen-year-old son, Husayn, who officially took charge in 1953.

During this time Britain continued to subsidize Jordan and Sir John Bagot Glubb still commanded the Arab Legion. Only in 1955 did the USSR consent to admitting Jordan to UN membership. There followed a brief period in which King Husayn flirted with Arab nationalism and the Palestinian Left, a subject I will cover in the next chapter. In my own view, Jordan would have benefited economically by making peace with Israel and gaining access to the Mediterranean. But the lesson of Abdallah's murder was clear. The Palestinians might have lost their homes and become second-class citizens in Jordan, but they could veto any attempt to bury their claims by a peace settlement. Never would Husayn publicly be the first to seek peace with Israel. The idea of a Greater Syria also faded like a desert mirage.

Syria and Lebanon

What did happen to the rest of Greater Syria? The impact of the war on Lebanon and Syria was different, but no less disruptive. What was now the republic of Syria had become embittered by a generation of unwanted French rule. After France's troops had defeated Faysal's Arab army in 1920 and taken control over all the areas mandated to France under the San Remo agreements, the French administration had done its best to suppress Arab nationalism in the land of its birth. Syria was never prepared for independence as Wilson's mandate scheme had envisaged; it was not even offered a constitution until 1936, and then the French parliament never ratified it! In the 1920s Syria was split up into fragmentary states to keep the Syrians from combining against the French mandate. Most of the divisions proved unworkable and had to be shelved, but two became permanent. One was the separation in 1938 of the region around Alexandretta and its formal annexation by Turkey in the following year. The other was the creation of Lebanon as a separate republic, for which I need to make a lengthy digression.

The predominantly Christian area around Mount Lebanon had enjoyed local autonomy from 1861 to 1914 within the Ottoman Empire, an arrangement that had been guaranteed by the European powers (but especially France). The Christians of Mount Lebanon were mostly Maronites in communion with the Roman Catholic church. They traded with France and sent their children to French mission schools. Unlike the other inhabitants of Syria, they welcomed the French occupation after World War I. Hoping to strengthen the Maronites politically, France created an enlarged Lebanon by adding the coastal towns of Tripoli, Beirut, and Sidon to the historic Mount Lebanon. The resulting entity, slightly over half Christian, proved sufficiently stable (meaning pro-French) to acquire a constitution and a little local autonomy in 1926. The French military occupation lasted until 1946, while the great landowning families of Lebanon evolved into an elite of bankers and merchants. Their government was "democratic" in the sense that its legislators were popularly elected, but I would call it a commercial oligarchy, since the wealth and power were concentrated in the leading families.

Lebanon's system also preserved confessional divisions by allocating to each religious sect a fixed share of seats in the parliament and posts in the bureaucracy. The apportionment was based on a census taken by the French in 1932. No other census has been taken since then, as the Maronites and several other sects fear that any head count would show their relative decline. The influx of about 150,000 Palestinian refugees in 1948 complicated the picture. Lebanon quickly assimilated those who were

Christian, but the Muslim majority was denied Lebanese citizenship and settled in large refugee camps. Had any census been taken that included the Palestinians and left out the Christians who had emigrated to Europe and America, Lebanon would have been proven predominantly Muslim since 1949. Instead, the system of proportional representation of religious sects continued to reflect what Lebanon had been under the French mandate. By unwritten agreement, the president was always a Maronite Christian, the prime minister a Sunni Muslim, and the other high posts went to the various smaller sects. The leaders also agreed to work together, despite their religious differences, to preserve the independence and territorial integrity of Lebanon. What this really meant was that the Christians would not try to keep the country tied to France or to recreate an autonomous Mount Lebanon under their own control, while the Muslims would not try to reunite Lebanon with Syria or any hypothetical pan-Arab state.

This understanding, to which all Christian and Muslim political leaders subscribed as their "National Pact" of 1943, guided Lebanon through a coup d'etat in 1952, a civil war in 1958 (see chapter 18), up to the more catastrophic breakdown of 1975-1976. Lebanon seemed to prosper under this system, but a few families continued to hold the lion's share of wealth and power, the government and army were too weak to protect the country or even to preserve order, Beirut's free press became a battleground for competing liberal, pan-Arab, and socialist ideologies, and the influx in 1948 of the unassimilable Palestinians eventually upset the system altogether.

My long digression on Lebanon will help me show how the creation of Israel affected Syria. The Syrians were angered not only by the amputation of Alexandretta and the creation of Lebanon during the time of the French mandate, but also by the decision of the Western powers to separate Palestine and Transjordan even before then. If Britain and France had cut up what was to have been Faysal's Arab kingdom in 1920 in order to serve their imperial interests, then ought (so hoped many Syrians) the imperialists' withdrawal to lead to the reunification of Greater Syria. But there were two flies in the ointment. One was the creation of a Jewish state, which to the Syrians was an imperialist plot to keep the area divided and under Western control. The other was Abdallah and his family. To be sure, a group of Syrians called the People's party wanted Arab unity restored under the Hashimites, probably an organic union of all Fertile Crescent countries, including Iraq. But the Syrians in power from 1945, the Nationalist party, wanted to keep Syria free of Hashimite rule. They too desired Arab unity, but under the aegis of the Arab League. Accordingly, Syria sent its army to fight against Israel in 1948 as an ally of Egypt and in competition with Abdallah and his Arab Legion. The poor showing of

Syria's troops led to allegations of scandals in Damascus. Discredited, the civilian government was overthrown by a military coup in 1949. Two more took place that year, and the leader who emerged from the pile was Colonel Adib Shishakli, whose populist dictatorship became the prototype for that of Egypt's Nasser and those of army officers in other Arab countries in the 1950s.

Deeply split by various religious and local differences, Syria became notorious for its own instability and disunity, yet its leaders aspired to unite all Arabs against Zionism (meaning Israel and its supporters) and imperialism. The overthrow of Shishakli in 1954 led to another attempt at civilian government, but the system was unresponsive to the country's need for economic and social reforms. An Arab socialist movement called the Ba'th ("renaissance") party became increasingly popular in Syria and among young people, army officers, and Palestinians in other Arab countries as well. It called for land reform, nationalization of basic industries, complete unification of the Arab world, and militant resistance to Israel and to all other vestiges of imperialism in the area. In such an atmosphere, no patriotic Syrian dared to argue for peace with Israel or even the absorption of the Palestine refugees, even though new farmlands were being developed in the northeastern part of the country. Indeed, Syria's own ethnic and religious minorities, such as the Armenians, various other Christian sects, Shi'i Muslims, Alawis (an offshoot of Shi'i Islam), Druze (described in chapter 6), and of course the Jews, generally fared badly in this period of rising Arab nationalism.

Iraq

Of all the Arab countries in southwest Asia the most populous is Iraq. With its two great rivers and its rising oil revenues, Iraq might have become the strongest Arab country. There are several reasons why it has not. First, it was put together from parts of three different Ottoman provinces by the British, who had conquered the area from the Turks during World War I. While its rivers might seem to unite these parts, keep in mind that the Tigris and Euphrates both start in Turkey and that the latter also flows through Syria. In addition, much of Iraq's arable land came under the control of the shaykhs of various quasi-independent bedouin tribes. The Muslim population was divided almost evenly between Sunnis and Twelve-Imam Shi'is, the latter having close ties with Iran next door. Religious minorities included Jews and Assyrians (or Nestorians, described in chapter 2). At least one-sixth of the population was Kurdish. A smaller share was Turkish. What these disparate groups had in common was four centuries of Ottoman rule, followed by a British military occupation and mandate between 1917 and 1932. The British wanted a ruler who would serve their interests and unite the peoples of the area. Faysal, driven by the French from Syria, served this purpose admirably, and so the British made him king of Iraq and quickly turned local power over to his government. In 1932 Iraq became the first mandated Arab country to become independent and join the League of Nations.

Unfortunately, Iraq's stability was upset by Faysal's premature death in 1933, an Assyrian uprising that the Iraqi army suppressed with a ferocity that seemed excessive to most outsiders, and a popular mood of strident Arab chauvinism in the late 1930s. Several coups brought military dictators into and out of power, culminating in the ardently nationalist and pro-Nazi regime of Rashid Ali al-Gaylani in 1941, which was crushed by the British. Meanwhile, Faysal's son and successor, Ghazi, had been killed in 1939 in a car crash (which many Iraqis blamed on the British), leaving his throne to his four-year-old son, Faysal II. A regency was set up under the boy's uncle, Abd al-Ilah, who worked closely with a shrewd Iraqi politician named Nuri al-Saʻid, whose policies were usually pro-British yet also Arab nationalist. Although trained as an Ottoman army officer, Nuri had joined the Arab revolt in 1916 and served the Hashimites from then on.

In 1942, with some British encouragement, Nuri proposed a union of Arab states in the Fertile Crescent: Syria, Lebanon, Palestine, Transjordan, and Iraq. Such a combination would have been dominated by Iraq. This Arab union appealed to few of the Jewish settlers in Palestine. The French, who were still clinging to Syria and Lebanon, were hostile. But the strongest opposition to Nuri's plan came from Egypt and Saudi Arabia, which did not want to see Baghdad and the Hashimites as leaders of the Arab world. As explained earlier, the Egyptian government, also with British backing, countered in 1944 by proposing the League of Arab States. Iraq, unable to gain enough support for its Fertile Crescent scheme, joined the Arab League and became the most vociferous Arab opponent of Zionism.

Iraq's army fought in the 1948 Palestine war, but the country was less directly affected by the defeat than Israel's immediate neighbors. Its rising oil revenues were being invested in river irrigation and other projects that promised prosperity in the long run. Cabinets might change with alarming rapidity, the various minority problems might keep on simmering (except for the Jews, nearly all of whom were allowed to emigrate, minus their property, to Israel by 1951), the socioeconomic gap between the landowning shaykhs and the masses of peasants and urban workers might widen, and the pro-Western monarchy might lose popular support. The West did not notice. Britain's remaining military presence was camouflaged politically in 1955 when Iraq joined with Turkey, Iran, Pakistan, and Britain to form an anti-Communist alliance commonly called the Baghdad

Pact. The fact that Iraq was supposed to be aligned militarily with the other members of the Arab League seemed irrelevant. Relations between Baghdad and Cairo were usually bad. Both competed for the support of Syria and Lebanon. To the West, though, Iraq was the very model of what a developing nation should be, that is until 1958. But this story must wait for the next chapter.

Egypt

As you may remember, I carried my chapter on Egypt up to the end of the British occupation in 1956. I did so because, for most politically conscious Egyptians at the time, their big concern was to free the Nile Valley from British rule. Egypt's involvement in the contest for Palestine after 1936 was really a struggle against the Hashimites for the leadership of the Arab world. Gaining control of the Sudan came to seem less important, as Cairo's attention shifted to preventing either the Jews or Abdallah from taking over Palestine. The 1952 revolution that eventuated in Nasser's rise to power can be viewed as the result of mounting frustration over either (1) Britain's continued occupation of the Nile Valley or (2) the Egyptian army's humiliating defeat by Israel. The latter interpretation is more common because, from 1948 until after the October 1973 war, Egypt's energies have been mobilized to fighting against Israel and competing for the leadership of the Arab world. On the one hand, American and Soviet pressure made the British give up their Suez Canal base in 1954. On the other, Egypt acquiesced to the Sudan's complete independence in 1956. Yet in 1977 the rapprochement between the Sudan and Egypt, followed by President Anwar al-Sadat's surprising visit to Jerusalem, led some observers to think that Egypt is turning away from Arab nationalism toward a revived emphasis on the unity of the Nile Valley.

It may help to put Egypt's role as an Arab country into a clearer historical perspective. Even though the Arabs have not been together politically since the fall of the Umayyads in 750—if indeed they were ever really united—the feeling has grown up in the last century that the people who speak Arabic really are one nation. They should unite in a single state, as the Germans tried to do under Bismarck and Hitler or the Italians under Mazzini and Mussolini. Arab unity must include Egypt, the largest Arab country, the link between the Arabs of North Africa and those of southwest Asia. Many Egyptians wanted to unify the Arabs not just out of local pride, but also because they believed that only a strong and united Arab world could withstand the domination of the Western powers. Israel's creation seemed to these Egyptians to be a Western imposition on the Arabs, an attempt to maintain British and American influence in the Middle East. This is not to say that they wanted Communist control either, but Russia had not ruled the Arab world in the past, and so Soviet diplomacy seized its chance to weaken Western influence: it turned away from Israel and began to back the militant Arabs.

President Nasser of Egypt emerged as the leader of pan-Arabism in 1955 because of (1) his leadership of the junta that had toppled the discredited Faruq regime in 1952, (2) his exposure to various Asian nationalist and Communist leaders at the 1955 Bandung Conference, (3) Iraq's joining the pro-Western Baghdad Pact, while Egypt stayed neutral in the cold war between the USSR and the West, and (4) Egypt's decision to purchase $200 million in weapons from the Communist countries, after the West had refused to sell arms that might be used against Israel. Arab nationalists outside Egypt, especially the Palestinians, now hailed Nasser as their savior. He would lead the refugees back to their usurped homeland, just as Salah al-Din in 1187 had driven the Crusaders from Jerusalem. Indeed, the Egyptian government started arming bands of *fidaiyin* ("commandos"), mainly Palestinian youths in the Gaza Strip, to raid Israel and provoke border incidents.

The U.S. government tried to discourage Nasser from his anti-Western drift by a policy that now seems curiously confused. On the one hand, Secretary of State John Foster Dulles wanted Nasser to zero in on Egypt's internal problems, so he offered technical and economic assistance, notably a large loan to finance the construction of the Aswan High Dam. On the other, Dulles resented Nasser's policy of "positive neutrality" between Communism and the West, his support of the Algerians fighting against French rule, his threats against Israel and pro-Western Arab governments, and his recognition of the People's Republic of China. In June 1956, just as Egypt decided to accept the Aswan Dam loan offer, Dulles, hoping to humiliate Nasser, yanked it away. The Egyptian leader responded by nationalizing the Suez Canal Company, claiming he would use its profits, most of which had previously gone to European investors since its opening in 1869, to finance the building of the High Dam. "O Americans," he shouted before an immense crowd, "may you choke to death in your fury!"

It was not the Americans who choked. After all, the British and French were the main users of the Suez Canal, especially for oil imports from the gulf. They now began thinking about diplomatic (or, if need be, military) measures to get it back. The summer and fall witnessed several well-publicized conferences, trips to Cairo, and other stratagems aimed at prying the canal from Nasser's grip. Meanwhile the Arabs hailed Nasser's defiance as just retribution for all the grief they had ever got from Western imperialism. When all diplomatic attempts to put the canal under international control had failed, the British and French resolved to take it back by force—and to topple Nasser from power if they could. Significantly, they turned to Israel as an accomplice.

ISRAEL'S EARLY YEARS

If the Arabs viewed Israel as an agent of Western imperialism, the Israelis saw themselves as an embattled nation seeking to assure the survival of the Jewish people in the wake of the Nazi Holocaust. They saw their war for independence as a struggle by an oppressed people for freedom from outside domination. The Arab states against which Israel had fought in 1948 were still mostly influenced by British advisers and dominated by kings and landlords. When revolutions later toppled the discredited regimes in Syria and Egypt, many Israelis were disappointed that the new leaders made no peace overtures to them. The republican Arab nationalists in uniform were no less bitter than the monarchical and feudal politicians in *kufiyahs,* fezzes, or turbans. Meanwhile, the Israelis had their hands full rebuilding a war-torn country. In addition, they had to absorb the thousands of Jewish refugees, survivors of the war and the death camps of Europe, those whom they had earlier tried to get Britain to admit. Besides, they had the unexpected influx of even greater numbers of Jewish refugees from the Arab countries, many of whom were transferred under complex secret agreements. Absorption of these new Israelis, so different in language and culture from the earlier Jewish settlers, placed severe strains on the country.

Problems of the Jewish State

Economic problems were severe. The currency, cut loose from the British pound, plummeted in value. The new government could borrow little money to pay its bills. But large amounts of U.S. government and private Jewish assistance, augmented by German restitution payments to Jewish survivors of the Hitler era, brightened the picture. In an extraordinary act of statesmanship, West German Chancellor Konrad Adenauer agreed with Israeli Prime Minister Ben Gurion to pay huge reparations to Israel for the Nazi Holocaust. All of this financial aid provided some capital for the development of Israel and reduced (though it could never eliminate) the balance of payments deficit.

But equally important to Israel's survival was its people's conviction that never again must the Jewish people face the threat of extinction, whether by Christian fanatics, totalitarian dictators, or Arab nationalists. To skeptics who wondered why the existence of tiny Israel, with a million Jews and as many problems, better guaranteed Jewish survival than the continued presence of perhaps ten million Jews in the West (of whom few seemed inclined to move to Israel), the Zionists countered that the Jews of Germany had prospered too, but who had protected *them* from Hitler? If the independence of Israel had created an Arab refugee problem, the Arab states were to blame. Israel now had its hands full absorbing Jewish refugees from Europe and the Arab countries themselves. If Israel could not have peace without letting the Palestinian refugees come back, as the United Nations insisted, then peace would have to wait. This, in essence, was the Zionist position.

Since the Israelis saw their war against the Arabs as a struggle for independence, we forget that up to 1948 few Jews in Palestine or anywhere else really expected the Jewish state to be born during their lifetime. As a minority group within a mainly Arab land, the early Zionist pioneers had toiled to start farms in the wilderness, to build Tel Aviv amid the sand dunes north of Jaffa, to transplant the schools, theaters, and newspapers they had known in eastern Europe, and to create new institutions, like Histadrut, which combined labor and capital within a collectively governed organization. They had formed political parties advocating various combinations of socialism, nationalism, and Judaism. They had revived Hebrew as a spoken language and modernized it as a medium of written communication. But they had apparently expected that the Jewish national home would remain part of the British Commonwealth, that its Jewish inhabitants would come mainly from Europe, and that the Palestinian Arabs would somehow get used to their presence and power. World War II, the Holocaust, and the 1948 war belied these expectations. Now Israel was an independent country, surrounded by Arab states implacably opposed to its existence, with Jews pouring in from all parts of the world (but mainly the Middle East and North Africa) and with a surprisingly small Arab minority. Despite their political inexperience and economic problems, though, the Israelis managed to build a nation-state with a relatively democratic government and a remarkable freedom from repression.

Politics in Israel

I do not mean to say that Israel's democracy is a carbon copy of what the British or the Americans have. Political parties, some of them holdovers from Jewish movements in pre-1914 Eastern Europe, proliferated. No party could ever command the support of a majority of Israel's voters, some of whom were doctrinaire socialists, others observant Orthodox Jews, others passionate Zionists, and others Arab nationalists. Furthermore, Israel did not adopt the system of geographical constituencies familiar to Anglo-Saxons, but rather a system of representation by which the percentage of votes cast in a general election for each party was exactly matched by the proportion of the seats it held in the following session of Israel's parliament, the Knesset. In other words, if 100,000 Israelis cast votes in an election and 30,000 of them supported a particular party; then, out of the 120 Knesset seats, 36 would go to candidates on that party's list. This would mean that the first 36 candidates listed by that party on the ballot would be seated in the Knesset, while those numbered 37 and beyond would not. The decision on how to rank the listed candidates would be made beforehand in a party caucus, not by the voters themselves. Following a pattern familiar to Europeans but not to Americans, executive power was vested in a council of ministers (or cabinets) responsible to the Knesset. This meant that the head of government, the prime minister, had to choose a cabinet acceptable to a majority of the Knesset members. Since no party has ever won a majority of the votes (hence the Knesset seats) in any general election, any political leader wanting to form a government would have to combine his party with one or two others, compromising some of his ideological principles or policy preferences in the bargain.

In the early years of the state, Israel's leading politician was David Ben Gurion, the leader of the moderate labor party known as Mapai. Even though Ben Gurion came to personify Israel in the minds of most foreigners and many Israelis, Mapai never got over 40 percent of the vote in any general election. In order to come up with a cabinet acceptable to a majority of the Knesset members, Ben Gurion always had to form a coalition with other labor parties and usually with the National Religious party, whose leaders were dedicated to making Israel a more truly Jewish state. Even though Ben Gurion and his Mapai followers were nonobservant in their private lives and secular in their public speeches, they had to make compromises with the National Religious party. The result was a socialist republic with no formal constitution, no official religion, no explicit reference to God in its declaration of independence; and yet the army and all government offices kept the kosher dietary laws, no buses ran on the Jewish sabbath (from sundown Friday to sundown Saturday) except in Haifa and predominantly Arab areas, and all marriages and divorces were handled by the religious courts! State school systems were maintained for Israelis who observed the laws of Judaism, for those who wanted their children to speak Hebrew and were nonobservant, and for the Arabs who wanted their children to be educated in their own language and culture.

What made such a complicated system work? With all Israel's economic problems, with a population so diverse in culture, and with no reliable Great Power to protect Israel against its numerous Arab foes, many foreigners shook their heads in disbelief. It seemed as if Israel survived because the Arabs were so hostile. But it would be fairer to say that Israel's system worked because its leaders, haunted by the memory of what Hitler had tried to do, felt that no personal or ideological preference was more important than the survival of the state, which they equated with the survival of the Jewish people. It was hard for a passionate Zionist like Ben Gurion to believe that anyone could really live a Jewish life outside Israel, though experience soon proved that Israel needed the political and financial support of a strong and prosperous Jewish diaspora. Observers of Judaism in America and other countries generally agreed that the rebirth of a Jewish state strengthened the faith and the practice of religion among Jews outside Israel, despite the corrosive effects of secularism and materialist ideologies in much of the modern world.

Israel's Foreign Relations

It is true, though, that Arab hostility made Israel's life harder. All road and rail connections between Israel and its neighbors were cut. Planes flying to or from Israel could not fly over Arab countries, let alone land in their airports. The Arab countries refused to trade with Israel and imposed a boycott against the products of any foreign firm that did business there. Israeli citizens, foreign Jews, and even foreign Gentiles whose passports showed they had visited Israel were barred entry to many of the Arab countries. Ships carrying goods to Israel could not pass through the Suez Canal or even enter certain Arab ports. Egypt blockaded the Straits of Tiran between the Red Sea and the Gulf of Aqaba, hampering the development of Israel's port at Eilat. Arab diplomats abroad publicly shunned their Israeli counterparts. Arabic books, newspapers, and radio broadcasts were often virulent in their hostility to Israel and its supporters.

In such a beleaguered condition, Israelis might be expected to develop symptoms of psychopathic hostility to outsiders. A few did. It was said (by Jews and Gentiles alike) that Israelis were rude and hard to get along with, like the native prickly pear or sabra that has a tough skin and is covered with spears, yet is sweet once you get through its defenses. Almost every part of Israel was near an Arab country, and border raids occurred often. Frequent, too, were Israel's retaliatory strikes against Arab villages and refugee camps considered responsible for the raids. The winding armistice line between Israel and Jordan posed special security problems, especially when it separated a village from its customary farming or grazing lands. And a massive retaliation raid by Israel into the Gaza Strip in 1955 convinced Nasser that Egypt must buy Communist weapons to strengthen its armed forces. Israel bought some of the arms it needed from friendly countries like France, but whenever possible it manufactured its own. The increased frequency of Arab *fidaiyin* ("commando") raids, plus the mounting fervor of hostile propaganda, led Israel's cabinet to take stronger military measures in 1956. When Britain and France prepared to attack Egypt, Israel was quick to join in their conspiracy. All three wanted to teach the Arabs, especially Nasser, a lesson.

The history of the Middle East since 1948 can easily be turned into just an account of the military and political struggle between the Arabs and Israel. When we do this, we tend to overlook the other developments that were taking place in the region. Not all peoples of the Middle East are Israelis or Arabs; there are Turks and Iranians who have countries and concerns of their own, there are minorities living in most Middle Eastern countries who do not share the preoccupations of their leaders, and there are times when even Zionists and Arab nationalists think about matters unrelated to their conflict. Even though limitations on my space and your patience prevent my elaborating on these facts, I hope you will keep them in mind.

OIL IN THE MIDDLE EAST

In any case, we must at least take note of a development that took place between 1948 and 1956 in Middle Eastern countries not contiguous with Israel. The export of oil was becoming the major source of income for some parts of the region. The greatest Middle Eastern oil producer for the first half of the twentieth century was Iran, which as you know is not an Arab country. In 1951, during a crescendo of nationalist agitation, Iran's prime minister, Dr. Mohammad Mosaddiq, nationalized the Anglo-Iranian Oil Company. In retaliation, Britain and most of its Western allies refused to buy any oil from Iran, leading to a dramatic increase in the demand for Arab oil to the benefit of Iraq, Saudi Arabia, and Kuwait. I hate to bore you with statistics, but I think some specific examples will make my point clearer. Iraq's oil production increased from 3.4 million long tons (3.8 regular or 3.5 metric tons) in 1948 to 33.1 in 1955. For Saudi Arabia, the increase was still more dramatic: from 1 million long tons in 1944 to 46 million in 1954. The champion, though, was Kuwait, which went up from 800,000 in 1946 to 54 million in 1956. Not only did the production and sale of oil (and natural gas) zoom upward, but the share of the profits going to the Arab governments also rose dramatically. In December 1950 the Arabian American Oil Company (usually called Aramco) announced that it had agreed with the government of Saudi Arabia on a fifty-fifty sharing of all revenues. Soon other oil-exporting Arab countries won comparable increases in their royalty payments from the foreign oil companies. Oil revenues became the main source of income for most states surrounding the Persian Gulf, enabling the more enlightened governments to embark on ambitious government schemes, while the more patriarchal rulers expanded their palaces and replaced their camels with air-conditioned

Cadillacs. In fairness I should point out that the principal prodigal was Saud, the king of Saudi Arabia from 1953 until his deposition in 1964. In due course, these oil-rich desert kingdoms would have the financial power to influence the policies of the other Arab states and even the Western countries. However, this potential was not realized in the 1950s, or indeed the 1960s, so I will have to treat the subject later on.

CONCLUSION

The period between 1948 and 1956 was one of rapid change in nearly all aspects of Middle Eastern life. Israel and several of the Arab countries either became independent or increased their political distance from their former rulers. The power of Britain and France waned, although their informal influence lingered on in many parts of the Middle East, while that of the United States and the USSR rose there as elsewhere in the world. Both countries tried to adopt policies that would give them supremacy in the Middle East. Both proposed to fill the "power vacuum" left by the declining British and French presence. But the peoples of the Middle East were becoming more assertive, more nationalistic, and more hostile to the presence of foreign troops in their land, or even to the implication that they might not yet be able to take care of themselves. The continuing clash between Arab nationalism and political Zionism created new opportunities and new dangers, as you will see in the following chapters.

18

From Suez to Aqaba

Over a decade separated the second from the third round of fighting between Israel and its Arab neighbors. Between the "Suez Affair" of October-November 1956 and the "Six Day War" of June 1967, the Arab-Israeli conflict was confined to debates, angry speeches, border incidents, and occasional threats of escalation. A UN peacekeeping force patrolled the Gaza Strip and parts of Sinai, reducing the likelihood of renewed hostilities between Egypt and Israel. Since the other Arab states could not—or at any rate would not—fight Israel without Egypt's participation, most experts thought the chances of a new war were remote. The Arab-Israeli conflict seemed to be giving way to a series of power contests among the Arab leaders themselves. Prominent in all these struggles were the personality and the policies of Egyptian President Nasser. Egypt's defiance of the West in the Suez Affair made Nasser popular throughout the Arab world, and this popularity tended to undermine the authority of other Arab leaders and their governments.

NASSER AND HIS POLICIES

What sort of a man was Nasser? During his sixteen years as Egypt's president, he became bigger than life in the words and images of those who loved and hated him. His personality defies easy generalization. He could be dictatorial or deferential, charismatic or suspicious, ingenuous or crafty. He reacted more than he acted. As the son of an Alexandria postal clerk and grandson of an Upper Egyptian peasant, Nasser had known poverty and humiliation in his youth. When he was eight, his mother died. Moody and withdrawn, young Nasser read widely, especially history books and the biographies of great men like Julius Caesar, Napoleon, and (closer to home) Mustafa Kamil. He became passionately attached to Egyptian nationalism, but not to the politicians and parties of the 1930s. Unable to afford law school and yet eager to lead his country's fight for independence, he secured admission to the military academy in 1937, just after young men without palace or aristocratic connections were first allowed to enter the officer corps.

Upon receiving his commission in 1938, Nasser served in various army posts and gradually brought together a group of young officers from equally modest backgrounds. Intensely patriotic, these men chafed at Britain's power and the weakness of their own army, shown by the British ultimatum to King Faruq in 1942 and Egypt's defeat in Palestine in 1948. The friendship of these officers became a conspiratorial movement, as they saw that only the overthrow of the rotten regime could liberate and redeem Egypt. As you know from chapter 15, they succeeded in overthrowing the monarchy in 1952. Nasser never lost this conspiratorial tendency. Even in power he kept a large corps of spies to observe and report on his friends as well as his enemies.

In the early years of the revolution he tended to lead from behind the scenes, but Nasser engineered the overthrow of President Muhammad Nagib once the latter seemed to become too popular. Ponderous as a speaker at first, Nasser did not gain popular support until he became a symbol of defiance against the West. Once he had achieved status as a leader, he cultivated his popularity assiduously and became intensely jealous of any would-be rival. His honesty, modest life-style, and devotion to Egypt's welfare were exemplary, but his authoritarian personality stifled free thought and tended to block the appearance of new leadership.

The Ideas of Nasserism

What did Nasser stand for? For many people in the Arab world—and some in other parts of Asia and Africa—he symbolized defiance of the power of Western imperialism. Not only Egyptians, but most Arabic-speaking people, indeed most nations of what we often call the "Third World," felt hurt and humiliated by their previous dealings with the West. From these feelings and, on a more positive note, the belief that the Arabs could build a better future for themselves, grew up an ideology often called "Nasserism." Its main ideas, as I see them, were pan-Arabism, positive neutralism, and Arab socialism. Let us study them one by one.

I would define pan-Arabism as Arab nationalism with a stress on political unification. Nasser and his supporters noted how foreign imperialism and dynastic rivalries had split up the Arabic-speaking peoples of the Middle East into a dozen or more countries. Thus divided, the Arabs had lost Palestine in 1948 and were still a prey for the machinations of outsiders. For instance, in the 1950s the benefits of Arab oil were going to a few hereditary monarchs and foreign oil companies when they should have been shared by all the Arabs. Political unification would increase the wealth and power of the Arab world as a whole. Nasser's opponents equated his pan-Arabism with Egyptian imperialism. They accused Nasser of trying to seize control of the rest of the Arab world to enrich Egypt in general and his own regime in particular.

Positive neutralism was Nasser's policy of not aligning Egypt with either the Communist bloc or the military alliances that were being promoted by the United States to oppose the spread of Communism. More than that, it also meant persuading other countries to join with Egypt in a loose association of nonaligned nations. Thus Egypt, together with countries like India and Yugoslavia, could derail American and Soviet efforts to line up the other countries of the world on opposing sides. Neutralism would reduce world tensions and possibly even resolve the cold war. Critics called it a policy of "working both sides of the street," a means by which Nasser could extract military and economic aid from the Communist bloc and the West at the same time.

Arab socialism has never been easy to define. It is not a coherent ideology that emerged, fully articulated, in Egypt or the other Arab countries at a given point in time. Rather, it evolved in reaction to the economic system prevalent in most of the Arab world up to the 1950s. In this system, "capitalism" really meant that most large business enterprises were owned by foreigners, and land, buildings, and other sources of wealth belonged to a small native elite (a system often misnamed "feudalism"), while the masses of Arab workers and peasants lived in dire poverty. To bring about reform, Arab socialists advocated government control of the major industries and public utilities, in order to divide the economic pie more evenly among the people. They also believed that the size of that pie can be enlarged by comprehensive state planning to expand manufacturing and modernize agriculture. While borrowing some of their ideas and much of their rhetoric from the Marxists, most Arab socialists opposed Communism for its atheism and tried to prove that their own ideology was compatible with Islam. They maintained that shopkeepers and other small businessmen (called "national capitalists") could play a constructive role in Arab socialism. They rejected the Marxian concept of class struggle; if it were stimulated, they feared, class war would divide the Arab world even more and dissipate energies needed to develop a modern economy. Critics of Nasser's formulation of Arab socialism argued that it lacked theoretical rigor, inflated Egypt's already swollen bureaucracy, and drove away badly needed foreign investment.

THE SUEZ WAR

In the summer of 1956, Nasser's government had, as you know, nationalized the Suez Canal Company amid Arab applause—and Western dismay. Britain, though it had agreed with Egypt in 1954 to evacuate its Suez Canal base, still viewed the canal itself as the same imperial lifeline it had been in the two world wars. Prime Minister Anthony Eden likened Nasser to Hitler and Mussolini. Recalling his own opposition to Britain's appeasement policies in the late 1930s, Eden wanted Nasser stopped before he could undermine the West's position throughout the Arab world. France also wanted to stop Nasser, mainly because Egypt was supporting, with words and weapons, the Algerian revolution. Both countries got most of their oil from ships passing through the canal and were sure the Egyptians could not run it efficiently. Many Americans, though less interested in the canal, wanted Nasser to be punished for his hostility to Israel and his growing friendship with the Communist countries. But President Eisenhower and Secretary of State Dulles did not want the issue to come to a military showdown. The U.S. government kept pressing for a diplomatic solution: a conference to consider international administration of the canal, a "Suez Canal Users Association" to help Egypt run it, or a UN Security Council resolution that would satisfy all parties. Keep in mind that Eisenhower was running for reelection that fall on a slogan of "peace and prosperity." This was no time for a Suez war.

War Preparations

Meanwhile, however, Britain and France prepared openly to recapture the canal by force, despite logistical problems that kept delaying the date of their joint attack. Israel, eager to clean out *fidaiyin* bases in Gaza and to break Egypt's blockade of the Gulf of Aqaba, also began to mobilize for a preventive strike against Egypt. While all this was going on, Egypt started operating the canal with surprising efficiency, rejected all proposals for internationalization, and treated those military preparations as a big bluff.

They were not. On 28 October Israel called up its reserves, thereby doubling the number of its citizens under arms, and attacked Egypt the following day. As the invaders cut off Gaza and drove into Sinai, Britain and France issued a joint ultimatum to both countries, calling for an immediate cease-fire and for troop withdrawals to positions ten miles (sixteen kilometers) from the Suez Canal! Since Israel's forces were still pushing through eastern Sinai at the time, the ultimatum was really directed against Egypt. When Nasser turned it down, a coordinated Anglo-French force bombarded Egypt's airfields, landed paratroops at Port Said, and occupied the northern half of the Suez Canal. The new supplies of Czech and Soviet weapons did not enable Nasser's army to defend Egypt against what he called the "tripartite aggression." Soon the Israelis had captured all of Sinai, and only a heroic but futile civilian resistance delayed the British capture of Port Said.

Results of the War

But Nasser was not turned out by his army or his people. Instead, his military defeat turned into a political victory because the United States joined the USSR in condemning the attack. The focus of the drama shifted to New York, where the General Assembly agreed to set up a United Nations Emergency Force (UNEF) to occupy the Egyptian lands taken by the invaders. In short, Britain and France did not get to keep the canal, Nasser was not discredited in the eyes of the Egyptians or other Arabs, and Israel could not get recognition and peace from the Arabs in exchange for withdrawal from the Sinai Peninsula and the Gaza Strip. Israel's main gain from the war was a vague guarantee that its ships could use the Gulf of Aqaba, hitherto blockaded by Egypt. A UNEF contingent was stationed at Sharm al-Shaykh, a fortified point controlling the Straits of Tiran between the Gulf of Aqaba and the Red Sea. This arrangement, backed by the Western maritime powers, lasted up to May 1967.

In effect, Nasser had survived the Suez Affair because the United Nations—and especially the United States—had saved him. The U.S. government expressed its opposition to the tripartite attack on Egypt in terms of its desire to support small nations of the "Afro-Asian bloc" against imperialist aggression. This happened to be the time of the abortive Hungarian revolution. It seemed inconsistent for America to condemn Soviet intervention to suppress a popular uprising in Budapest while condoning a Western attack on Port Said. A more cogent reason, though, is that the crisis came to a head only days before the presidential election, hardly the time for a possible confrontation with the USSR. Thus the U.S. government managed to antagonize the British, the French, and the Israelis. It won little gratitude from Nasser and the Arabs.

THE COLD WAR IN THE ARAB WORLD

The U.S. government thought that its pro-Arab tilt in the Suez Affair would persuade the Arab governments to side with the West against Communism. The loss of British and French prestige in the Arab world seemed likely to create a power vacuum which, if America did not move in resolutely, would be filled by the USSR and its supporters. Only Iraq had formally joined an anti-Communist military alliance—what was then commonly called the Baghdad Pact—and no other Arab state was likely to commit itself so strongly to the West.

The Eisenhower Doctrine

Still it was thought that an American aid offer might win over some Arab governments. Thus the Eisenhower Doctrine was born, essentially a program by which the U.S. government offered military and economic assistance to any Middle Eastern country trying to withstand Communist aggression, whether direct or indirect. When it was proclaimed in January 1957, the Eisenhower Doctrine probably helped impress the American public with the importance of the Middle East and possibly deterred the USSR from a more forward policy in the area, but its reception in Arab capitals was decidedly mixed. Some Arab governments (such as Lebanon) accepted it. But Arab nationalists viewed it as an attempt by U.S. Secretary of State Dulles to take over Britain's role as policeman of the Middle East. To them, the Suez Affair had proved that Zionism and imperialism posed greater dangers to the Arab world than any theoretical threat of Communist aggression. Nasser in Egypt and the Ba'th party in Syria vehemently denounced the Eisenhower Doctrine, while Nuri al-Sa'id of Iraq strongly approved of it. He thought he knew what was best for the Arabs. After all, as he was apt to point out, he had helped to lead an Arab nationalist revolt before Nasser and his "free officers" were even born!

Trouble in Jordan and Lebanon

The struggle between the neutralist and pro-Western Arabs was especially strong in Jordan. The annexation of the rump of Arab Palestine (the West Bank) by what had up to 1949 been Transjordan created severe strains in that country. The Palestinians were more urbanized, educated, and politicized than the Transjordanians. They bitterly resented the existence of Israel, the Western governments that they blamed for creating and maintaining it, and the Arab leaders who had failed to prevent or to destroy it. Many Palestinians opposed Hashimite rule; to them King Husayn was a playboy, a pro-Western puppet propped up by the Arab Legion with its bedouin soldiers and British officers.

In an effort to win greater Palestinian support, Husayn had given in to Arab demands to keep Jordan out of the Baghdad Pact in 1955. Early in 1956 he had relieved General Glubb of his command of the Arab Legion. Free elections that October resulted in the formation of a popular front cabinet including several Arab nationalists and even one Communist minister. Also at that time, Britain began pulling its troops out of Jordan. It stopped subsidizing the government as well, but Egypt, Saudi Arabia, and Syria agreed to take up the slack. Ba'thist and pro-Nasser officers within Jordan's army began to replace royalists, and early in April 1957 they attempted to seize Husayn's palace. A few days later the Arab nationalists tried to capture a major Jordanian army base, but King Husayn rallied loyal troops to his side and personally faced down the threat to his rule. He then dismissed the popular front cabinet, declared martial law, dissolved parliament, and established what amounted to a royal dictatorship. Dulles then declared that the territorial integrity of Jordan was a vital American interest and sent the U.S. Sixth Fleet to the eastern Mediterranean. In effect, the Eisenhower Doctrine was first used to thwart an Arab nationalist takeover in Jordan. Even with American backing, though, Husayn's position remained precarious. The Palestinian Arabs, especially the refugees, still opposed the monarchy, which was violently assailed in widely heard broadcasts from Radio Cairo.

Meanwhile, the Lebanese government under President Kamil Sham'un decided to accept the Eisenhower Doctrine, despite objections from Arab nationalists that to do so would violate Lebanon's neutrality. The pro-Western Lebanese, mainly Christians, held a slight edge in political power over the Arab nationalists, most of whom were Muslim. Some detractors accused Sham'un's government of increasing that edge by rigging the 1957 parliamentary elections, in which many opposition leaders failed to be reelected. The Arab nationalits, supported both by Palestinians living in Lebanon's refugee camps and by Egypt and Syria, continued to oppose the government's pro-Western orientation and accused Sham'un of trying to perpetuate his own power. The stage was being set for the outbreak of Lebanon's 1958 civil war.

The Struggle for Mastery in Syria

A British journalist named Patrick Seale has written a perceptive account of Arab politics from 1945 to 1958 called *The Struggle for Syria*. As the title implies, his main thesis is that any power, whether local or foreign, seeking to dominate the Middle East must first control Syria. Although geographical Syria includes also Lebanon, Israel, and Jordan, even the republic of Syria has become a cockpit of international rivalries. Between the two world wars France and Britain competed for control of Syria, and in recent years the United States and USSR have been contenders for its support. Rivalries among other Arab governments have been even stronger. After World War II Abdallah of Transjordan aspired to rule a "Greater Syria" and so sought political backing inside the country, as did his main rivals, Kings Faruq and Ibn Saud. Geography has almost dictated Iraq's interest in Syria, which Egypt has usually tried to counter no matter who was ruling in Baghdad and Cairo.

Sensitive to these rivalries, Syrian politicians have tended to identify with the various contenders in their own struggle for power in Damascus. It should also be remembered that Syrians have usually been in the vanguard of Arab nationalism. As mentioned earlier, some young Syrian intellectuals formed a movement called the Ba'th ("renaissance") party, pledged to work for the complete unification of all Arabic-speaking peoples from the Atlantic Ocean to the Persian (or Arab) Gulf, within a political framework that would protect individual freedom and build a socialist economy. According to the Ba'th party constitution, "the Arab nation has an immortal mission which has manifested itself in renewed and complete forms in the different stages of history and which aims at reviving human values, encouraging human development, and promoting harmony and cooperation among the nations of the world."

To enable the Arab nation to achieve this mission, the Ba'th must gain control of as many Arab governments as possible and bring them together into an organic unity. Its first success was in Syria. Early in 1957, immediately after the Suez war had compromised the country's pro-Western politicians, a coalition of Ba'thists and other Arab nationalists won control of the government. Encouraged by Radio Cairo broadcasts and generous Soviet loans, Syria's new rulers moved toward what the Western countries took to be a pro-Soviet stance. Scarred by previous military coups backed by outsiders, Syria suspected the U.S. government of plotting its overthrow and expelled several embassy officials. As Turkey massed troops on its Syrian border, both America and the USSR threatened to intervene on opposite sides. The crisis cooled off, but some Americans began viewing Syria as a Communist satellite.

The United Arab Republic

The belief that Syria was a Communist satellite was erroneous. Syria's leaders were Arab nationalists, not Communists. A Communist takeover in Damascus would have stifled the Ba'th or set off a conservative countercoup like that of Husayn in Jordan. The Ba'thists saw their salvation in a union with Nasser's Egypt. Nasser might have preferred a gradual federation of the two countries, but Syria's leaders could not wait. On 1 February 1958 Syrian President Quwatli met with Nasser in Cairo and agreed to the marriage of their two countries. Henceforth, Syria and Egypt would be the "northern region" and the "southern region" of a new state, the United Arab Republic (UAR). Plebiscites held later that month in both regions ratified the agreement. The people voted almost unanimously for Nasser as their first president. Contrary to Western suspicions about a Nasserite *Anschluss,* it was the Syrians who rejoiced most at their union with Egypt.

The union settled Syria's internal problems, for a while anyway, but it put great pressure on other Arab governments to follow suit. The Hashimite kings, Jordan's Husayn and Iraq's Faysal II, reacted to the United Arab Republic by forming a rival union of their own, one more homogeneous but much less popular. Saudi Arabia kept aloof, but may have shown its nervous hand when a powerful Syrian politician, Colonel Abd al-Hamid Sarraj, accused King Saud of bribing him to assassinate

Nasser and rupture the union with Egypt. As I mentioned in chapter 14, this led to Saud's fall from power, as his brother and heir apparent, Faysal, took control of the finances and foreign affairs of Saudi Arabia. Although he was widely thought to be pro-Nasser in 1958, Faysal did not join the UAR, preferring not to share his country's huge oil revenues. Meanwhile, Yemen's ultraconservative government agreed to federate with the UAR, but Yemen's internal politics were virtually unaffected. The Palestinian Arabs were jubilant over the union between Egypt and Syria. They hailed Nasser as the new Salah al-Din who would soon, like his illustrious predecessor, restore their usurped homeland. The government and people of Israel reacted calmly to this sudden upsurge of Arab unity.

The 1958 Civil War in Lebanon

By contrast, the other non-Muslim state east of the Mediterranean, namely Lebanon, really felt the winds of Arab nationalism. The lure of Arab unity was strong among several groups in Lebanon: the Palestinians, especially those living in refugee camps; the Muslim Lebanese who felt that the status quo favored the Christians; the young people, mainly university students, who believed that Lebanon's aloofness from Arab nationalism served the interests of Western imperialism; and those Lebanese politicians who were excluded from power by the Sham'un regime. Many groups made the short trip to Damascus to hail the union with Egypt. Demonstrations were held in various cities and villages. When Muslim sections of Beirut displayed Nasser posters, Christians festooned their quarters with pictures of Sham'un. Tensions built up during the spring.

The spark that lit the fire was the assassination of a pro-Nasser newspaper editor in May 1958. Arab nationalists were quick to blame the government and to accuse Sham'un of plotting to amend Lebanon's constitution to assure himself a second term as president. A heterogeneous opposition, led by city politicians and rural grandees, banded together as a "national front." Shooting incidents and ancient feuds erupted in the countryside, the government declared a curfew, and the first Lebanese civil war began. In some ways, the war was like a comic opera: bombs exploded at random, rebel leaders continued to use the government's phone and postal facilities, and the army stayed out altogether. But the Sham'un regime accused Nasser of encouraging the rebels by smuggling arms across the Syrian border and appealed to the Arab League and then to the UN Security Council to stop this threat to Lebanon's independence. A UN observer group was unable to corroborate charges of massive infiltration from Syria, but the observers confined their operations to daylight hours on major roads.

The civil war in Lebanon might just have run down, once President

Sham'un agreed to let the parliament choose his successor. The rebel leaders did not really want to turn the country over to Nasser (though they welcomed his support), or the Palestinians, or the Communists. What brought the Lebanese conflict into the wider arena was a concurrent event in another Arab country, the Iraqi revolution of 14 July 1958. In a sudden coup, a group of army officers seized control of the police camps, the radio station, and the royal palace in Baghdad. They murdered King Faysal II and his uncle, Abd al-Ilah, hunted down and shot Nuri al-Sa'id, and declared Iraq a republic. While most Arabs rejoiced at the fall of the monarchy, the West was horrified. The new regime seemed the embodiment of both Arab nationalism and Communism, a triumph for Nasser, a harbinger of the fate awaiting Jordan and Lebanon, and a stalking horse for Soviet imperialism in the Middle East. If only America had helped to topple Nasser in 1956!

American Military Intervention

Immediately the U.S. government dispatched marines to Lebanon, responding to Sham'un's plea for aid under the Eisenhower Doctrine, and British troops were landed in Jordan, where Husayn's regime seemed to be in peril. It is highly probable that the West would have intervened in Iraq if there had been any hope of restoring the monarchy, and this may explain why Nasser suddenly flew to Moscow to seek Soviet aid. But the rule of the Hashimites was finished in Baghdad. The new military junta assured its own popularity by instituting land reform, proclaiming its support for Arab unity, and renouncing its military alliance with the West. When the fiery young nationalist who was second-in-command, Abd al-Salam Arif, flew to Damascus to meet Nasser, it seemed only a matter of time before Iraq would join the UAR. But the supreme revolutionary leader, Colonel Abd al-Karim Qasim, seems to have realized that Iraq's oil revenues would go a lot farther at home without being shared with thirty million Egyptians and six million Syrians. Arif was eased out of power, and Qasim settled into playing an unstable balancing game between the Arab nationalists and the Communists. The Iraqi government did try to better the lives of the masses, but many problems, especially the Kurdish rebellion in the oil-rich north, proved no more soluble for Qasim than they had been under Nuri al-Sa'id and the Hashimites.

The Ebb of the Pan-Arab Tide

In retrospect, the summer of 1958 was a high point for pan-Arabism. Just as Iraq under Qasim soon went its own way, so too did Saudi Arabia under Crown Prince Faysal. The American marines in Lebanon confronted more Coke vendors than Communists. In due course, its parliament elected neutralist Fuad Shihab, the general who had kept Lebanon's army out of the civil war, as the replacement for the pro-Western Sham'un. American troops pulled out, all factions agreed to respect the independence and neutrality of Lebanon, and their leaders resumed their favorite activity, making money. Britain likewise withdrew its troops from Jordan, but the Husayn regime did not fall. Experts have been predicting his overthrow ever since. A military coup in the Sudan in November 1958, initially thought to be pro-Nasser, did not unify the Nile Valley. Some Syrians began to wonder why no other country followed theirs into the United Arab Republic. During 1959 and 1960 Egypt's heavy-handed bureaucracy made further inroads into Syria's hitherto capitalistic economy. Even the Ba'th party chafed under Nasser's insistence that it, like all other Syrian parties, must be absorbed by the National Union.

For a while Nasser mended his fences with the West, mainly because Iraq repudiated the Arab nationalist parties in favor of the Communists. But the USSR was playing a growing role in the UAR economy, and Nasser was coming to believe that state planning and control of all major industries would be needed to fulfill a promise he had made to double the national income within ten years. In his July Laws of 1961, Nasser nationalized nearly all manufacturing firms, financial institutions, and public utilities in Egypt and Syria, reduced to about 100 acres the maximum landholding allowed an individual, and put a ceiling on the salary a UAR citizen could earn. These laws so antagonized bourgeois Syrians that, a few months later, a military coup in Damascus ended their union with Egypt. Soon after that, the UAR terminated its federation with Yemen, when its imam allegedly composed satirical verses against Nasser. At the end of 1961, Nasser, the leader who aspired to unite the Arab world, stood alone.

Arab Socialism and Nasser's Comeback

The tide of Nasserism had now reached its ebb. Within Egypt the focus was on building a new order under Arab socialism. Nasser called together a National Congress of Popular Forces to draw up the National Charter, which was published amid great fanfare in May 1962. A new single party, the Arab Socialist Union, replaced the flagging National Union, and half the seats in its national council were set aside for workers and peasants. Workers were put on the managing boards of some nationalized companies. For the first time in Egypt's history a worker and a woman took charge of cabinet ministries. If his socialist experiment led to economic growth and greater social equality, Nasser reasoned, other Arab countries would follow his example. Defying Egypt's political isolation, Nasser adopted as his newest slogan, "Unity of goals, not unity of ranks."

The first sign of a change was Algeria's independence in July 1962 after a bitter eight-year struggle against France. The Algerian leader, Ahmad Ben Bella, strongly supported Nasser and all revolutionary Arab causes. The second was the revolution that broke out in Yemen that September, only a week after the old imam died and Prince Badr took over. A group of Yemeni army officers seized control in San'a and proclaimed a republic. Elated, the Egyptian government hailed the new regime and assumed that Badr had been killed. Actually, he and his followers had taken to the hills, where monarchist tribesmen were ready to fight for their imam, backed by the Saudis who did not want a Nasserite republic on their southern border. Nasser sent an Egyptian force to shore up the new republican regime, but its leaders were inexperienced and Yemen's civil war proved intractable. What seemed to be a contest between the followers of the young imam (mainly Shi'is in the hills) and republican officers (mainly Shafi'i rite Sunnis living near the coast) became a five-year struggle by proxy between Saudi Arabia and Egypt.

More heartening news for Nasser came in early 1963 when Ba'thist officers brought off two successive coups: the overthrow of Qasim in Iraq that February in favor of Abd al-Salam Arif (who, after his break with Qasim, had spent most of the last four years in jail) followed by the toppling a month later of the separatist government in Syria. Soon Iraq and Syria adopted identical flags and sent delegations to Cairo to negotiate a union with Nasser. Popular enthusiasm for Arab unity reached its peak in April 1963, as the three leading Arab countries drew up plans for a new United Arab Republic. But again people's hopes were dashed, as Nasser's differences with the Ba'th party proved unbridgeable. For the rest of the year, Arab governments, newspapers, and broadcasters hurled invectives at one another.

The Jordan Waters Dispute

An Israeli move brought the Arabs back together. Ever since the birth of modern Israel, its scientists and engineers had worked on the problem of getting more fresh water to meet its irrigation needs. American hydrologists had long argued that the Jordan River could be harnessed to irrigate both Israel and Jordan. An American emissary named Eric Johnston had actually secured an agreement from both countries on the technical aspects of a plan to share the Jordan waters, but the government of Jordan finally rejected it on political grounds in 1955. For a few years Israel hoped that Jordan might relent, but finally decided to go ahead and build a national water carrier to meet its own needs, taking from Lake Kinneret (the Sea of Galilee) the share of Jordan River waters that would have been allocated to Israel under the Johnston Plan.

Israel's tapping the Jordan waters galvanized the Arab countries into action. Perhaps Jordan, Syria, and Lebanon could divert the main tributaries of the Jordan River and thus deter Israel from completing its national water carrier. Nasser invited all Arab kings and presidents to Cairo to discuss the issue, and they met at the Nile Hilton in January 1964. Although unable to agree on immediate action against Israel, the Arabs did consider their summit successful enough to hold others in Alexandria in September 1964 and in Casablanca the following year. The basic consensus was that the Arab armies were not yet strong enough to confront Israel, but that they would develop their military capability so that Syria and Jordan could build and defend diversionary projects on the tributaries of the Jordan.

Formation of the Palestine Liberation Organization

Another act of the 1964 summit meetings drew relatively little outside attention, but it would become fateful for the Arab world. The Arab leaders voted to set up the Palestine Liberation Organization (PLO). This group was to serve as an umbrella organization for all clubs, societies, and parliamentary organizations serving the Palestinian Arabs. With Nasser's encouragement, Palestinian representatives met in 1964, charged an influential lawyer named Ahmad al-Shuqayri with appointing an executive committee for the PLO, and adopted a national charter. Its main principles were that the Palestinian Arabs must fight to regain their homeland within what had been the British mandate boundaries, and that only they had the right of self-determination within Palestine, although Jews of Palestinian origin might continue to live in the liberated country. In other words, the state of Israel was to be destroyed. For foreign consumption, at least, the Palestinians advocated a "secular democratic state" in which Jews, Christians, and Muslims would live together in peace.

The PLO started assembling a conventional army, made up of refugees in Gaza, Jordan, and Syria. But a more dramatic and effective force was a guerrilla movement called al-Fatah, led by Yasir Arafat, which signaled its existence on 1 January 1965 by trying to sabotage part of Israel's national water carrier. Arafat, who claimed to have been born in Jerusalem, had fought against the creation of Israel in 1948, later became the leader of the Palestinian students in Egypt, and lived for several years in Kuwait. More than Shuqayri, he spoke for the militant younger Palestinians. The attacks by al-Fatah, supported by Syria but generally launched from Jordan, caused serious casualties and property damage within Israel. The Israel government, headed since 1963 by Levi Eshkol, decided to put pressure on the Arab governments to curb these commando operations. In November 1966 the Israel army made a devastating retaliatory raid into the Jordanian

West Bank, striking at commando bases in the village of al-Samuʻ. This set off a noisy outcry against Israel from Western countries as well as the Arabs. The UN Security Council passed a unanimous resolution condemning the Israeli raid. Even many Israelis wondered whether it would not have been wiser to attack Syria, which gave material and vocal support to the commandos, instead of Jordan.

BACKGROUND TO THE JUNE 1967 WAR

By the mid-1960s Syria had once again emerged as the most radical Arab nationalist state. Unable to form a union with Egypt or even with Iraq in 1963, its Baʻth party government continued to press for Arab unity and for military action against Israel. It spearheaded attempts to divert the headwaters of the Jordan, fired from the Golan Heights down on Israelis farming the no-man's-land at the Syrian border, and armed various Palestinian commando groups. A military coup in February 1966 brought to power an even more radical wing of the Baʻth party. Many of the new leaders belonged to a rather mysterious minority, the Alawi religious sect, many of whose young men had joined the Syrian officer corps. Hoping perhaps to overcome Sunni Syrian suspicions and to enlist their cooperation, they tried even harder to uphold the principles of Arabism and hence of the struggle against Israel. By this time Nasser had come to realize that his army, much of which was still bogged down in the Yemen conflict, would not be ready to fight against Israel for quite a while. His relations with America had sunk to a new low as President Johnson (whom Nasser detested) cut off the sale of surplus wheat to Egypt. The USSR continued to support Nasser, but not to supply offensive arms in sufficient quantities for an attack against Israel. Nevertheless, Nasser decided that he could best restrain Syria's new leaders by making a military alliance with them.

Nasser's Actions against Israel

Nasser's decision to ally Egypt militarily with Syria was a serious miscalculation. In April 1967 Syrian planes got into an aerial dogfight with the Israelis and came out a poor second. Levi Eshkol made it clear that his government would take stronger retaliatory measures against Syria unless it stopped firing on Israeli settlements near its borders. In early May the Russians led Nasser to believe that Israel was despite its denials massing troops in the north for an attack on Syria. Egypt started calling up reserve units, routing tanks through its main cities and into Sinai, and making threats against Israel. Perhaps Nasser was bluffing to impress the Syrians, but no one else thought so at the time. For months Nasser's rivals, especially King Husayn, had taunted him for hiding behind UNEF in Gaza and Sinai. On 16 May Nasser demanded that the United Nations withdraw its peacekeeping force. Secretary General U Thant promptly heeded Nasser's demand without even consulting with the Security Council. Once UNEF was removed from all key points in Gaza and Sinai, Egyptian military units moved in. Among the strategic points they occupied was Sharm al-Shaykh, from where they resumed the Arab blockade against Israeli shipping through the Gulf of Aqaba. Nasser's prestige soared once again throughout the Arab world.

The Arab blockade of the Straits of Tiran, illegal in the opinion of Israel's supporters, has come to be seen as the main cause of the ensuing war of June 1967. Israel could not allow its trade from the port of Eilat, important in establishing closer ties with south Asia and East Africa (though minor in comparison with its Mediterranean trade), to be throttled in this way. Besides, as Arab newspapers and radio stations were clearly calling for a war to bring about the destruction of the Jewish state, the Israelis could hardly assume that the blockade of the Gulf of Aqaba was the only belligerent act the Arab governments were planning. But what should they do? Their right to navigate through the Straits of Tiran had been guaranteed by the Western maritime powers. The U.S. government, mired in the Vietnam war, counseled caution. The European governments had cooled toward Israel since the Suez Affair, perhaps because nearly all their oil came from the Arab world. It seemed futile to wait for a Western flotilla to force open the Straits of Tiran or to expect resolute action from the UN Security Council. While Israel's leaders were willing to seek peace by diplomatic means, they were not eager to commit national suicide.

When King Husayn flew to Cairo on 30 May to conclude an agreement with Nasser over a joint Arab military command, Israel's cabinet assumed that war was inevitable. Most reserve units were called up, the entire economy was put on a war footing, and Israel's political leaders buried their quarrels in order to come up with a new cabinet that would represent nearly all shades of opinion within the state. Especially significant was the appointment on 2 June of General Moshe Dayan as defense minister, despite his long-standing personal and political differences with Prime Minister Eshkol. A hero in the 1948 war of independence and the 1956 Sinai Campaign, Dayan gave new hope to the Israelis in what seemed to be their moment of peril.

Epilogue

Israel's preemptive air strike against its Arab neighbors and the war that ensued, which I will describe in the next chapter, lasted only six days. Its outcome was a devastating Israeli victory. Nasser's air force was wiped out on the ground and his army was scattered in Sinai. Israeli troops reached the banks of the Suez Canal in the west and of the Jordan River in the east. After trying to pin the blame for his defeat on the Americans, Nasser addressed his people over Radio Cairo, offering to resign from the presidency. Huge popular demonstrations throughout Egypt persuaded him to reconsider. But, if Nasser survived to lead Egypt for another three years, Nasserism never regained the vigor or the appeal it had enjoyed up to those six disastrous days of June 1967.

CONCLUSION

The history of the Middle East since May 1967 has been so dominated by the Arab-Israeli conflict that the preceding decade now seems relatively serene. Yet this chapter has shown that its political history was turbulent indeed. We may place some of the blame on outsiders for fishing in troubled waters, but how and why were those waters troubled in the first place? Younger readers may indeed be confused by the personalities and policies that clashed, especially in the eastern Arab world. Are there no simple shortcuts, no tidy generalizations, no keys to understanding all this history?

Thousands of books and articles cover some parts of the Middle East during this era, yet I still do not think that we have found that key. Rapid changes, especially in education and technology, were breaking down the customary modes of life and thought. Masses of people, mostly the poor and the young, flocked to the big cities. Alien ideas and customs, first embraced in those growing urban centers, spread everywhere by means of that important invention, the transistor radio, plus of course newspapers, magazines, schools, rural health centers, motion pictures, and (in some countries) television. Ideas of nationalism and progress seemed to be gaining at the expense of religion and respect for tradition, much as the car and the truck replaced the camel and the donkey.

Was this good? It is easy to say so, and yet I would now argue that many of the political slogans and ideologies of that era have proven false. Nasserism (as a blend of traditional and modern values) now seems more like a personality cult than Kemalism (with its positive commitment to westernization). Positive neutrality was a natural reaction to the cold war, but rejecting the Communist and Western blocs belied its name and worked well only as long as both were competing for Arab favor. Pan-Arabism failed to consider the deep-seated differences within the Arab world, not just among leaders but also their peoples, and also between countries that had oil and those having none. It tended to antagonize religious and ethnic minorities, like the Maronites of Lebanon and the

Kurds of Iraq. Parliamentary democracy broke down when the masses were hungry and uneducated and when the military officers or the new technicians were impatient to govern. Arab socialism failed to transform Arab society from its traditional individualism and clannishness into a collectivist economic system serving the common good. Many citizens failed to grasp its meaning, like the Cairo merchant who told me that Arab socialism meant lowering his prices for a foreigner (instead of jacking them up!) in order to give him "a good idea about Egypt."

Remember the early chapters of this book, when Islam as a doctrine and a way of life had inspired the Arabs and their converts to submerge their cares and desires into a grand collective enterprise: the great conquests, the High Caliphate, and Islamic civilization. How sad that no new Muslim leader has come forth to recharge those batteries, to enlist the minds and muscles of men and women to rebuild the *ummah,* to harness the tools and techniques of modern industry to create an egalitarian society, and to make Islam a guide for right thoughts and actions in the modern world! There have been many Muslim thinkers, from Muhammad Abduh to Sayyid Qutb, but their voices have been drowned out by those who spoke louder or tuned out by those who would not hear. Who can say what the Arabs might have done with stronger guidance and a more coherent belief system?

Israel had problems too. Political Zionism had achieved its goal of creating a Jewish state, but was it truly a light unto the Gentiles? In *The United States and Israel* (1963), Nadav Safran remarked that the most successful product coming from Israel since its foundation was the Uzi submachine gun. Judaism as practiced during centuries of dispersion meant little or nothing to Israel's leaders. Ben Gurion (among others) was puzzled that so few Jews came to Israel from the advanced Western countries. With half of Israel's Jewish population made up of immigrants from Middle Eastern countries, were the Israelis becoming a "Levantine" people? Reacting against this danger (which might have benefited the country by making it more truly Middle Eastern), Israelis developed cults of physical fitness and military might, of archeological quests to affirm their ties to the land, and of reclamation through the planting of crops and trees. No consensus emerged on how Jewish the Israelis should be, so they ranged from the ultraobservant (some even refused to recognize the Jewish state because the Messiah had not arrived) to those who denied the existence of God and the Bible's relevance to modern life. Jewish religious leadership was no better than its Muslim and Christian counterparts elsewhere. And what part ought the Arabs, 10 percent of Israel's population, play in a state whose flag portrayed the Star of David and whose anthem expressed the Jews' longing for the land of Zion? What about the Arabs who fled from Israel in 1948 and still claimed the right to return? If the Jews had remembered Zion for two thousand years, could the Palestinian refugees forget it in less than twenty?

Amid the mists of ideological confusion and the dust of political combat brewed the storms that have raged in the heart of the Middle East since 1967. They will be the dominant theme of my last two chapters.

19

From June to October

Israel's victory over Egypt, Syria, and Jordan in the June 1967 war was swift and surprising. It refuted the belief, common since 1956, that the Jewish state could not defeat the Arabs without Western allies. It exploded the myth that "unity of goals" among the Arab states would lead them to victory over Israel, and it proved that the Israel Defense Forces could attain high levels of skill, coordination, and valor in order to assure their country's survival. It also created a new myth, shared by both supporters and detractors of the Jewish state, that Israel was invincible. This myth lasted up to October 1973.

MAJOR MIDDLE EAST ISSUES: 1967-1973

Before I cover the military and political aspects of the 1967 war, let me try to point out some of the overarching themes of Middle East history between June 1967 and October 1973. This is not yet an easy task for we lack the perspective of distance. Therefore, feel free to look at the events and weigh them for yourself, as all historians of the Middle East will do in the years to come. I expect that more of the main actors will write their memoirs, some governments will publish documents, and future events will shed new light on those of the recent past. Historians will sift through the evidence, analyze what they think is important, and arrive at new syntheses. Some, like Walter Laqueur and Hisham Sharabi, have already begun to delineate what they see as the main trends.

The Arab-Israeli Conflict

We can all agree that since June 1967 the Arab-Israeli conflict has constantly held center stage in the Middle East drama, more so than ever it did before. Many diaspora Jews hitherto uninvolved in Israel have become ardent Zionists, while the question of Palestine has gained new importance in such remote Arab countries as Morocco and Kuwait. The quarrels among Arab states and the power struggles within some of them have continued as before 1967, but they have tended to become subsidiary to the Arab-Israeli conflict. Other Middle East news, such as the Greek-Turkish conflict over Cyprus, the Kurdish revolt in Iraq, the shah's reported violations of human rights in Iran, and the skyrocketing wealth and power of the oil-exporting countries, have made headlines from time to time; but hardly a month has gone by since June 1967 without some prediction that a new war was about to break out between the Arabs and Israel. Up to 1973 most people assumed that Israel—if adequately armed by the United States—would win any conventional war. For this reason, the Palestinian *fidaiyin* (variously translated as "terrorists" and "freedom fighters") came to play a greater role than ever before in the Arab struggle against Israel.

The Soviet Role

In addition, the USSR stepped up its role as arms supplier and adviser to many of the Arab states, especially Egypt, Syria, and Iraq. The period between 1967 and 1973 was one in which the rising superpower involvement in the Middle East conflict often threatened to escalate into World War III. Since neither the United States nor the USSR wanted so drastic a confrontation, they conferred frequently together and with other powers over possible solutions to the Arab-Israeli conflict.

War or Peace

During that six-year period, as since then, many people put forth solutions and formulas for peace. Neither the Arabs nor the Jews wanted the wars, the threats, and the tensions to go on forever. But at what price could each side agree to make peace with the other? The old Arab issue about the displaced Palestinians tended to give way to two others: return of Arab lands taken by Israel in June 1967 and recognition of the national rights of the Palestinian Arabs. The Israelis continued to demand security and Arab recognition, but could not agree among themselves how many of the captured lands—Jerusalem, the West Bank (which the Israelis call Judea and Samaria), the Gaza Strip, Sinai, and the Golan Heights—they should give back in exchange for peace. From Israel's point of view, the United Nations was no longer the credible peacemaker it had been in 1948-1949 and 1956 because of its tilt toward the Arabs, but there was no international forum and no disinterested arbiter to take its place. Arms purchases took a growing share of every Middle East government's budget, more young men in uniform risked dying before their time, and people's mental and physical energies increasingly shifted from constructive to essentially destructive endeavors. "*Ma'lesh,*" said the Arabs; "*Ma la'asot,*" said the Israelis—never mind—surviving and dignity are worth more than the highest costs we (and our supporters) could ever be forced to pay!

THE JUNE 1967 WAR

The story of Israel's lightning victory over the Arabs in June 1967 will be told and retold for years to come. In essence, what happened was that Israel's air force attacked the main airfields of Egypt, followed by those of Jordan, Syria, and Iraq, on the morning of 5 June and wiped out virtually all their war-making potential. Upon gaining control of the air in the first few hours, Israel's army moved into Sinai and, in four days' fighting, captured the entire peninsula. Nasser again blocked the Suez Canal (as he had done in 1956), but Israel was able to lift the blockade of the Gulf of Aqaba.

Since King Husayn had made a pact with Nasser a week before the war that effectively put his army under Egyptian command, it was hardly surprising that Jordan entered the war, firing into Israeli sections of Jerusalem. Israel's army then invaded the northern part of the West Bank (or Samaria) and also the northern areas of Arab Jerusalem to secure Mount Scopus (an Israeli enclave since the 1949 armistice) and to attack the Old City from its eastern side. On 7 June the Israelis took the Old City, after heavy and difficult fighting, and prayed at the Western Wall for the first time in nineteen years. Elsewhere on the West Bank, Israel's forces pushed back the Jordanians, under Husayn's direct command, in extremely tough fighting. The Arabs accused Israel of dropping napalm on Jordanian troops and of using scare tactics to clear out some refugee camps and West Bank villages. Such allegations are hard to prove or to refute, but over 200,000 Arabs did take refuge on the East Bank, and new tent camps ringed the hills around Amman. Many Palestinian Arabs, after hearing promises from the Arab radio stations that Israel would be wiped out and that they would be allowed to return home, must have wondered why the various Arab armies failed to work together to achieve victory.

Syria was the least helpful. Because of recent border clashes with Jordan, Syria did nothing to help Husayn until it was too late, which then left Israel free to storm Syria's well-fortified positions on the Golan Heights—no easy task—when no other Arab country would or could do anything for the Damascus regime. If Israel and Syria had not agreed to a UN cease-fire on 10 June, the Israelis could have marched into Damascus itself. Let me share with you the conclusion by Abdel Latif Tibawi (a Palestinian Arab) to his *Modern History of Syria*: "Syria had often in history marched under the banner of Islam to victory and glory; it had yet to prove that it could do so under the banner of Arab nationalism."

Reasons for the Outcome

The June 1967 war did indeed tend to discredit the ideas of Arab nationalism. Before the war the Arab forces had seemed superior on paper:

Egypt's armed forces alone outnumbered Israel's, even with all its reserve units mobilized; the Arabs had 2700 tanks to Israel's 800; 800 fighter planes to Israel's 190; 217 ships to Israel's 37; and the population ratio was about 25 to 1. The Arabs had the unequivocal support of the Communist bloc and most Asian and African countries at a time when America's position was (to quote a State Department spokesman) "neutral in thought, word, and deed." Many Americans would have disputed this characterization, but with half a million troops in Vietnam there was little chance they could have intervened even if Israel had asked them to do so.

Why then did Israel win? One obvious reason is that Israel attacked first, destroyed most of the Arab fighter planes, and then kept complete control of the air. Another is that Egypt still had many of its best troops stationed in Yemen, helping the republican side in the civil war. The *New York Times* reported during the war that Israel probably had more troops on the field than its enemies and definitely was superior in firepower and mobility during the battles fought. Israel also had rapid internal transport and communication. The technical sophistication of Israel's soldiers—or even just the fact that they all could read and write—helped. Israel's culture encourages creative thinking under pressure, ability to improvise solutions, and democratic camaraderie between officers and fighting men. This is not to argue that the Israeli soldier is "better" than his Arab counterpart in strength, motor skills, or even bravery, but he could work better with and rely more on his comrades-in-arms. By contrast, Arab armies were riven with factionalism, just as Arab governments distrusted one another. I have described earlier how this helped cause the Arabs' defeat in 1948. In 1967, even after most of the anachronistic monarchies and landowning elites had fallen from power, even after some fifteen years of pan-Arabism and social reform in Egypt and Syria, and even after billions of dollars worth of Soviet and Western arms had poured into the Arab world, the Arabs' divisiveness led to a swifter, more devastating defeat in 1967 than in 1949. Small wonder that Nasser, the chief spokesman for radical Arab nationalism, tried to resign!

The War's Aftermath

When the guns fell silent on 10 June, Israel had expanded its land area to three times what it had been six days earlier, having occupied the Gaza Strip, the Sinai Peninsula, the West Bank, and the Golan Heights. Almost a million Arabs, mostly Palestinians, had come under Israeli rule. Neither the Israelis nor anyone else had expected this to happen. No one had drawn up contingency plans. Defense Minister Dayan and other Israeli officials had said during the war that they were not trying to expand the borders of Israel. Probably most Israelis were relieved just to find that they had not

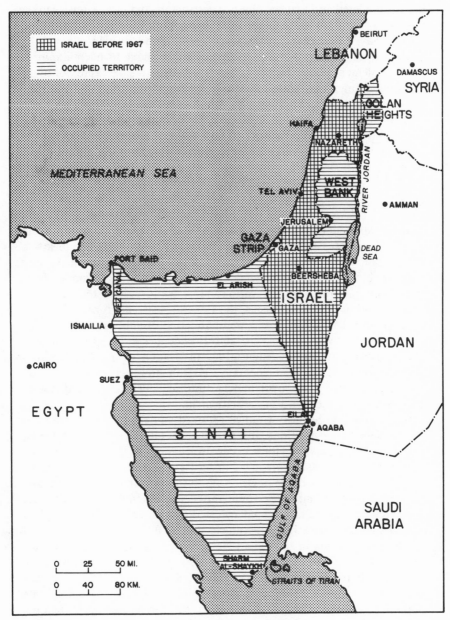

Map 10. Israel and the Occupied Territories, 1967-1973

been annihilated and that the physical destruction and loss of Jewish lives, though certainly bad enough, were less than anyone had anticipated. Many hoped that the militant Arab leaders would be overthrown by the moderates or that the Arab governments would agree to negotiate for a peace settlement. Looking back, it is too bad both sides were not more accommodating. The Arabs refused to negotiate from weakness (after all, some said, Hitler could not persuade Churchill to talk peace in 1940), while the Israelis thought it prudent to hold the occupied lands as bargaining counters in the peace talks they still hoped would ensue. Besides, the new frontiers were shorter and much more defensible than the old ones had been. Some Israelis started to speak of keeping the occupied lands, strengthening Arab fears about Zionist expansionism.

The United Nations

The Arabs believed that a just solution was more likely to come from the United Nations (as in 1956) than from direct negotiations. In response to a Soviet call, a special session of the General Assembly was held that summer, but its deliberations ended inconclusively, because none of the resolutions put forth by the various blocs could muster the necessary majority. After five futile weeks, the General Assembly turned the issue back to the Security Council. A well-publicized summit meeting between Soviet Premier Alexei Kosygin and President Lyndon Johnson also accomplished nothing. In August 1967 the leaders of the various Arab countries (none of whom, incidentally, fell from power because of the war) held a summit of their own in Khartum, at which they voted not to negotiate with Israel for a peace settlement.

By the time the Security Council resumed its deliberations, both sides had hardened their positions. Just as the Arabs refused to talk with Israel, the Israelis were making their occupation more visible in the captured territories. Arab houses were razed in Jerusalem's Old City to enlarge the open area in front of the Western Wall. Suspected terrorists in Gaza and the West Bank were imprisoned or deported, and in some cases their houses were blown up as well. Some villages and towns (e.g., parts of Qalqilya) were wiped out. With full government approval, Jewish settlers started building settlements in the Golan Heights, outside Hebron, and in East Jerusalem, especially on the hills connecting Mount Scopus with the western half of the city. East Jerusalem, including the Old City, was annexed by Israel, defying a nearly unanimous General Assembly vote opposing the move. The USSR started to rearm Syria and Egypt, sending in more technicians and advisers, and the danger of a new war was rising.

Security Council Resolution 242

The Security Council had to come up with a peace formula acceptable to both Israel and the Arabs, as well as the United States and the USSR.

During the lengthy debates, Britain's Lord Caradon devised a formula with the necessary ambiguity—the famous Security Council Resolution 242—that all the permanent members could accept. It emphasized "the inadmissibility of acquiring territory by war" and called for a just and lasting peace based on (1) withdrawal of Israeli armed forces from territories occupied in the recent conflict and (2) recognition of the right of every state in the area to "live in peace within secure and recognized boundaries free from threats and acts of force." Other points included free navigation through international waterways, a "just settlement to the refugee problem," and a guarantee of the territorial integrity of every state in the Middle East.

Since Resolution 242 has joined the Husayn-McMahon Correspondence and the Balfour Declaration in that special gallery of ambiguous diplomatic documents complicating the Arab-Israeli conflict, I think you should know what the parties to the conflict read into it. The Arabs saw the resolution as a call to Israel to hand back, as a precondition for peace, *all* the territories captured in the June war. Israel claimed that the resolution meant withdrawal from *some* of the territories, since each country was to live at peace within *secure* and recognized borders. Some Arabs interpreted the "just settlement to the refugee problem" to mean repatriation by Israel of all displaced Palestinians wishing to return (indeed, the General Assembly had passed resolutions to that effect almost annually since 1948), while Israel contended that the Palestinian refugees should be settled in the Arab countries. After all, the Israelis said, the Arab states had expelled their Jews, most of whom had settled in Israel, and no one suggested that they be allowed to return to Iraq, Yemen, or Morocco.

Egypt, Jordan, and Israel all agreed to abide by Resolution 242 (Syria, which saw it as amounting to de facto recognition of Israel, did not do so until much later), but Arabs and Israelis did not interpret it the same way. A UN mediator, Dr. Gunnar Jarring, was charged by the UN secretary-general with bringing the two sides closer together. But, even as his ultimately fruitless mission got under way in late 1967 and early 1968, the deficiencies of the resolution were becoming apparent. One obviously was that each side expected the other to give in first. Another was that no limitations would be put on the arms race, which was as feverish and financially debilitating as ever. Still another was that the Arabs could still wage economic warfare against Israel and its supporters—the boycott would go on. Finally, though this became clear only gradually, the resolution ignored the rights and interests of the Palestinian Arab people.

THE PALESTINIAN ARABS

The emergence of the Palestinians as a separate factor in the Arab-Israeli conflict has been one of the most dramatic developments of the post-1967 era. The idea that the Palestinians constitute a distinct people is novel. Never before in Middle East history had the Arabs living in Palestine desired or achieved status as a separate and independent state. Quite the contrary, the Arabs of that region had generally chosen, to the extent they could express or exercise any choice at all, to be part of a larger state: Islamic, Arab, or at least Syrian. Before the creation of Israel, the term "Palestinian" was often used by Jews or by foreigners for the inhabitants of the British mandate of Palestine, but rarely by the Arabs themselves. Between 1948 and 1967, the Arabs from Palestine, especially the refugees in neighboring countries, were apt to be the most ardent advocates of pan-Arabism, which would presumably obliterate the distinctions between them and, say, Egyptians, Syrians, Saudis, and Iraqis.

But, by virtue of certain common shared experiences and ideas, Palestinians could come to see themselves as a people and then as a nation, just as surely as the East European Jews had turned into Zionists in the early twentieth century. The Jewish settlers in Palestine had rejected the local Arabs before they had a state, expelled them during the 1948 war, and then refused to admit them back into what had become Israel. The Palestinians noted that the other Arab countries would not, could not, and indeed should not, absorb them. No country wanted them. But these Arabs did not want to see themselves or to be seen as objects of pity, wards of the UN Relief and Works Agency, or sources of embarrassment to other Arab countries. Now that the 1967 war had proven the inadequacy of the armies of the Arab governments, the Palestinians must get arms, train themselves, and liberate their usurped homeland for themselves.

The Palestine Liberation Organization

Thus the Palestine Liberation Organization, set up in 1964 at the behest of the Arab governments, emerged after the Arabs' defeat as a much more militant group. The older leaders, notably the loquacious lawyer Ahmad al-Shuqayri, gave way to younger ones who, though no less determined to get rid of Israel by force of arms, were more adept at using the Western media to publicize their cause. Getting support from most of the Communist countries was no problem; what the PLO wanted was to win public opinion in Western Europe and North America over the Palestinian cause. To do this, they must stop harping on the destruction of Israel and the Jewish bloodbath or mass exodus that might be expected to ensue, and stress instead their goal to set what had been Palestine before 1948 free from the false ideology of Zionism, which debased the Jewish faith and oppressed the Christian and Muslim Arabs who had formerly made up the majority of Palestine's native population. Israel's leadership was likened to that of the white settler regimes of Rhodesia and South Africa. The

Palestinian *fidaiyin,* whom the Israelis called "terrorists," should instead be viewed as "freedom fighters" comparable to the Algerian FLN or the French Partisans during the Nazi occupation. American young people, opposed to the senseless Vietnam war, might be persuaded to identify Yasir Arafat, leader of al-Fatah (the largest group of *fidaiyin*), with such contemporary heroes of the New Left as Che Guevara, Ho Chi Minh, and Eldridge Cleaver. Some did. But many Jewish students and intellectuals in the New Left could not quite swallow the equation of Zionism (which their parents believed in) with such demonstrable evils as capitalism, racism, and fascism.

The Rise of the Fidaiyin

Early in 1968 Israel's army, stung into retaliatory action by *fidaiyin* raids and bombings within Israel, attacked the Jordanian village of Karamah, some twenty-five miles (forty kilometers) west of Amman. Israel reportedly lost six jet fighters and twelve tanks in the battle, before both sides agreed to a new cease-fire. Many of Jordan's casualties were Palestinians from al-Fatah. Its role in resisting the Israelis gave new luster to Yasir Arafat and his supporters. Certainly it looked better than the regular armies of Egypt, Syria, and Jordan. Young men in refugee camps and in many Arab cities and villages started volunteering for al-Fatah. Even King Husayn announced, after an Israeli air raid east of the Jordan River, "We are all *fidaiyin* now." Foreign journalists flocked to interview Arafat and to visit his training camps. Some, impressed by his unswerving nationalism, extolled his vision of a liberated, unitary Palestine that would be secular and democratic, a state where Jews, Christians, and Muslims might live together in peace. Skeptics wondered, though, whether any existing Arab country was secular, democratic, or preserving concord among the various religious groups living within its borders. The Palestinians agreed that many Arab leaders were rather reactionary, bigoted perhaps, and tied to landowning or bourgeois class interests; but the guerrillas were young, well educated, and free from these ties to the past. Many even took on code names as a symbolic gesture. Who would be so uncouth as to point out the family tie between Yasir Arafat and the Husaynis, the family of Jerusalem's former mufti, who had thrown in his cause with Hitler?

AMERICAN PEACE EFFORTS

Meanwhile, between 1967 and 1969 the U.S. government undertook several well-intentioned efforts to solve the Arab-Israeli conflict in quite a different way, by an agreement among the major outside powers. It would be fatuous to try to cover all the conferences held in those years, but it is useful to remember that President Johnson, Secretary of State Dean Rusk, and many other leading Americans hoped they could somehow reach agreements with the Soviet leaders, plus perhaps Harold Wilson of Britain and Charles de Gaulle of France, on a set of principles for an Arab-Israeli settlement. To the extent that I can reconstruct it, the logic of the American plan was that the USSR could influence the leading Arab countries, while America could use its leverage on Israel, probably by selling or withholding advanced weapons, in order to bring both sides together in a settlement based on Resolution 242. Presumably the Soviets would be glad to stop pouring weapons into Egypt, Syria, and Iraq, arms that might never be paid for and that required sending large Russian training missions. However, the Soviets liked having armies in Egypt and Syria, athwart what had been the main oil routes to the West up to 1967. The naval and air facilities they got in those countries contributed to their buildup in the Mediterranean, where the U.S. Sixth Fleet had been dominant before the June 1967 war.

During the war the USSR had ruptured diplomatic relations with Israel, and many of the Arab countries had likewise broken with the United States. This limited the ability of the superpowers to play a balancing role in the Middle East. Besides, Israel argued that a peace settlement imposed by the powers would last only so long as the Arab states were too weak to defy it. Look at what had happened to the peace settlement imposed on Egypt after the 1956 Suez war. Many Arabs, too, doubted that the United States and USSR would work for a just solution once they had taken care of their own interests in the Middle East.

Nixon's Policies

Richard Nixon's victory in the November 1968 elections gave some hope to the Arabs, if only because a new administration in Washington would be freer to take initiatives favorable to their interests. Nixon sent a special envoy to the area, former Pennsylvania Governor William Scranton, who added a new expression to American parlance when he returned calling for a more "evenhanded" approach to the Middle East conflict, implying that the Johnson administration had been unfair to the Arabs. One of the central issues in debates over U.S. Middle East policy was the degree to which the government should arrange arms sales to Israel or, for that matter, to such moderate Arab states as Jordan. The Johnson administration had arranged to sell Phantom jets to Israel; but the Nixon administration held up the transaction for a while, apparently hoping that its leverage over Israel might help to bring about a peace settlement.

The War of Attrition

But the Egyptians, perhaps because of growing press coverage given to *fidaiyin* raids and Israeli retaliations, did not wait. In March 1969 Nasser announced that Egypt would step up the shooting that had been going on across the Suez Canal ever since the end of June 1967, thus beginning the so-called war of attrition. Nasser, a chess player in his spare time, hoped to wear down the Israelis east of the canal by picking off men and planes every now and then. What actually happened, though, was that far more Egyptians than Israelis got killed, the Egyptian cities west of the canal got shelled so badly that their civilian populations had to be evacuated, Israeli commandos crossed over and picked off Egyptian military targets at will, and Israeli planes flew sorties over Cairo and bombed various military bases and munitions factories in the Nile Delta. Many Egyptians worried about the Aswan High Dam, which Soviet money and technicians had build for Nasser. By 1970 Israeli troops were securely dug in behind the "Bar Lev line" just east of the canal; while Egypt was becoming increasingly vulnerable to Israel's planes, including the Phantom jets that Nixon, despairing of his projected peace plan, had supplied in September 1969. Nasser flew to Moscow to persuade the USSR to supply Egypt with more weapons, planes, missiles, and advisers. By the summer of 1970 Israeli fighter pilots engaging in dogfights high above the Suez Canal began to suspect that Russians, not just Egyptians, were flying the enemy MIGs.

POLITICAL CHANGES: 1967-1970

Let us put aside the war of attrition to look at some other political developments. I wrote earlier that no Arab government was overthrown as a result of the June 1967 defeat. Nevertheless, leadership changes were taking place, and the alignments of Arab countries remained kaleidoscopic.

Yemen and South Yemen

In the Khartum summit meeting of 1967, the Egyptian and Saudi governments agreed to wind down the five-year-old civil war in Yemen. Soon after Nasser pulled out his troops, the republican regime he had backed fell from power. A new regime then emerged that edged closer to accommodation with the imam, his tribal supporters, and the Saudis. Farther south, the British had tried for years to combine the more urban and politicized citizens of Aden Colony with the tribal shaykhs and sultans of the southern Arabian peninsula (the part long known as the Aden Protectorate). The combination was to be called the South Arabian Federation. The tribal leaders, most of them friendly to Britain, were supposed to keep the urban radicals under control, but during the 1960s several nationalist groups arose among the unionized workers of the port of Aden. This outpost of empire was becoming more costly than it was worth, and so Britain's labor government decided in 1966 to let it go. Once it announced its intention of pulling all troops out of southern Arabia, the federation's Arab supporters became disenchanted and the two leading nationalist groups began fighting each other for control. Late in 1967 Britain handed over southern Arabia to the victorious faction, the National (Liberation) Front. The new country was renamed the People's Republic of Southern Yemen. Later, as an expression of its leaders' hope that it might some day be reunited with northern Yemen, it became the People's Democratic Republic of Yemen. It has since been among the most radical Arab states. Its politics still interact with those of northern Yemen; in the summer of 1978 the leaders of both countries were assassinated two days apart, possibly by the same man. Unification now seems far off.

Iraq

In Iraq, Abd al-Rahman Arif, who had replaced his brother, Abd al-Salam Arif (who died in a plane crash in 1966), was overthrown by a rightist coup in July 1968. Two weeks later another faction of the Ba'th party seized power in Baghdad. Iraqi politics and policies often mystify foreigners. Basically, the new government did not get along well with Syria (while both were ruled by the Ba'th party, the dominant factions were different) because of their dispute over the use of Euphrates River waters. Relations with Iran were strained because both countries wanted to control the Shatt al-Arab, where the Tigris and Euphrates meet before they empty into the gulf. In addition, Iraq criticized Egypt and Jordan for having accepted Resolution 242, tacitly recognizing Israel. In northern Iraq, the Kurds went on fighting for their independence, and the new regime tried to distract popular opinion at home by publicly hanging fourteen convicted Israeli spies (nine of whom happened to be Jewish) in Baghdad. A tentative settlement was made with the Kurds in 1970, but it did not last. Iraqis alleged that the shah of Iran was arming the Kurdish rebels.

Libya

In 1969 military coups overthrew moderate or pro-Western governments in the Sudan, Libya, and Somalia. Of these changes, the most interesting was the revolution in Libya, which brought to power an impetuous, articulate, and devout army colonel named Mu'ammar al-Qadhafi (or Gaddafi in the vernacular of Libya). This twenty-seven-year-old officer soon emerged as the new beacon of militant Arab nationalism. He made the Americans leave Wheelus Air Base, forced all tourists to carry travel documents written in Arabic, and volunteered his troops for duty alongside Nasser's on the Suez Canal and the *fidaiyin* in Jordan and Lebanon. Nasser was especially impressed by the Libyan revolutionary, who reminded him of what he had been like fifteen years earlier, but of course Qadhafi had not yet worn himself out fighting against Zionism and imperialism.

Israel

In Israel, meanwhile, Ben Gurion's successor as prime minister, Levi Eshkol, died suddenly in March 1969. He was replaced by the former foreign minister and secretary-general of Mapai, Golda Meir. Although she was only supposed to serve in a caretaker capacity until the November 1969 elections, the differences among other politicians and factions within Israel's ruling labor alignment made her the most acceptable standard-bearer for her party. Thus, following the elections she formed a broad coalition government. She proved to be a remarkably strong-willed and capable leader. Mrs. Meir, born in Russia and educated in Milwaukee, Wisconsin, was especially adept at keeping Israel's prima donnas (like Yigal Allon and Moshe Dayan) from each other's throats and also at persuading Americans to see what was happening in the Middle East through Israeli glasses.

The Rogers Peace Plan

As always, though, the State Department was less influenced by Israel than any other branch of the U.S. government. In yet another effort to break the Middle East impasse, Secretary of State William Rogers made a major speech in December 1969 in which he laid down the peace plan that has come to bear his name. Basically, the Rogers Peace Plan called for a renewal of the cease-fire between Egypt and Israel and for a resumption of Dr. Jarring's efforts to mediate between them. Rogers envisaged a lasting peace "sustained by sense of security on both sides," with borders that "should not reflect the weight of conquest," presumably meaning that Israel should pull out of just about everything it had taken in the war. He also said that "there can be no lasting peace without a just settlement of the refugee problem," although he did not specify what that might be. As for Jerusalem, Rogers stated the United States "cannot accept unilateral actions by any party to decide the final status of the city," but it should be unified and allow free access to all faiths and nationalities. Nasser initially rejected the Rogers Peace Plan, but the summit meeting of Arab leaders held that month in Rabat gave him little reason to hope that the other Arab countries would increase their military or economic aid to Egypt during the war of attrition.

The steady escalation of this war during the first half of 1970 and the growing danger of direct U.S. and Soviet involvement evidently made the Rogers Peace Plan look better to Nasser; perhaps the Americans could obtain by peaceful pressure what Egypt's armed forces had failed to gain by war. In a dramatic policy shift, Nasser announced Egypt's acceptance of the Rogers Plan on 23 July. Jordan, harassed more and more by the activities of the *fidaiyin* on its soil, quickly followed suit. Israel had severe doubts about the wisdom of America's new policy, but reluctantly went along. A ninety-day cease-fire went into effect, and Dr. Jarring resumed his rounds of the various Middle Eastern capitals. Damascus was the one exception; Syria still would not accept Resolution 242. Israel's suspicions seemed confirmed when Egypt moved some of its new surface-to-air missiles to within firing range of the Suez Canal, a violation of the cease-fire agreement, but Egypt insisted it had planned to move them before the cease-fire was arranged. In the October 1973 war, the benefit to Egypt of these new missile sites would become apparent, but in 1970 the United States did not want to force a pullback. Israel then refused to continue peace talks with Gunnar Jarring, even though the United States offered $500 million in credits, largely for the purchase of more Phantom jet fighters.

Clashes in Lebanon and Jordan

The Rogers Peace Plan caused a severe disruption within Jordan. The root of the trouble was the Palestinian problem. The PLO and other guerrilla organizations could not maintain bases of operation within Israel or its occupied lands because of Israel's strict security arrangements and the harsh measures it usually took against suspected terrorists. This meant, in effect, concentrating the guerrilla bases in refugee camps and peasant villages in southern Lebanon and east of the Jordan River. Because guerrilla activities led to Israeli retaliatory raids across the border, many Lebanese and Jordanians resented the Palestinian presence in their countries. Several clashes took place in Lebanon in the fall of 1969. An agreement worked out in Cairo between the PLO and the Lebanese government severely limited the Palestinians' freedom of action in Lebanon, causing a stepping up of their activities in Jordan in early 1970. This inevitably led to trouble between the PLO and King Husayn's soldiers, many of whom were former bedouin who had never really liked the Palestinians.

The big blowup was started by a Marxist splinter group, the Popular Front for the Liberation of Palestine (PFLP), headed by Dr. George Habash. He believed that the Palestinians could only get what they wanted if they first struck against Western governments and civilians in order to dramatize their cause. The form of action chosen by Habash's group was hijacking civilian airliners, starting with an El Al jet that it diverted to Algeria in 1968. In early September 1970 the PFLP brought its campaign to a climax by hijacking four Western planes, all filled by summer travelers headed for home, and forcing them to land in a desert airstrip near Amman. The harsh treatment of the passengers (especially those who happened to be Jewish) so embarrassed the Jordanian government that King Husayn's army began fighting against the Palestinians, civilians as well as *fidaiyin,* destroying many sections of Amman and other cities and towns. Syria sent an armored column into Jordan to help the Palestinians, but withdrew after a few days when Israel (with U.S. encouragement) threatened to intervene in the fighting. The Egyptian government stepped in again, as it had done in Lebanon, but it took literally all the strength Nasser had left in him to make peace between Arafat and Husayn. The following day he died of a heart attack. Considering his career as an Arab militant, it is ironic that his last act was to rescue Husayn from the PLO and thus give the Rogers Peace Plan an additional lease on life. However, his own death threw the whole Middle East situation into doubt.

Egypt after Nasser

Nasser's death set off an extraordinary wave of public mourning in Egypt. *The Guinness Book of World Records* lists Nasser's funeral as having had more participants (four million is a conservative estimate) than any other in history. Anwar al-Sadat, Nasser's vice-president and one of the last of the original "free officers" group, was chosen to succeed him, but many doubted he would last long in power. Other Nasserites continued to compete with Sadat and with one another. Not until 15 May 1971 did Sadat eliminate all major contenders from his government in a purge known as the "corrective revolution." While feigning loyalty to the principles for which Nasser had stood, Sadat soon began to make far-reaching changes. Nasser's elaborate security apparatus was dismantled. Sadat tried to encourage native and foreign capitalists to invest in Egyptian enterprises, even though it meant a step away from socialism. The official name of the country, which had remained the United Arab Republic even after the Syrian breakaway, was changed to the Arab Republic of Egypt. Although Egypt's ties with the USSR were seemingly strengthened by a fifteen-year treaty of alliance signed in June 1971, they were in fact becoming strained because of Soviet reluctance to supply Sadat with offensive weapons for use against Israel. In another year, Sadat's patience would become so frayed that he would order most of the Soviet advisers and technicians to leave Egypt.

The End of the Rogers Peace Plan

But what happened to America's efforts to bring peace to the Middle East? The temporary cease-fire was renewed several times during the fall and winter of 1970-1971, as Jarring resumed his mission between the two sides. In February 1971 he sent notes to both Egypt and Israel, asking them to accept certain points as a necessary preliminary to negotiations. Egypt would have to sign a "peace agreement" with Israel embodying the final settlement. Israel would have to withdraw to what had been the frontier between Egypt and Palestine (which meant that Egypt would not regain control of the Gaza Strip). Sadat actually agreed to sign a contractual agreement on the terms of a peace with Israel, which was something Nasser had never done. But Israel refused in principle to withdraw to the pre-June 1967 armistice lines. This put an end to the Rogers Peace Plan. Both Israel and Egypt did express interest in a partial settlement that would have included reopening the Suez Canal (closed since 1967), with Israel pulling its forces back some distance from its east bank. America tried hard to obtain agreement on this partial settlement, and I must say that, given the hindsight of the October 1973 war, it seems a pity that neither Egypt nor Israel accepted it in 1971. In the latter half of that year, Sadat took to speaking of 1971 as "the year of decision" in which Egypt and Israel would either make peace or go to war. But in fact 1971 was not the year of decision, and neither was 1972.

It seems now that America's attempts to mediate an Arab-Israeli settlement through indirect negotiations, however well-meant they may have been, failed to get to the roots of the problem: Israel's fear of attack (and hence extinction) by the Arabs, and the Arabs' fear of expansion (and hence domination) by the Israelis. Israel could not risk its security by agreeing in advance to make concessions that might be matched by only some—or possibly none—of its Arab opponents. What if Israel gave up all or part of Sinai, only to find out that Sadat did not want peace after all or was overthrown by more militant Egyptian officers? What if Israel's withdrawal from the West Bank (presumably the sequel to abandoning Sinai) led not to Jordanian rule but rather to the emergence there of a small, unviable, and discontented Palestinian state? Besides, the right-wing parties had left Israel's broad coalition government at the time it accepted the cease-fire for the Rogers Peace Plan. Any ill-conceived concession might bring down on Golda Meir's head the scathing condemnation of Menachem Begin, leader of the conservative Herut party, plus many other Israelis who cared about national security.

As for Egypt, Sadat felt he had bent as far as he could by agreeing in principle to making peace with Israel. A separate peace would probably isolate Egypt from the rest of the Arab world and cause the oil-exporting countries to have second thoughts about supporting the faltering Egyptian economy, which was sliding dangerously close to bankruptcy. Jordan would have made peace with Israel in return for its complete withdrawal from the West Bank, including the Old City of Jerusalem. In 1972 King

Husayn proposed a federation between these Palestinian areas and the rest of Jordan, to be called the United Arab Kingdom. Neither Israel nor the West Bank Palestinians endorsed the idea. Syria maintained that Israel, as an expansionist state, would never give up peacefully what it had taken by force. The USSR did not directly oppose America's peacemaking efforts, since it wanted to move toward détente with the West, but it also did not encourage them. Instead, it continued to cultivate its own friends in the area, including both Syria and Iraq, as well as the chastened PLO and related guerrilla groups.

DANGER SIGNS IN THE MIDDLE EAST

Knowing what would happen in October 1973, we are inclined to look back on the two preceding years as the lull before the storm. Actually, there were danger signals. Qadhafi, having agreed in principle to a union with Sadat's Egypt, started putting heavy pressure on him to take a more active stance against Israel. Busloads of Libyans tried to enter Egypt in the summer of 1973 to urge Sadat to get moving. This resulted in an indefinite postponement of the proposed union and in Qadhafi's exclusion from Sadat's conferences with other Arab leaders where they discussed precisely what Qadhafi had been urging him to do. Palestinian *fidaiyin* continued to dramatize their cause in ways especially obnoxious to both Israel and the West. Their targets included Puerto Rican pilgrims in Israel's Lod Airport, Israeli athletes at the 1972 Olympic Games in Munich, the U.S. ambassador in Khartum, and a trainload of Jewish emigrants from the USSR entering Austria. Israeli bombers would periodically strike back at Palestinian strongholds, also taking many innocent lives. The United Nations continued to condemn these Israeli reprisals against Arabs, but not Palestinian actions such as those I have just listed.

Rising Oil Prices

At this time, the Western press and people began to worry about the impending energy crisis and the possible hazards of overdependence on imported Arab oil. Europe and Japan felt especially vulnerable. Since World War II the industrialized countries had shifted from coal to oil as their main energy source. As Middle Eastern production skyrocketed, the oil companies had kept their prices low. In fact, they had actually lowered them in 1959 and 1960 without consulting the host governments. Because the two sides had by then agreed to split oil profits fifty-fifty, this unilateral action by the companies reduced the governments' revenues. It may have reflected market conditions, but petroleum and natural gas are irreplaceable resources and, for some of the exporting countries, their main source of national income. Five of them (Iran, Iraq, Kuwait, Saudi Arabia, and Venezuela) met in Baghdad in 1960 and formed the Organization of Petroleum Exporting Countries (OPEC). Later they were joined by Qatar, Libya, Indonesia, Abu Dhabi (now the United Arab Emirates), Algeria, Nigeria, and Ecuador.

During the 1960s, while world oil supply kept up with demand, OPEC kept a low profile. But as its members came to know one another and learned more about the economics of oil, the organization became more assertive. In 1968 it recommended that its members explore for new resources on their own, buy shares in the oil companies, restrict their concession areas, and set posted (or tax reference) prices on their products (so that an oil price drop would not reduce government revenues). Two years later the companies agreed to work toward uniform (and higher) posted prices and to raise the tax rates on oil company earnings. As world demand kept going up, the oil exporters were starting to flex their economic muscle.

What did this mean in specific prices? Since there are many kinds of oil and pricing arrangements, it would be hard to quote representative figures, but let me try. One barrel (42 U.S. gallons or 159 liters) of Iraqi crude oil sold in 1950 for U.S. $2.41, dropping to $2.15 by 1960. The price rose back to $2.41 by 1970, reached $3.21 in 1971, and $3.40 in 1972. Since much attention has been paid to the fourfold price hike late in 1973, I should point out that oil had stayed cheap for a generation. Had the prices of other raw materials or manufactured goods stayed the same between 1950 and 1970? The international accounting unit for oil is the U.S. dollar, whose value has dropped considerably since the U.S. government stopped selling gold at $35 per ounce. The value of an ounce of gold has risen more than five times in terms of dollars, just between 1970 and 1978. The industrialized world must learn to get along without cut-rate oil prices.

CONCLUSION

The period from June 1967 to October 1973 was one of continued tension in the Middle East, one in which fighting was frequent and often escalating. Military expenditures soared. The United States and USSR found themselves increasingly involved in the Arab-Israeli conflict, despite frequent attempts to cooperate in seeking a solution as part of their own move toward détente. Israel seemed to be the most powerful state in the Middle East. The Arabs were weakened by factionalism, internal strife, differences over their goals and methods for achieving them, and a general mood of self-doubt caused by their catastrophic defeat in the 1967 war. Under such circumstances, is it not remarkable that American peace-making efforts got any positive response from such disparate rulers as Nasser, Husayn, and Sadat? Have the Arabs become more responsive since the October 1973 war and has the oil embargo improved their bargaining position? I hope to discuss this in the following chapter.

20

The Quest for Peace

The war that broke out on Saturday afternoon, 6 October 1973, was the most intensely fought, the most costly in lives and equipment, and the most dangerous of the five Arab-Israeli wars that have occurred since 1948. It changed people's perceptions of the relative strength of the parties to the conflict. It also precipitated a fourfold increase in the price of Middle East oil, and nearly caused a military showdown between the United States and the USSR. Its aftermath enlarged the American role in trying to resolve the conflict. These attempts at first moved Israel and the Arabs only slightly toward a peace settlement, but they did lead to a considerable improvement in U.S. relations with some of the Arab countries, notably Egypt. It may seem odd that this improvement was effected by America's first Jewish secretary of state and by an Egyptian leader who had once sought Nazi German aid to free his country from British rule. But Israel did withdraw its forces from some of the lands it had won in 1967 and 1973 as a result of agreements negotiated by Secretary Kissinger's "shuttle diplomacy," and at least some Arabs began to envision peace with Israel as a possibility.

In the wake of the October 1973 war the Palestinian Arabs, though not directly involved in the fighting, became more prominent. The Arab states and many other countries came to believe that their interests could best be served by setting up a new Palestinian state, within lands relinquished by Israel, under the aegis of the Palestine Liberation Organization. But the PLO still refused publicly to recognize and make peace with Israel, which in turn argued that it could hardly negotiate with—let alone relinquish land to—an organization that willed its destruction. The problem of the Palestinians took on added urgency as they became involved in a protracted and bloody civil war in Lebanon, worse than the one they had precipitated earlier in Jordan.

A change of administrations in Washington brought to power an American president eager to win fame as the man who brought peace to the Middle East. Carter's advisers thought that the road to peace would pass through a general conference of the main parties to the conflict. But how could the United States bring Israel and the Palestinians to the same bargaining table? Finally Egypt's President Sadat tried to break the impasse by making a highly publicized trip to Jerusalem, the first time any Arab leader had openly visited Israel, and speaking before the Knesset about his hopes for peace. A flurry of peace conferences and high-level meetings ensued, but the progress toward peace was very slow. The United States found it had to intervene often to preserve the momentum. Even so, the chances of a comprehensive peace settlement seemed, when I wrote these lines at the end of 1978, pretty remote.

PREFATORY REMARKS: PERSPECTIVE AND PEACE

A historian who writes about the recent past walks on eggs. Things happen suddenly in the Middle East, and projections for the future are always hazardous. Even without a major breakthrough toward peace or a new drift into war, who knows what the twenty-first-century reader will see as the main Middle Eastern events and trends from 1973 to 1978? Obviously, the intervening years will highlight some issues at the expense of others. Let me give an example by looking backward. At the beginning of the twentieth century, the building of the Berlin to Baghdad railway by a German company was a major diplomatic issue. Our forebears saw that it would enhance German power within the Ottoman Empire at the expense of Britain, France, and Russia. Meanwhile, few people noticed that in 1901 a British subject obtained from the Iranian government a concession that led to the first major oil discovery in the Middle East. Yet today we see Middle East oil as much more important than a railroad that was never completed. By the same token, I wonder if what we see as a major event today may seem insignificant in 2001. Having unburdened myself of this caveat, I venture to suggest that the major theme of the time span from the October 1973 war to the writing of these lines is the quest for peace between Israel and the Arabs.

But what do we mean by peace? In earlier chapters, I have assumed that you and I know what peace is. Or do we? One simple answer is that peace is the absence of conflict. But in the Middle East many conflicts smolder for years, then suddenly flare up. The Arab-Israeli conflict was dormant most of the time between 1956 and 1967, and yet there was no peace. Or we could define peace in another way: it is a conditon of harmony within and between every person, every group, and every nation in the world. Two people cannot be at peace with each other unless they feel at peace with themselves. If the members who make up a group disagree among themselves, they will not be able to agree with some other group. A country riven with factional, sectional, or ethnic hostility cannot reach a lasting peace with another state. Such idyllic conditions are rare in human life, though. Many past disputes have died down, enabling the parties to stop fighting each other, and yet they have never reached an agreement.

When addressing the question of peace with Israel, some Arabs say they will accept *salam* but not *sulh*. What is the difference? Both Arabic words mean "peace," but in modern usage *salam* carries an undertone of a temporary cessation of hostilities. Two closely related words are *salamah* (meaning "safety") and *islam* ("submission" or "surrender"). The word *sulh* means "reconciliation." Those Arabs who make this distinction may envisage an armistice with Israel, a respite from hostilities in which they can regain their political and economic strength, but not a true reconciliation with the Jewish state. Since this distinction naturally arouses the fears of Israel and its supporters, it hardly seems likely to lead to peace. But then is Israel simply a Jewish state? It is in fact a country inhabited by Jews and Arabs who must somehow find a just basis of coexistence that does not involve domination or repression of one side by the other. Let us not kid ourselves. Arab Israelis—let alone Palestinians under Israel's administration—do not enjoy the same power, rights, and status as Jewish Israelis. Zionists who ignore the feelings of these 1.7 million Arabs also impede the quest for *sulh* and maybe even *salam*. There can be no peace without security. There can be no peace without justice. For both sides. Period.

PRELUDE TO WAR

In September 1973 the Middle East seemed calm, and an Arab-Israeli war seemed highly improbable. The Israelis, having just celebrated their country's twenty-fifth birthday, were getting ready for another Knesset election. It seemed likely that power would remain with the same group that had ruled Israel since 1948. Now known as the Ma'arach ("alignment"), it was a bloc of moderate and socialist political parties (excluding, however, the Arab and Jewish Communists). Leading the Ma'arach was Mapai, the "Workers Party of Israel" formerly headed by Ben Gurion and then Golda Meir. The ruling alignment was also in coalition with the National Religious party, for which many of Israel's Orthodox Jews tended to vote. Menachem Begin, leader of the right-wing nationalists, had participated in coalition governments backed by the Ma'arach from 1967 to 1970, when he resigned in protest against Israel's acceptance of the Rogers Plan. He was now combining Israel's various conservative parties into a new coalition called the Likud.

American Concerns

The United States, having withdrawn its forces from Vietnam, seemed to be losing interest in foreign affairs. Most Americans were preoccupied with the scandals surrounding high figures in the Nixon administration—mainly the Watergate affair. Those concerned with long-range issues noted the growing gap between America's consumption and production of petroleum and other fossil fuels, a deficit that was being met by rising imports of oil and natural gas from the Middle East. Some oilmen argued that, unless the U.S. government took a more evenhanded approach to the Middle East conflict, the Arabs would stop selling these products to the West. As I mentioned in the last chapter, oil prices were beginning to rise, while the value of the dollar was falling.

In an attempt to ward off a crescendo of criticism about Watergate, President Nixon had just appointed his national security adviser, Dr. Henry Kissinger, as the new secretary of state. A few Arabs thought that Kissinger, being Jewish, would favor Israel, but he publicly expressed views similar to those of his predecessor, William Rogers. Eager to promote "détente," a relaxation of tensions between the Communist countries and the West, Kissinger hoped that the superpowers would put an end to the arms race and bring peace to the Middle East, the area where they would be most apt to confront each other.

Arab Frustrations

Both America and Israel underestimated how frustrated the Arab governments felt because of Israel's continuing and deepening occupation of the lands taken in 1967. Many pro-Israel observers knew this frustration existed, but assumed that the Arabs harped on the territorial issue to distract outsiders from their real aim of destroying the state of Israel and asserted that they lacked the will and the power to make the Israelis pull out. After all, the Arabs had never fought against Israel without having Egypt in their vanguard. Anwar al-Sadat seemed to have weakened his ability to fight by expelling his Soviet advisers and technicians in 1972. Several times Sadat warned American and European journalists that he might soon attack Israeli positions somewhere in Sinai to create a crisis in which the superpowers would have to intervene. This brought back derisive memories of his fatuous threat that 1971 would be the "year of decision." Critics claimed that Sadat was incapable of decision, either to wage war or to make peace with Israel.

Actually, Sadat wanted both. A war with Israel would be costly to Egypt, but if his army and air force, equipped with an impressive arsenal of Soviet tanks, planes, and missiles, could regain some of the lands Nasser had lost in 1967, Egypt would be in a better position (and a better frame of mind) to make peace with Israel. True, Egypt's economy was sliding toward bankruptcy, but any peace overtures to Israel without such a war would cause the richer Arab states to cut off all aid to Egypt. While Sadat had purged his government of any of Nasser's henchmen who might have opposed his own policies, he could be overthrown by the military. Many officers and men had been in a state of alert ever since 1967 and were thirsting for either battle action or a chance to return to civilian life. The policy of "no war no peace" (an expression taken from the decisions of the 1967 Khartum summit) had outlived its usefulness. The Egyptians followed Israel's election campaign, in which both the Ma'arach and the Likud made glowing promises about Jewish settlements and development towns in Sinai, especially in the areas nearest to the Gaza Strip. Sadat eloquently expressed his own reaction, "Every word spoken about Yamit [Israel's new port near Rafah] is a knife pointing at me personally and at my self-respect."

War Preparations

Sadat therefore began to confer publicly and privately with other Arab heads of state about an attack on Israel. For various personal and political reasons, he could no longer cooperate with Qadhafi, who made frequent and often unannounced visits to Cairo to harangue the Egyptian people about the Arabs' duty to fight Zionism, the proper role of women in Islam, and the wickedness of Cairo's nightclubs. The projected union between Egypt and Libya, due to take effect on 1 September 1973, was put off and finally forgotten.

Instead Sadat looked to King Faysal of Saudi Arabia, Egypt's main financial backer, and to the other confrontation states, Syria and Jordan. These two countries had been on bad terms with each other ever since the days of Abdallah's "Greater Syria" scheme. However, Hafiz al-Assad, Syria's president since late 1970, was more interested than his predecessors in building up his country's economy and less inclined to subvert the politics of Jordan. Husayn wanted to end his kingdom's isolation in the Arab world. Thus, in early September Sadat brought the two leaders together for a mini-summit at which they agreed to revive the "eastern front" against Israel. The next day Israel announced it had shot down thirteen Syrian jets and lost one in an air battle over the Mediterranean (Syria admitted to a score of eight to five). Was this a show of power, Israel's effort to discredit the new solidarity vaunted by the Arab confrontation states? I do not know. But it appears that high-level Syrian and Egyptian officers started planning for a coordinated surprise attack on the Israeli occupied territories in the Golan Heights and the east bank of the Suez Canal.

Not until we have more published memoirs and documents will we know for sure if Syria and Egypt really hoped to invade and defeat Israel, presumably to liberate Palestine. This was not their stated purpose. The Arab leaders counted on catching Israel off guard. They thought that

America, paralyzed politically by the Vietnam debacle and the Watergate scandals, would not intervene. They also agreed that Jordan, lacking a missile defense system against Israeli aircraft, should stay out of the early phases of the war. Did Syria and Egypt deliberately choose Yom Kippur (the Jewish Day of Atonement) as the date of their attack? Again I am not sure. The original plan was to launch it just after sundown, with a nearly full moon. The fact that the Russians had just sent up a new spy satellite may have helped to set the timing.

THE OCTOBER (YOM KIPPUR) WAR

The outbreak of the war was signaled by a massive Egyptian air and artillery assault on Israel's Bar Lev line east of the Suez Canal together with a large-scale Syrian tank invasion into the Golan Heights. With 600 officers and soldiers on the Bar Lev line and 70 tanks to guard the Golan, Israel could hardly blunt the initial Arab assault. Within an hour thousands of Egyptians had crossed the Suez Canal, having used their surface-to-air missile system to shoot down Israeli planes, thus denying the enemy its customary control of the air, and had overrun most of the Bar Lev line. The Syrians had retaken Mount Hermon and were making rapid inroads into the southern half of the Golan Heights.

Israel's Unpreparedness

Mobilizing Israel's reserves was quick and easy; most were either at home or at prayer in the synagogues. Soon hundreds of units were grouping and heading toward the two fronts. Had the surprise attack occurred on any day other than Yom Kippur, it would have been harder for the Israel Defense Forces to call up the reserves. Still, Israel was taken by surprise. Both Israeli and American intelligence had noted the massing of Egyptian and Syrian troops during the preceding week, but had assumed that they were on routine maneuvers, and in any case would Muslim armies attack during the month of Ramadan? Israel did not want to call up its reserves, having done so at great expense only a few months earlier. By the time it realized that war was inevitable, it was too late to bring its front-line units up to the necessary level of strength. In an emergency cabinet meeting on the morning of 6 October, the idea of a preemptive air strike was brought up, but Golda Meir ruled out such an action, which might cause the U.S. government to cut off all assistance to Israel.

The Course of the Fighting

The Arab assault worked at first but slowed down later. The Egyptians might well have pushed deep into Sinai and the Syrians down the Golan

Heights into the Jezreel Valley. In retrospect, it seems they had not expected to start off so well and had not planned what to do next. The Israelis, many of them hardened veterans of three or four previous wars, fought back. Seeing that Egyptian infantrymen carried lightweight surface-to-air missiles capable of knocking out a low flying jet, Israel's pilots developed new evasive maneuvers. Some threw pieces of aluminum foil out of their planes to confuse missiles guided by TV cameras.

During the first week of fighting the Israelis concentrated their forces in the north, fearing what might happen if Syrian forces broke through into mainly Arab areas, such as the Galilee or the occupied West Bank. The Syrians were soon driven back beyond the 1967 armistice line. Israeli units reached Sasa, a town half way between Kunaitra and Damascus. They advanced no farther, partly for fear of Soviet intervention or a massive onslaught by Jordan or Iraq, but also because the main thrust of Israel's effort shifted to the Egyptian front. Two Egyptian armies had crossed the canal and occupied positions about 10 kilometers deep into Sinai, but Israeli intelligence found a weak spot in the middle, between the two armies. In the second week of fighting, amid tank battles as large in scale and as costly in lives and equipment as any that had been fought in World War II, the Israelis penetrated the middle zone, reached the canal, and crossed it. Few of the men in the advance units survived the Egyptian fire and bombardment, but a land bridge was eventually built, and hundreds of Israelis crossed over to the west side of the canal. Egypt tried to play down the crossing, but as the Israelis continued to advance southward toward Suez, Sadat became apprehensive.

Arms Supplies and the Oil Embargo

One major factor in turning the tide was America's resupply of arms to Israel. The U.S. government had held off sending ammunition and supplies during the first week of the war, fearing to antagonize the Arabs and perhaps hoping to push Israel into a more accommodating mood, but in the second week a massive arms airlift started. How could the Arabs discourage this operation? The weapon that had gone begging for years, an embargo on the sale of oil to the United States, now beckoned. To be sure, Arab oil-exporting countries had cut off sales to the West in the June 1967 war, but that oil boycott had fizzled after a few weeks. The difference was that the world market had been glutted with oil in 1967, whereas even before October 1973 there was growing concern about oil supplies in most of the industrialized countries, which showed up in speeches and popular writings about the "energy crisis." Egypt had long urged the oil-rich gulf states to deny oil to America as a means of putting pressure on Israel to withdraw. An editorial in *al-Ahram* argued that American university students, if forced to attend classes in unheated lecture rooms, would demonstrate for the Arab cause as they had for troop withdrawals from Indochina.

Anyway, the day after America started flying arms to Israel, the Arab oil-producing states, meeting in Kuwait, announced that they would cut back their production 5 percent that month and that these cutbacks would continue until Israel had withdrawn from all the occupied territories and recognized the national rights of the Palestinians. Various OPEC members then took to announcing sudden price hikes of up to 50 percent. Finally, the Arab states (but not Iran) agreed to place an embargo on the United States and any European country considered to be excessively pro-Israel. As things turned out, the Netherlands was singled out, not so much due to the Dutch government's policies, but rather because much of the oil supplied to northern Europe came in at the port of Rotterdam. The oil embargo failed to halt the U.S. airlift, but it caused many European countries to deny landing rights to American planes carrying arms to Israel. All hastened to issue statements backing the Arab interpretation of Resolution 242. Even so, oil supplies ran short. With winter coming, the European countries had to adopt austerity measures to cut oil consumption.

The Superpowers and the Cease-fire

By the third week of the war, the longest the Arabs and Israelis had fought since 1948, both Egypt and Syria were in military trouble. The USSR, anxious to avert their collapse, invited Kissinger to Moscow. The U.S. government might have played on the Russians' panic, but it had troubles of its own. Aside from American fears of the Arabs' oil weapon and the danger that more Arab countries might enter the war, Washington was in disarray. Vice-President Agnew had just resigned. President Nixon fired his special Watergate prosecutor and accepted his attorney general's resignation in the "Saturday night massacre." Hastening to Moscow, Kissinger hammered out with Communist party chief Leonid Brezhnev the terms for a mutually acceptable UN Security Council resolution. There was to be a cease-fire in place, a reaffirmation of Resolution 242, and immediate negotiations between the parties to the conflict. This resolution was adopted by the Security Council and accepted by Egypt and Israel—but not Syria. Heavy fighting continued on both fronts, however, with Egypt and Israel accusing each other of bad faith. By the time the Security Council had come up with a new document, Resolution 338 of 24 October 1973, Israel's forces in Egypt had reached the outskirts of Suez itself and in Syria had gained more land around Mount Hermon.

Many Israelis resented the imposed cease-fire. Egypt's third army was trapped in Sinai east of Suez, and Israel was in a position to nullify its effectiveness. But Kissinger reasoned that Egypt would be more apt to make peace if it was allowed to leave the war with some of its initial gains. The cease-fire was shaky. The troop lines seemed hopelessly intermingled, and most people expected the fighting to resume at any time. The United States put its armed forces on a "red alert" the next day, reportedly because Soviet ships were unloading nuclear warheads at Alexandria. Despite these and other scares, though, the cease-fire held.

THE WAR'S AFTERMATH

The June 1967 war had destroyed whatever influence the United States had in Egypt and Syria. One of the remarkable results of the October 1973 war was that America actually regained most of that lost influence. The man responsible for this feat was Kissinger. Even though he had never spent time in the Arab countries or shown much interest in them before he became secretary of state, he managed to deal shrewdly and yet compassionately with their leaders, to persuade them to back down from their uncompromising stance toward Israel, and to strengthen their ties with the United States, which alone could put real pressure on Jerusalem. He was willing to try various methods of bringing the Arabs and the Israelis together; if one failed, he came up with another. In early November Egyptian and Israeli commanders actually met in a tent pitched near Kilometer 101 on the Cairo-Suez road, to see if they could identify and unsnarl the lines between the Egyptian and Israeli troops and arrange for sending food and medical supplies to Egypt's trapped third army. When this fell short of his hopes, Kissinger began organizing a general conference, to be held in Geneva in late December. Even though Syria refused to attend on the grounds that the PLO had been left out, Egypt and Israel came. After a day for opening speeches, the conference adjourned and a technical committee started working on the urgent problem of disentangling the Israelis and the Egyptians around Suez. The Geneva Conference has remained in suspension ever since.

Shuttle Diplomacy

In January 1974 Kissinger began flying between Jerusalem and Aswan, finally hammering out a "separation of forces" agreement by which Israel's troops withdrew from all lands west of the canal and established its armistice line about twenty miles (thirty-five kilometers) east of Suez. A new UN Emergency Force patrolled a buffer zone east of the canal. This enabled Sadat to keep the lands his forces had taken while regaining those they had lost in the October war, while the Israelis could then demobilize most of their reserve soldiers, who were needed in their factories, shops,

Map 11. The Territorial Situation at the End of the October 1973 War

offices, and classrooms back home. So pleased were the Egyptians with this arrangement that Sadat helped Kissinger persuade King Faysal to lift the oil embargo. In fact, Syria too was persuaded to negotiate a disengagement with Israel. This agreement proved even tougher to work out. It kept Kissinger in the Middle East for almost all of May 1974, but finally the Israelis agreed to give back to Syria what they had taken in the October war, plus the Golan Heights' principal city, Kunaitra. A UN Disengagement Observer Force was admitted into the Golan Heights, but only for a six-month period that would have to be renewed by the agreement of both sides. Despite some anxious moments as each six-month period drew to a close, Syria and Israel have maintained this agreement since May 1974. Kissinger returned home to a hero's welcome. Nixon, now in deep trouble at home over Watergate, toured several Arab countries and Israel in June, trying to reap some of his glory.

Israel's Domestic Crisis

While Kissinger was practicing his virtuoso diplomacy, the government of Israel underwent a severe political crisis. The general election, planned for October 1973, had been postponed until late December because of the war. When it was held, the right-wing Likud coalition made serious inroads into the majority of Knesset seats held by the Ma'arach and its allies, apparently a voter reaction against bungling by Golda Meir's cabinet in the beginning of the war. During the early months of 1974 she struggled to set up a new cabinet, but her efforts were hampered by arguments between secularist and Orthodox parties over the question of "who is a Jew?" A hoary issue in Israel's politics, it basically revolves around whether the government can confer citizenship rights on any Jewish immigrant desiring them (the position of the secularists) or whether it may do so only for an immigrant who can prove that he/she had a Jewish mother or has been converted in accordance with Jewish law. Many North American Jews, belonging to the Conservative or Reform movements, object to such a definition, which implies that Israel does not recognize their rabbis' authority to perform conversions to Judaism. On the other hand, the Orthodox Jews argued that Israel should strive to be a truly Jewish state, not just one in which the people who call themselves Jews happen to form a majority. Golda Meir, unable to get a consensus on whether to include the National Religious party in her cabinet, and stung by criticism about the war, finally offered her resignation. As soon as the disengagement agreement with Syria took effect, she stepped down in favor of Yitzchak Rabin, formerly Israel's ambassador in Washington.

Effects of the Oil Embargo

The oil crisis of 1973-1974 caused serious economic and political problems for the industrialized world. The price of crude oil fluctuated wildly for a time, as various countries proceeded to bid against one another to secure adequate supplies to run their factories, drive their cars, and heat their houses. At one point the price per barrel got up as high as $20, a far cry from the average posted price of $3 charged in January 1973, but eventually it settled at about $11.65. The United States was less directly affected than Europe or Japan, simply because it produces some oil and can import from Canada, Mexico, and Venezuela, but speed limits had to be lowered, thermostats turned down, and clocks set forward in midwinter. Drivers formed long lines at gas stations, and many suspected the oil companies of holding back supplies in order to bring up the prices charged to the consumer. In the Middle East, the sudden increase in oil revenues opened new vistas for industrial development and political leverage to countries like Saudi Arabia, Kuwait, and Iran. Libya, for example, had ample funds to influence African governments to change their policies toward Israel or to support revolutionary causes in Ireland or Ethiopia. But even the oil exporters had problems, as Western businessmen jammed their hotels and the waiting rooms of government offices, as ships loaded with machinery and consumer goods lined up around the inadequate ports of the Persian (or Arabian) Gulf countries, and as poorer countries like Egypt (to say nothing of the PLO!) importuned them for economic assistance.

Countries without oil, including some Arab ones like Jordan, Yemen, and the Sudan, were hard pressed to pay the new prices. India, Pakistan, and Bangladesh had to shelve many of their needed development plans just to pay for oil. The European countries, Japan, and America all experienced higher unemployment and "double digit inflation" in 1974. These problems naturally had repercussions on everyone buying from those industrialized nations or trying to sell to them. Arabs and Iranians started investing heavily in corporate stocks and bonds, real estate, treasury bills, and other forms of Western capital. At the rate they were acquiring "petrodollars," some observers feared that the oil-exporting countries would soon own most of the world's major assets. These fears proved unwarranted, but the economic power of Saudi Arabia, Kuwait, Iran, and the United Arab Emirates has continued to grow and to be translated into political—and military—power. U.S. arms sales to the Middle East, to mention a sensitive topic, reached $9 billion in 1977.

PLO Power at Its Zenith

Foreign countries, hoping to improve their ties with the Arabs, began to support the Palestinian cause to a degree far greater than ever before. Even though they had taken little part in the October 1973 war, the Palestinians increased their leverage over other Arab governments. Many had migrated into the oil-producing countries to find a living and now contributed heavily to both the elite and the work force of countries like Kuwait (where Palestinians are now a quarter of the whole population). Not surprisingly, the Kuwaiti government has contributed heavily to the PLO. In October 1974 the Arab heads of state, meeting in Rabat, recognized the PLO as the "sole legitimate representative of the Palestinian people on any liberated Palestinian territory." Even King Husayn conceded to the PLO the right to negotiate for the West Bank (though later it turned out that Jordan never really gave up hope of regaining control over that territory). In addition, the UN General Assembly invited PLO leader Yasir Arafat to speak, and later approved a resolution both recognizing the right of the Palestinians to independence and sovereignty and giving the PLO observer status at the United Nations. Meanwhile UNESCO voted to cut off financial aid to Israel because of its "persistence in altering the historical features of Jerusalem." In 1975 Israel would become even more isolated in the world community, as the UN General Assembly passed a harsh resolution condemning Zionism as a form of racism.

The UN actions have been attacked by many Westerners, who often infer that oil diplomacy has swayed the world body against Israel and Zionism. But there is a logic to the Palestinian position and the support it has received from most UN member states. To them, the state of Israel is made up largely of Jewish settlers (and their descendants) who have usurped lands once occupied by Palestinian Arabs. These settlers, in the various wars they have fought, tried to expand into other Arab lands, subjugating or displacing their inhabitants. Israel still tries to bring in new Jewish settlers from abroad as a means of strengthening the state. Religious observance is not the criterion by which most Israelis determine who is a Jew; rather, it is "Jewish identity," a rather broad term encompassing parentage, culture, and even physical appearance. To supporters of the Arab cause, Zionism is the movement that has led and still leads to the oppression of Arabs in a settler state comparable to South Africa, where the whites are unquestionably racist. Not surprisingly, the Palestinians court the support of Blacks and other oppressed peoples for their own cause. Supporters of Israel see the equation of Zionism with racism as a means of delegitimizing the state and possibly encouraging the persecution of Jews in other countries, such as the USSR.

The PLO has portrayed itself as a movement struggling for national liberation, seeking a democratic Palestinian state where Christians, Jews, and Muslims will live together in justice, equality, and fraternity. It denied Zionist attempts to discredit the movement as terrorist. Acts of sabotage and murder against Israeli civilians, which became especially virulent in the spring of 1974, were explained as necessary steps toward the liberation of Palestine, although objective observers wondered whether their real purposes were not to stop Kissinger's peace efforts and to provoke Israeli air raids against the *fidaiyin* in southern Lebanon (which also took innocent lives). Some argued that giving the Palestinians a state on the West Bank and in the Gaza Strip would force them to become more responsible, precisely because of their vulnerability to retaliation if they did not police themselves. Few Israelis were prepared to take the chance.

A Return to Shuttle Diplomacy

In the winter of 1975 Kissinger began a new series of talks with Egypt and Israel aimed at an interim Sinai agreement that would preserve the momentum of the peace negotiations and possibly strengthen moderates like Sadat at the expense of Yasir Arafat and the extremists. Kissinger tried again his shuttle diplomacy that had worked so well in 1974. However, the talks broke down because Israel did not want to hand back the oilfields at Abu-Rudays or the strategic Gidi and Mitla passes, while Egypt refused to give a pledge of nonbelligerency. When King Faysal was shot to death by a deranged nephew, many observers expected a new period of political instability in the Arab countries. The U.S. government began "reassessing" its Middle East policy, and some inferred that this would mean a tilt toward the Arabs in an effort to buy peace. Arms deliveries to Israel were slowed down, and there were hints that American economic aid, amounting to about $2 billion per year since the 1973 war, might be lowered considerably.

In due course, though, both Egypt and Israel became more accommodating. In June 1975 Sadat reopened the Suez Canal and allowed ships carrying Israeli cargoes to pass through. Later in the summer the talks resumed. After yet another round of shuttle diplomacy Kissinger obtained a new Sinai agreement. Israel pulled back from the passes and the oilfields, and a hundred U.S. civilian technicians joined the UN Emergency Force inside the buffer zone separating the Egyptian and Israeli armies. Some members of Congress questioned letting Americans serve as a trip wire in case of a sudden Arab or Israeli attack, but the new agreement was ratified. Egypt did agree to a renunciation of war as a means of resolving the Middle East conflict, a statement widely interpreted in other Arab capitals as a sellout, but neither the Palestinians nor any other Arab government could effectively oppose Egypt.

LEBANON: THE ARENA FOR A NEW ARAB STRUGGLE

Meanwhile, a separate but related crisis arose in Lebanon: a civil war more lasting, costly, and bitter than that of 1958. The issues are complex, and perhaps it would be best to look at them from various angles.

The Religious Angle

The conflict is usually seen as one between Christians and Muslims. Lebanon was a country deeply divided along confessional lines, one in which the Maronites, the largest single Christian sect, had long exercised power disproportionate to their actual share of the population. Lebanon's Muslims, really a majority of the country's people, sought equal rights for themselves. We should not assume that all Christians lined up on the side of the Maronites (many of the Greek Orthodox did not) or that all Muslims had the same interests. Shi'i Muslims were gaining in numbers, relative to the historically predominant Sunnis, and at times they sought recognition of their status. It is also awkward to explain that the leading spokesman of the "Muslim" side was Kamal Jumblat, a Druze.

The Nationalist Angle

Some experts viewed the civil war as a struggle between Lebanese nationalists, who viewed their country as a link between the West and the Middle East, and Arab nationalists, who wanted closer ties with Syria and other Arab states. Not surprisingly, this aspect of the conflict drew various Arab countries to fish in troubled waters. Since no other Arab state would say in public that it favored Lebanese particularism over Arab nationalism, the policy adopted by any given Arab country was apt to depend on whether it was friendly to Syria or not. And Syria's policy, as I will soon explain, did not stay the same. Supporters of Israel tended to watch the Palestinians, whom they viewed as fighting against the Lebanese (meaning the Maronites). At least 300,000 Palestinians live in Lebanon, mainly in the south and in refugee camps around Beirut. Many at this time felt shut out of Lebanon's political and economic life. Christian Arabs from Palestine had been quickly assimilated after 1948, but not the Palestinian Muslims, who would have helped create a Lebanese Muslim majority. Since 1971 the PLO had its main base of operations in Lebanon. It did not want to get involved in a civil war, but it tended to sympathize with any group that espoused Arab nationalism and the eventual liberation of Palestine. As some of you may remember, it was a Christian attack on a busload of Palestinians that touched off the fighting in April 1975. From then on, the PLO was committed to the Arab nationalist side.

The Economic Angle

The Lebanese conflict was also a struggle between a privileged class of landowners and businessmen trying to preserve the status quo and a large mass of poor people (mainly Muslim) striving for greater equality. The gap between rich and poor, especially in Beirut, was scandalous. High-rise luxury apartment buildings stood beside shacks made of cinder blocks and corrugated iron. Unable to collect income taxes from the rich, the government tried to make up its loss by excise taxes on cigarettes and other consumer goods. Many employers evaded paying the minimum wage, as there were always Palestinian refugees or newcomers from the mountains who were desperate for work and could be hired cheaply.

The Ideological Angle

With social conditions like these, some journalists and scholars saw the civil war as one between the "Right" (guardians of the status quo) and the "Left" (those who wanted change). In a way this was true. Those who were rich, well connected, and Christian *tended* to support the Right; those who were not *generally* became Leftists. But many exceptions existed. There is also the international aspect. Although Americans no longer look for Communists behind every tree, doubtless some Marxist "Progressives" did enter the struggle. Besides, the rifles and grenade launchers used by the Left tended to be of Soviet manufacture, while American weapons predominated among the forces of the Right. Since all Middle Eastern countries have armed themselves to the teeth for years, and since Lebanon is a smuggler's haven, no one should wonder that bombs and guns were plentiful in that civil war.

An Attempted Synthesis

All of these angles have some truth. None is wholly true. People fight for many reasons other than religion, nationality, class interest, or ideology. There are also loyalties based on family, patronage, habit, or even neighborhood. Old grudges and dormant feuds were revived. Past favors or slights were paid back in kind—or worse. Lebanon had dozens of armed factions, ranging from youth gangs to private armies; for many Lebanese felt insecure, even in the best of times, without a gun and a group to defend them. Sticking to basics, the two main Lebanese parties to the conflict were the Phalangists, a well-established and largely Maronite force, and the Murabitun, a predominantly Muslim army that rose to prominence in late 1975, when the two sides fought for control of Beirut's hotel district. Lebanon's president, Sulayman Franjiyah, clearly supported the "Christian" side. The "Muslim" side had several leaders, best known among whom was Kamal Jumblat, a Druze landowner, and of course Yasir Arafat, as head of the PLO, also helped. Savage fighting alternated with shaky cease-fires over a period of eighteen months. It was most intense in and around Beirut, where neighborhoods became battle zones, and both sides, using bazookas and grenades never intended for street fighting, reduced buildings to rubble. It is estimated that 70,000 people (mostly civilians) were killed, over half a million were left homeless, and property damage exceeded a billion dollars.

Syria's Role in the War

The most puzzling aspect of the Lebanese civil war was Syria's policy shift in 1976. Syria's stand should have been obvious. It had deeply resented France's separation of Lebanon during the mandate, and ever since independence most Syrians had hoped that some day the two countries would be reunited. Predominantly Muslim and historically the bellwether of Arab nationalism, Syria had tended to side with any faction that would weaken the rule of the pro-Western Maronite Christians there. Naturally, then, President Hafiz al-Assad should have supported the rebel group during the 1975-1976 civil war. At first he did, both morally and militarily. But in January 1976 he managed to get both Franjiyah and his opponents to accept a cease-fire and a political settlement involving a slight shift in Lebanon's power balance in favor of the Muslims. But the Muslim Lebanese, abetted by the PLO, rebelled against this compromise settlement. Soon Syria had to send in tanks and troops to enforce the arrangement it had hammered out. Syrian troops attacked Lebanese Muslims and the PLO, battering them into submission by the early fall of 1976.

An Arab summit meeting, held in Riyad that October, devised a formula by which Lebanon would continue to be occupied by an Arab League peacekeeping force, most of which would in fact consist of Syrians. Elias Sarkis, a moderate, was elected to succeed Franjiyah as president, but it was strange for a Syrian leader like Assad, supposedly a champion of Arab nationalism and socialism, to be protecting Christian interests in Lebanon. It may be that Assad did not want the PLO to gain so much power and prestige from the Lebanese civil war that no Arab government could control it. Or perhaps he just disliked Yasir Arafat. Lebanon settled down into an uneasy truce, but the fighting had created a de facto partition of the country—even of Beirut itself—between Christians and Muslims. While some Christians still lived peacefully in "Muslim" zones such as western Beirut, the Maronites started building a new harbor and airport north of the city and treating their area as a Christian counterpart to Israel. Indeed, the Israelis seemed to agree. As a foretaste of their massive invasion two years later, Israeli forces in 1976 started going into southern Lebanon to wipe out Palestinian guerrilla bases and warned Syria not to send its troops too close to the Lebanese border. Christian Lebanese in the south—cut off from their coreligionists in the rest of the country—began crossing over into Israel to sell their produce, seek work, or obtain medical care.

CARTER'S POLICIES

The U.S. government became less active in the search for a Middle East settlement during 1976 because of its presidential elections. Both Ford and Carter pledged their support to a strong and independent Israel and played down the need to find some arrangement for the Palestinian Arabs. The United States was not unaffected by the war, as the American ambassador was assassinated in June 1976 and the PLO assisted the U.S. embassy in evacuating American civilians. Some Americans wondered if their government was starting to recognize the PLO in the process. Later on, once Carter had been elected, the time seemed ripe for a new American initiative to settle the Arab-Israeli conflict and perhaps, as a result, the Lebanese civil war and other problems as well.

Early Attitudes

If we need a key to the thinking of the new American administration on the Middle East, the most important is a report prepared by the Brookings Institute and published in February 1976. Called *Towards Peace in the Middle East,* it recommends that the Arab countries recognize Israel within its pre-June 1967 boundaries (with a few minor border adjustments) and that Israel should turn over the West Bank and the Gaza Strip to a government of Palestinian Arabs, though not necessarily the PLO. In order to achieve these agreements the Geneva Conference should be revived. One of the scholars involved in drafting the Brookings Report was a political scientist, William Quandt, who went to serve under Carter's national security adviser, Zbigniew Brzezinski. President Carter and his secretary of state, Cyrus Vance, put high priority on the Middle East conflict and started holding talks with various heads of state during 1977, with the goal of reconvening the Geneva Conference before the end of the year.

Problems of American Policy

New snags soon developed. One problem was that the Israelis were intensely suspicious of any conference in which the USSR would join the United States as cochairman. Formerly, Kissinger's shuttle diplomacy had effectively kept Moscow out of the peacekeeping process. Now Washington seemed determined to invite the Russians back in, embarrassing the Israelis and reportedly even Sadat. In addition, the Arab states insisted on representation of the Palestinians at the proposed conference. If they were left out altogether, they might well try to sabotage the settlement, as it has become axiomatic that some Palestinian individual or group will kill someone or blow up something whenever a peace is in sight that might bypass the interests and aspirations of the Palestinian Arabs. If they were to be included, would the PLO represent them, as provided for by the decision of the Arab leaders at Rabat in 1974? This would be totally unacceptable to Israel, which viewed Arafat as a murderer and the PLO as the umbrella for a collection of terrorist groups. As far as Israel was concerned, Jordan was a Palestinian state and there was no need for another, especially one that would try to destroy Israel. On the other hand, every Palestinian of stature looked to the PLO as his representative. As of 1976, all the newly elected mayors of West Bank towns were avowed supporters of the PLO. The PLO was ambiguous in its public policy statements about recognizing Israel, but it definitely wanted to speak for the Palestinians at the Geneva Conference.

America learned the hard way not to take the Israelis for granted. While the Carter administration was seeking peace, new general elections were held in Israel in May 1977. The ruling alignment had become weakened by internal dissension between Prime Minister Rabin and Defense Minister Shim'on Peres. The situation was made worse by scandals within the government, as when a disgraced cabinet officer committed suicide, and Rabin was embarrassed by the revelation that his wife had disobeyed Israel's currency regulations by keeping a dollar account in a Washington bank. Inflation was going on at an annual rate of over 30 percent. Social problems were mounting. Israel's electorate therefore decided to vote out the Ma'arach. Some switched to a new party calling for peace and major reforms, the Democratic Movement for Change, while others voted for the right-wing Likud. When the votes were counted, the Likud had won an upset victory. Its leader, Menachem Begin, managed to form a viable coalition with the National Religious party and to take over as prime minister, the first time that the post had ever been held by an Israeli not belonging to one of the labor parties. Begin's election seemed to be a step backward from peace, as he was quick to assert that the West Bank (which he called Judea and Samaria) was an integral part of Eretz Israel that had been liberated, not captured, in June 1967. He encouraged Jewish settlements in strategic parts of what was otherwise a predominantly Arab area. Most Arabs called Begin a terrorist. As former leader of the Irgun, he had been the man responsible for the Dayr Yasin massacre of April 1948. It seemed highly unlikely that any Arab leader would want to talk to such a chauvinistic Israeli.

But, to everyone's surprise, one did. In a speech before Egypt's National Assembly, Anwar al-Sadat stated, somewhat theatrically, that he was willing to go before the Israeli Knesset to argue Egypt's case for peace.

Questioned by American TV journalists, Begin indicated that he would be pleased to receive the Egyptian president in Jerusalem at any time. Arrangements were made rapidly, faster than anyone had expected, and on 19 November 1977 Sadat flew to Israel. The following day he delivered before the Knesset a speech that was carried to most parts of the world by radio and television. He told the Israelis that Egypt would make peace with them in return for a complete withdrawal from all territories occupied in the 1967 war and recognition of a Palestinian state. Many people thought that Sadat's visit was so drastic a step toward peace that Israel should have made comparable concessions to Sadat. The problem with this was that no other Arab leader seemed to want a reconciliation with Israel as much as Sadat did, and some, like Qadhafi and (predictably) Yasir Arafat, were calling him a traitor to the Arab cause. Israel would gladly have made a separate peace with Egypt, but Sadat wanted a comprehensive settlement involving Syria, Jordan, and the Palestinians.

To follow up on his Jerusalem visit, Sadat convoked a general peace conference in Cairo in December 1977, but only Israel and the United States agreed to come, so it was kept at a low level of diplomatic representation and ended inconclusively. It became obvious to the Israeli visitors, though, that Egyptians, badly pinched by economic austerity because of the heavy burden of maintaining a large defense establishment, welcomed them cordially as harbingers of peace and eventual prosperity. In addition, Begin flew to Ismailia to meet with Sadat on Christmas day, and the two leaders agreed to have concurrent sets of negotiations: military talks in Cairo and political talks in Jerusalem. By the time the negotiations began in January 1978, though, the initial enthusiasm of both sides had cooled. Begin was upset by what he construed as anti-Semitic remarks in the government-controlled Egyptian press. Sadat was angered by Israel's insistence on maintaining settlements and industrial towns in the Sinai Peninsula, to be protected by the Israeli army (much as the British had retained a base at the Suez Canal up to 1956), and so he decided to recall his political negotiating team from Jerusalem.

Combined with these territorial issues were differences of opinion between the two sides of the Palestine question. Begin offered self-rule (limited by a continuing Israeli military presence) to the Arabs of the West Bank and Gaza. Sadat called for self-determination by the Palestinian people. Each leader seemed blind to the other's fears. How could Begin expect Sadat to accept indefinite Israeli domination over the Palestinians, when the Arabs had been struggling for most of this century to achieve their independence from foreign rule? How could Sadat expect Begin to jeopardize his country's security by committing his government, before any substantive negotiations, to return strategic areas to the control of Arabs who had not yet recognized Israel's right to exist? Jewish Israelis did not care to admit that the Arabs of Palestine wanted freedom and dignity as much as they did, while Egypt (and the other Arab countries) did not fully realize how Israel's concern for security resulted from Jewish fears of extinction after the Nazi Holocaust and years of tension resulting from the Middle East conflict.

Such tunnel vision was tragic, for both sides needed peace. The burden of military expenditures was more than either could bear. Some Israelis were voting with their feet, leaving for other countries because they could no longer live with confiscatory taxes, constant calls to military reserve duty, and ceaseless tension. Many Arabs, too, had gone abroad, especially highly educated men and women seeking greater intellectual freedom and professional opportunities. Egypt especially needed to free funds committed to arms in order to build (or repair) its limping economy. Large-scale bread riots had broken out in Cairo in January 1977, drawing world attention to Egypt's economic problems. Anyone who has tried lately to ride a Cairo bus or to get a dial tone on an Egyptian phone knows how serious they have become.

The U.S. government has become more involved than ever before in the quest for peace. Americans feel that another Arab-Israeli war would be terribly destructive and dangerous, that the USSR stands to gain if direct talks fail (during 1978 Russia seemed to strengthen its position in Libya, Ethiopia, South Yemen, and Afghanistan), and that Arab oil must keep flowing to Western consumers. President Carter and many of the members of his administration have devoted a disproportionate share of their time and energy to the Arab-Israeli conflict. This has meant flying visits, compromise formulas, balanced sales of strategic weapons, and top-level meetings in various places.

A spectacular summit, consisting of Sadat, Begin, and Carter, with numerous cabinet officers and advisers from all three countries, met at Camp David (Maryland) in September 1978. Twelve days of intense negotiations produced documents called "A Framework for the Conclusion of a Peace Treaty Between Egypt and Israel" and "A Framework for Peace in the Middle East." The latter was intended to bring other parties into the settlement. But Jordan, Saudi Arabia, and (not too surprisingly) Syria and the PLO refused to join this proposed love feast. After long and bitter debate, Israel's Knesset agreed to pull its troops out of Sinai and hence to remove its settlements from the lands it would give back to Egypt. Negotiations then opened at Blair House, not far from the White House (a clear sign of Carter's indispensability). But the Washington talks foundered on Egypt's attempt to link the establishment of full diplomatic relations with Israel's progressive loosening of its control over the Arabs of

Map 12. Political Map of the Middle East, 1978

Gaza and the West Bank. The three-month deadline, accepted by both
Sadat and Begin at Camp David, passed without a peace treaty between the
two sides.

Meanwhile, OPEC announced that, during 1979, it would raise posted
oil prices by 14.5 percent (later, after the Iranian revolution, it would hike
them farther and faster), adding to the West's balance-of-payments
deficits. Fighting a war of nerves against each other, Egypt and Israel
continued to court Carter, Congress, and the American people. Peace was
a must, but could the two sides pay the political costs of a compromise?
Concerned about his falling popularity at home and America's eroding
position in the Middle East, Carter finally decided to fly to Cairo and
Jerusalem to sew up the loose ends of the peace accord. This risky venture

paid off, as Carter and his aides managed to reconcile the major differences between Sadat and Begin. A complex treaty, formally ending the state of war between Israel and Egypt, was signed on the White House lawn on 26 March 1979. It was an expensive undertaking for the United States, Begin and Sadat disagreed almost at once on the meaning of the document they had signed, and almost all the other Arab governments condemned it. Most of all, the Palestinians accused Sadat of betraying their quest for justice and self-determination by agreeing to negotiate with the Israelis on the future of Gaza and the West Bank. Prospects for peace between Israel and the Arabs are as stable as a rollercoaster ride. But when will the ride ever end?

EPILOGUE

In looking at the history of the Middle East from the rise of Islam to the present, I think you may have noticed, as I have, the degree to which our attention has been drawn to confrontations and especially to wars. There is a danger, when you survey the history of any country or region, that you will become bogged down in its struggles and never get to its cultural achievements or the everyday lives of its people. I feel this keenly in the case of the Middle East. Indeed, the closer we have moved to current history, the more narrowly I am forced to concentrate on conflicts in the Middle East: United States versus USSR, oil producer versus oil consumer, Christian versus Muslim, but especially Arab versus Israeli.

It is one of the occupational diseases of textbook writers to draw up lists, but I feel I must now enumerate what I see as the main causes of conflict in the Middle East: (1) the incomplete transition from communities based on religion and obedience to divine law to nation-states enforcing laws made by human beings to increase their security and well-being in the world, (2) the quest for freedom and dignity by highly articulate peoples (or nations) who have gone through centuries of subordination to outsiders and are determined never to be subjected again, (3) the involvement of outside governments and individuals who, however good their intentions, cannot deal with the hopes and fears of Middle Eastern peoples and, in the worst cases, exploit them to serve their own needs, (4) the concentration of highly destructive weapons in countries that are both volatile and vulnerable, and (5) the rising gap between the world's need for food and fossil fuels and the amounts available for consumption, which may seem good to certain Middle Eastern countries blessed with large oil reserves, but is actually a mixed blessing.

The Middle East is a region that has always been vulnerable to invasion and exploitation, that has never been able to escape from the ambitions of local or foreign rulers, and that has been prized for its natural resources or courted for its strategic location. It has also produced more than its share of scholars and poets, artists and architects, philosophers and prophets. Some call it the cradle of human civilization. Let us hope that it will not become its grave.

Glossary

Abbas I, Shah (awb-BOSS): Safavid ruler (1587-1629)

Abbas II, Khedive (ab-BASS): Viceroy of Egypt (1892-1914)

Abbasid dynasty (ab-BAS-sid): Arab family, descended from an uncle of Muhammad named Abbas, which ruled from Baghdad over parts of the Muslim world (750-1258)

Abd al-Ilah (AB-dul ee-LAH): Regent of Iraq (1939-1953)

Abd al-Malik (AB-dul MA-lik): Umayyad caliph ruling in Damascus (685-705), who ended the second *fitnah*

Abdallah, Emir (ab-DULL-ah): Son of Emir Husayn of Mecca, participant in the Arab Revolt, and ruler of Transjordan (1921-1951)

Abdallah ibn al-Zubayr (ab-DULL-ah ibn el-zoo-BAYR): Challenger to the Umayyads (ca. 683-692)

Abduh, Muhammad (AHB-doo, moo-HOM-mad): Egyptian Muslim reformer (d. 1905)

Abdulaziz (AB-dul-a-ZEEZ): Ottoman sultan (1861-1876)

Abdulhamid II (AB-dul-ha-MEED): Ottoman sultan (1876-1909), strong advocate of pan-Islam and opponent of constitutional government

Abdulmejid I (AB-dul-me-JEED): Ottoman sultan (1839-1861)

Abu al-Abbas ("al-Saffah") (AH-bull-ab-BASS e-saf-FAH): Abbasid caliph (750-754)

Abu-Bakr (AH-boo-BEKR): First caliph (632-634), who suppressed tribal revolts and began conquests outside the Arabian peninsula

Abu-Ja'far al-Mansur (AH-boo JAH-far el-man-SOOR): Abbasid caliph (754-775), responsible for construction of Baghdad

Abu-Kir, Battle of (ah-boo-KEER): British victory over Napoleon (1798)

Abu-Muslim (AH-boo-MOOS-lim): Persian leader of the Abbasid revolt

Abu-Rudays (AH-boo-ro-DAYCE): Sinai oil field held by Israel (1967-1975)

Abu-Talib (AH-boo-TAW-lib): Muhammad's uncle and protector (d. 619)

343

Achaemenid (ak-a-MEE-nid): Ancient Persian dynasty (550-330 B.C.)

Aden (AH-den): Port city between the Red and Arabian seas, ruled by Britain (1839-1967), now in the People's Democratic Republic of Yemen

Adli Yakan (ODD-lee YEH-ghen): Egypt's prime minister in 1921

Afghan (AF-gan): Pertaining to Afghanistan, a mountainous country east of Iran

al-Afghani, Jamal al-Din (el-af-GHAW-nee, je-MAWL ed-DEEN): Influential pan-Islamic agitator and reformer (d. 1897)

Agha Khan (AH-gha KHAWN): Modern leader of Isma'ili Shi'i Muslims

Aghlabid dynasty (AGH-la-bid): Family ruling Tunisia (800-909)

Ahd (AH-d): Nationalist secret society of Arab officers in the Ottoman army before and during World War I

Ahmad ibn Hanbal (AH-mad ibn-HAM-bal): Muslim jurist and theologian

Ahmad ibn Tulun (AH-mad ibn-to-LOON): Turkish founder of the Tulunid dynasty of Egypt (868-908)

Ahmad Shah (Ah-mad SHAH): Last Qajar ruler of Iran (1909-1925)

Ahmed III (ah-MET): Ottoman sultan (1703-1730)

al-Ahram (el-ah-RAHM): Influential Cairo daily newspaper

Aishah (ah-EE-sha): Daughter of Abu-Bakr, one of Muhammad's wives, and leader of forces opposing Ali at the Battle of the Camel (656)

akhi (AH-khee): Turkish mystic

Alawi (AH-la-wee): Pertaining to an offshoot of Shi'i Islam prevalent in parts of northern Syria

Aleppo (ah-LEP-po): City of northern Syria

Alexander the Great: Macedonian general and empire builder (d. 323 B.C.)

Alexandretta: Mediterranean coastal city and its hinterland, now held by Turkey but claimed by Syria, and currently called "Iskenderun"

Alexandria: Egyptian city on the Mediterranean coast

Ali (AH-lee): Fourth of the early caliphs (656-661), regarded by Shi'i Muslims as the first imam ("leader") after Muhammad

Alid: Pertaining to Ali, his descendants, or to partisans of their role as Muslim imams

aliyah (ah-lee-YAH): Immigration of Jews to Palestine or Israel

Allenby, Edmund: Commander of Egyptian Expeditionary Force in World War I, conqueror of Palestine, later high commissioner for Egypt (1919-1925)

Alliance Israelite Universelle: French-Jewish educational foundation

Allon, Yigal (al-LOAN, yeeg-AHL): Israeli general and political leader

Amin (ah-MEEN): Abbasid caliph (809-813)

amir (ah-MEER): See *emir*

amir al-muminin (ah-MEER el-muh-men-NEEN): Commander of the true believers, a title given to the caliph

Amman (am-MAN): Capital of Jordan (formerly Transjordan)

Amr ibn al-As (AHM-r ibn el-AHS): Early Arab general, conqueror of Egypt

Anatolia: Peninsula between Mediterranean, Black, and Aegean seas

Anglo-American Commission of Inquiry: Committee that visited Palestine in 1946, urged continuation of mandate and admission of 100,000 Jews

Anglo-Egyptian Treaty: 1936 pact defining Britain's military position in Egypt, denounced by Egypt in 1951, officially terminated in 1954

Anglo-Ottoman Commercial Treaty: 1838 agreement limiting Ottoman tariffs

Anglo-Persian Oil Company: Firm holding petroleum exploration, drilling, and refining rights in Iran, renamed Anglo-Iranian Oil Company, nationalized by Mosaddiq in 1951

Ankara: (1) Site of Timur's victory over Bayezid I in 1402; (2) capital of Turkey since 1923

ansar (ahn-SAWR): Medinan Muslim converts

Antichrist: Great antagonist of Jesus Christ who Christians and Muslims believe will fill the world with evil just before Christ's return

Antioch: Ancient city in southern Anatolia, important early Christian center

anti-Semitism: Popular term for prejudice against or persecution of Jews

anti-Zionism: Opposition to the idea that Jews constitute a nation, or hostility to the State of Israel

Aqaba (AH-ka-ba): (1) Inlet from the Red Sea; (2) city in southern Jordan

al-Aqsa (el-AHK-sa): Important Jerusalem mosque

Arab: (1) Native speaker of Arabic; (2) person who identifies with Arabic cultural tradition; (3) inhabitant of Arabia; (4) citizen of a country in which the predominant language and culture are Arabic; (5) camel nomad

Arab Higher Committee: Palestinian nationalist organization of the 1930s

Arab League: Political association of Arab states, founded in 1945

Arab Legion: Former name of the army of Transjordan or Jordan

Arab nationalism: Movement or ideology working toward unification of all Arab countries and their independence from non-Arab control

Arab-Ottoman Friendship Society: Ephemeral Arab group after 1908 Young Turk Revolution

Arab Revolt: British-backed rebellion of Arabs, mainly in the Hijaz, against Ottoman rule (1916-1918)

Arab socialism: Ideology calling for state control of Arab economies

Arab Socialist Union: Egyptian political party (1962-1978)

Arabia: Original Arab homeland, a peninsula bounded by the Red Sea, Arabian Sea, Persian Gulf, and the Fertile Crescent

Arabic: (1) Semitic language spoken by Arabs; (2) pertaining to the culture of Arabs

Arafat (ah-rah-FAT): Hill near Mecca

Arafat, Yasir: Palestinian Arab nationalist, founder of al-Fatah, and PLO leader since 1968

Aral Sea: Large lake in central Asia

Aramaic: Ancient Semitic language

Aramco: Arabian American Oil Company, developer of petroleum industry in Saudi Arabia

Aramean (ah-rah-MEE-an): Native speaker of Aramaic

Ardabil (ar-da-BEEL): City in northwestern Iran, where Safavids started

Arian: Pertaining to the belief of some early Christians that Jesus Christ was human, not of the same substance as God the Father

Arif, Abd al-Rahman (AH-ref, AB-der-rah-MAN): Leader of Iraq (1966-1968)

Arif, Abd al-Salam (AH-ref, AB-des-sa-LAM): Arab nationalist leader of Iraq (1958, 1963-1966)

Arkam (ar-KAM): An early Meccan convert to Islam

Armenia: (1) Mountainous region of eastern Anatolia; (2) the kingdom of the Armenians, conquered by the Turks in the eleventh century

Aryan: Pertaining to the Indo-European language family (often used in juxtaposition with "Semitic")

asabiyah (ah-sah-BEE-ya): Feeling of group solidarity

al-Ash'ari (el-ASH-ah-ree): Early Muslim theologian (d. 935)

Ashkenazim (ash-ke-na-ZEEM): Jews whose recent ancestors came from Eastern Europe

al-Assad, Hafiz (el-Es-sed HAW-fez): President of Syria (1970-)

Assassin: Member of a militant group of Isma'ili Shi'is who fought against the Seljuks and other Sunni rulers between the eleventh and thirteenth centuries

Assyrian: Pertaining to Nestorian Christians in Syria, Iraq, and Iran

Aswan (ass-WAHN): (1) City in Upper Egypt; (2) site of the High Dam, built for Egypt by the USSR (1958-1969)

Ata Malik Juvaini (AH-ta MA-lik jo-VAY-nee): Administrator in Mongol Iran

Ataturk: See *Kemal*

attrition, war of: Artillery and air struggle between Egypt and Israel (1969-1970)

Ayatollah (AYE-uh-tol-lah): High-ranking Shi'ite legal expert.

Ayn ud-Dowleh (AYN-od-DOE-leh): Qajar minister opposed to 1906 Iranian Constitutionalist Revolution

Ayn Jalut (AYN-ja-LOOT): Crucial Mamluk victory over Mongols in 1260

Ayyubid dynasty (eye-YOO-bid): Salah al-Din and his descendants, who ruled in Egypt (1171-1250) and Syria (1174-1260)

Azerbaijan (AH-zur-bye-JOHN): Mountainous region of northwestern Iran

al-Azhar (el-OZ-har): Muslim mosque-university in Cairo

Babak (BAH-bek): Ninth-century Persian revolutionary

Babur (BAH-ber): Founder of the Timurid ("Moghul") dynasty in India

Badr, Battle of: Muhammad's first victory over the Meccans (624)

Badr, Imam (BEDR, ee-MAHM): Yemen's ruler (1962), overthrown by military coup

Badreddin (bed-red-DEEN): Popular rebel against Sultan Mehmet I

Baghdad (bagh-DAD): Capital of Iraq, seat of Abbasids (762-1258)

Baghdad Pact: Anti-Communist military alliance formed in 1955, now CENTO

Bahrain (bah-RAYN): (1) Persian Gulf island country; (2) name for eastern Arabia during caliphal period

bakhshish (bakh-SHEESH): Gift, tip, bribe, or payment for services

Balfour Declaration: Official statement in 1917 by Britain's foreign secretary supporting Jewish national home in Palestine

Balkans: Mountainous region of southeastern Europe

Baluchistan (ba-LOOCH-i-stan): Region of eastern Iran and Pakistan

Bandung Conference: Meeting of Asian and African leaders (1955)

Bani Murrah (ben-ee-MUR-ra): Very poor eastern Arabian tribe

al-Banna, Hasan (el-BEN-na, HAS-san): Leader of the Society of the Muslim Brothers, which flourished in Egypt during the 1930s and 1940s

Bar Lev line: Israel's defense line east of the Suez Canal (1967-1973)

Barmakid (BAR-ma-kid): Persian family of vizirs under early Abbasids

al-Barudi, Mahmud Sami (el-bah-ROO-dee, mah-MOOD SA-mee): Egyptian nationalist prime minister (1882)

Basle: Swiss city, site of first international Zionist congress (1897)

Basrah (BOSS-ra): Town in southern Iraq

bast (BAWST): Act of taking refuge in a mosque or other public place to evade arrest

Ba'th (BAHTH): Arab nationalist and socialist party ruling Syria and Iraq

Baybars (BAY-barce): Mamluk general and sultan (1260-1277)

Bayezid I (BYE-zeh-zeet): Ottoman sultan (1389-1402), strong expansionist

Bayezid II: Ottoman sultan (1481-1512)

Bayt al-Hikmah (BAYT el-HIK-ma): Muslim center of learning under Abbasids

bazaar: (bah-ZAWR): (1) Large trading and manufacturing center; (2) urban merchants as a corporate body, especially in Iranian cities

bedouin (BED-a-win): Arab camel nomad(s)

Begin, Menachem (BAY-gin, me-NAH-khem): Leader of Israel's right-wing Herut party and Likud coalition, and prime minister (1977-)

Beirut (bay-ROOT): Port city, commercial center, and capital of Lebanon

Bektashi (bek-TAH-shee): Sufi order, popular among Ottoman janissaries

Ben Bella, Ahmad: Algerian nationalist leader and president (1962-1965)

Ben Gurion, David: Zionist pioneer, writer, politician, defense and prime minister of Israel (1948-1953 and 1955-1963)

Berber: Native inhabitant of parts of North Africa

Berlin to Baghdad railway: Projected rail line that, if completed, would have enhanced Germany's power in the Ottoman Empire before World War I

Bernadotte, Folke: Swedish UN mediator during 1948 Palestine war

Bethlehem: Judean (or West Bank) city, south of Jerusalem

Bilal (bee-LAL): Muhammad's first muezzin, a Black Ethiopian

Biltmore Program: American Zionist resolution (1942) openly demanding a Jewish state in Palestine

BILU (BEE-loo): Late nineteenth-century Russian Zionist movement

Black Sheep Turcomans: Shi'i Turkish dynasty ruling in Iran (1378-1469)

Bosporus: Straits connecting Black Sea and Sea of Marmora

British Agency: Offices and residence of Britain's chief political and diplomatic officer in Cairo to 1914, later called the Residency

Bukhara (boo-KHAH-ra): Central Asian city

bulgur: Parched cracked wheat used in Middle Eastern cooking

Bunche, Ralph: American diplomat and UN mediator in Palestine (1948-1949)

Bursa: City in northwestern Anatolia, an early Ottoman capital

Buyid dynasty (BOO-yid): Family of Shi'i Persians that settled south of the Caspian, then conquered and ruled Iran and Iraq (932-1055), sometimes also called "Buwayhid"

Byzantine Empire: Roman Empire of the East (330-1453), having its capital at Constantinople and professing Greek Orthodox Christianity

Cairo: Capital of Egypt, founded by the Fatimids (969)

caliph (KAY-lif): Successor to Muhammad as head of the Islamic *ummah*

Camel, Battle of the: First clash between two Muslim armies (656), in which Talhah, Zubayr, and Aishah challenged Ali unsuccessfully

Canaanite: Member of Semitic group living in Palestine before the Jews

capitulations: System by which Muslim rulers conceded extraterritorial immunity from local laws and taxes to subjects of Western countries

Caradon, Lord: British diplomat who drafted Security Council Resolution 242 (1967)

Casablanca: Moroccan city, site of an Arab summit conference (1965)

Caucasus: Mountain range between the Black and the Caspian seas

Chalcedon: Site of Christian council (451) at which the Orthodox bishops condemned the Monophysite view of the nature of Christ

Chaldiran, Battle of (chawl-dee-RAWN): Major Ottoman victory over Safavid Iran (1514)

Chingis Khan (CHING-giss-KHAWN): Mongol commander and ruler of most of Asia (d. 1227), sometimes also "Genghis Khan"

Chovevei Tzion (kho-ve-VAY tsee-YON): Early Russian Zionist group

Churchill memorandum: Official statement of British Palestine policy (1922), limiting Jewish immigration to the country's absorptive capacity

Cilicia (si-LISH-ya): Region of southwestern Anatolia, "Little Armenia"

Circassian: Native (or descendant of a native) of the Caucasus region east of the Black Sea

clan: Large family, or subgroup of a tribe

Committee of Union and Progress: See *Young Turks*

Constantine: Roman emperor (306-337)

Constantinople: City on the Bosporus and Sea of Marmora, originally named Byzantium, which became capital of the Byzantine Empire (330-1204 and 1262-1453) and of the Ottoman Empire (1453-1922), renamed Istanbul

constitutionalist: Person who believes that governments should follow a set of basic laws limiting the rulers' powers, especially applied to an Iranian nationalist around 1906

Copt: Egyptian (or Ethiopian) Monophysite Christian

Córdoba (KOR-do-va): Spanish city, capital of later Umayyads (756-1030)

cossack: (1) Horse soldier of southern Russia, (2) member of a Persian brigade trained and largely officered by Russian cossacks up to 1921

Crane, Charles: American plumbing manufacturer and philanthropist

Crimea: Region north of the Black Sea, formerly Turkish and Muslim

Crimean War: Conflict among powers having imperial interests in the Middle East (1853-1856), in which Russia was defeated by Britain, France, and the Ottoman Empire

Cromer, Lord: British consul in Egypt (1883-1907), a financial and administrative reformer, but resented by Egyptian nationalists

Crusades: European Christian military expeditions against Muslims (sometimes Greek Orthodox Christians) between the eleventh and fifteenth centuries

Ctesiphon (TESS-a-fawn): Sasanid capital, southwest of modern Baghdad

Curzon, Lord: Britain's main representative at 1923 Lausanne Conference

Cyprus: Mediterranean island near Anatolia and Syria

Cyrenaica (sir-e-NAY-ka): Region corresponding to eastern Libya

Damascus: Capital of Syria, seat of the early Umayyads (661-750)

al-Darazi, Shaykh (ed-da-RAH-zee): Syrian founder of the Druze religion

Dardanelles: Straits connecting the Aegean Sea to the Sea of Marmora

Dayan, Moshe (die-YAN, mo-SHEH): Israeli general and political leader

Dayr Yasin (dare-ya-SEEN): Palestinian village near Jerusalem, site of massacre of Arab civilians by the Irgun (April 1948)

Demirel, Suleyman (deh-mir-REL): Turkish political leader

Democratic Movement for Change: Israeli reformist party led by General Yigael Yadin, in ruling coalition with Begin's Likud (1977-)

Demokrat party: Turkish political party in power during the 1950s

devshirme (dev-shir-MEH): Ottoman system of recruiting Christian boys, converting them to Islam, and training them for military or administrative service

Dhahran (dhuh-RAHN): East Arabian city, site of first oil strike (1936)

Dinshaway Incident (den-sha-WYE): British atrocity against Egyptian peasants (1906)

diwan (dee-WAHN): (1) List of Arab troops entitled to share booty during early conquests; (2) council of ministers; (3) collection of poems

Dome of the Rock: Muslim shrine in Jerusalem, built (692) on site of Jewish Temple, Abraham's sacrifice, and Muhammad's miraculous night journey

Druze: Pertaining to the secret religion, practiced by some Arabs in Syria, Lebanon, and Israel, founded by Shaykh al-Darazi, who preached that the Fatimid al-Hakim was the last of a series of emanations from God

Dual Control: Joint Anglo-French financial control in Egypt (1876-1882)

Ecevit, Bulent (eh-ja-VEET, boo-LENT): Turkish political leader

Eden, Anthony: British diplomat, prime minister during Suez Crisis (1956)

Edessa: Town in northwestern Mesopotamia and a Crusader state (1098-1144)

Egyptian Expeditionary Force: British group charged with capturing Palestine and Syria during World War I

Eilat (ay-LOT): Israel's port on the Gulf of Aqaba

Eisenhower Doctrine: Official U.S. policy statement opposing spread of Communism in the Middle East (1957)

Elburz (el-BORZ): Mountain range in northern Iran

emir (eh-MEER): Muslim ruler or prince, also "amir"

Enver (EN-ver): Young Turk revolutionary leader

Ephesus (EH-fuh-suss): Town in western Anatolia, important in early Christian times, site of council of bishops that condemned Nestorianism (430)

Ertogrul (AIR-tuh-rule): Turkish *ghazi* leader (d. ca. 1280), father of Osman I

Erzurum (AIR-zuh-room): City in eastern Anatolia, site of Turkish nationalist congress (1919)

Eshkol, Levi (ESH-kol, LEH-vee): Israel's prime minister (1963-1969)

Ethiopia: East African country, mainly Christian since the fourth century, heavily involved in Arabian politics up to Muhammad's time

Euphrates: The more western of Iraq's two rivers

Faruq (fa-ROOK): Pleasure-loving king of Egypt (1936-1952)

al-Fatah (el-FET-ah): Palestinian guerrilla group founded by Yasir Arafat

al-Fatat (el-fa-TAT): Arab nationalist student group before World War I

Fath Ali Shah (FATH-aw-lee-SHAH): Qajar ruler (1797-1834)

Fatimah (FAW-tee-ma): Muhammad's daughter, who married Ali

Fatimid dynasty: Arab family of Isma'ili Shi'is claiming descent from Ali and Fatimah and ruling North Africa (909-972) and Egypt (969-1171), also competing with other dynasties for control of Syria, Hijaz, and Yemen

Faysal (FAY-sul): Son of Abd al-Aziz ibn Saud and king of Saudi Arabia (1964-1975)

Faysal I: Son of Amir Husayn of Mecca, leader in the Arab Revolt, headed provisional Arab government in Damascus (1918-1920), ousted by French, and later king of Iraq (1921-1932)

Faysal II: King of Iraq (1939-1958)

Feast of Abraham's Sacrifice: Id al-Adha (Arabic) or Kurban Bayram (Turkish), annual Muslim holiday commemorating Abraham's obedience to God's command by offering his son, Ishmael (Isma'il)

Feast of the Fast-Breaking: Id al-Fitr (Arabic) or Ramazan Bayram (Turkish), annual Muslim holiday following the month of Ramadan

Ferid, Damad (fe-REED, da-MAWD): Ottoman prime minister backed by the sultan (his brother-in-law) and the Western powers after World War I

Fertile Crescent: Modern term for the lands extending from the eastern Mediterranean through Syria and Mesopotamia to the Persian Gulf

fez: Crimson brimless head covering worn in the later Ottoman Empire and in some successor states, outlawed in Turkey by Kemal Ataturk

fidaiyin (fe-DA-ee-yeen): People who sacrifice themselves for a cause, now most often applied to Palestinian Arabs fighting against Israel

fiqh (FIKh): The science of Islamic law (jurisprudence)

fitnah (FIT-na): Civil war in early Islam

Four Reserved Points: Britain's limitations on its unilateral declaration of Egypt's independence (1922)

Fourteen Points: President Wilson's plan to resolve the issues that had caused World War I, calling for self-determination of subject peoples

Franjiyah, Sulayman (fran-JEE-ya, slay-MAHN): Lebanon's president (1970-1976)

free will: Religious doctrine preaching that God has created human beings capable of choosing their own actions

Fuad I (foo-ODD): King of Egypt (1917-1936)

Fustat (foos-TAHT): Egyptian garrison town in early Islamic times, later an administrative center, near modern Cairo

Gabriel: Angel who transmitted the Quran to Muhammad

Galilee: Mountainous area of northern Israel, containing many Arab villages

garrison town: City set up by the early caliphs to house Arab soldiers when they were not out on campaigns, such as Basrah, Kufah, and Fustat

al-Gaylani, Rashid Ali (el-gay-LA-nee, ra-SHEED AH-lee): Leader of 1941 Arab nationalist government in Iraq overthrown by the British

Gaza Strip: Small part of southwest Palestine held by Egyptian forces in 1948 and inhabited wholly by Arabs, administered by Egypt (1948-1956 and 1957-1967), and captured by Israel in both 1956 and 1967

Geneva Conference: December 1973 meeting of Israel, Egypt, and Jordan, cochaired by the United States and the USSR, technically in adjournment ever since

Gezira Sporting Club (geh-ZEER-a): Cairo social club that used to exclude Egyptians from membership

al-Ghazali (el-gha-ZA-lee): Major Muslim theologian (d. 1111)

Ghazan Khan (gha-ZAWN KHAWN): First Muslim Il-Khanid ruler (1295-1304)

ghazi (GHAH-zee): Muslim military adventurer or border warrior

Ghazi: King of Iraq (1933-1939)

Ghazna: City in Afghanistan south of Kabul, basis of the Ghaznavid Empire

Ghaznavid (GHAHZ-na-vid): Turkish empire comprising Afghanistan, parts of Iran and central Asia, and conquering much of India (977-1186)

ghulam (GHOO-lum): Male slave, usually in the army or administration

Gibraltar: (1) Mountain in southern Spain; (2) straits between the Atlantic and the Mediterranean (originally Jebel Tariq, named for the Berber commander of the Muslim conquest of Spain)

Gidi Pass: Strategic point in western Sinai, captured by Israel in 1956 and 1967 and relinquished to a UN force in the 1975 Sinai agreement

Gilan (gee-LAWN): Region of northwestern Iran

Glubb, John Bagot: British author and former commander of the Arab Legion

Gobi Desert: Large arid region of Mongolia

Goha: Legendary figure in Arabic humor

Gokalp, Ziya (GEUK-alp, ZEE-ya): Theoretician of Turkish nationalism (d. 1924)

Golan Heights (go-LAHN): Mountainous area of southwestern Syria, occupied by Israel since 1967 and scene of intense fighting in 1973

Golden Horde: Muslim Mongol group ruling Russia from the 13th to 15th century

Granada: Capital of the last Muslim state in Spain

Grand National Assembly: Representative legislature of first Turkish republic

Great Khan: Title of chief Mongol emperor during the thirteenth century

Great Silk Route: Trade route connecting Iran with China, crossing the steppes and mountain passes of central Asia

Greek fire: Naphtha derivative that ignited upon contact with water, used by Byzantine and later by Muslim sailors to destroy enemy ships

Greek Orthodox: Pertaining to the branch of Christianity that accepts the spiritual authority of the patriarch of Constantinople and espouses the Christological doctrines adopted at Nicaea (325) and Chalcedon (451)

Gurganj (goor-GAWNJ): Persian city located southeast of the Caspian Sea

Habash, George (HOB-osh): Leader of the Popular Front for the Liberation of Palestine, a Marxist Palestinian Arab group

Habsburg (HOPS-burg): Pertaining to a German family ruling over the Holy Roman Empire (1273-1806) and Austria (up to 1918)

hadith (ha-DEETH): A statement, documented by a chain of reliable witnesses, concerning a saying or action of Muhammad, or an action of one of his companions that he approved, hence an authoritative source of the Shari'ah

Hafiz (ha-FEZ): Persian poet (d. 1389)

Haganah (ha-ga-NAH): Jewish army in Palestine (1920-1948)

Hagar (HAH-gar): Abraham's second wife, mother of Ishmael, ancestor of Arabs

Haifa: Israel's main port city

al-Hakim (el-HACK-em): Fatimid caliph (996-1021), venerated by the Druze

hajj (HODGE): Muslim rite of pilgrimage to Mecca, or (with a lengthened vowel) a Muslim who has completed the pilgrimage rites

al-Hajjaj (el-haj-JAJ): General and governor of Iraq under Abd al-Malik

Hamdanid dynasty: Arab family with branches ruling in Aleppo and Mosul during the tenth century

Hanafi (HAH-na-fee): Rite of Sunni Muslim jurisprudence, originating in Iraq, making heavy use of communal consensus as a source

Hanbali (HAM-ba-lee): Rite of Sunni Muslim jurisprudence, very strict, requiring that all rules of conduct be based on the Quran and *hadith.*

Hanif (ha-NEEF): An Arab true believer before the rise of Islam

harem: The portion of a Muslim house used by women and young children, off limits for male strangers and guests

Harun al-Rashid (ha-ROON er-ra-SHEED): Abbasid caliph (786-809)

al-Hasa (el-HOSS-a): Persian Gulf coast region of Saudi Arabia

Hasan (HAH-san): Older son of Ali and Fatimah, nominated by Ali as his successor, but pensioned off by Mu'awiyah

Hashimite (HA-she-mite): (1) Member of the family descended from Hashim; (2) supporter of an extremist mawali Shi'i sect in late Umayyad times; (3) member of the dynasty ruling the Hijaz (1916-1925), Syria (1918-1920), Iraq (1921-1958), and Jordan (1921-)

Haskalah (hoss-ka-LAH): Period of Jewish enlightenment (eighteenth to nineteenth centuries)

Hebrew: Semitic language spoken in ancient and modern Israel

Hebron (HEB-run): Town in Judea (the West Bank), revered by both Jews and Muslims

Hellenistic: Pertaining to the society and culture of the Mediterranean area that used Greek as its main literary and administrative language

Heraclius (he-RACK-lee-us): Byzantine emperor (610-641), who pushed back the Sasanids, but later lost Syria and Egypt to the Arabs

Herat (heh-RAWT): Historic Persian city, now in western Afghanistan

Hermon (hair-MOAN): Mountain in southwestern Syria, partly occupied by Israel since 1967, scene of heavy fighting in October 1973

Herut (khay-ROOT): Israel's right-wing nationalist party, headed by Menachem Begin

Herzl, Theodor (HAIR-tsul, TAY-a-dor): Writer and founder of political Zionism (d. 1904)

Hess, Moses: Early German socialist and advocate of a Jewish state

Hijaz (he-JAZZ): Mountainous area of western Arabia

hijrah (HIJ-ra): Emigration of Muhammad and his followers from Mecca to Medina in 622 (year 1 of the Muslim calendar)

Hira (HEE-ra): Capital of pre-Islamic Lakhmid kingdom

Hisham (he-SHAM): Umayyad caliph (724-743)

Histadrut (hiss-ta-DROOT): Israel's main labor union, owner of many business enterprises, and manager of the largest sick fund

Holy Sepulcher: Jesus' reputed burial place, a major church in Jerusalem

Hudaybiyah (hoo-day-BEE-ya): Treaty made by Muhammad with the Meccans in 628 enabling Muslim emigrants to make the hajj

Hulegu (HEW-le-gew): Chingis Khan's grandson, who continued the Mongol conquest of the Middle East and founded the Il-Khanid dynasty

Hunayn ibn Ishaq (hu-NAYN ibn iss-HOCK): Muslim scientist and translator (d. 873)

Hunkar-Iskelesi (HOON-kyar-iss-KELL-e-see): 1833 treaty making the Ottoman Empire virtually a Russian protectorate

Hunyadi, John (hoon-YAH-dee): Hungarian military leader (d. 1456)

Husayn (hoo-SAYN): Younger son of Ali and Fatimah, killed in an anti-Umayyad revolt at Karbala (680), hence a martyr for Shi'i Muslims

Husayn: Emir and sharif of Mecca (1908-1924), king of the Hijaz (1916-1924), and standard-bearer of the Arab Revolt against the Ottomans

Husayn: King of Jordan (1953-)

Husayn Kamil: Sultan of Egypt (1914-1917)

Husayn-McMahon correspondence: Letters exchanged by Emir Husayn and the British high commissioner in Cairo in 1915, offering British aid for Arab independence in exchange for Arab support against the Ottoman Empire

al-Husayni, Hajj Amin (el-hoo-SAY-nee, HODGE a-MEEN): Mufti of Jerusalem and Palestinian Arab nationalist leader in 1930s and 1940s

Ibn Khaldun (ibn-khal-DOON): Noted historian and social thinker (d. 1406)

Ibn Rushd (ibn-ROOSHD): a Muslim philosopher (d. 1198), "Averroes" in Latin

Ibn Saud (ibn-sa-OOD): Arab leader (d. 1953) who conquered most of the Arabian peninsula between 1902 and 1930

Ibn Sina (ibn-SEE-na): Muslim philosopher, theologian, and scientist

(d. 1037), "Avicenna" in Latin

Ibrahim (ib-ra-HEEM): Ottoman sultan (1640-1648)

Ibrahim: Son of Mehmet Ali, conqueror of Syria and its governor (1832-1840)

Ibrahim, Damad (da-MAHD): Ottoman vizir under Ahmed III

ijtihad (ij-tee-HAD): Use of individual reasoning to determine a specific Muslim rule

Ikhwan (ikh-WAHN): (1) Sedentarized bedouin soldiers for Ibn Saud; (2) members of the Society of the Muslim Brothers

Il-Khanid (il-KHAW-nid): Mongol successor dynasty in Iran (1256-1353)

imam (ee-MAHM): (1) Muslim religious or political leader; (2) one of the succession of Muslim leaders, beginning with Ali, regarded as legitimate by Shi'is; (3) leader of Muslim congregational worship

Imperial Rescript: Ottoman government promise of equal rights and status to all subjects, regardless of religion (1856), sometimes called the "Hatt-i-Humayun"

India Office: Agency in London supervising government of India (to 1947)

Inonu (ee-neu-NIEW): (1) Site of two Turkish battles against the Greeks in western Anatolia (1921); (2) surname adopted by Ismet, the Turkish commander in these battles

iqta' (ik-TAH): Land grant from a ruler for military or administrative services performed by a client

Iran (ee-RAWN): Preferred name for what used to be called Persia

Iraq (ee-ROCK): Arabic name for Mesopotamia

Irgun Tzvei Leumi (eer-GOON TSVAY le-oo-MEE): Right-wing Zionist guerrilla group, commanded by Menachem Begin, active in the 1940s

Isfahan (iss-fa-HAWN): City in central Iran, Safavid capital (1597-1736)

Islam (iss-LAM): The religion, now prevalent in the Middle East and many other parts of Asia and Africa, based on belief in a single, all-powerful God who revealed Himself to a series of prophets, ending with Muhammad, to whom He vouchsafed the Quran

Isma'il (iss-ma-EEL): Seventh legitimate imam, for Seven-Imam Shi'is

Isma'il, Khedive: Viceroy of Egypt (1863-1879)

Isma'il, Shah: Founder of the Safavid dynasty (1501-1524)

Isma'ili (iss-ma-EE-lee): Pertaining to Seven-Imam Shi'ism

Ismailia (iss-ma-ee-LEE-ya): Egyptian city on the Suez Canal

Ismet (iss-MET): Turkish general, chief representative of Turkey at the Lausanne Conference (1923), president of the republic (1938-1950)

isnad (iss-NAD): Chain of witnesses authenticating a *hadith*

Israel: (1) surname of Jacob and hence of his descendants; (2) the ancient northern Jewish kingdom; (3) the modern Jewish state, located in what used to be Palestine

Israelites: Descendants of Jacob, or Jews

Istanbul (iss-tahn-BOOL): Modern name for Constantinople

Ivan III (ee-VAHN): Russian ruler (1462-1505) who married the niece of the last Byzantine emperor

Izmir (iz-MEER): West Anatolian city, formerly called Smyrna

Jabotinsky, Vladimir (zha-buh-TIN-skee): Founder of the Revisionist (right-wing) Zionist movement (d. 1940)

Jacob: Son of Isaac and mythic ancestor of the Jews

Jacobite: Syrian Monophysite Christian

Jaffa: Port city in Palestine/Israel, now absorbed by Tel Aviv

janissary: Christian conscript foot soldier in the Ottoman army, converted to Islam and trained to use firearms

Jarring, Gunnar (YAR-ring, GUN-nar): UN mediator between Israel and the Arab states from 1967 to 1971

Jawhar (JOW-har): Arab general who conquered Egypt for the Fatimids (969)

Jehovah: Anglicization of Y-hv-h, the Hebrew name for God

Jem: Brother and rival (d. 1495) to Ottoman Sultan Bayezid II

Jemal (je-MAWL): Young Turk leader and governor of Syria (1915-1918)

Jerusalem: Main city in Judea, major religious center for Jews, Christians, and Muslims, proclaimed by Israel to be its capital

Jewish Agency: Organization provided for in the Palestine mandate to work with Britain to set up Jewish national home, later became the main organization facilitating Jewish immigration and absorption into Israel

Jewish National Fund: Zionist land purchasing and development agency in Palestine/Israel, founded in 1901

Jezreel (jez-REEL): Major valley in northern Israel

jihad (jee-HAD): Muslim struggle against evil within oneself, one's associates, and the *ummah*; also its defense against non-Muslim aggression

jinn: Invisible creatures living on earth, capable of doing good or harm

jizyah (JIZ-ya): Per-capita tax paid by non-Muslim males under Muslim rule

Johnston, Eric: American businessman sent by Eisenhower in 1953 to negotiate Jordan River development scheme for Israel and Jordan

Jordan, Hashimite Kingdom of: State formed from the Emirate of Transjordan and parts of Arab Palestine (commonly called the "West Bank") annexed by Abdallah in 1948

Jordan River: River flowing through Syria, Jordan, and Israel

Judea: Mountainous area of eastern Palestine/Israel

Jumblat, Kamal (jum-BLOT, ke-MAL): Lebanese Druze leader (d. 1977)

Junayd, Shaykh (joo-NAYD): Turcoman Shi'i Sufi leader of the Safavids in Azerbaijan (d. 1460), grandfather of Shah Isma'il

Jundishapur (joon-dee-shah-POOR): Sasanid and Muslim center of learning

Justice party: Turkey's conservative party since 1961, led by Suleyman Demirel

Ka'bah (KAH-ba): Muslim shrine in Mecca, housing the Black Stone, serving as focal point for the hajj and direction for formal worship

Kabul (KAW-bul): Capital of Afghanistan

kalam (ka-LAM): Muslim science of theology

Kalb (KELB): Southern Arab tribe important in early Umayyad times

Kamil, Mustafa (KA-mel, moos-TAH-fa): Egyptian nationalist (d. 1908)

Kapi Kullar (KAH-puh kul-LAWR): "slaves of the gate," or servants of the Ottoman sultan, hence members of the Ottoman elite

Kara-Khitay (KAH-ra-khee-TIE): Early thirteenth-century confederation of Mongol and Turkish tribes in central Asia

Karamah (ka-RAH-may): Jordanian village, site of 1968 Israeli attack, in which Palestinian *fidaiyin* claimed victory

Karbala (KAR-ba-la): City of Iraq, site of Husayn's rebellion and martyrdom (680), and since then a Shi'i pilgrimage center

Karlowitz, Treaty of: 1699 pact in which Ottomans ceded Hungary to Austria

al-Kawakibi, Abd al-Rahman (el-ka-WA-ke-bee, ab-der-rah-MAHN): Arab nationalist writer (d. 1902)

Kayi (KY-eh): Central Asian Turkish tribe, from which Ottomans claim descent

Kemal, Mustafa ("Ataturk") (ke-MAWL, MOSS-ta-fa [a-ta-TEWRK]): Turkish general, statesman, and westernizer of Turkey (d. 1938)

Kemalism: Principles of Turkish nationalism and westernizing reform advocated by Kemal Ataturk

Kerman (kayr-MAWN): City in southeastern Iran

Khadijah (kha-DEE-jah): Muhammad's first wife (d. 619)

Khalid ibn al-Walid (KHA-lid ib-nel-wa-LEED): Brilliant Arab general, conqueror of northern Arabia, Syria, Iraq, and Iran (d. 644)

kharaj (kha-RODGE): Land tax paid by peasants on agricultural produce

Kharijite (KHA-re-jite): "Seceder" who opposed Ali after he accepted arbitration of Battle of Siffin (657) and killed him (661), later an anarchist group believing that any sinless Muslim could be caliph

Khartum (khar-TOOM): (1) Capital of the Sudan; (2) site of August 1967 Arab summit conference opposing peace negotiations with Israel

Khazar (KHAH-zar): Turkish tribe that converted to Judaism

khedive (khe-DEEV): "Viceroy," title of Egypt's ruler (1867-1914)

Khomeini, Ayatollah Ruhollah (kho-may-NEE): Religious leader of Iran's revolution (1978-1979)

Khurasan (kho-ra-SAWN): Persian province east of the Caspian

Khuzistan (khoo-ze-STAWN): Oil-rich province of southwestern Iran

Khwarizm (KHAW-rezm): Region south of the Aral Sea

Khwarizm-Shah (khaw-rezm-SHAH): Central Asian Turkish dynasty (1077-1231) defeated by Chingis Khan

kibbutz: (kee-BOOTS): Jewish settlement, formerly agricultural, now increasingly industrial, in which most property is collectively owned

Kilometer 101: Site of Egyptian-Israeli military talks following 1973 war

Kinda (KIN-da): Central Arabian tribe prominent in the sixth century

al-Kindi (el-KIN-dee): Muslim philosopher and scientist (d. 873)

King-Crane Commission: American committee sent by 1919 Paris Peace Conference to ascertain Syrian and Palestinian Arab political aspirations, but its report, sympathetic to Arab nationalism, was not acted upon

Kinneret, Lake: Sea of Galilee, between northeast Israel and Golan Heights

Kipchak (KIP-chock): Central Asian Turkish tribe, source of many Mamluks

Kitchener, Lord: Commander of Anglo-Egyptian army that retook the Sudan (1896-1898), later British consul-general in Egypt (1911-1914)

kizilbash (kee-zel-BOSH): Shi'i Turks, especially Safavid horse soldiers

Knesset: Israel's unicameral parliament, having 120 members

Konya: City in southern Anatolia, capital of Seljuks of Rum (1077-1300)

Koprulu (KUH-prew-lew): Seventeenth-century family of Ottoman vizirs

kosher: Pertaining to the dietary laws of traditional Judaism

Kosovo, Battle of (kuh-SO-vo): Site of Ottoman defeat and conquest of Serbia (1389)

Kufah (KOO-fa): Garrison town on lower Euphrates founded by Umar, later an important commercial and intellectual center

kufiyah (kef-FEE-ya): White or colored headcloth worn by men in Arabia and parts of the Fertile Crescent

kuftah (KOOF-ta): Spiced ground lamb or beef usually baked over coals

Kunaitra (koo-NAYT-ra): Main city in Golan Heights, captured by Israel in 1967, fought over in October 1973, returned to Syria in 1974

Kurd: Member of linguistic-cultural group concentrated in southeastern Turkey, northern Iraq, northwestern Iran, and parts of Syria

Kurdistan: Autonomous state for Kurds projected by Treaty of Sèvres (1920)

Kuwait (koo-WAYT): Small oil-rich principality on Persian Gulf

Ladino (la-DEE-no): Spanish dialect spoken by Sephardic Jews and written in Hebrew characters

Lakhmid (LAHKH-mid): Arab tribe near Iraq prominent before Islam and usually allied with the Sasanids

Lampson, Miles: British high commissioner and ambassador in Egypt (1934-1946), later "Lord Killearn"

al-Lat (el-LAT): Meccan goddess before Islam

Lausanne (loe-ZAHN): (1) 1923 conference and treaty between Turkey and the World War I Allies, replacing the Treaty of Sèvres; (2) abortive 1949 peace conference between Israel and the Arab states

Lawrence, T. E.: British World War I intelligence officer who helped inspire the Arab Revolt, gifted writer and advocate of Arab nationalism

Lazar (la-ZAHR): King of Serbia (d. 1389)

Lebanon: Small country north of Israel and west of Syria

Lepanto, Battle of (le-PAHN-toe): European naval victory over Ottoman Empire (1571)

Levantine (le-van-TEEN): Pertaining to the Levant or the eastern shores of the Mediterranean, or to its inhabitants, especially non-Muslims

Liberation Army, Arab: Palestinian-Syrian group fighting against Israel (1948)

Likud (lee-KOOD): Coalition of Israel's right-wing parties, led by Menachem Begin, in power since May 1977

Lloyd, Lord: British high commissioner in Egypt (1925-1930)

Lydda: City in Israel, renamed Lod, site of the main civil airport

Ma'arach (ma-a-RAKH): Coalition of Israeli labor parties, in power up to May 1967

Macedonia: Area of northern Greece and southern Yugoslavia, often disputed

madhhab (MEDH-heb): Sunni legal rite or school

madrasah (MED-ra-sah): Muslim secondary school, formerly Sunni law school

mahdi (MEH-dee): Rightly guided one, precursor of the Judgment Day

Mahdi: Abbasid caliph (775-785)

Mahdi (of the Sudan): Muhammad Ahmad (d. 1885), leader of successful Sudanese rebellion against Egyptian rule

Mahmud I (mah-MOOD): Ottoman sultan (1730-1754)

Mahmud II: Ottoman sultan (1808-1839) and major westernizing reformer

Mahmud of Ghazna: Ghaznavid ruler (998-1030)

Majlis (MODGE-liss): Iran's bicameral parliament

Maliki (MA-li-kee): Rite of Sunni Muslim jurisprudence, originating in

Medina, making heavy use of *hadith*s as an authoritative legal source

Malikshah (ma-lik-SHAH): Seljuk sultan (1072-1092)

Mamluk (mem-LOOK): (1) Turkish or Circassian slave soldier; (2) member of a military oligarchy controlling Egypt and Syria (1250-1517) and retaining local power in some areas up to the nineteenth century

Mamun (ma-MOON): Abbasid caliph (813-833)

al-Manat (el-ma-NAT): Meccan goddess before Islam

mandate: Commission given by the League of Nations to a Western power to train a former territory of Germany or the Ottoman Empire for eventual self-rule, or a country governed under this tutelary relationship

Manichaeism (ma-ni-KEE-izm): Dualistic religion formulated by Mani, a third-century Persian, calling for the liberation of the body from the soul by various ascetic spiritual exercises, strong in Iraq, Iran, and some parts of central and eastern Asia

Mansur: See *Abu-Ja'far*

al-Mansurah (el-man-SOOR-a): Egyptian city besieged in Seventh Crusade

Manzikert, Battle of (MAN-zi-kurt): Seljuk victory over Byzantines (1071)

Mapai (ma-PIE): Israel's moderate labor party, now part of the Ma'arach

marches: Frontier areas between two countries or cultures

Maronite: Pertaining to a Christian sect, mainly in northern Lebanon, whose distinguishing belief is that Christ contained two natures within one will, and which has been in communion with Roman Catholicism since the seventeenth century, possibly earlier

Marwa: Small hill in Mecca, important in the rituals of the hajj

Marwan I (mar-WAHN): Umayyad caliph (684-685)

Marxism: System of socialist thought, developed by Karl Marx and others, arguing that capitalism must be overthrown by a revolution leading to a workers' state, which will later wither away and be replaced by a classless and harmonious society

mawla (MOW-la), pl. **mawali** (ma-WA-lee): (1) Client member of an Arab tribe, entitled to protection but not a full-fledged member; (2) a non-Arab convert to Islam during the early period of the conquests

Mazandaran (ma-zan-da-RAWN): Province in northern Iran

McMahon, Henry: British high commissioner in Egypt (1914-1916)

Mecca: Birthplace of the Prophet Muhammad and chief commercial and pilgrimage center of western Arabia

Medina (me-DEE-na): Farming oasis of northwest Arabia, formerly named Yathrib, to which Muhammad and his followers went in 622

Mehmet I (meh-MET): Ottoman sultan (1413-1421)

Mehmet II: Ottoman sultan (1451-1481), conqueror of Constantinople (1453)

Mehmet Ali: Turkish/Albanian adventurer who gained control of Egypt and instituted many westernizing reforms (1805-1849)

Meir, Golda (may-EER): Israel's prime minister (1969-1974)

Mersin (mur-SEEN): Port city in southern Anatolia

Merv: City in Khurasan

Mesopotamia: Greek name for land between the Tigris and Euphrates rivers

Messiah: According to the Bible, the expected deliverer of the Jewish people, and, according to Christians, Jesus Christ

Middle East Supply Center: Cairo-based British organization coordinating manufacturing and distribution in Arab states and Iran in World War II

Midhat (mid-HOT): Turkish liberal reformer (d. 1884)

millet (mil-LET): Ottoman political-social community based on religious membership, semiautonomous with leaders appointed by the sultan

Milner, Lord: British statesman who headed commission of inquiry to Egypt (1919) and later negotiated unsuccessfully with Sa'd Zaghlul

minaret: Turkish name for the mosque tower from which the muezzin calls Muslims to worship five times daily

Mithraism: Ancient Persian religion, involving various mystery rites to which only men were admitted, popular among Roman soldiers and competing in the empire against Christianity during the third century

Mitla Pass: Strategic mountain pass in western Sinai, captured by Israel in 1956 and 1967, relinquished to a UN buffer force in 1975

mixed courts: Egyptian tribunals for civil cases involving foreign nationals (1876-1949)

Mohammad Reza Shah Pahlavi (moe-HAHM-mad RAY-za shah PAH-la-vee): Shah of Iran (1941-1979)

mollah (MUL-la): Persian Muslim teacher

Mongol: Nomadic horseman from northeastern Asia; member of a group of tribes who, under Chingis Khan and his descendants, overran most of Asia in thirteenth century

Monophysite (muh-NAW-fiz-zite): A Christian (usually Middle Eastern) who believed that Christ had only one nature, wholly divine, in his person, a view condemned by the Council of Chalcedon in 451

monotheistic: Pertaining to belief in a single god, as in Judaism, Christianity, and Islam

Morea (mo-REE-a): The Peloponnesus, or southern Greece

Mosaddiq, Mohammad (moss-sa-DEGH): Iranian nationalist prime minister (1951-1953), who nationalized the Anglo-Iranian Oil Company, later was overthrown in a coup engineered by the shah (and possibly the CIA)

mosque: Place of communal worship for Muslims

Mosul (MOE-sel): City in northern Iraq

Mu'awiyah (moo-AWE-wee-ya): Umayyad caliph (661-680)

Mudros (MOOD-ross): Aegean island where Ottoman Empire formally surrendered to World War I Allies in October 1918

muezzin (moo-EZ-zin): Man who calls other Muslims to communal worship, usually from an elevated part of a mosque, e.g., balcony of a minaret

mufti (MOOF-tee): (1) Sunni Muslim legal consultant; (2) nowadays the leader of the ulama in a Muslim state

Muhammad (moo-HOM-mad): Arab religious leader, born in Mecca about 570 and founder of the Islamic *ummah* (in 622 at Medina), regarded by Muslims as the last of God's messengers, whose divine revelations were compiled and preserved in the Quran

Muhammad ibn Abd al-Wahhab (ibn ab-dul-wa-HAB): Founder of the Wahhabi movement (d. 1787)

Muhammad al-Muntazar (el-moon-TUZ-zer): Last of the twelve legitimate imams, who disappeared about 878 and is expected to return someday

Muhammad, Prince: Leader of a Turkish state in central Asia, that of the Khwarizm-Shah dynasty, who fought against Chingis Khan

muhtasib (MOH-ta-sib): Muslim market inspector

Mu'izz (moo-IZZ): Fatimid caliph (953-975)

mujtahid (MOOJ-ta-hid): Learned Muslim who interprets the Shari'ah, especially in Shi'i jurisprudence

Mukhtar (mookh-TAHR): Leader of rebellion in Kufah (685-687)

multezim (MOOL-te-zim): Ottoman tax collector allowed by the government to keep a share of what he collected

Murad I (moo-ROT): Ottoman sultan (1360-1389)

Murad II: Ottoman sultan (1421-1451)

Murad IV: Ottoman sultan (1623-1640)

muruwwah (mu-ROO-wa): Pre-Islamic code of Arab virtues

Muscat (muss-KOTT): City in Oman

Muslim (MOOS-lim): (1) A person who submits to God's will; (2) anyone who believes that God revealed the Quran to Muhammad

Muslim Brothers, Society of: Political group, strong in Egypt (1930-1952) and several other Arab countries, calling for an Islamic political and social system, and opposing Western power and cultural influences

Mustafa II (MOOS-ta-fa): Ottoman sultan (1695-1703)

al-Mu'tasim (el-MOOH-ta-sim): Abbasid caliph (833-842)

Mu'tazilah (mooh-TA-zi-la): Rationalist formulation of Islamic theology, best known for stressing that God created all things, including the Quran

Nader Afshar (NAW-der awf-SHAWR): Persian military leader who became shah (1736-1747), drove out Afghan invaders, and conquered part of India

Nagib, Muhammad (ne-GEEB): Titular leader of 1952 Egyptian revolution

al-Nahhas, Mustafa (en-na-HASS, moos-TAH-fa): Leader of Egypt's Wafd party (1927-1952)

Najaf (NED-jef): City in Iraq where Ali was assassinated (661), hence a Shi'i pilgrimage center

Najran (nej-RAHN): Southern Arabian city, important in early commerce

Nasiruddin Shah (NAW-sir ud-DEEN): Qajar ruler (1848-1896)

Nasiruddin Tusi (NAW-sir ud-DEEN TOO-see): Muslim astronomer (d. 1274)

Nasser (Gamal Abd al-Nasir) (ga-MAL ABD en-NAW-sir): Leader of 1952 military coup that overthrew Egypt's monarchy, later prime minister, then president (1954-1970)

Nasserism: Western term for the political philosophy and program of Nasser including nationalism, neutralism, and Arab socialism

National Charter: 1962 Egyptian document describing goals of Arab socialism

National (Liberation) Front: Aden's successful independence movement

National Pact: 1943 agreement among Lebanon's religious and political groups

National party: Egyptian movement demanding independence from foreign control, a name applied to followers of Urabi in 1881-1882 and of Mustafa Kamil from 1895, though not formally until 1907

National Religious party: Main party of observant Jews in Israel

Nationalist party: Syria's leading party just after World War II

nationalism: Desire of a group of people to preserve or obtain common statehood, or ideology stressing loyalty to the nation-state or devotion to the cause of independence of a particular national group

Negev (ne-GEV): Desert in southern Israel

Neoplatonist: Supporter of the philosophical system, founded in the third century, based on the ideas of Plato and common in the Middle East up to the Arab conquests

Nestorian (ne-STOR-ee-an): Pertaining to Christians believing in the two separate (divine and human) natures of Christ, a view condemned by the Council of Ephesus (431)

New Ottomans: Turkish political movement in 1870s demanding a constitution, parliamentary government, and other Ottoman westernizing reforms

Nicaea (nye-SEE-ya): City in northwest Anatolia, site of the Christian church council in 325 that accepted the trinitarian view of the nature of God: father, son, and holy spirit

Nishapur (NEE-sha-poor): City in Khurasan

Nizam-i-Jedid (ne-ZAWM-e-je-DEED): Military and political reform program promulgated by Selim III but crushed by the janissaries in 1807

Noble Rescript of the Rose Chamber: Ottoman government promise of judicial and administrative reforms (1839), sometimes called the "Hatt-i-Sherif of Gulhane"

Nur al-Din (NOOR-ed-DEEN): Sultan of Mosul and Damascus (1146-1174)

Nuri al-Sa'id (NOOR-ee es-sa-EED): Pro-Western Iraqi leader (d. 1958)

October war: War started by Egypt and Syria in 1973 to regain lands occupied by Israel since 1967, also called "Yom Kippur war" or "Ramadan war"

olim (o-LEEM): Jewish immigrants to Israel

Oljeitu (uhl-JAY-tu): Il-Khanid ruler (1304-1317)

Oman (oh-MAN): Country in southeast Arabian peninsula

OPEC: Organization of Petroleum Exporting Countries, group formed in 1960 to maintain minimum price for oil

Orhan (or-HAHN): Ottoman sultan (1326-1360)

Orkhon (or-KHOHN): River in Mongolia, site of eighth-century inscriptions

Osiris (oh-SIE-ris): The king and judge of the dead in ancient Egyptian religion

Osman I (oss-MANN): Ottoman sultan (ca. 1280-1326)

Osman II: Ottoman sultan (1618-1622)

Osmanli (oss-MAHN-lee): Pertaining to descendants of Osman I, or to their soldiers and administrators, or to the language they used

Ottoman Decentralization party: Liberal political movement favored by moderate Arab nationalists before World War I

Ottoman Empire: A multinational Islamic state (1299-1922), which began in northwest Anatolia and spread through the Balkans, most of southwest Asia and the North African coast

Ottomanism: Idea of loyalty to the Ottoman state (as opposed to separatist nationalism) encouraged by nineteenth-century Ottoman westernizers

Oxus River: Roman name for the Amu-Darya, a central Asian river flowing from the Pamir Mountains northwest toward the Aral Sea

Pahlavi (PAH-la-vee): (1) Pre-Islamic Persian language; (2) ruling family of Iran (1925-1979)

Palestine: (1) Geographical term for southern Syria; (2) name of the British-mandated country from 1922 to 1948; (3) term preferred by many Arabs for some or all of the lands currently governed by the state of Israel

Palestine Liberation Organization: Group set up in 1964 by Arab heads of state; now the umbrella organization for most Palestinian military, political, economic, and social organizations

Palestine White Paper: British statement of policy in 1939 limiting Jewish immigration and land purchase rights within its mandate of Palestine

Palestinian: Inhabitant of Palestine, now used mainly for Arabs

Palmyra: Ancient Arab city in central Syria that challenged Roman power in the third century

pan-Arabism: Movement to unite all Arabs in one state, especially popular since World War II

pan-Islam: Idea or movement calling for unity of all Muslims, cultivated by late nineteenth- and early twentieth-century Ottoman governments

pan-Slavism: Movement to unite all Slavs, especially under Russian leadership

pan-Turanism: Attempt to unite all peoples speaking Turkic languages

Paris Peace Conference: Meeting of victorious Allies after World War I to establish peace in Europe and the Middle East

Parthian: Persian dynasty (248 B.C.–226 C.E.) preceding the Sasanids

Partition Plan for Palestine (UN): Proposed division of the Palestine mandate into Jewish and Arab states, approved by the UN General Assembly in 1947; the Jewish state became the basis for the state of Israel

Passfield White Paper: British official report, blaming Jews as well as Arabs for the 1929 riots in Palestine

Peel Commission: British committee that visited Palestine in 1937, first to recommend partition of the mandate into Jewish and Arab states

People's Democratic Republic of Yemen: Current name for what used to be Aden and the Aden Protectorate, then the South Arabian Federation, and then South Yemen; abbreviated PDRY

Peres, Shim'on (PAIR-es, shim-OWN): Leader of Israel's labor alignment (1977-)

Permanent Mandates Commission: League of Nations body supervising administration of mandates

Persia: Older name for the country now generally called Iran

Persian: Pertaining to the main language or culture of Persia

Persian Gulf: Also called the Arab Gulf, the body of water separating Iran from the Arabian peninsula and connecting the Shatt al-Arab to the Arabian Sea

Petra (PET-ra): City in southern Jordan carved from stone by Nabatean Arabs in the first century C.E.

petrodollars: Dollars earned by oil-exporting countries

Philip "the Arab": Roman emperor (244-249), actually Syrian and possibly Christian

Philip II (Augustus): King of France (1180-1223), who fought in Third Crusade

Pinsker, Leo: Russian Zionist, author of *Auto-Emancipation*

pogrom (puh-GRAWM): Organized massacre of Jews

Popular Front for the Liberation of Palestine: Marxist Palestinian group led by George Habash, noted for its extremism and airplane hijackings

Port Said (sa-EED): Egyptian city where Suez Canal meets the Mediterranean

positive neutralism: Nasser's policy of not siding with either the Communist countries or the West, but seeking to reconcile the two blocs

predestination: The belief that God has determined what will happen to every living person, the opposite of "free will"

Prester John: Mythic Christian ruler in East Asia or Ethiopia, thought by some medieval Western Christians to be an ally against the Muslims

Punjab (poon-JAWB): A region of northwestern India, now partly in Pakistan

al-Qadhafi, Mu'ammar (el-gad-DOF-fee, mu-AHM-mer): Libyan president (1969-)

qadi (KAW-dee): A Muslim judge

al-Qadisiyah (el-KAW-de-SEE-ya): A region of central Iraq, site of a battle in which the Arabs defeated the Sasanid Persians in 637

Qajar dynasty (KAW-jar): Family of Turkic origin ruling Iran (1794-1925)

Qalqilya (kal-KEEL-ya): Arab border village in central Palestine between the West Bank (or Samaria) and Israel

qanat (ka-NAWT): Canal, especially one carrying irrigation water underground

qanum (ka-NOON): A law promulgated by a ruler, as opposed to the rules or laws contained in the Shari'ah

Qarmatian (kar-MAHT-e-an): Member of an Isma'ili Shi'i group that established a republic, allegedly practicing communism of property and spouses, in tenth-century Bahrain and Arabia

Qasim, Abd al-Karim (KAW-sem, AB-del-ka-REEM): President of Iraq (1958-1963), Nasser's rival in Arab politics

Qayrawan (kye-ruh-WAHN): City in northeastern Tunisia; also called Kairouan

Qays (KICE): Northern Arabian tribe

Qazvin (kaz-VEEN): City in northwestern Iran, briefly the Safavid capital

Qubilai Khan (KOO-bi-lie KHAHN): Mongol ruler in the late thirteenth century

Quran (koor-AWN): The collection of revelations that Muslims believe God vouchsafed to Muhammad via Gabriel, and one of the main sources of Islamic law, literature, and culture; also "Koran"

Quraysh (koo-RAYSH): Leading tribe of northwest Arabia, especially Mecca

Qutb, Sayyid (KOTB, SAY-yid): Egyptian Muslim fundamentalist (d. 1966)

Qutuz (ko-TOOZ): Mamluk general

al-Quwatli, Shukri (el-koo-WOT-lee, SHOOK-ree): Syrian leader in 1950s

Rabat Summit (ra-BAWT): 1974 meeting of Arab heads of state, where they resolved to make the PLO the sole spokesmen for Palestinians

Rabin, Yitzchak (ra-BEEN, yits-KHAWK): Israeli prime minister (1974-1977)

racism: Any doctrine saying that one race is superior to another

Rafah (RAH-fah): Sinai village near Gaza Strip

Ragib, Mehmet (raw-GHIP, meh-MET): Eighteenth-century Ottoman vizir

Ramadan (ra-ma-DAWN): Month of the Arabic calendar during which Muslims abstain from eating, drinking, and sexual intercourse from daybreak until sunset, in commemoration of Muhammad's first revelations of the Quran

Ramleh (RAHM-leh): Strategically located village in central Palestine/Israel

Rashid al-Din (ra-SHEED ed-DEEN): Muslim historian who served as vizir to the Il-Khanids (d. 1318)

Rashid dynasty: Ruling family in northeastern Arabia and rival of the Saudis in the early twentieth century

Rashidun caliphs (ra-shee-DOON): First four successors to Muhammad as leaders of the *ummah,* namely Abu-Bakr, Umar, Uthman, and Ali

re'aya (re-AH-ya): Member(s) of the Ottoman subject class

refugees, Palestinian: Arabs who were forced or who chose to leave their homes in areas now part of Israel, during the 1948 or 1967 wars

Republican People's party: Liberal Turkish party founded by Kemal Ataturk and now headed by Bulent Ecevit

Reshid, Mustafa (re-SHEED, MOOS-ta-fa): Westernizing Ottoman reformer in the early Tanzimat era

Residency: See *"British Agency"*

Reuter, Baron de: British businessman offered a lucrative concession in Iran by Nasiruddin Shah in 1873

Revisionist party: Right-wing Zionist movement founded by Jabotinsky

Reynaud de Chatillon (ray-NO duh SHA-tee-yon): French military leader in the Latin Kingdom of Jerusalem

Reza Shah (RAY-za SHAH): Ruler of Iran (1925-1941)

Rhodes: Mediterranean island, site of 1949 "proximity talks" between some Arab states and Israel, mediated by Ralph Bunche

Richard I, "The Lionhearted": King of England (1189-1199)

riddah (RID-da): Rebellion of the Arab tribes against rule from Medina after Muhammad's death, quelled during caliphate of Abu-Bakr

Riyadh (ree-YOD): (1) Capital of Saudi Arabia; (2) site of 1976 Arab summit meeting, creating a peacekeeping force (mainly Syrian) to end the Lebanese civil war

Rogers Peace Plan: American proposal (1969-1970) to end the war of attrition, calling on Israel to withdraw from lands occupied since 1967

Rum (ROOM): Arabic, Persian, and Turkish word for Anatolia, sometimes also used collectively for Greek Orthodox Christians

Rushdi, Husayn (ROOSH-dee, hu-SAYN): Egypt's prime minister (1914-1919)

Russo-Turkish War: 1877-1878 conflict between Russia and the Ottoman Empire, in which the latter lost land in Anatolia and the Balkans

Saba (SAH-ba): Ancient Arabian kingdom in Yemen

sabra (SOB-ra): Jewish native of Israel

al-Sadat, Anwar (es-sa-DAT, AN-war): President of Egypt (1970-)

Sa'di (sah-DEE): Persian poet (d. 1291)

Safa (SAH-fa): Small hill in Mecca, important in the hajj ritual

Safavid dynasty (SAH-fa-vid): Initially Sufi Azerbaijani Turkish family that ruled over Iran (1501-1722), strengthening Twelve-Imam Shi'ism and Persian culture

Safed (sah-FED): City in northern Israel

Saffarid dynasty (saf-FAR-id): Persian family of coppersmiths, who took control of parts of Iran in the late ninth century

Sa'id (sa-EED): Viceroy of Egypt (1854-1863)

Salah al-Din (sa-LAH ed-DEEN): Arabic name for a Kurdish military adventurer who gained control of Egypt from the Fatimids (1171) and of Syria from the Zengids (1174), defeated the Crusaders in 1187 and regained Jerusalem from Islam, but failed to expel them from Acre

salam (sa-LAM or suh-LAWM): (1) Peace; (2) greeting(s)

Samanid dynasty (sa-MAN-id): Persian family that took over Khurasan and Transoxiana in the late ninth century and later imported Turkish tribesmen, such as the Ghaznavids and the Seljuks, to serve as border guards

Samaria: Israeli term for the northern half of the West Bank

Samarqand (sa-mar-KAWND): Major city in Transoxiana

Samarra (sa-MAR-ra): City in northern Iraq, Abbasid capital (836-889)

al-Samu' (es-sa-MOO-ah): Arab village subjected to harsh Israeli reprisal following Palestinian border raids in 1966

Samuel, Herbert: British high commissioner in Palestine (1920-1925)

San'a: Capital of the Yemen Arab Republic

San Remo: Site of 1920 Anglo-French agreement on the mandate borders

Sanskrit: The classical language of India

Saracen: Medieval European word for "Arab" or "Muslim"

Sarkis, Elias (sar-KEES, il-YAS): President of Lebanon (1960-)

Sarraj, Abd al-Hamid (sar-RODGE, AB-del-ha-MEED): Syrian Arab nationalist

Sasa (SAH-sa): Syrian town southwest of Damascus, site of heavy fighting during October 1973 war

Sasanid dynasty (sa-SAW-nid): Persian ruling family (227-651)

Saud (ibn Abd al-Aziz) (sa-OOD): King of Saudi Arabia (1953-1964)

Saud dynasty: Arab family of Najd, supporting Wahhabi doctrines since the reign of Muhammad ibn Saud (1746-1765), rulers of most of the Arabian peninsula during the twentieth century

Saudi Arabia (SOW-dee): Kingdom in the Arabian peninsula ruled by the Saud dynasty

SAVAK (sa-VAWK): Iran's secret police

al-Sayyid, Ahmad Lutfi (es-SAY-yid, AH-mad LOOT-fee): Egyptian liberal nationalist (d. 1963)

Scopus, Mount: Hill northeast of Jerusalem, site of first Hebrew University campus and Hadassah Hospital, surrounded by Jordanian-held land (1949-1967)

Sebuktegin (suh-BEWK-tuh-geen): Central Asian Turkish chieftain (d. 997), vassal of the Samanids, and founder of the Ghaznavid dynasty (977-1186)

Security Council Resolution 242: November 1967 statement of principles for achieving peace between the Arabs and Israel, accepted by both sides but with differing interpretations

Security Council Resolution 338: Cease-fire resolution ending October 1973 war, calling for direct talks between Israel and the Arab states

Selim I (se-LEEM): Ottoman sultan (1512-1520), surnamed "the Inexorable"

Selim II: Ottoman sultan (1566-1574), surnamed "the Sot"

Selim III: Ottoman sultan (1789-1807), noted for his reforms

Seljuk (sel-JOOK): (1) Central Asian Turkish tribal leader who converted to Islam (ca. 960), correctly Selchuk; (2) ruling family descended from Seljuk

Semitic: Pertaining to a subgroup of Asian languages, including Arabic and Hebrew, having consonantal writing systems, inflected grammars, and structured morphologies, or to a speaker of one of these languages

Separation of Forces Agreement: Formula adopted by Kissinger to secure Israel's withdrawal from Arab lands taken in the October 1973 war

Sephardim (se-FAR-dim or sfa-ra-DEEM): Jews whose ancestors came from Spain or Portugal, or from the Middle East or North Africa

Serbia: Ancient Balkan kingdom, now part of Yugoslavia

Seven-Imam Shi'i: Any Muslim who believes that the true leadership of the *ummah* was passed from Ali through a line of heirs ending in Isma'il; also called "Isma'ilis" or "Seveners"

Sèvres, Treaty of (SEVr): Abortive treaty imposed by the World War I Allies on the Ottoman Empire in 1920, later replaced by the Treaty of Lausanne

Shafi'i (SHA-fi-ee): Rite of Sunni Muslim jurisprudence, originating in Cairo, making considerable use of analogy

shahid (SHA-hid): Professional witness or notary, in Muslim law

Shajar al-Durr (SHA-jar ed-DOR): Woman ruler of Egypt (1250)

shaman (sha-MAHN): Pre-Islamic Turkish wizard, soothsayer capable of communicating with the dead, healing the sick, keeping tribal lore

Sham'un, Kamil (sham-OON, ka-MEEL): President of Lebanon (1952-1958)

Shari'ah (sha-REE-a): The highly articulated code of Muslim behavior, based primarily on the Quran and *hadith,* secondarily on analogy, consensus, and judicial opinion, that is binding on all Muslims

sharif (sha-REEF): Descendants of Muhammad

Sharm al-Shaykh (sharm esh-SHAYKH): Fortified point near Straits of Tiran

Shatt al-Arab (shot-el-AH-rab): Confluence of Tigris and Euphrates rivers

shaykh (SHAYKH): (1) Arab tribal leader; (2) ruler; (3) learned Muslim

shaykh al-Islam (SHAY-khul-iss-LAHM): Chief Muslim legal and religious officer in the Ottoman Empire, appointed by the sultan

Shihab, Fuad (she-HAB, foo-ODD): Lebanon's president (1958-1964)

Shi'i (SHEE-ee): Muslim who believes that the leadership of the *ummah* should have gone, after Muhammad's death, to Ali, to whom special legislative power and spiritual knowledge were vouchsafed

Shiraz (shee-RAHZ): City in southern Iran

Shishakli, Adib (shi-SHEK-lee, a-DEEB): Syria's president (1949-1954)

shofar (SHOW-fer): Ram's horn blown by Jews on religious occasions

al-Shuqayri, Ahmad (esh-shoo-KAY-ree): First PLO leader (1964-1968)

shura (SHOO-ra): Council chosen by Umar to elect his successor in 644

shuttle diplomacy: Kissinger's method of mediating between the Arab countries and Israel

Shu'ubiyah (shoo-oo-BEE-yah): eighth-ninth century literary and political movement in which Persians sought equal power and status with Arabs

Sidon: City in southern Lebanon

Sidqi, Isma'il (SID-kee, iss-ma-EEL): Egyptian royalist politician

Siffin, Battle of (sif-FEEN): Indecisivie clash in 657 between partisans of Ali and Mu'awiyah, who wished to avenge the death of Uthman

Sinbad the Magean (sin-BAWD): Leader of eighth-century Persian revolt

Sind: Region of lower Indus River valley, now part of Pakistan

sipahi (se-PAW-hee): Ottoman horse soldier supported by *timar* or *iqta'*

Skanderbeg: Albanian military leader, also called George Castriota

Smyrna: See *Izmir*

Sogut (suh-EWT): Northwest Anatolian town where Ottoman Empire started

squinch: Small arch or corbeling built across the internal angle between two walls to help support an arch or spire

Stern Gang: Zionist group, also called "Lehi," which carried out various guerrilla actions in Palestine in the 1940s

Suez Affair: British, French, and Israeli attack on Egypt (1956), following Nasser's nationalization of the Suez Canal Company

Suez Canal: Man-made channel connecting the Mediterranean and Red seas

Suez Canal Users Association: Group proposed by Dulles to run the canal

Sufi (SOO-fee): Pertaining to Muslim mystics, or their beliefs, practices, or organizations

Sufism: Organized Muslim mysticism

Suleyman the Magnificent (soo-lay-MAHN): Ottoman sultan (1520-1566)

sulh (SOOLh): Reconciliation, or comprehensive peace settlement

sultan (sool-TAWN): Title for ruler of various Muslim states, including the Seljuk and Ottoman empires

Sultaniyah (sool-ta-NEE-ya): Il-Khanid capital city in northern Iran

sunnah (SOON-na): The sayings and actions of Muhammad relating to correct Muslim belief or behavior

Sunni (SOON-nee): (1) Muslim accepting the legitimacy of the caliphs who succeeded Muhammad and adhering to one of the legal rites developed in the early caliphal period; (2) conscientious followers of Muhammad's sunnah

Sykes-Picot Partition Plan (pee-KOE): 1916 secret treaty between Britain, France, and Russia, planning to partition the Ottoman Empire into colonies or spheres of influence

Syria: (1) Region east of the Mediterranean, including parts of southern Turkey, the republic of Syria, Lebanon, Israel, Jordan, and northern Sinai, also called "the Levant"; (2) the republic of Syria

Syrian Protestant College: American University of Beirut, before 1920

Tabaristan (ta-BAHR-i-stahn): Persian region between the Elburz mountains and the Caspian Sea

Tabatabai: See *Ziya*

Tabriz (ta-BREEZ): City in Azerbaijan

Tahirid dynasty (TAW-her-id): Ruling family in eastern Iran (820-873)

Taif (TA-if): Mountain city in western Arabia, near Mecca

Talal (ta-LAL): King of Jordan (1951-1952)

Talat (TULL-aht): The most influential of the Young Turk leaders

Talhah (TULL-ha): Muhammad's associate who challenged Ali in the Battle of the Camel, in which he died (656)

Talmud (TAHL-mood): Collection of Jewish law and tradition

T'ang dynasty (TONG): Strong Chinese ruling family (618-937)

Tanzimat (tan-zee-MOTT): Program of intensive westernizing reform enforced by the Ottoman government, especially from 1839 to 1876

Taurus (TOR-us): Mountain range in southern Anatolia

Tawfiq (tow-FEEK): Viceroy of Egypt (1879-1892)

Tehran (teh-RAWN): Iran's capital under the Qajar and Pahlavi dynasties

Tel Aviv: Coastal city in Israel

Temple: When capitalized, one of several edifices built in Jerusalem as main centers of Jewish worship in Biblical times

Tengri (TENG-gree): The Turkish and Mongol god of the blue sky

Thrace: Area on northern shore of the Aegean Sea

Tiberias: City in northeastern Israel

Tigris: The more eastern of Iraq's two rivers

timar (tee-MAHR): Land grant by Ottoman sultans for military service

Timur (Leng) (tee-MOOR): Central Asian Turkish conqueror of Kurasan, Iran, Iraq, and Syria (1379-1405), also called "Tamerlane"

Timurid dynasty: Ruling family descended from Timur, holding central Asia in the fifteenth century, and later India (often called "Moghuls")

Tiran (tee-RAHN): Straits linking Gulf of Aqaba to the Red Sea

Trans-Iranian Railway: Line linking Caspian Sea and Persian Gulf, built under Reza Shah

Transjordan: Emirate or principality east of the Jordan River excised by the British from their Palestine mandate in 1921

Transoxiana: Land northeast of the Oxus River, conquered by the Arabs in the eighth century, later invaded successively by Turks and Mongols

Transylvania: Mountainous region between Rumania and Hungary

Trench, Battle of the: Unsuccessful Meccan siege of Medinan Muslims (627)

tribe: Group of people (often nomadic) sharing real or fictitious descent from a common ancestor, also common traditions, customs, and leaders

Tripoli: (1) City in northern Lebanon; (2) twelfth-century Crusader state; (3) capital city of Libya

T'u-chüeh (TOO-jway): Chinese name for the sixth-century Turkish empire

Turk: (1) Speaker of a Turkic language; (2) citizen of Turkey

Turkish: Pertaining to the language and culture of the Turks

Twelve-Imam Shi'i: Any Muslim who believes that leadership of the *ummah* should have gone to Ali and his descendants, of whom the twelfth is hidden but will some day return to restore righteousness; also called "Imami," "Ja'fari," or "Twelver"

Twitchell, Karl: American geologist who looked for oil in Saudi Arabia in the 1930s

Ubaydullah, "the Mahdi" (oo-bay-DUL-la): Founder of the Fatimid dynasty (909-934), having his capital at Mahdiyah, near modern Tunis

Uhud, Battle of (OH-hood): Muslim defeat by pagan Meccans (625)

Uighur (WEE-goor): Turkic people of northwestern China, who ruled a large and sophisticated kingdom in the eighth and ninth centuries

Ukaz (oo-KAHZ): Town near Mecca, site of pre-Islamic poets' fair

Ukraine: Rich agricultural region north of the Black Sea

ulama (OO-le-ma): Collective term for Muslim scholars and jurists

Umar I (OH-mar): Second of the Rashidun caliphs (634-644), leader of the early Arab conquests

Umar II: Umayyad caliph (717-720), who reduced discrimination against non-Arab converts to Islam

Umayyad dynasty (om-MYE-yad): Clan of the Quraysh tribe that ruled the Muslim world as a whole (661-750) and Spain until 1030

ummah (OOM-ma): The political, social, and spiritual community of Muslims

Uniat Catholics: Christians of various Eastern rites that have chosen to go into communion with the Roman Catholic Church

Unionist: Member or supporter of the Committee of Union and Progress

United Arab Emirates: Federation of Arab principalities on Persian Gulf

United Arab Republic: Union of Egypt and Syria (1958-1961)

United Nations Disengagement Observer Force: International army stationed between Syria and Israel (1974-)

United Nations Emergency Force: International army between Egypt and Israel (1957-1967 and 1974-)

United Nations Relief and Works Agency (UNRWA): International organization providing aid and education to Palestinian Arabs since 1949

Urabi, Ahmad (oo-RAH-bee): Egyptian army officer and nationalist, who led revolution against Dual Control (1881-1882)

Urban II: Pope (1088-1099) who called the First Crusade

Uthman (oth-MAHN): Third of the Rashidun caliphs (644-656)

Uzbek: Central Asian Turkish people, rivals to Safavids in the sixteenth century

al-Uzza (el-OZ-za): Meccan goddess before Islam

Varna: Bulgarian port city, site of Crusader defeat by Ottomans (1444)

Venizelos, Eleutherios: Greek prime minister during invasion of Anatolia (1919-1922) and strong advocate of a greater Greece

vizir (ve-ZEER): Government minister in a Muslim country; also "wazir"

wadi (WAH-dee): Valley

Wafd (WAHFT): Unofficial Egyptian delegation to 1919 Paris Peace Conference, later Egypt's main nationalist party up to the 1952 revolution

Wahhabi (wa-HAH-bee): Fundamentalist Muslim sect, founded by Muhammad ibn Abd al-Wahhab (d. 1787), now dominant in Saudi Arabia

Wailing Wall Incident: Fracas in Jerusalem (1929) leading to widespread Arab attacks against Jews there and elsewhere in Palestine

Walid I (wa-LEED): Umayyad caliph (705-715)

Wallachia (wal-LAY-ke-ya): Balkan region now part of Rumania

waqf (WAHKF): Muslim endowment of land or other property, usually set up for a beneficent or pious purpose

Wassmuss, Wilhelm: German consul in Iran who led anti-British and anti-Russian revolts during World War I

Weizmann, Chaim (VITES-man, KHIME): British Zionist leader who helped to bring about Balfour Declaration; Israel's first president (1948-1952)

West Bank: Area of Arab Palestine annexed by Jordan in 1948 and captured by Israel in 1967, called "Judea and Samaria" by some Israelis

White Revolution: Radical reform program proclaimed by Iran's shah (1963)

Wingate, Reginald: British high commissioner in Egypt (1916-1919)

Yad Mordechai (yod MOR-de-khye): Israeli kibbutz near Gaza Strip

Yamit (ya-MEET): Israeli industrial town built in occupied Sinai

Yarmuk River (yar-MOOK): Tributary of Jordan, site of Arab victory (636)

Yathrib (YATH-rib): Original name of Medina

Yazd (YEZD): City in central Iran

Yazid I (ye-ZEED): Umayyad caliph (680-683)

Yemen (YEH-men): (1) Mountainous region of southwestern Arabia, (2) the Yemen Arab Republic, (3) the People's Democratic Republic of Yemen

Yom Kippur war: See *October war*

Young Egypt: Egyptian nationalist movement, popular in the 1930s, having strong Fascist leanings

Young Turks: Group of Turkish nationalist students and army officers who took control of the Ottoman government in 1908, restored its constitution, and instituted westernizing reforms; their main organization was the Committee of Union and Progress

Zaghlul, Sa'd (zagh-LOOL, SOD): Egyptian nationalist leader (d. 1927)

Zagros (ZAW-gross): Mountain range in southwestern Iran

zakat (ze-KAT): Fixed share of income or property that all Muslims must pay as tax or charity for the welfare of the needy

Zayd ibn Harithah (ZAYD-ibn-ha-REE-tha): Adopted son of Muhammad

Zayd: Fifth Shi'i imam, leader of an unsuccessful revolt (d. 740)

Zaydi Shi'i (ZAY-dee): Any Muslim who believes that the leadership of the *ummah* was passed on from Zayd to his descendants

Zaynab (ZAY-nub): Wife of Muhammad's adopted son, Zayd, who divorced her to let Muhammad marry her

Zengi (ZENG-gee): Turkish general and founder of a state in Mosul (1127-1146)

Zindiq (zin-DEEK): (1) Muslim heretic; (2) Manichaean or supporter of some other pre-Islamic Persian religion

Zionism: (1) Nationalist ideology stressing solidarity of the Jewish people; (2) movement to create or to maintain a Jewish state, especially in Palestine/Israel

Zionist: Believer in Zionism

Ziya Tabatabai, Sayyid (zee-YA ta-ba-ta-BAW-ee): Civilian leader of Iranian nationalist revolt (1921)

Ziyad ibn Abihi (zee-YAD ibn-a-BEE-hee): Arab governor of Iraq under Caliph Mu'awiyah

Zoroastrianism: Iranian religion, founded in the sixth-century B.C. by Zarathustra/Zoroaster, preaching the existence of a supreme deity and of a cosmic struggle between Good and Evil

Zubayr (zoo-BAYR): Muhammad's associate who challenged Ali in the Battle of the Camel, in which he died (656), and father of Abdallah

Bibliographic Essay

Since this book is supposed to introduce the history of the Middle East to college students primarily and to the public secondarily, the books and articles that I will recommend are chosen for their readability and their reliability. Professional historians, including instructors using this work as a textbook, can benefit more from a recent publication by the Research and Training Committee of the Middle East Association, namely Leonard Binder, ed., *The Study of the Middle East* (New York: Wiley, 1977), especially the section on history by Albert Hourani. I hope that someday we will have a teacher's handbook for Middle East history. This essay is intended to serve students and nonspecialist readers and also to acknowledge my indebtedness to many scholars whose publications have influenced what I wrote.

First, a number of general histories of the Islamic Middle East have influenced the overall structure of *A Concise History of the Middle East.* Listed in order of their initial publication in English, they are: Philip K. Hitti, *History of the Arabs* (New York: Macmillan, 1937; 10th ed., 1970); Carl Brockelmann, *History of the Islamic Peoples,* trans. Joel Carmichael and Moshe Perlmann (New York: G. P. Putnam, 1947); George Kirk, *A Short History of the Middle East* (London: Methuen, 1949; 7th ed., New York: Praeger, 1964); Sydney Nettleton Fisher, *The Middle East: A History* (New York: Knopf, 1958; 3rd ed., 1978); Philip K. Hitti, *The Near East in History* (Princeton: Van Nostrand, 1961); William Polk, *The United States and the Arab World* (Cambridge: Harvard University Press, 1965; 3rd ed., 1975); Sir John Bagot Glubb, *A Short History of the Arab Peoples* (New York: Stein & Day, 1969); Yahya Armajani, *Middle East Past and Present* (Englewood Cliffs, N.J.: Prentice-Hall, 1970); P. M. Holt, Ann K. S. Lambton, and Bernard Lewis, eds., *The Cambridge History of Islam,* 2 vols. (Cambridge: University Press, 1970); and Marshall G. S. Hodgson, *The Venture of Islam,* 3 vols. (Chicago: University of Chicago Press, 1975). Of these, I consider Hodgson's work to be the most thought provoking and Fisher's the best for beginning students, but I am especially indebted to the *Cambridge History*'s early chapters in my work.

Having suggested in my preface that this book might be read in conjunction with a collection of original sources in translation, I have several in mind: Arthur J. Arberry, *Aspects of Islamic Civilization* (London: George Allen & Unwin, 1964); Marshall G. S. Hodgson, ed., *Introduction to Islamic Civilization,* 3 vols. (Chicago: University of Chicago Press, 1958-1959); Arthur Jeffery, *Islam: Muhammad and His Religion* (New York: Liberal Arts Press, 1958) and *Reader on Islam* (The Hague: Mouton, 1962); James Kritzeck, *An Anthology of Islamic Literature* (New York: Holt, Rinehart, and Winston, 1964); Bernard Lewis, *Islam: From the Prophet Muhammad to the Capture of Constantinople,* 2 vol. (New York: Harper & Row, 1974); Eric Schroeder *Muhammad's People* (Portland, Me.: Bond Wheelwright Press, 1955); and John Alden Williams, *Islam* (New York: Braziller, 1960) and *Themes of Islamic Civilization* (Berkeley and Los Angeles: University of California Press, 1971).

GENERAL RESEARCH AIDS

A good reference tool for beginning students is Jere Bacharach's *A New East Studies Handbook,* 2nd ed. (Seattle: University of Washington Press, 1976), which contains dynastic tables, lists of rulers, maps, a chronology, glossary, and other aids. There are several more specialized handbooks: Michael Adams, ed., *The Middle East: A Handbook* (New York and Washington: Praeger; London: Anthony Blond, 1971); Peter Mansfield, ed., *The Middle East: A Political and Economic Survey,* 4th ed. (London and New York: Oxford University Press, 1973); C. H. Philips, *Handbook of Oriental History* (London: Offices of the Royal Historical Society, 1951); Jean Sauvaget, *Introduction to the History of the Muslim East,* rev. Claude Cahen (Berkeley and Los Angeles: University of California Press, 1965); and Colin Legum, ed., *Middle East Contemporary Survey* (New York: Holmes and Meier, 1978).

Since the modern period is naturally more changeable, a yearbook may serve both beginners and specialists as well as a handbook. One that is especially useful is *The Middle East and North Africa* (London: Europa Publications, 1950-). Reeva Simon, *The Modern Middle East: A Guide to Research Tools in the Social Sciences* (Boulder: Westview Press, 1978) can serve as the modern counterpart to Sauvaget. The most established periodical publication in our field is the *Middle East Journal* (Washington, 1947-), which includes a quarterly chronology of events and bibliography of new books and periodical articles. Historians of the Middle East now use the *International Journal of Middle East Studies* (New York and London, 1970-) and the *Middle East Studies Association Bulletin* (New York, 1967-). Recent events are covered in various newsletters, such as the *Middle East Economic Digest* (London, 1957-) and *Arab Report and Record* (London, 1966-), as well as the *New York Times* and the *Christian Science Monitor.*

In preparing this book, I relied heavily on *The Encyclopaedia of Islam* (Leiden: E. J. Brill, 1913-1938; 2nd ed., 1954-), but it may be easier for beginners to use Stephen and Nandy Ronart's *Concise Encyclopedia of Arabic Civilization,* 2 vols. (New York: Praeger, 1960-1966). Also useful are Evyatar Levine and Yaacov Shimoni, *Political Dictionary of the Middle East in the Twentieth Century* (Jerusalem: Jerusalem Publishing House, 1972); Raphael Patai, ed., *Encyclopedia of Zionism and Israel,* 2 vols. (New York: Herzl Press and McGraw-Hill, 1971); and the monumental *Encyclopaedia Judaica,* ed. Cecil Roth, 16 vols. (Jerusalem: Keter Publishing House, 1972).

Until John Woods's projected historical atlas appears, we must continue to use R. Roolvink's *Historical Atlas of the Muslim Peoples* (Cambridge: Harvard University Press, 1957). A good modern one is the *Atlas of the Arab World and the Middle East* (London: Macmillan; New York: St Martin's Press, 1960). The best physical map is still Bartholomew's *The Middle East,* but a good political map of the area was published with the September 1978 issue of *National Geographic.*

Librarians, students, and general readers will welcome the new and heavily annotated bibliography by David Littlefield, *The Islamic Near East and North Africa* (Littleton, Colo.: Libraries Unlimited, 1977). Somewhat less annotated but more extensive in its coverage is George N. Atiyeh, *The Contemporary Middle East, 1948-1973* (Boston: G. K. Hall, 1975), which, despite its title, covers a lot of history.

INTRODUCTION AND CHAPTER 1

Students wanting to know how some well-known writers on the Middle East view history might read Sir Hamilton Gibb, *Studies on the Civilization of Islam,* eds. Stanford J. Shaw and William R. Polk (Boston: Beacon Press, 1962); Albert Hourani, *A Vision of History* (Beirut: Khayat's, 1961); Bernard Lewis, *History—Remembered, Recovered, Invented* (Princeton: Princeton University Press, 1975), or Denis Sinor, ed., *Orientation and History* (Bloomington: Indiana University Press, 1970).

For a general introduction to the area's geography, beginners should read Stephen H. Longrigg and James Jankowski, *The Middle East: A*

Social Geography (Chicago: Aldine, 1970). More technical works include Peter Beaumont, Gerald Blake, and J. Malcolm Wagstaff, *The Middle East: A Geographical Study* (New York: Wiley, 1976); W. B. Fisher, *The Middle East: A Physical, Social, and Regional Geography,* 6th ed. (London: Methuen; New York: Barnes & Noble, 1971); and Xavier de Planhol, *The World of Islam* (Ithaca: Cornell University Press, 1959). The societies and cultures of the traditional Middle East are surveyed in Carleton Coon, *Caravan: The Story of the Middle East,* 2nd ed. (New York: Holt, Rinehart, and Winston, 1959; reprint ed., 1976); Daniel Lerner, *The Passing of Traditional Society* (New York: Free Press, 1959); Ailon Shiloh, ed., *Peoples and Cultures of the Middle East* (New York: Random House, 1969); and T. Cuyler Young, ed., *Near Eastern Culture and Society* (Princeton: Princeton University Press, 1951).

CHAPTER 2

The history of the Middle East before Muhammad is, as you probably know, a field unto itself. The best introduction currently available is William W. Hallo and William Kelly Simpson, *The Ancient Near East: A History* (New York: Harcourt Brace Jovanovich, 1971), but see also Milton Covensky, *The Ancient Near Eastern Tradition* (New York: Harper & Row, 1966) and two works by Henri Frankfort: *Before Philosophy* (Harmondsworth, Middlesex: Penguin Books, 1951) and *The Birth of Civilization in the Near East* (Bloomington: Indiana University Press; London: Williams & Norgate, 1951).

The most comprehensive introduction to Byzantine history is George Ostrogorsky, *History of the Byzantine State,* trans. Joan Hussey (New Brunswick, N.J.: Rutgers University Press, 1957). Beginners might try Joan Hussey, *The Byzantine World* (London: Hutchison, 1957; New York: Harper & Row, 1961); and Tamara Talbot Rice, *Everyday Life in Byzantium* (London: B. T. Batsford; New York: G. P. Putnam's Sons, 1967).

On the Eastern Christian churches, see Aziz S. Atiya, *A History of Eastern Christianity* (London: Methuen; South Bend, Ind.: Notre Dame University Press, 1968); and Donald Attwater, *The Christian Churches of the East,* 2 vols. (Milwaukee: Bruce, 1947-1948). There is very little on Zoroastrianism, but try Robert C. Zaehner, *The Dawn and Twilight of Zoroastrianism* (London: Weidenfeld and Nicolson, 1961).

General books on Iran (or Persia) require special attention. Best for beginners are probably Richard N. Frye, *Persia* (London: George Allen and Unwin, 1968); and Donald Wilber, *Iran: Past and Present,* 8th ed. (Princeton: Princeton University Press, 1976). On the early period, see

Frye's *Heritage of Persia* (Cleveland and New York: World Publishing Co., 1963). Advanced students should use *The Cambridge History of Iran* (Cambridge: University Press, 1968-) of which volumes 1, 4, and 5 have appeared so far. I also acknowledge the help I received from Taghi Nasr, *The Eternity of Iran* (Tehran: Iranian Ministry of Culture and Arts, 1974).

The classic description of the Arabian desert is Charles Doughty, *Travels in Arabia Deserta* (Cambridge: University Press, 1888; many reprints). On the domestication of the camel, read Richard Bulliet, *The Camel and the Wheel* (Cambridge: Harvard University Press, 1975). Translations of early Arabic poetry, traditionally considered "pre-Islamic," include Arthur J. Arberry's *The Seven Odes* (New York: Macmillan, 1957) and Charles J. Lyall's *Translations of Ancient Arabian Poetry* (London and Edinburgh: Williams & Norgate, 1885).

Surveys of early Arab or medieval Islamic history include H. M. Balyuzi, *Muhammad and the Course of Islam* (Oxford: George Ronald, 1976); E. A. Belyaev, *Arabs, Islam, and the Arab Caliphate in the Early Middle Ages,* trans. Adolphe Gourevitch (New York: Praeger, 1969); John B. Christopher, *The Islamic Tradition* (New York: Harper & Row, 1972); Bernard Lewis, *The Arabs in History* (London: Hutchinson's University Library, 1950; 4th ed., 1966); Francis E. Peters, *Allah's Commonwealth* (New York: Simon & Schuster, 1973); John J. Saunders, *A History of Medieval Islam* (New York: Barnes & Noble, 1965); Bertold Spuler, *The Muslim World: An Historical Survey,* pt. 1, trans. F.R.C. Bagley (Leiden: E. J. Brill, 1960); Gustave Von Grunebaum, *Classical Islam: A History, 600-1258,* trans. Katherine Watson (London: George Allen & Unwin, 1970); and W. Montgomery Watt, *The Majesty That Was Islam* (New York: Praeger, 1974). Beginners should try Saunders or Lewis first.

CHAPTER 3

A good life of the Prophet for beginners is Betty Kelen's *Muhammad: A Messenger of God* (Nashville, Tenn.: T. Nelson, 1975). Students should go on to W. Montgomery Watt's *Muhammad: Prophet and Statesman* (London: Oxford University Press, 1961), based on his two longer works *Muhammad at Mecca* (Oxford: Clarendon Press, 1953) and *Muhammad at Medina* (same publisher, 1956), which stress the social and economic environment. A more psychologically oriented study is Tor Andrae's *Mohammed: The Man and His Faith,* trans. Theophil Menzel (London: George Allen & Unwin; New York: Barnes and Noble, 1935; reprinted several times). See also Sir John Bagot Glubb, *The Life and Times of Muhammad* (New York: Stein & Day, 1970). Biographies by Muslims are numerous but tend to be too detailed and subjective for most non-Muslim readers; try Zeinolabedin Rahnema, *Payambar: The Messenger,* trans. L. P. Elwell-Sutton, 3 vols. (Lahore: Shaykh Muhammad Ashraf, 1964-); or Abdul Hamid Siddiqui, *The Life of Muhammad* (Lahore: Islamic Publications, 1969).

The Quran cannot really be translated, but English versions may help the reader who knows no Arabic. Arthur J. Arberry, *The Koran Interpreted,* 2 vols. (New York: Macmillan, 1955), is the most literary. *Bell's Introduction to the Qur'an,* rev. W. Montgomery Watt (Edinburgh: University Press; Chicago: Aldine, 1970), is the most technically accurate. These may be supplemented by Watt's *Companion to the Qur'an* (London: George Allen & Unwin; New York: Humanities Press, 1967).

CHAPTER 4

Books by Western writers about Islamic beliefs and practices often betray assumptions that offend Muslims, while those written by Muslims may confuse instruction about their faith with religious indoctrination. Among the best books in the former group are Sir Hamilton Gibb, *Mohammedanism: An Historical Survey,* 2nd ed. (London: Oxford University Press, 1952; many reprints); Philip K. Hitti, *Islam: A Way of Life* (Minneapolis: University of Minnesota Press, 1970); and Arthur S. Tritton, *Islam: Beliefs and Practices* (London: Hutchinson's University Library, 1951). Among the latter, see Abd al-Rahman Azzam, *The Eternal Message of Muhammad,* trans. Caesar Farah (New York: Devin-Adair, 1964); Sayyid Abul A'la Maudoodi, *Towards Understanding Islam* (Lahore: Islamic Publications Ltd. [Karachi], 1960); Seyyed Hossein Nasr, *Ideals and Realities of Islam* (London: George Allen & Unwin, 1966; New York: Praeger, 1967); and Fazlur Rahman, *Islam* (New York: Holt, Rinehart, and Winston, 1966). The pilgrimage rites are described in Ahmad Kamal, *The Sacred Journey* (New York: Duell, Sloan & Pearce, 1961).

CHAPTER 5

For the history of the caliphate as an institution, see Thomas W. Arnold, *The Caliphate* (Oxford: Clarendon Press, 1924; reprint ed., 1965, with a concluding chapter by Sylvia Haim); and Sir William Muir *The Caliphate: Its Rise, Decline, and Fall,* 3rd ed. (London: Smith, Elder, 1898; reprint ed., 1963). A provocative recent work is M. A. Shaban, *Islamic History A.D. 600-750 (A.H. 132): A New Interpretation* (Cambridge: University Press, 1971). Short and readable biographies of Umar and Mu'awiyah (plus other early "greats") can be read in Philip Hitti,

Makers of Arab History (New York: Harper & Row, 1968). On the early conquests, the best military history in English is Sir John Bagot Glubb, *The Great Arab Conquests* (London: Hodder & Stoughton, 1963; Englewood Cliffs, N.J.: Prentice-Hall, 1964), which should be supplemented by Elias Shoufani, *Al-Riddah and the Muslim Conquest of Arabia* (Toronto: University of Toronto Press, 1973). R. N. Frye, ed., *The Cambridge History of Iran,* vol. 4 (London and New York: Cambridge University Press, 1975), contains scholarly articles on various aspects of Iranian history from 637 to 1055.

CHAPTER 6

For the period of the High Caliphate, in addition to the general histories by Hitti, Hodgson, Lewis, Saunders, and Von Grunebaum already cited, see Julius Wellhausen, *The Arab Kingdom and Its Fall,* trans. Margaret Graham Weir (Calcutta: University of Calcutta, 1927; reprint ed., 1963); and Sir Hamilton Gibb, *The Arab Conquests in Central Asia* (London: Royal Asiatic Society, 1923). Controversial but well worth reading are two recent books by M. A. Shaban: *The Abbasid Revolution* (London and New York: Cambridge University Press, 1971) and the second part of *Islamic History: A New Interpretation* (London and New York: Cambridge University Press, 1976). The most readable histories are by Sir John Bagot Glubb: *The Empire of the Arabs* (Englewood Cliffs, N.J.: Prentice-Hall, 1963); *The Course of Empire* (London: Hodder and Stoughton, 1965); and *Haroon er-Rasheed and the Great Abbasids* (London: Hodder & Stoughton, 1976). This illustrious caliph is the subject of H. St. John Philby's *Harun al-Rashid* (New York and London: D. Appleton-Century, 1934). See also Harold Bowen, *The Life and Times of Ali ibn Isa, "The Good Vizier"* (Cambridge: University Press, 1928; reprint ed., 1975). On Baghdad, see Jacob Lassner, *Topography of Baghdad in the Early Middle Ages* (Detroit: Wayne State University Press, 1970); and Gaston Wiet, *Baghdad: Metropolis of the Abbasid Caliphate,* trans. Seymour Feiler (Norman: University of Oklahoma Press, 1971). Important for history as well as art is Oleg Grabar, *The Formation of Islamic Art* (New Haven: Yale University Press, 1971).

CHAPTER 7

As I wrote in the text, this is a difficult period to study. A good starting point is from the general histories already cited, followed by Sir John Bagot Glubb, *The Lost Centuries* (London: Hodder & Stoughton, 1967); and D. S. Richards, ed., *Islamic History 950-1150* (Oxford: Cassirer, 1973). Since

Iran looms larger in importance, see volume 5 of *The Cambridge History of Iran* edited by J. A. Boyle (Cambridge: University Press, 1968). Also good for this period is Richard N. Frye, *Bukhara: The Medieval Achievement* (Norman: University of Oklahoma Press, 1965).

A good general introduction to Turkish history is Roderic Davison, *Turkey* (Englewood Cliffs, N.J.: Prentice-Hall, 1968), to be supplemented for the early period by Claude Cahen, *Pre-Ottoman Turkey*, trans. J. Jones-Williams (London: Sidgwick & Jackson; New York: Taplinger, 1968); and Clifford E. Bosworth's *The Ghaznavids* (Edinburgh: University Press, 1963) and *The Later Ghaznavids* (New York: Columbia University Press, 1977).

Abundant literature on the Crusades is available from a Western point of view. Start with Hans Eberhard Mayer, *The Crusades,* trans. John Gillingham (New York and Oxford: Oxford University Press, 1972); then Steven Runciman's very readable *History of the Crusades,* 3 vols. (Cambridge: University Press, 1951-1954). On the more advanced level, I recommend Kenneth Setton, ed., *A History of the Crusades,* 4 vols. to date (Madison: University of Wisconsin Press, 1955-1977). A Muslim perspective appears in Philip K. Hitti, and trans., *An Arab-Syrian Gentleman and Warrior in the Period of the Crusades* (New York: Columbia University Press, 1929; reprint ed., 1964). Among the many books on Salah al-Din, see Andrew Ehrenkreuz, *Saladin* (Albany: State University of New York Press, 1972); and Sir Hamilton Gibb, *The Life of Saladin* (Oxford: Clarendon Press, 1973).

Background to the Mongols can be picked up from Rene Grousset, *The Empire of the Steppes,* trans. Naomi Walford (New Brunswick: Rutgers University Press, 1970). The same author wrote a biography of Chingis Khan—*The Conqueror of the World,* trans. Marion McKellar and Denis Sinor (New York: Orion Press, 1967). See also John J. Saunders, *The History of the Mongol Conquests* (London: Routledge & Kegan Paul; New York: Barnes & Noble, 1971). Some contemporary sources have been translated and edited in Bertold Spuler's *History of the Mongols,* trans. Helga and Stuart Drummond (London: Routledge & Kegan Paul, 1972).

CHAPTER 8

Many authors, both Muslim and Western, have tried to write synoptic descriptions of Islamic civilization. Other than works cited earlier, these include Edward W. Lane, *Arabian Society in the Middle Ages* (London: Curzon Press, 1883; reprint ed., 1971); Reuben Levy, *The Social Structure of Islam,* 2nd ed. (Cambridge: University Press, 1957); and Gustave Von Grunebaum, *Medieval Islam,* 2nd ed. (Chicago: University of Chicago

Press, 1953; numerous reprints). Collaborative efforts include C. E. Bosworth and Joseph Schacht, eds., *The Legacy of Islam* (London and New York: Oxford University Press, 1974); Nabih Amin Faris, ed., *The Arab Heritage* (Princeton: Princeton University Press, 1944); Bernard Lewis, ed., *Islam and the Arab World* (New York: Knopf, 1976); Roger Savory, ed., *Introduction to Islamic Civilization* (London, New York, and Melbourne: Cambridge University Press, 1976); and the second volume of *The Cambridge History of Islam,* cited earlier.

On the Shari'ah, see Joseph Schacht, *An Introduction to Islamic Law* (London: Oxford University Press, 1964); and Noel J. Coulson, *A History of Islamic Law* (Edinburgh: University Press, 1965). On theology generally, start with W. Montgomery Watt, *Islamic Philosophy and Theology* (Edinburgh: University Press, 1962). Sufism is sympathetically covered in Seyyed Hossein Nasr, *Sufi Essays* (Albany: State University of New York Press, 1972); and Annemarie Schimmel, *Mystical Dimensions of Islam* (Chapel Hill: University of North Carolina Press, 1975).

On the literature of Muslim peoples, see Edward G. Browne, *A Literary History of Persia,* 4 vols. (Cambridge: University Press, 1928); Sir Hamilton Gibb, *Arabic Literature: An Introduction,* 2nd ed. (Oxford: Clarendon Press, 1963); and Reynold A. Nicholson, *A Literary History of the Arabs* (New York: Scribner's, 1907; London: Unwin, 1914; many reprints). I have already suggested some anthologies of original literary works in English translation. Ibn Khaldun's *Muqaddimah* has been translated into three volumes of English by Franz Rosenthal (New York: Bollingen, 1958) and abridged by N. J. Dawood (Princeton: Princeton University Press, 1967). Rosenthal also wrote *A History of Muslim Historiography* (Leiden: E. J. Brill; New York: Humanities Press, 1968).

The most readable introduction to Islamic art, profusely illustrated, is Ernst Grube's *The World of Islam* (New York and Toronto: McGraw-Hill, 1966).

CHAPTER 9

I derived my views on the significance of gunpowder from Carlo M. Cipolla, *Guns, Sails, and Empire* (New York: Minerva Press, 1965); and from Hodgson, *The Venture of Islam,* cited earlier.

The Il-Khanid phase of Mongol history is covered by Bertold Spuler in *The Muslim World: A Historical Survey, Part II: The Mongol Period,* trans. F. R. C. Bagley (Leiden: E. J. Brill, 1960). A readable introduction to the Mamluks is Sir John Bagot Glubb, *Soldiers of Fortune: The Story of the Mamlukes* (New York: Stein & Day, 1973). It should be followed by Ira M. Lapidus, *Muslim Cities in the Later Middle Ages* (Cambridge:

Harvard University Press, 1967). On specific cities of this era, see A. J. Arberry, *Shiraz: Persian City of Saints and Poets* (Norman: University of Oklahoma Press, 1960); Gaston Wiet, *Cairo: City of Art and Commerce,* trans. Seymour Feiler (Norman: University of Oklahoma Press, 1964); and Nicola Ziadeh, *Damascus under the Mamluks* (Norman: University of Oklahoma Press, 1964).

The latest general history of the Ottoman Empire, based heavily on Turkish sources, is Stanford J. Shaw (with Ezel Kural Shaw in volume 2), *History of the Ottoman Empire and Modern Turkey,* 2 vols. (London, New York, and Melbourne: Cambridge University Press, 1976-1977). Since this history may seem formidable to beginners, I also suggest Lord Eversley and Sir Vallentine Chirol, *The Turkish Empire from 1288 to 1922* (London: T. Fisher Unwin, 1922); Bernard Lewis, *Istanbul and the Civilization of the Ottoman Empire* (Norman: University of Oklahoma Press, 1963); and Raphaela Lewis, *Everyday Life in Ottoman Turkey* (London: Batsford; New York: G. P. Putnam's Sons, 1971).

On Ottoman institutions, Albert Howe Lybyer's *The Government of the Ottoman Empire in the Time of Suleiman the Magnificent* (Cambridge: Harvard University Press, 1914), well written and still often cited, has been superseded by later works, especially H.A.R. Gibb and Harold Bowen, *Islamic Society and the West,* vol. 1, pts. 1-2 (London: Oxford University Press, 1950-1957). A vivid account of the Ottoman conquest of Istanbul is Steven Runciman's *The Fall of Constantinople, 1453* (Cambridge: University Press, 1965). On Mehmet II, see Franz Babinger, *Mehmed the Conqueror and His Time,* trans. William C. Hickman and Ralph Manheim (Princeton: Princeton University Press, 1977). Another great sultan is studied in Roger B. Merriman, *Suleiman the Magnificent, 1520-1566* (Cambridge: Harvard University Press, 1944); and, more lightly, in Harold Lamb, *Suleiman the Magnificent* (Garden City: Doubleday & Co., 1951; reprint ed., 1978). See also Paul Cole's *The Ottoman Impact on Europe* (London: Thames & Hudson, 1968); Halil Inalcik, *The Ottoman Empire: The Classical Age, 1300-1600* (London: Weidenfeld & Nicolson, 1973); and L. S. Stavrianos, *The Balkans since 1453* (New York: Rinehart & Co., 1958).

There are no good books in English on the Safavids, except of course on Isfahan, for which see Wilfrid Blunt, *Isfahan: Pearl of Persia* (New York: Stein & Day, 1966). Until volume 6 of *The Cambridge History of Iran* comes out, look for scattered articles by Roger M. Savory. Incidentally, the standard reference tool indexing periodical literature on Islam and the Middle East is J. D. Pearson's *Index Islamicus, 1906-1955* (Cambridge: Heffer & Sons, 1958) with its quinquennial, later annual, and now quarterly supplements.

A good reader for this era is John J. Saunders, ed., *The Muslim World on the Eve of Europe's Expansion* (Englewood Cliffs, N.J.: Prentice-Hall, 1966).

CHAPTER 10

The Eastern Question is a staple of European diplomatic historians. The most thorough, if at times arduous, treatment is Matthew S. Anderson, *The Eastern Question, 1774-1923* (London: Macmillan; New York: St. Martin's Press, 1966). On British Middle East policy, see especially H. L. Hoskins, *British Routes to India* (London: Longman's Green, 1928; reprint ed., 1966); Harold W. V. Temperley, *England and the Near East: The Crimea* (London and New York: Longman's Green, 1936; reprint ed., 1964); V. J. Puryear's *England, Russia, and the Straits Question* (Berkeley: University of California Press, 1931); and Sir Charles Webster, *The Foreign Policy of Palmerston*, 2 vols. (London: G. Bell, 1951; reprint ed., 1969). On the Middle Eastern rivalry between England and France, see John Marlowe [pseud.], *Perfidious Albion* (London: Elek, 1971); and on their activities in Egypt, David S. Landes, *Bankers and Pashas* (Cambridge: Harvard University Press, 1958).

The work I cited in the text on Russia is Robert J. Kerner, *The Urge to the Sea* (Berkeley and Los Angeles: University of California Press, 1942), to be supplemented by Barbara Jelavich, *A Century of Russian Foreign Policy* (Philadelphia and New York: Lippincott, 1964). On the Balkan crisis of 1875-1878, see William L. Langer, *European Alliances and Alignments, 1871-1890*, 2nd ed. (New York: Knopf, 1950); Mihailo D. Stojanovic, *The Great Powers and the Balkans* (Cambridge: University Press, 1939); and B. H. Sumner, *Russia and the Balkans, 1870-1880* (Oxford: Oxford University Press, 1937; reprint ed., 1962).

For the Middle East during the eighteenth and nineteenth centuries, in addition to works cited elsewhere, see P. M. Holt, ed., *Political and Social Change in Modern Egypt* (London: Oxford University Press, 1968) and his *Egypt and the Fertile Crescent, 1516-1922* (Ithaca: Cornell University Press, 1966); Thomas Naff and Roger Owen, eds., *Studies in Eighteenth Century Islamic History* (Carbondale and Edwardsville: Southern Illinois University Press, 1977); and William Polk and Richard Chambers, eds., *The Middle East in the Nineteenth Century* (Chicago: University of Chicago Press, 1967). A great collection of horror stories about the later Ottoman Empire is Noel Barber's *The Sultans* (New York: Simon and Schuster, 1973).

Original sources in English translation include M. S. Anderson, ed., *The Great Powers and the Near East, 1774-1923* (London: Edward Arnold,

1970); and J. C. Hurewitz, ed., *The Middle East and North Africa in World Politics,* 3 vols. (New Haven: Yale University Press, 1975-), an update of his *Diplomacy in the Near and Middle East,* 2 vols. (Princeton: Van Nostrand, 1956).

CHAPTER 11

The early westernization of Egypt can be traced through Christopher Herold, *Bonaparte in Egypt* (New York: Harper & Row, 1962); Henry Dodwell, *The Founder of Modern Egypt* (Cambridge: University Press, 1931; reprint ed., 1967); and Helen Rivlin, *The Agricultural Policy of Muhammad Ali in Egypt* (Cambridge: Harvard University Press, 1961). General surveys of modern Egyptian history include Robert Collins and Robert Tignor, *Egypt and the Sudan* (Englewood Cliffs, N.J.: Prentice-Hall, 1967); Tom Little, *Modern Egypt* (New York: Praeger, 1968); and P. J. Vatikiotis, *The Modern History of Egypt* (London: Weidenfeld & Nicholson; New York: Praeger, 1969). On intellectual changes, see Nadav Safran, *Egypt in Search of Political Community* (Cambridge: Harvard University Press, 1961).

A study of the westernization of the Ottoman Empire should start with Bernard Lewis, *The Emergence of Modern Turkey,* 2nd ed. (London and New York: Oxford University Press, 1968). On Selim III, read Stanford J. Shaw, *Between Old and New* (Cambridge: Harvard University Press, 1971). On the Tanzimat era, see Roderic H. Davison, *Reform in the Ottoman Empire, 1856-1876* (Princeton: Princeton University Press, 1963; reprint ed., 1972); and Serif A. Mardin, *The Genesis of Young Ottoman Thought* (Princeton: Princeton University Press, 1962). Also useful is Niyazi Berkes, *The Development of Secularism in Turkey* (Montreal: McGill University Press, 1964).

On nineteenth-century Iran, start with Peter Avery, *Modern Iran* (London: Benn; New York: Praeger, 1965); then Hamid Algar, *Religion and State in Iran: The Role of the Ulama in the Qajar Period* (Berkeley and Los Angeles: University of California Press, 1972).

Two collections of sources useful for this and the following chapters are Robert G. Landen, ed., *The Emergence of the Modern Middle East* (New York, Cincinnati, etc.: Van Nostrand Reinhold, 1970); and George Lenczowski, ed., *The Political Awakening of the Middle East* (Englewood Cliffs, N.J.: Prentice-Hall, 1970).

CHAPTER 12

The rise of Egyptian nationalism during the heyday of British imperialism is covered in Peter Mansfield, *The British in Egypt* (New York: Holt, Rinehart, and Winston, 1972); John Marlowe's *Spoiling the Egyptians* (New York: St. Martin's Press, 1975) and *Cromer in Egypt* (London: Elek; New York: Praeger, 1970); Afaf Lutfi al-Sayyid [Marsot], *Egypt and Cromer: A Study in Anglo-Egyptian Relations* (London: John Murray, 1968; New York: Praeger, 1969); Robert Tignor, *Modernization and British Colonial Rule in Egypt, 1882-1914* (Princeton: Princeton University Press, 1966); and Charles Wendell, *The Evolution of the Egyptian National Image* (Berkeley, Los Angles and London: University of California Press, 1972). The recent book on Urabi mentioned in the text is Alexander Schölch, *Ägypten den Ägyptern!* (Zurich: Freiberg i. Br., 1972).

On nationalism in Turkey, see Kemal Karpat, *Inquiry into the Social Foundations of Nationalism in the Ottoman State* (Princeton: Center for International Studies, 1973); David Kushner, *The Rise of Turkish Nationalism, 1876-1908* (London: Frank Cass, 1977); and the works already cited by Niyazi Berkes, Bernard Lewis, and Stanford and Ezel Kural Shaw. A popular biography of Abdulhamid is Joan Haslip's *The Sultan* (New York: Holt, Rinehart, and Winston, 1958). Ernest Ramsaur, *The Young Turks* (Princeton: Princeton University Press, 1957; several reprints) covers the CUP before it took power; for the later period, see Feroz Ahmad, *The Young Turks: The Committee of Union and Progress in Turkish Politics, 1908-1914* (Oxford: Clarendon Press, 1969). Ziya Gokalp's *Turkish Nationalism and Western Civilization*, trans. Niyazi Berkes (New York: Columbia University Press, 1959) should be supplemented by Robert Devereux, *The Principles of Turkism* (Leiden: E. J. Brill, 1968).

On both Egypt and Turkey, see also the essays edited by William Haddad and William Ochsenwald, *The Nationalism in a Non-National State* (Columbus: Ohio State University Press, 1977). On Jamal al-Din al-Afghani, see Nikki Keddie, *Sayyid Jamal al-Din "al-Afghani"* (Berkeley and Los Angeles: University of California Press, 1972). She has written many articles on early Iranian nationalism, but see also the writings of Algar, Avery, and Cottam cited elsewhere. The classic account of the constitutionalist movement is E. G. Browne, *The Persian Revolution of 1905-1909* (Cambridge: University Press, 1910; reprint ed., 1966).

CHAPTER 13

On the origins and rise of Arab nationalism, the classic account is George Antonius's *The Arab Awakening* (Philadelphia and New York: J. P. Lippincott, 1939; many reprints). It has been corrected in some details by

Sylvia Haim's introduction to *Arab Nationalism: An Anthology* (Berkeley: University of California Press, 1962; reprint ed., 1976); Albert Hourani's *Arabic Thought in the Liberal Age* (London, New York, and Toronto: Oxford University Press, 1962; reprint ed., 1970); Hisham Sharabi's *Arab Intellectuals and the West: The Formative Years, 1875-1914* (Baltimore: Johns Hopkins University Press, 1970); and Zeine N. Zeine's *The Emergence of Arab Nationalism* (Beirut: Khayat's, 1966).

Anglo-Arab relations during World War I have recently been studied by Elie Kedourie in *England and the Middle East, 1914-1921* (London: Bowes and Bowes, 1956), *The Chatham House Version and Other Middle Eastern Studies* (London: Weidenfeld & Nicholson, 1970), and *In the Anglo-Arab Labyrinth* (London, New York, and Melbourne: Cambridge University Press, 1976). As an antidote to his hostile attitude toward Arab nationalism, read C. Ernest Dawn, *From Ottomanism to Arabism* (Urbana, Chicago, and London: University of Illinois Press, 1973); and Abdel Latif Tibawi, *Anglo-Arab Relations and the Question of Palestine* (London: Luzac & Co., 1977).

Many books have been written about T. E. Lawrence, of which I recommend John E. Mack, *A Prince of Our Disorder: The Life of T. E. Lawrence* (Boston: Little, Brown, 1976); Philip Knightley and Colin Simpson, *The Secret Lives of Lawrence of Arabia* (New York: McGraw-Hill, 1969); and Desmond Stewart, *T. E. Lawrence* (New York: Harper & Row, 1977). Lawrence's own account of the Arab revolt, a classic, is *The Seven Pillars of Wisdom* (Garden City: Doubleday, Doran & Co., 1935; numerous reprints). Also interesting is Ronald Storrs' *Orientations* (London: Ivor Nicholson & Watson, 1937), also published as *The Memoirs of Sir Ronald Storrs* (New York: Putnam, 1937; reprint ed., 1973).

On the diplomacy of World War I and its aftermath, see Briton Cooper Busch, *Britain, India, and the Arabs, 1914-1921* (Berkeley: University of California Press, 1971); Aaron S. Kliemann, *Foundations of British Policy in the Arab World: The Cairo Conference of 1921* (Baltimore: Johns Hopkins University Press, 1970); Elizabeth Monroe, *Britain's Moment in the Middle East, 1914-1956* (London: Chatto & Windus; Baltimore: Johns Hopkins University Press, 1963); Jukka Nevakivi, *Britain, France, and the Arab Middle East, 1914-1920* (New York: Oxford University Press, 1968); and Howard M. Sachar, *Emergence of the Middle East, 1914-1924* (New York: Knopf, 1969).

Stephen Longrigg has written two good histories of the mandates: *Syria and Lebanon under French Mandate* (London, New York, and Toronto: Oxford University Press, 1958), and *Iraq, 1900 to 1950* (same publisher, 1953).

CHAPTER 14

As this book moves into the modern period, I would like to recommend some general books on various aspects of the Middle East in the twentieth century. The most serviceable, though very detailed, surveys are George Lenczowski, *The Middle East in World Affairs,* 3rd ed. (Ithaca: Cornell University Press, 1962); and Don Peretz, *The Middle East Today,* 3rd ed. (New York: Holt, Rinehart, and Winston, 1978). The society and culture of the Arab countries are well covered in Morroe Berger, *The Arab World Today* (New York: Doubleday & Co., 1962); and Jacques Berque, *The Arabs: Their History and Future,* trans. Jean Stewart (New York: Praeger, 1964).

No book better captures the life and character of the Middle East's most renowned westernizer of the twentieth century than Lord Kinross's *Atatürk* (London: Weidenfeld & Nicolson, 1964; New York: William Morrow, 1965). Among contemporary accounts, H. C. Armstrong's *Gray Wolf* (London: A. Barker, 1932; New York: Minton, Balch, 1933) is readable but gossipy. Halide Edib [Adivar], *Turkey Faces West* (New Haven: Yale University Press, 1930; reprint ed., 1973); Irfan Orga, *Phoenix Ascendant: The Rise of Modern Turkey* (London: R. Hale, 1958); and Ahmed Amin Yalman, *Turkey in My Time* (Norman: University of Oklahoma Press, 1956) give Turkish views of the Kemalist era. In addition to general histories of Turkey cited earlier, I also recommend Geoffrey Lewis's *Modern Turkey,* 4th ed. (New York: Praeger, 1974).

The best account of the life of Ibn Saud is David Howarth's *The Desert King* (New York: McGraw-Hill, 1964). It can be supplemented by the idiosyncratic *Arabian Jubilee* by Harry St. John B. Philby (London: Robert Hale, 1952). Good introductions include George Kheirallah's *Arabia Reborn* (Albuquerque: University of New Mexico Press, 1952); Philby's *Sa'udi Arabia* (London: Benn; New York: Praeger, 1955); Karl Twitchell's *Saudi Arabia, with an Account of the Development of Its Natural Resources,* 3rd ed. (Princeton: Princeton University Press, 1958); and D. Van der Meulen's *The Wells of Ibn Saud* (London: John Murray, 1957). The best available background study is R. Bayly Winder, *Saudi Arabia in the Nineteenth Century* (New York: St. Martin's, 1965). On Aramco's beginnings, see Wallace Stegner, *Discovery: The Search for Arabian Oil* (Beirut: Middle East Export Press, 1971), which also appeared serially in *Aramco World* in 1968-1969; and also David Finnie, *Desert Enterprise* (Cambridge: Harvard University Press, 1958). On Ibn Saud's successors, read Gerald de Gaury, *Faisal, King of Saudi Arabia* (New York and Washington: Praeger, 1966).

Because the Pahlavi dynasty has been so controversial, unbiased biographies of Reza Shah are rare. I used Donald N. Wilber, *Riza Shah Pahlavi: The Resurrection and Reconstruction of Iran, 1878-1944* (Hicksville, N.Y.: Exposition Press, 1975); supplemented by Hassan Arfa, *Under Five Shahs* (London: John Murray, 1964; New York: William Morrow, 1965); and Amin Banani, *The Modernization of Iran, 1921-1941* (Stanford: Stanford University Press, 1961). On modern Iran generally, see Richard Cottam, *Nationalism in Iran* (Pittsburgh: University of Pittsburgh Press, 1964); George Lenczowski, ed., *Iran under the Pahlavis* (Stanford: Hoover Institution, 1978); and Gerald de Villiers, *The Imperial Shah: An Informal Biography,* trans. June P. Wilson and Walter B. Michaels (Boston and Toronto: Atlantic-Little, Brown, 1976).

CHAPTER 15

Much of the best writing on twentieth-century Egypt has been done by French authors, such as Jacques Berque, *Egypt: Imperialism and Revolution,* trans. Jean Stewart (London: Faber; New York: Praeger, 1972); Marcel Colombe, *L'Evolution de l'Egypte, 1924-1950* (Paris: G. P. Maisonneuve, 1951); and Jean and Simonne Lacouture, *Egypt in Transition,* trans. F. Scarfe (New York: Criterion Books, 1958). Other good books for this period include Charles Issawi, *Egypt at Midcentury* (London and New York: Oxford University Press, 1954); Afaf Lutfi al-Sayyid Marsot, *Egypt's Liberal Experiment, 1922-1936* (Berkeley, Los Angeles, and London: University of California Press, 1977); Barrie St. Clair McBride, *Farouk of Egypt: A Biography* (London: Hale, 1967; South Brunswick, N.J.: A. S. Barnes, 1968); Richard Mitchell. *The Society of Muslim Brothers* (London and New York: Oxford University Press, 1969); Mahmud Zayid, *Egypt's Struggle for Independence* (Beirut: Khayat's, 1965); and works by Little, Monroe, and Vatikiotis cited earlier.

Several leaders of the 1952 revolution wrote personal accounts: Gamal Abdel Nasser, *Egypt's Liberation: The Philosophy of the Revolution* (Washington: Public Affairs Press, 1955); Mohamed Neguib, *Egypt's Destiny: A Personal Statement* (London: Gollancz; Garden City: Doubleday, 1955); and Anwar El Sadat, *Revolt on the Nile* (London: Allan Wingate; New York: John Day, 1957).

CHAPTER 16

Literature abounds on the contest for Palestine, but it is hard to separate scholarship from propaganda. Among the works closest to the former, I recommend Isaiah Friedman, *The Question of Palestine, 1914-1918* (New

York: Schocken, 1973); J. C. Hurewitz, *The Struggle for Palestine* (New York: Norton, 1950; reprint ed., 1968); John Marlowe, *The Seat of Pilate* (London: Cresset, 1959); relevant portions of Howard M. Sachar's *Emergence of the Middle East* (cited earlier) and *Europe Leaves the Middle East, 1936-1954* (New York: Knopf, 1972); Leonard Stein, *The Balfour Declaration* (New York: Simon & Schuster, 1961); and Christopher Sykes, *Crossroads to Israel, 1917-1948* (Cleveland: World Publishing Company, 1965; reprint ed., 1973). Personal accounts of the period include Robert John and Sami Hadawi, *The Palestine Diary,* 2 vols. (New York: New World Press, 1970) for the Arabs; Storrs's *Orientations* (already cited) for the British; and Chaim Weizmann's *Trial and Error* (New York: Harper, 1949) for the Zionist viewpoint. Putting Britain's Palestine policy in a larger context are Richard Allen, *Imperialism and Nationalism in the Fertile Crescent* (London, New York, and Toronto: Oxford University Press, 1974); and George Kirk, *The Middle East in the War* (London and New York: Oxford University Press, 1972).

Among general histories of Israel, useful also for my last chapters, the best are Howard Sachar, *A History of Israel from the Rise of Zionism to Our Time* (New York: Knopf, 1976); and Nadav Safran, *Israel: The Embattled Ally* (Cambridge, Mass., and London: Belknap Press, 1978). Especially readable are Abba Eban, *My Country* (New York: Random House, 1972); and Amos Elon, *The Israelis: Founders and Sons* (New York: Holt, Rinehart, and Winston, 1971). See also Walter Z. Laqueur, *A History of Zionism* (New York: Holt, Rinehart, and Winston, 1972), to be supplemented by Arthur Hertzberg, ed., *The Zionist Idea* (Philadelphia: Jewish Publication Society, 1960).

The politicizaton of Palestine's Arabs can be traced in Yehoshua Porath, *The Emergence of the Palestinian National Movement, 1918-1929* (Jerusalem: Hebrew University Press, 1973) and *The Palestine Arab National Movement, 1929-1939. II: From Riots to Rebellion* (London: Frank Cass, 1978).

The Arabs have been at a disadvantage in competing for the attention of Western scholarship, but Abdelwahab M. Elmessiri has recently written a trenchant critique of political Zionism called *The Land of Promise* (New Brunswick, N.J.: North American, Inc., 1977), to be read in conjunction with Walid Khalidi, ed., *From Haven to Conquest* (Beirut: Institute for Palestine Studies, 1971). See also the works by Antonius, Khouri, and Tibawi, cited elsewhere, as well as Sami Hadawi, *Bitter Harvest: Palestine between 1914-1967* (New York: New World Press, 1967); and Ibrahim Abu-Lughod, ed., *The Transformation of Palestine* (Evanston, Ill.: Northwestern University Press, 1971). Sympathetic to the Arabs of Palestine is David Hirst, *The Gun and the Olive Branch: The Roots of*

Violence in the Middle East (New York and London: Harcourt Brace Jovanovich, 1977).

CHAPTER 17

On the 1948 Palestine war, or Israel's war of independence, see Jon and David Kimche, *A Clash of Destinies* (New York: Praeger, 1960), also published as *Both Sides of the Hill* (London: Secker, 1960); and Dan Kurzman, *Genesis, 1948: The First Arab-Israeli War* (New York: World Publishing Co., 1970). Sir John Bagot Glubb eloquently defends his role in *The Story of the Arab Legion* (London: Hodder & Stoughton, 1948) and *A Soldier with the Arabs* (London: Hodder & Stoughton, 1957; New York: Harper Brothers, 1958). The *Journal of Palestine Studies* has published relevant memoirs by several Arab leaders, including Fawzi al-Qawuqji (in 1972) and Gamal Abdel Nasser (in 1973). See also Larry Collins and Dominique Lapierre, *O Jerusalem* (New York: Simon & Schuster, 1972). On the aftermath, see Earl Berger, *The Covenant and the Sword* (Toronto: University of Toronto Press, 1965); E.L.M. Burns, *Between Arab and Israeli* (New York: Ivan Obelensky, 1962); George Kirk, *The Middle East, 1945-1950* (London and New York: Oxford University Press, 1954); Don Peretz, *Israel and the Palestine Arabs* (Washington: Middle East Institute, 1956); and Nadav Safran, *From War to War* (New York: Pegasus, 1969). On the new state of Israel, see David Ben Gurion, *Rebirth and Destiny of Israel,* trans. Mordekhai Nurock (New York: Philosophical Library, 1954); Norman Bentwich, *Israel Resurgent* (London: Benn; New York: Praeger, 1960); and James G. McDonald, *My Mission to Israel* (New York: Simon & Schuster, 1951). On the Arab countries at this time, see Jon Kimche, *Seven Fallen Pillars* (New York: Praeger, 1953); also Albert Hourani, *Syria and Lebanon: A Political Essay* (London, New York, and Toronto: Oxford University Press, 1946; several reprints); Majid Khadduri, *Independent Iraq, 1932-1958,* 2nd ed. (London, New York, and Karachi: Oxford University Press, 1960); Edith Penrose and E. F. Penrose, *Iraq: International Relations and National Development* (Boulder: Westview Press, 1978); Fahim Qubain, *The Reconstruction of Iraq, 1950-1957* (London: Stevens; New York: Praeger, 1958); and Nichola Ziadeh, *Syria and Lebanon* (London: Benn; New York: Praeger, 1957).

On the events leading up to the 1956 Suez war, see Erskine Childers, *The Road to Suez: A Study in Western-Arab Relations* (London: Macgibbon & Kee, 1962); Sir Anthony Eden, *The Suez Crisis of 1956* (Boston: Beacon Press, 1968), reprinted from *Full Circle* (London: Times Publishing Co.; Boston: Houghton Mifflin, 1960); Anthony Nutting, *No End of a Lesson:*

The Story of Suez (London: Constable; New York: C. N. Potter, 1967); Ernest Stock, *Israel on the Road to Sinai* (London: Gollancz; Ithaca: Cornell University Press, 1967); and Hugh Thomas, *Suez* (New York and Evanston: Harper & Row, 1966).

CHAPTER 18

Since Gamal Abdel Nasser and his policies take up so much of this chapter, the following books may be useful: R. Hrair Dekmejian, *Egypt under Nasir: A Study in Political Dynamics* (Albany: State University of New York Press, 1971); Jean Lacouture, *Nasser,* trans. Daniel Hofstadter (New York: Knopf, 1973); Anthony Nutting, *Nasser* (London: Constable; New York, E. P. Dutton, 1972); Robert H. Stephens, *Nasser: A Political Biography* (New York: Simon & Schuster, 1972); and Wilton Wynn, *Nasser of Egypt: The Search for Dignity* (Cambridge, Mass.: Arlington Books, 1959). His Arab policies are treated sympathetically in Charles D. Cremeans, *The Arabs and the World: Nasser's Nationalist Policy* (New York: Praeger, 1963). Mohamed Heikal, *The Cairo Documents* (Garden City, N.Y.: Doubleday, 1972) covers mainly Nasser's relations with foreign leaders. On his relations with Washington, see especially Miles Copeland [pseud.], *The Game of Nations* (New York: Simon & Schuster, 1969). On the dynamics of inter-Arab politics during this period, read sequentially Patrick Seale, *The Struggle for Syria: A Study of Postwar Arab Politics, 1945-1958* (London: Oxford University Press, 1965); and Malcolm H. Kerr, *The Arab Cold War: Gamal Abd al-Nasir and His Rivals, 1958-1970,* 3rd ed. (London, Oxford, and New York: Oxford University Press, 1971).

Nasser's rival in Iraq is sympathetically treated by Uriel Dann, *Iraq under Qassem: A Political History, 1958-1963* (London: Pall Mall; New York: Praeger, 1969). King Husayn justifies his policies in *Uneasy Lies the Head: An Autobiography* (London: Heineman; New York: Bernard Geis Associates, 1962). The standard account of Lebanon's 1958 civil war is Fahim Qubain, *Crisis in Lebanon* (Washington: Middle East Institute, 1961). A good survey of Syria is A. L. Tibawi, *A Modern History of Syria, Including Lebanon and Palestine* (London: Macmillan; New York: St. Martin's Press, 1969). Books on the Ba'th include Kamal S. Abu-Jaber, *The Arab Ba'th Socialist Party: History, Ideology, and Organization* (Syracuse: Syracuse University Press, 1966); John F. Devlin, *The Ba'th Party: A History from Its Origins to 1966* (Stanford: Hoover Institution Press, 1976); and Itamar Rabinovitch, *Syria under the Ba'th, 1963-1966* (Jerusalem: Israel Universities Press, 1972). Western opposition to Arab nationalism is criticized in Michael Ionides, *Divide and Lose: The Arab*

Revolt of 1955-1958 (London: Geoffrey Bles, 1960) and supported in George Kirk, *Contemporary Arab Politics* (New York: Praeger, 1961).

On the events leading up to the June 1967 war, see Theodore Draper, *Israel and World Politics* (New York: Viking Press, 1967); Walter Laqueur, *The Road to Jerusalem* (New York: Macmillan, 1968) also published as *The Road to War* (London: Weidenfeld & Nicolson, 1968); and Kennett Love, *Suez: The Twice-Fought War* (New York and Toronto: McGraw-Hill, 1969). The memoirs of U Thant, published posthumously in 1978, try to shift some of the blame from himself to Nasser.

CHAPTER 19

Since Israel made more facilities available to foreign journalists than Egypt or Syria did, we have far more literature on Israel's version of the June 1967 war. Best for beginners is Randolph and Winston Churchill, *The Six Day War* (London: Heinemann; Boston: Hougton Mifflin, 1967); then Edgar O'Ballance, *The Third Arab-Israeli War* (London: Faber & Faber; Hamden, Conn.: Archon, 1972). Moshe Dayan's daughter writes her impressions of the front in *Israel Journal, June 1967* by Yael Dayan (New York: McGraw-Hill, 1967) also published as *A Soldier's Diary: Sinai 1967* (London: Weidenfeld & Nicolson, 1967). Jordan's role is described by two journalists interviewing King Husayn (Vick Vance and Pierre Lauer) in *My "War" with Israel,* trans. J. P. Wilson and W. B. Michaels (New York: Morrow; London: Own, 1969). A general "feel" for the Arabs' reaction to the war can be gleaned from Halim Barakat's novel, *Days of Dust,* trans. Trevor Le Gassick (Wilmette, Ill.: Medina University Press International, 1974). See also Elias Sam'o, ed., *The June 1967 Arab-Israeli War: Miscalculation or Conspiracy?* (Wilmette, Ill.: Medina University Press International, 1971); and Fred J. Khouri, *Arab Israeli Dilemma,* 2nd ed. (Syracuse: Syracuse University Press, 1976).

A rather pro-Israel and anti-Soviet account of this period is Walter Z. Laqueur's *The Struggle for the Middle East,* rev. ed. (New York: Macmillan, 1972). Soviet policies are analyzed in Michael Confino and Shimon Shamir, eds., *The U.S.S.R. and the Middle East* (Jerusalem: Israel Universities Press, 1973). America's pro-Israeli policy during and after the 1967 war is criticized in Maxime Rodinson, *Israel and the Arabs,* trans. Michael Perl (New York: Pantheon, 1968); Hisham Sharabi, *Palestine and Israel: The Lethal Dilemma* (New York: Pegasus Press, 1969); and David Waines, *The Unholy War: Israel and Palestine, 1897-1971* (Wilmette, Ill.: Medina University Press International, 1971). An interesting personal account by a Palestinian is Leila Khaled's *My People*

Shall Live: The Autobiography of a Revolutionary, ed. George Hajjar (London: Hodder & Stoughton, 1973). See also Fawaz Turki, *The Disinherited: Journal of a Palestinian Exile* (New York and London: Monthly Review, 1972; reprinted with an epilogue in 1974). On Palestinian politics generally, read William Quandt, Fuad Jabber, and Ann Mosley Lesch, *The Politics of Palestinian Nationalism* (Berkeley and Los Angeles: University of California Press, 1971).

CHAPTER 20

It may surprise you to learn that so much has come out on the October (Yom Kippur) war and its aftermath that there is already a bibliography: Michael Rubner, *The Middle East Conflict from October 1973 to June 1977: A Selected Bibliography* (Los Angeles: California State University Press, 1977). On the background, from the Arab side, see Mohamed Heikal's *The Road to Ramadan* (New York: Quadrangle, 1975); and, for the Israelis, Michael Handel's *Perception, Misperception, and Surprise: The Case of the Yom Kippur War* (Jerusalem: Hebrew University, 1975). On the events of the war itself, I recommend *Insight on the Middle East War* (London: Deutsch, 1974), edited by the "Insight Team of the *Sunday Times.*" On the political side, see Walter Z. Laqueur, *Confrontation: The Middle East War and World Politics* (London: Abacus; New York: Quadrangle, 1974) and the essays edited by Naseer Aruri called *Middle East Crucible: Studies on the Arab-Israeli War of 1973* (Wilmette, Ill.: Medina University Press International, 1975).

Kissinger's role in the postwar peace negotiations is praised in Edward Sheehan's *The Arabs, Israelis, and Kissinger* (New York: Reader's Digest Press, 1976) and attacked by Matti Golan's *Secret Conversations of Henry Kissinger* (New York: Quadrangle, 1976). On America's Middle East policies generally, see Joseph Churba, *The Politics of Defeat: America's Decline in the Middle East* (New York: Cyrco Press, 1977); and William B. Quandt, *Decade of Decisions: American Policy toward the Arab-Israeli Conflict, 1967-1976* (Berkeley, Los Angeles, and London: University of California Press, 1977).

Several major actors on the Middle Eastern scene have written their memoirs. Especially interesting are Golda Meir, *My Life* (New York: Dell, 1976); and Anwar al-Sadat, *In Search of Identity: An Autobiography* (New York: Harper & Row, 1978).

OPEC and Middle Eastern oil have received a lot of attention since 1973. See Dankwart Rustow and John R. Mugno, *OPEC: Success and Prospects* (New York: New York University Press, 1976); George Lenczowski, *Middle East Oil in a Revolutionary Age* (Washington:

American Enterprise Institute, 1976); Abdul Amir Kubbah, *OPEC Past and Present* (Vienna: Petro-Economic Research Centre, 1974); and J. C. Hurewitz, ed., *Oil, The Arab-Israeli Dispute, and the Industrial World: Horizons of Crisis* (Boulder: Westview Press, 1976). More attention is now being paid to oil-producing countries rarely mentioned in my book, such as the United Arab Emirates. See John Duke Anthony, *Arab States of the Lower Gulf: People, Politics, Petroleum* (Washington: Middle East Institute, 1975).

On the Middle East arms race, see Robert Pranger and Dale R. Tahtinen, *Implications of the 1976 Arab-Israeli Military Status* (Washington: American Enterprise Institute, 1976).

The best book I have seen so far on the 1975-1976 Lebanese civil war is John Bulloch's *Death of a Country: The Civil War in Lebanon* (London: Weidenfeld & Nicolson, 1977). Its background is ably sketched by Kamal S. Salibi in *Crossroads to Civil War: Lebanon, 1958-1976* (Delmar, N.Y.: Caravan Books, 1976).

Of the textbooks now available on Middle East politics, the best is James Bill and Carl Leiden, *The Middle East: Politics and Power* (Boston: Allyn & Bacon, 1974), of which a new edition will come out in 1979. It can be supplemented by Michael Hudson, *Arab Politics: The Search for Legitimacy* (New Haven: Yale University Press, 1977); Malcolm Kerr, ed., *The Elusive Peace in the Middle East* (Albany: State University of New York Press, 1975); Peter Mansfield, *The Arab World: A Comprehensive History* (New York: Crowell, 1977); and Frank Tachau, ed., *Political Elites and Political Development in the Middle East* (New York: John Wiley & Sons, 1975). For keeping abreast of very recent political and economic events, my favorite sourcebook is *The Middle East: U.S. Policy, Israel, Oil, and the Arabs,* 3rd ed. (Washington: Congressional Quarterly, 1978).

Lest we forget that the peoples of the Middle East do lead lives outside the realms of politics and economics, I end this essay with two anthologies of recent literature, both Mentor paperbacks: James Kritzeck, ed., *Modern Islamic Literature* (New York: Holt, Rinehart, and Winston, 1970); and Leo Hamalian and John D. Yohannan, eds., *New Writings from the Middle East* (New York: New American Library, 1978).

Index